POLITICS AND THF ˉ
REVOLUTIONAR

After the collapse of the Romanov dynasty in February 1917, Russia was subject to an eight-month experiment in democracy. Sarah
Badcock studies its failure through an exploration of the experiences
and motivations of ordinary men and women, urban and rural, military and civilian. Using previously neglected documents from regional
archives, she offers a new history of the revolution as experienced in the
two Volga provinces of Nizhegorod and Kazan. She exposes the confusions and contradictions between political elites and ordinary people
and emphasises the role of the latter as political actors. By looking
beyond Petersburg and Moscow, she shows how local concerns, conditions and interests were foremost in shaping how the revolution
was received and understood. She also reveals the ways in which the
small group of intellectuals who dominated the high political scene of
1917 had their political alternatives circumscribed by the desires and
demands of ordinary people.

SARAH BADCOCK is Lecturer in History at the University of
Nottingham.

NEW STUDIES IN EUROPEAN HISTORY

Edited by
PETER BALDWIN, University of California, Los Angeles
CHRISTOPHER CLARK, University of Cambridge
JAMES B. COLLINS, Georgetown University
MIA RODRÍGUEZ-SALGADO, London School of Economics and Political
Science
LYNDAL ROPER, University of Oxford

The aim of this series in early modern and modern European history is to publish outstanding works of research, addressed to important themes across a wide geographical range, from southern and central Europe, to Scandinavia and Russia, from the time of the Renaissance to the Second World War. As it develops the series will comprise focused works of wide contextual range and intellectual ambition.

For a full list of titles published in the series, please see the end of the book.

POLITICS AND THE PEOPLE IN REVOLUTIONARY RUSSIA

A Provincial History

SARAH BADCOCK

University of Nottingham

CAMBRIDGE UNIVERSITY PRESS

CAMBRIDGE UNIVERSITY PRESS
Cambridge, New York, Melbourne, Madrid, Cape Town, Singapore,
São Paulo, Delhi, Dubai, Tokyo, Mexico City

Cambridge University Press
The Edinburgh Building, Cambridge CB2 8RU, UK

Published in the United States of America by Cambridge University Press, New York

www.cambridge.org
Information on this title: www.cambridge.org/9780521182256

First published 2007
First paperback edition 2010

A catalogue record for this publication is available from the British Library

ISBN 978-0-521-87623-0 Hardback
ISBN 978-0-521-18225-6 Paperback

This book is dedicated to my grandparents,
Ted and Freda Ellis

Contents

List of figures and table   *page* viii
Notes on the text   ix
Acknowledgements   x
Maps   xii

1   Introduction   1

2   The February revolution: whose story to believe?   30

3   The Socialist Revolutionary Party and the place of
    party politics   56

4   Choosing local leaders   87

5   Talking to the people and shaping revolution   123

6   Soldiers and their wives   145

7   'Water is yours, light is yours, the land is yours, the wood
    is yours'   181

8   Feeding Russia   211

    Conclusions   238

Bibliography   244
Index   257

Figures and table

FIGURES

1.1	Great Russian population (%) in Kazan province, by *uezd*	*page* 7
1.2	Political constitution of Town Dumas after re-elections in 1917	26
3.1	Dates of membership and first arrest of PSR members	63
3.2	Election results in Sormovo for July, September and November 1917	82
4.1	Education levels of local leaders in 1917	89
4.2	Occupations of local leaders in 1917	90
7.1	Livestock (per head) held in Nizhegorod and Kazan provinces, by *uezd*, for 1916	184
7.2	Sown areas (in *desiatins*) in Nizhegorod and Kazan provinces, by *uezd*, showing crop types, for 1916	185
7.3	Land sown (in *desiatins*) by peasant and private owners, 1916	187
7.4	Ownership of woodland in Nizhegorod province	193

TABLE

1.1	The Provincial Government's five incarnations	12

Notes on the text

All dates before 31 January 1918 are given according to the Julian (old-style) calendar, which ran thirteen days behind the Gregorian (new-style) calendar in use in Western Europe. The Gregorian calendar was adopted in Russia on the day following 31 January 1918, which was declared to be 14 February, though many regional Soviet newspapers began to give new dates, with old dates in brackets, in their publications, after the Bolshevik seizure of power on 25 October 1917.

In transliterating Russian titles, quotations and names, I have used the Library of Congress system, except in the case of well-known persons, or names that are familiar in other spellings, such as Alexander Kerensky and Rimsky-Korsakov. Soft signs at the ends of words have been omitted.

I have tried to keep the use of Russian terms and abbreviations in the text to an absolute minimum. There are a number of terms, however, which translate clumsily, and have been given in Russian throughout.

Each province is divided into *uezdy* and each *uezd* subdivided into *volosti*.

desiatina: measurement of area, equivalent to 2.7 acres

narodnyi dom: People's house

otrub (pl. *otruba*): peasant household farm with enclosed field strips

PSR: Socialist Revolutionary Party

pud: measurement of weight, equivalent to 36.113 pounds

samosud: mob law

skhod: village or communal gathering

soldatka (pl. *soldatki*): soldier's wife

soslovie (noun), *soslovnyi* (adj.): social categories applied in tsarist period

SD: Social Democrat

SR: member of the Socialist Revolutionary Party

uezd: district; subdivision of province

volost: rural district; subdivision of *uezd*

zemstvo (pl. *zemstva*): local self-government organ

Archival materials are referred to by their collection *fond* (f.), section *opis* (op.), file *delo* (d.) and page number *listok* (l.). Unless otherwise indicated, all translations are my own.

Acknowledgements

This study has been made possible by the financial and moral support that I have received from a wide variety of sources. Funding from scholarly bodies and from my indefatigable parents enabled me to pursue my research interests. The Arts and Humanities Research Board, the University of Durham, the British Foundation of Women Graduates and the Royal Historical Society all provided me with financial support in the course of my doctoral research, on which this work is partly based. The financial support of the Leverhulme Trust enabled me to spend an invaluable year in Russia furthering my research. The study leave afforded me by the University of Nottingham gave me the time I needed to complete this manuscript.

I could not have completed this book without the help of the staff of various archives and libraries, in Moscow, St Petersburg, Kazan, Nizhnii Novgorod, London and Nottingham. I'm only sorry I don't remember the names of the many archivists who were so kind and helpful to me, especially the reading room staff who bore my amateurish spoken Russian and my fixation on 1917 with good humour. I spent many months in the newspaper room of the Russian National Library on the Fontanka in St Petersburg and the then head of the section, Victor Victorovich, brightened my day with his cheery hellos and chocolate treats. I am particularly grateful to the director of Nizhnii Novgorod's State Archive, Victor Alekseevich Kharmalov, and the director of the National Archive of the Republic of Tatarstan, Liudmila Vasil'evna Gorokhova, for permitting me to use their wonderful archives.

The scholars of revolutionary Russia are an exceptionally welcoming and friendly bunch. Michael Hickey has offered more support than I should really have dared to ask for. His painstaking comments and criticisms of my work over the last few years have improved this book beyond measure. Geoff Swain and Chris Read have generously and patiently read and commented on very many versions of this work. They have also offered me a lot of support right through my career. Dan Orlovsky's insightful comments on a final version of this manuscript helped me clarify my ideas. The detailed evaluation from the anonymous reader consulted by Cambridge University Press improved this book significantly. The Study Group on the Russian Revolution provided a knowledgeable and support-ive forum for the exchange of ideas. I have bludgeoned too many people into conversation about 1917 to name them all here. I would however like to thank, in no particular order, Aaron Retish, Liudmila Novikova, Murray Frame, Jimmy White, Ian Thatcher, Cath Brennan, Paul Dukes, Bob Mc-Kean, Peter Gatrell, Boris Kolonitskii, David Saunders, John Slatter, David Moon, David Longley, Michael Melancon, Mark Baker, John Morison and Maureen Perrie. Any shortcomings and errors in this work are, of course, my own and have endured despite all these individuals' best efforts.

Finally, I'd like to thank my friends and family, who may not have read the mountains of paper I've generated over the last few years, but have offered the trappings of sanity in my ivory tower world. My mam and dad Louise and Ernie, and my sister Zoe, have been unflagging in their support for me through all the ups and downs of academic study. My boon companions Louise, Lolly, Becky, Karen, Sam and of course the infamous Ben Aldridge have conspired to keep things in perspective, and life cheery over the last few years. Graham Tan has borne the brunt of my scholarly anxieties with forbearance and love.

A portion of chapter 6 appeared in the *International Review of Social History* 49 (2004), 47–70, and a version of chapter 5 appeared in the *Russian Review* 65 (October 2006), 2–21. I thank both publishers for permission to reprint this material.

Maps

Map 1. The Russian Empire, *c.* 1900

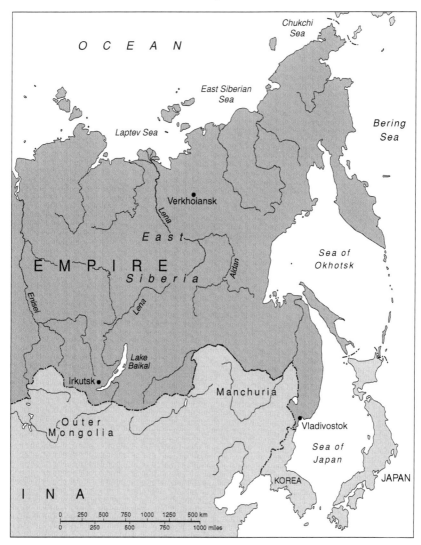

Map 1. (*cont.*)

Map 2. European Russia, *c.* 1900

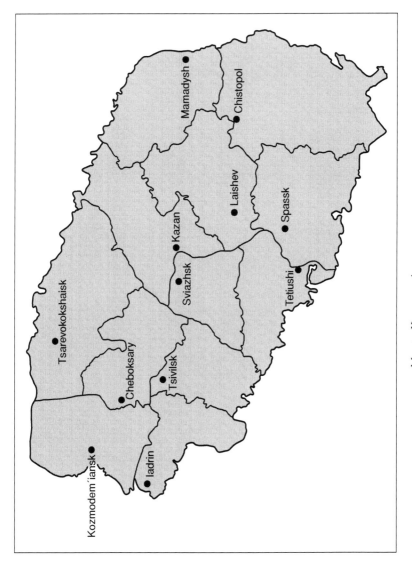

Map 3. Kazan province, c. 1900

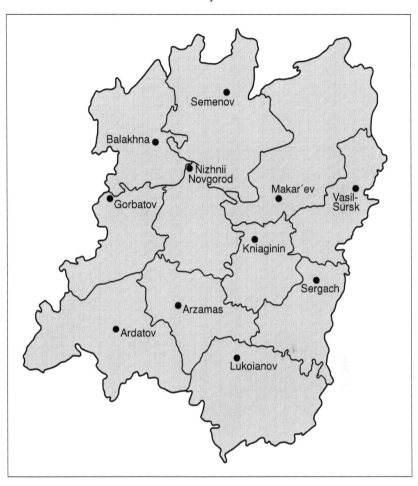

Map 4. Nizhegorod province, *c.* 1900

CHAPTER I

Introduction

The catastrophic failure of the Provisional Government's attempts to govern Russia and to safely usher in a democratically elected national assembly overshadows any study of 1917. The democratic party political system that was used as a basis for the new regime failed to take root, and was swept away by the Bolshevik seizure of power in October 1917. This book will look at the roots of Russian democracy's collapse after only eight brief months, by exploring the experiences of ordinary people in 1917. The evidence from Nizhegorod and Kazan suggests that localism overwhelmed national interests in 1917, and that, as Donald Raleigh put it, 'Russia was breaking into local economic units'.[1] This study argues that ordinary people displayed autonomy and direction in 1917, but that their motivations and short-term goals did not coincide with those of the state. For Nizhegorod and Kazan, February 1917 began the process of a complete collapse of central governmental power. The Provisional Government's faith in democratic government, and in the potential of Russia's people to govern themselves, proved to be incompatible with their other goals of maintaining domestic peace and order, and continuing Russia's involvement in the war effort.

There is a massive body of literature tackling the events of 1917, and a number of recent works have provided full and balanced accounts of the course of events.[2] Despite the rich historiography of the Russian revolution, however, the focus of historical study has been on the capitals, and the urban, organised population. There is a wealth of Russian experience still

[1] Raleigh used this phrase to describe the situation in Saratov by summer (Donald J. Raleigh, 'The revolution of 1917 and the establishment of Soviet power in Saratov', in Rex A. Wade and Scott J. Seregny (eds.), *Politics and society in provincial Russia: Saratov, 1590–1917* (Columbus, OH, 1989), pp. 277–306, p. 293).
[2] See, for example, Tsuyoshi Hasegawa, *The February revolution: Petrograd 1917* (Seattle, 1981); Orlando Figes, *A people's tragedy: the Russian revolution 1891–1924* (London, 1996); Christopher Read, *From tsar to soviets: the Russian people and their revolution* (London, 1996); Rex A. Wade, *The Russian revolution, 1917* (Cambridge, 2000); Steve A. Smith, *The Russian revolution: a very short introduction* (Oxford, 2002).

to be explored, away from the urban centres and political elites, that can alter our perceptions of Russia's revolutionary year. This book, by taking a regional perspective, and by concentrating on the political experiences of ordinary Russians, aims to provide a counterbalance to the many, and excellent, histories of Russia which have privileged events in the capital cities, and the experiences of the urban and the organised population.

Historians have focused on the activities of the organised and the 'conscious' within the population, namely political elites, workers and to some extent soldiers. These groups were important, and their activities undoubtedly had disproportionate impact on the course of revolutionary events. The focus of this work, however, will be on understanding the revolutionary experience of the elusive 'average Joe'. Much of this book is concerned with Russia's peasant population, which formed the vast majority of the population, but it does not deal exclusively with the experiences of rural Russia. I have tried to consider ordinary people together, men and women, urban and rural, and military and civilian, in order to get a more rounded picture of the revolution's implications. This approach brings its own problems, and necessitates a loss of the sharp focus and insights that have been drawn from more specific studies. It does, however, emphasise the loose and uncertain identities that were a feature of the late Imperial and especially the revolutionary period. By looking at urban and rural experiences of revolution alongside one another, a more holistic version of 1917's events emerges. Where the political elite is considered, it is in their attempts to communicate with ordinary people. These channels of communication help us understand that ordinary people participated in the political process in rational ways, but in ways that often did not correspond with the aspirations of Russia's political elite. Far from an elite few conducting the masses along their revolutionary path, the small group of intellectuals who dominated the high political scene of 1917 had their political alternatives circumscribed by the desires and demands of ordinary people.

With some notable exceptions, studies of 1917 have concentrated on events in Petrograd and to a lesser extent Moscow. When I started this project one senior authority in the field told me that study of the provinces was pointless, because 'when the bell tolls in Petersburg, the bell tolls all over Russia'. This common misperception of Russia, that events in the provinces simply followed the course set by the capitals, is one that recent historiography has been challenging, and that this work, with its focus on life in two of Russia's provinces, Kazan and Nizhegorod, seeks to further undermine. These provinces, despite their position as neighbours in central eastern European Russia, provide examples of Russia's tremendous geographic, ethnic and economic diversity. Kazan and Nizhegorod cannot be taken as exemplars for every Russian province, or even for the Volga region. If we are to understand revolutionary events at grass-roots level, we need to look at different provinces individually.

This work shows conclusively that local concerns, conditions and interests dominated the ways that the revolution was received and understood by ordinary people in Nizhegorod and Kazan. Few direct comparisons between the two provinces have been made, as the differences within *uezds* of each province were often greater than differences between the two provinces as a whole. Only in more specific cases, as between Kazan town and Nizhnii Novgorod town, can direct comparisons be drawn. Ordinary people's responses to revolution need to be understood in their local context, and these contexts defy straightforward comparisons and summaries. This is not grand history that comes to elegant and sweeping conclusions. It is small and messy, very much like ordinary people's lives.

This study focuses on an extremely narrow chronological window, from the February revolution up until the Bolshevik seizure of power in October. Recent works by, amongst others, Peter Holquist and Joshua Sanborn have stressed the importance of seeing 1917 in a 'continuum of crisis' with the years of the First World War that preceded it and with the civil war that followed it.[3] Studying 1917 as part of a broader chronological picture has provided an important corrective to the tendency to see 1917 in isolated and exceptionalist terms. The narrow chronological focus of this study can, however, also contribute to our understanding of the revolution. The eight-month term of the Provisional Government did not occur in an historical vacuum, but it can be considered on its own terms, and as more than just a stepping stone to its ugly and historically significant postscript, the Bolshevik seizure of power and subsequent civil war. The Bolshevisation of revolutionary history, in which the history of the victors seems to dominate the whole historical process, is hard to avoid. By looking at ordinary people's responses to the exceptional circumstances of 1917, with its rapid formation of local governmental forms and unique opportunities for popular self-government and autonomy, we can make some progress in our attempts to understand ordinary people's responses to revolutionary events, and ultimately the failure of the Provisional Government on its own terms, rather than on the terms of the Bolshevik victors.[4]

---

[3] Peter Holquist, *Making war, forging revolution: Russia's continuum of crisis, 1914–1921* (Cambridge, MA, 2002); Joshua A. Sanborn, *Drafting the Russian nation: military conscription, total war, and mass politics, 1905–1925* (DeKalb, IL 2003).

[4] Michael Melancon expressed similar concerns about 'Bolshevised' history (Michael Melancon, 'The Neopopulist experience: default interpretations and new approaches', *Kritika* 5 (2004), 195–206).

When studying Russia's revolution, it is often difficult to discern the perspectives of ordinary Russian people. We are drawn into revolutionary events by the grand narratives of revolution, but in doing so we sometimes lose individuals. A collection of documents edited by Mark Steinberg sought to find the individual in revolution by seeking out ordinary people's voices in their letters and proclamations.[5] The quest for the ordinary person's perspective is a frustrating one. The vast majority of Russia's ordinary people did not express their views and feelings in the written word. The voices heard in Steinberg's collection, in letters to newspapers or ministers that expressed individuals' opinions, demands and desires, are not representative of Russia's whole population. In particular, the voices of male, urban and often armed Russians far outnumbered and overpowered female, rural and civilian voices. This study explores the environment in which ordinary men and women lived, and the challenges they faced in making political decisions and getting on with daily life. In this way we can gain an insight into the revolutionary year for ordinary people.

This book looks at the dialogues between political elites and ordinary people, and the confusions and contradictions these dialogues exposed. One of the problems we have in trying to understand ordinary people's experiences of 1917 is that most of the historical sources were constructed by the political elite. As James Scott commented, the peasantry often appeared in the historical records not as actors in their own right, but as contributors to statistics.[6] The rich records of police surveillance that historians have mined for the Soviet period to uncover 'hidden transcripts', is not available for the revolutionary period, when the state was at its weakest ebb.[7] What we know, especially of rural life in revolutionary Russia, is seen through a filter of the political elite's perceptions of events. This study has drawn on a wide range of sources but has relied particularly on local newspapers and on records of local government, grass-roots administration and soviet organisations. Many of these sources are dominated by the urban political elite, but by evaluating them carefully, we can challenge the assumptions and misconceptions inherent in the sources, and a subtly altered picture of the revolutionary year emerges. We need to start by challenging the tropes used to describe the countryside. Peasants and rural life are described

---

[5] Mark D. Steinberg, *Voices of revolution, 1917* (New Haven, CT, 2001).

[6] James Scott, *Weapons of the weak: everyday forms of peasant resistance* (New Haven, CT, 1985), p. 29.

[7] The work of Lynne Viola and Sheila Fitzpatrick used *svodki*, secret police reports, extensively in their attempts to penetrate the experience of daily rural life in Soviet Russia (Lynne Viola, *Peasant rebels under Stalin: collectivisation and the culture of peasant resistance* (New York, 1996); Sheila Fitzpatrick, *Stalin's peasants: resistance and survival in the Russian village after collectivisation* (Oxford, 1994)).

repeatedly in newspapers, literature and local government sources as 'dark', 'ignorant' and needing 'enlightenment'. These value judgements are put to one side here and the perspectives of ordinary people themselves are considered. Ordinary people made rational and informed choices about their best interests in 1917, and they engaged in political life consciously and pragmatically.

Throughout this book reference is made to 'ordinary people' and the 'political elite'. 'Political elite' refers both to the political elite at the centre of power in Petrograd, and to those individuals who were in positions of authority in regional politics. The term 'ordinary people' is used with reservations, but because it was the least judgemental and broadest way to describe those individuals who were not active in the formal political and administrative structures that developed in 1917. Stephen Frank and Mark Steinberg used the term 'lower class' in their collection of essays to try and embrace the same range of people, but I have avoided this because of its negative connotations.[8] The Russian word most closely associated with my understanding of ordinary people is the difficult to translate *narod*. I have deliberately avoided using *narod*, because it is often used to refer only to rural people. The distinctions between peasant, worker and soldier were fluid and difficult to pinpoint with accuracy. A better Russian word to use is probably *trudiashchiesia*, or working people, but this might exclude the unemployed or other marginal groups. This broad term 'ordinary people' is not intended to place all those included in it in an easily lumped together mass. Ordinary people were in no way homogenous, and the term allows room for the huge range of different identities that were adopted by them. These terms are intended to be understood loosely, even amorphously, and are not necessarily mutually exclusive. Some 'ordinary people' could also be described as members of the political elite, if, for example, they participated in local administration or leadership. These general groupings are, however, helpful in understanding grass-roots politics, and communication between political leaders and their constituents.

A SKETCH OF NIZHEGOROD AND KAZAN

Nizhegorod and Kazan as they were in 1917 shared some boundaries and were situated in the central eastern belt of European Russia, and both were bisected by the Volga river, Russia's main artery. Both provinces occupied

---

[8] Stephen P. Frank and Mark D. Steinberg, *Cultures in flux: lower-class values, practices and resistance in late Imperial Russia* (Princeton, NJ, 1994).

key geographical locations for transport and trade and were served by the Trans-Siberian railway and water transportation on the Volga and the Kama rivers. Both capital cities had reputations as the country's foremost trading centres, with Kazan being described as the gateway to Siberia, and Nizhnii Novgorod renowned for its annual fair. Both provinces were considered to be part of Russia's fertile 'black earth' belt and had correspondingly high levels of agricultural production, though Kazan was a net exporter of grain, whereas Nizhegorod imported grain. Nizhegorod province was split into 11 *uezds* and 249 *volosts*. The population of Nizhegorod province in 1917 was around 2 million,[9] of which only 361,000 lived in the thirteen towns of the province. Of these, 204,000 lived in Nizhnii Novgorod itself, a large and highly industrialised city. There were some 70,000 workers based in Nizhegorod province in 1917, most of whom where active in heavy and metallurgical industries. The biggest industrial centres were situated in the suburbs of Nizhnii Novgorod, in Kanavin and Sormovo. Kazan province was split into twelve *uezds*, with a population of nearer 3 million. Kazan was home to one of Russia's oldest universities and had a large and active student population. Industry in Kazan was less developed than in Nizhnii Novgorod.

These profiles are useful in giving us a general impression of these provinces' economic output, but without more detailed consideration, they mask the diversity that was a feature of both provinces. Kazan's twelve *uezds*, and Nizhegorod's eleven, each had very distinct geographic features and economic development, which makes any generalisations about them difficult, as forms of agriculture and industry were often specific to their local geography. Another factor that makes straightforward comparisons and generalisations about these two provinces difficult was their diverse ethnic profiles. While Nizhegorod was predominantly Great Russian in make-up, Kazan was included in the mid-Volga region, which was home to large non-Russian communities. Non-Russians made up 35 per cent of the mid-Volga population in the 1897 census. Kazan had the highest proportion of non-Russians of all the mid-Volga provinces. It is worth outlining in more detail Kazan's ethnic diversity, since it played an important part in shaping her responses to 1917. Only around 40 per cent (887,000) of Kazan's population were Great Russian. Tatars made up 32 per cent of the population (721,000), Chuvash 22 per cent (507,000) and Cheremis

[9] P. A. Golub, I. E. Korabliev, M. E. Kuznetsov and I. I. Fignater, *Velikaia Oktiabr'skaia Sotsialisticheskaia Revoliutsiia: entsiklopediia* (Moscow, 1987), p. 334, cites 2,081,200 population in 1917; N. P. Oganovskii (ed.), *Sel'skoe khoziaistvo Rossii v XX veke: sbornik statistiko-ekonomicheskikh svedenie za 1901–1922g.* (Moscow, 1923), pp. 20–1, cites 2,051,700 in 1916.

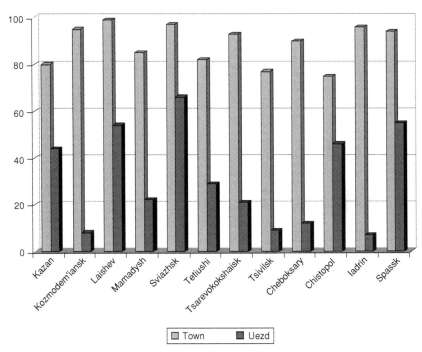

Figure 1.1. Great Russian population (%) in Kazan province, by *uezd*
Source: Iskandr M. Muliukov, 'Rukovodstvo sovetov kul'turno-prosvetitel'nymi uchrezhdeniami v pervye gody Sovetskoi vlasti, 1917–1920gg. po materialam Kazanskoi gubernii', unpublished PhD thesis, Institut iazyka, literatury i istorii imeni G. Ibragimova Kazanskogo filiala ANSSSR (Kazan, 1990), p. 227.

5 per cent (124,000). These different ethnic groups had diverse cultural and linguistic traditions that make any generalisations about popular feeling in Kazan difficult.

The ethnic composition of town and country and of different *uezds* differed significantly around Kazan, as we see in figure 1.1. Non-Russian groups were often scattered rather than concentrated in one particular region, and some villages were ethnically mixed.[10] Communities' ethnic identities offer indications of their dominant occupations, social networks and responses to 1917's political processes. It is, however, difficult to make generalisations about particular regions because of the level of ethnic mixing, and the uneven patterns of ethnic distribution around the region. One point on

---

[10] Robert Geraci, *Window on the east: national and Imperial identities in late tsarist Russia* (Ithaca, NY, 2001), p. 33.

which we can be confident is that non-Russians were not proportionately represented in the region's towns. In Kozmodem'iansk *uezd*, for example, though Great Russians made up only 8 per cent of the *uezd* population, they made up 95 per cent of the population in Kozmodem'iansk town, which meant that Great Russians dominated the administration of the *uezd*. This pattern is replicated in other *uezds* around Kazan province. Non-Russian communities' lack of connection to urban culture was to have important implications for them in 1917, when formal power structures crystallised around towns, leaving non-Russian groups effectively isolated from the political elite centred in the towns. We should also take note of the diversity of languages and letters seen among Kazan's non-Russian community, which greatly complicated communications in 1917. As the revolutionary tides swirled around Kazan, non-Russian communities were left to some extent isolated as a result of the difficulties the political elite faced in communicating with them.

Russia's largest Tatar community was based in Kazan. Their language was Turkic in origin, one of the oldest literary languages of the former Soviet Union, and used the Arabic script. Tatars practised Sunni Muslim religion. A distinct subdivision of the Tatar language, using the Cyrillic script, was developed in the eighteenth century by the small number of Tatars who formally converted to the Russian Orthodox Church in the seventeenth and eighteenth centuries. These converts were known as baptised Tatars (*Kreshchennyi tatary*), also referred to as Kryashen, and formed a distinct subdivision within Tatars who spoke Tatar but could not read Arabic script. Muslim Tatars were easy to distinguish by their clothing and grooming, and unlike other non-Russian groups, who were predominantly peasant, Tatars spanned the social spectrum, had a well-developed merchant class and were the most urbanised of Kazan's non-Russian groups.[11]

The Chuvash people also spoke a Turkic-based language, though theirs included an admix of words from Persian, Arabic and Russian. Their literary language was not established until the 1870s and was written in the Cyrillic script. Tatars and Chuvash could understand one another's languages, but with difficulty. The vast majority of Chuvash were listed as practising the Orthodox religion, and those who were not Christians were more likely to practise Animist faith than Muslim faith. The Chuvash were considered to be highly skilled agriculturalists, and they enjoyed a relatively high standard of living. They were the most urbanised, after the Tatars, of Kazan's non-Russian community.

---

[11] Ronald Wixman, *The peoples of the USSR: an ethnographic handbook* (London, 1984), pp. 186–7; Geraci, *Window on the east*, pp. 36–44.

The Cheremis, also referred to as the Marii, are a Finnic people, whose language belonged to the Finno-Ugric group and was established in a literary form by the Russian Orthodox Church in their attempts to convert the Marii. The Marii practised Shamanist-Animist religion, though some did convert to the Orthodox Church. They were divided into two subgroups that shared cultural practices but had mutually unintelligible dialects. The highland, or forest Marii, lived mostly on the right bank of the Volga, while the lowland, or meadow Marii, settled mainly on the left bank of the Volga. The meadow Marii were often forest dwellers and engaged in beekeeping, hunting and basic agriculture. They were often employed as barge haulers or fishermen. The highland Marii tended to practise more advanced agriculture than their meadow cousins and were considered to be more assimilated to the Great Russian population.[12] Kazan's ethnic diversity is not the main focus of the study, but the region's ethnic make-up was an important feature of its social and political responses to the revolutionary year and therefore forms an integral part of the analysis presented here.

CENTRAL POWER AND AUTHORITY IN 1917

This book will concentrate on events outside the capitals and is structured thematically rather than chronologically. This presents a real challenge to the book's structure, as the complex chronology of 1917 informed the events that unfolded in the provinces, and the climate of daily life. The following section offers a brief overview of central government and the challenges to it over the course of the Provisional Government's eight months in power. The February revolution occurred when workers' demonstrations and a mutiny in the garrison at the end of February caused the tsarist government to collapse.[13] The events of 1917 can be framed around key chronological events; the February revolution and the abdication of the tsar; the April crisis over war aims that led to Miliukov's resignation and the formation of the first coalition government; the June offensive, Kerensky's attempt to galvanise the army; the July days, a series of demonstrations and disturbances on the streets of Petrograd between 3 and 5 July, characterised by their forceful demands for 'All power to the Soviet'; the Kornilov affair of August, when the army's supreme commander was implicated in a plot to take over government, and Kerensky's own credibility was severely damaged by his own involvement in the affair; September's Democratic

---

[12] Wixman, *The peoples of the USSR*, p. 132; Geraci, *Window on the east*, pp. 33–4.
[13] The authorative view of February is probably Hasegawa, *The February revolution*. For a masterful discussion of agency in the February revolution, see Michael Melancon, *Rethinking Russia's February revolution: anonymous spontaneity or socialist agency?* (Pittsburg, 2000).

Conference, called at the initiative of the soviets as a last gasp attempt to unite democratic forces, and finally, of course, the Bolshevik seizure of power on 25 October 1917, in the name of the soviets. These events marked shifts in the elite political climate that had immediate ramifications on provincial political life. The chapters that follow will dwell repeatedly on two key themes that defined these crises and dogged Russia's administrators both at the centre and in the provinces. These two inextricably linked themes are Russia's participation in the First World War and economic crisis.

The First World War placed an unprecedented strain on Russia's economy and society. We can see the war as the Provisional Government's midwife, but also its executioner. Having contributed in no small part to the collapse of the tsarist regime, involvement in the war was too great a burden for the new Provisional Government. The war's implications for Russia were massive and profound. Mass warfare demanded total mobilisation, of men, of industry and of the economy at large. Peter Gatrell estimates that 12 per cent of Russia's population, or 17.5 million people, were displaced by the war.[14] This population displacement placed unprecedented strain on the economy and society. The state was required to train, feed and equip the army, to provide subsidies for soldiers' families and to care for the wounded. On the home front, the loss of male workers placed pressure on agriculture and on the families who depended on their labour. Russia's transport system groaned under the strain of moving men, provisions and equipment across Russia's extensive front lines. The fighting drove large numbers of civilians away from their homes and into heartland Russia. These refugees placed further pressure on transport, on provisioning and on the state's infrastructure. Socially, the war was fundamentally politicising, causing ordinary workers, soldiers and peasants to redefine their relations with the state.[15]

Russia's economy moved towards meltdown in 1917. Exports of goods were virtually halted, both by the need to mobilise industry into military production, and by the disruption of trade routes. The balance of trade collapsed both on internal and external markets. By 1915–16, four-fifths of government expenditure was covered by deficit. This proportion actually worsened in 1917.[16] It is easy to forget that the Provisional Government's

---

[14] Peter Gatrell, *Russia's first world war: a social and economic history* (London, 2005), p. 222. Gatrell comes to these figures by estimating numbers of mobilised soldiers, prisoners of war and refugees.

[15] See Sanborn's penetrating analysis of the social impact of war in Russia (Joshua A. Sanborn, 'Unsettling the empire: violent migrations and social disaster in Russia during World War I', *Journal of Modern History* 77 (2006), 290–324).

[16] Gatrell, *Russia's first world war*, p. 134.

policy options were gravely constricted by the financial crisis it presided over. This financial crisis manifested itself harshly in ordinary people's lives. As the government printed more and more money to cover the deficit, inflation surged out of control. One economist estimated that a basket of household goods in the second half of 1917 cost about five times what it had in 1913.[17] Ordinary people in the towns and countryside found it increasingly difficult or even impossible to obtain life's daily necessities. Ordinary Russians were politicised, empowered and filled with hope by the February revolution. In the catastrophic economic climate, their hopes were unrealisable. Ordinary people became increasingly frustrated and angry as their demands were not met.

Two sources of central power and authority emerged to preside over Russia's collapsing economy. The Provisional Government rose from the rubble of the tsarist government. It was formed from negotiations between the Temporary Committee, an informal meeting of Duma members, and the Petrograd Soviet, and its members were drawn predominantly from the State Duma. It was to be reformed five times in the course of its eight-month life but was initially dominated by Kadets and Progressives, both moderate Liberals (see table 1.1). The Petrograd Soviet was constructed on the initiative of several socialist Duma members, and members of the central workers' group who had just been released from prison. The Petrograd Soviet's executive body was dominated from the outset by intelligentsia figures, but its mass constituency was elected representatives from Petrograd's workers and soldiers. Power and authority in 1917 is often described as 'dual power'. This describes the division of authority between the Provisional Government and the Petrograd Soviet. Initially, the Petrograd Soviet offered provisional support to the Provisional Government in so far as it defended the interests of revolutionary democracy. When the first Provisional Government collapsed at the end of April over War Minister Miliukov's secret note to the allies over Russia's war aims, the leaders of the Soviet agreed to shore up the Provisional Government more firmly by entering into coalition with it. Key Soviet leaders entered the Provisional Government, including the leaders of the Socialist Revolutionary Party (PSR) and the Mensheviks. Though the Soviet leaders themselves withdrew from the coalition at the end of July, Soviet members continued to play key roles in the Provisional Government until its demise.

The Petrograd Soviet was perceived to have real power by dint of its popularity and alleged authority among ordinary people, while the Provisional

[17] M. P. Kokhn, *Russkie indeksi tsen* (Moscow, 1926), p. 18.

Table 1.1. *The Provisional Government's five incarnations*

Dates of the formation of the new governments, and the political affiliation of the members

Ministerial post	3 March	5 May	25 July	1 September	25 September
Prime minister	Prince G. E. Lvov — IND	Prince G. E. Lvov — PROG	A. F. Kerensky — IND	A. F. Kerensky — SR	A. F. Kerensky — SR
Foreign affairs	P. N. Miliukov — KAD	M. I. Tereschenko — PROG	M. I. Tereschenko — PROG	M. I. Tereschenko — PROG	M. I. Tereschenko — PROG
War	A. I. Guchkov — KAD	A. F. Kerensky — SR	A. F. Kerensky (Savinkov) — SR (SR)	General Verkhovskii — IND	General Verkhovskii — IND
Army	A. I. Guchkov — KAD	A. F. Kerensky — SR	A. F. Kerensky (Lebedev) — SR (SR)	General Verkhovskii — IND	General Verkhovskii — IND
Navy	A. I. Guchkov — KAD	A. F. Kerensky — SR	A. F. Kerensky — SR	Admiral Verderevskii — IND	Admiral Verderevskii — IND
Transport	N. V. Nekrasov — PROG	N. V. Nekrasov — PROG	Yurenev — PROG		Liverovskii — SR
Trade and industry	A. I. Konovalov — KAD	A. I. Konovalov — KAD	Prokopovich — KAD		A. I. Konovalov — KAD
Finance	M. I. Tereschenko — PROG	A. I. Shingarev — KAD	N. V. Nekrasov — KAD		Bernadskii — RD
Education	A. A. Manuilov — KAD	A. A. Manuilov — KAD	Ol'denburg — KAD		Salazkin — IND
Holy Synod	V. N. Lvov — NAT	V. N. Lvov — NAT	Kartashev — NAT		Kartashev — KAD
Agriculture	A. I. Shingarev — KAD	V. M. Chernov — SR	V. M. Chernov — SR		Maslov — SR
Justice	A. F. Kerensky — SR	P. N. Pereverzev — SR	Zarudnyi — SR		Maliantovich — MEN
Labour		M. I. Skobelev — MEN	M. I. Skobelev — MEN		Gvozdev — MEN
Post and telegram		I. G. Tsereteli — MEN	A. M. Nikitin — MEN	A. M. Nikitin — PS	A. M. Nikitin — PS
Food		A. V. Peshekhonov — PS	A. V. Peshekhonov — PS		Prokopovich — IND
Welfare		Prince D. I. Shakhovskoi — KAD	Yefremov — PROG		Kishkin — KAD
State Controller	I. V. Godnev — KAD	I. V. Godnev — KAD	Kokoshkin — KAD		Smirnov — MEN
Interior			Avksentev — SR		Nikitin — PS

Key to abbreviations in table: IND – Independent, with no party affiliation; NAT – Nationalist Party; SR – Socialist Revolutionary Party; PS – Popular Socialist Party; KAD – Kadet Party; PROG – Progressive Party; MEN – Menshevik Party; RD – Radical Democrat

Government lacked popular support but could claim legitimacy from its origins in the State Duma, and more importantly as the only body that was willing to tackle the Sisyphean task of governing Russia. The Provisional Government and Petrograd Soviet were in conflict over a number of key issues during the Provisional Government's governance of Russia, in particular over war aims and government personnel. At times their conflicts verged on open hostility. If we look at the broader picture, however, the Provisional Government and Petrograd Soviet shared key aims. Both desired a restoration of civic order and calm, the establishment of civil liberties, the convocation of a Constituent Assembly and Russia's continued participation in the world war. Their grounds for collaboration were ultimately more powerful than their grounds for conflict. This common ground between the Petrograd Soviet and Provisional Government was even larger and more pronounced in the soviets and Provisional Government organisations in Nizhegorod and Kazan.

Tsuyoshi Hasegawa pinpointed the problem of dual power as lying with the inconsistency between the wishes of the Soviet leaders and the wishes of their mass support.[18] This study of Nizhegorod and Kazan suggests that Hasegawa's point needs to be developed and highlighted further. In Kazan and Nizhegorod, dual power did not exist between soviet and Provisional Government bodies. There were, however, divisions between local leaders and their constituents. Though the theoretical locations of power were traceable, in practice power was situated with those who had the ability to operate it. Authority did not spring from legitimacy in 1917, or at least not legitimacy in legal terms. Authority, that is, the ability to enforce obedience, was notable for its absence for the better part of 1917. Even the Petrograd Soviet, commonly credited with having 'power', and therefore authority, was swept away by the tide of public opinion. When decisions were made that were not popular, the effect was that the Soviet leadership lost credibility, not that they asserted their authority. Where local leaders were unable to win the support of their constituents, they had almost no coercive measures open to them and were therefore exposed to the vagaries of popular will.

Leopold Haimson argued that dual power was nothing more than a reflection of the profound rift in society that had emerged between the propertied classes and the workers, particularly in Petrograd.[19] This view is

---

[18] Tsuyoshi Hasegawa, 'The problem of power in the February revolution of 1917 in Russia', *Canadian Slavonic Papers* 14 (1972), 611–33, p. 626.

[19] Leopold J. Haimson, 'The problem of social identities in early twentieth-century Russia', *Slavic Review* 47, 1 (1988), 1–20.

supported by Ronald Suny who argued that dual power was an active model of polarisation within society.[20] These conclusions are not supported when we look at the balance of power outside Petrograd. Although the Provisional Government's lack of solid support can be seen as a vote of no-confidence from the people it professed to represent, dual power did not display any neat polarisation of views, and the balance of power in Petrograd did not represent the balance of power outside the capital. Though soviet and Provisional Government administrations coexisted in Kazan and Nizhegorod, they were too closely intertwined to conform to the model of 'dual power'.[21]

THE 'DEMOCRATISATION' OF POWER IN THE PROVINCES

The February revolution initiated an unprecedented and dramatic root and branch transformation of local government, and the watchword of revolutionary local government structures was democratisation. Democracy had a raft of different meanings in the revolutionary lexicon. It could refer to democracy as a political system, or it could refer to 'the democracy', political power for ordinary people. Boris Kolonitskii remarks that 'Democratisation was looked upon as a solution to all possible problems.'[22] The old regime's structures were denounced as inefficient and corrupt, and systematically removed. The implicit assumption was that the old regime's failings could be righted, so long as the new mantra of democracy and representative government was applied to every aspect of government and administration. This assumption was challenged in the course of 1917 by the grave problems facing Russia's new administrators. The Provisional Government attempted to establish a local government network responsible to central government through the appointment of provincial and *uezd* commissars, and the creation of locally selected executive committees at every level from province down to *volost* and village. The basis for establishment of this new order was the old Town Dumas and town councils in urban areas and *zemstva* committees in rural areas. Ad hoc public committees, formed in the immediate aftermath of revolution and often named 'committees of public safety', in some places continued to operate alongside the commissar system, or even

[20] R. G. Suny, 'Towards a social history of the October revolution', *American Historical Review* 88 (1983), 31–52, p. 36.
[21] Donald Raleigh came to the same conclusions in his study of Saratov in 1917 (Donald J. Raleigh, *Revolution on the Volga: 1917 in Saratov* (New York, 1986), pp. 92–3).
[22] Boris I. Kolonitskii, '"Democracy" as identification: towards the study of political consciousness during the February revolution', in Madhavan K. Palat (ed.), *Social identities in revolutionary Russia* (London, 2001), pp. 161–73, p. 161.

replaced it. The soviets of workers', soldiers' and peasants' deputies evolved autonomously.[23] The soviets were large councils, with representatives usually elected from their constituency by open vote.[24] These unwieldy bodies elected an executive committee and a presidium that governed the soviet. Activists usually initiated the formation of soviets, put out calls for elections and often went on to dominate the soviets' executive committees.

Urban groups enjoyed a heavy predominance in the new power structures. Town-based 'committees of public safety' often formed the nucleus of provincial power by supplementing their urban membership with some representatives from the *uezds*. The soviet structures that formed alongside these Provisional Government bodies evolved predominantly from workers and soldiers, and only affiliated with the always later-forming peasant soviets as an afterthought. The vast majority of the provincial population was rural-based and was decidedly under-represented in regional power structures. The political elite complained repeatedly in newspapers, appeals and official reports that peasant Russia had not adopted the mantras of committees, democracy and organisation that formed the backbone of the new revolutionary order. Certainly when compared with urban environments, the countryside looked under-organised. Factories and garrisons, already organised into tightly functioning units, were quick to form their own committees, which could then feed representatives into the regional power structures. The network of committees that could provide delegates for regional power structures was much thinner in rural than in urban areas. The formation of specifically revolutionary organisations in the countryside went on patchily and seemed to leave the rural population adrift from the drive for organisation that was such a feature of 1917.

We must be careful, however, not to misunderstand this apparently under-structured countryside. The shortage of specifically revolutionary organisations in the countryside was partly due to the existence of pre-revolutionary village organisations that continued to operate in 1917, making specifically revolutionary organisations rather superfluous. Communal and village councils in their original pre-revolutionary forms provided

---

[23] Generally speaking, the soviets of workers' and soldiers' deputies met together, or had a joint executive committee (as in Nizhnii Novgorod), but the soviet of peasants' deputies tended to retain independence, even if it participated in joint soviet meetings, or publications (as in Tambov).

[24] The standard reference work on the formation of soviets is Oskar Anweiler, *The soviets: the Russian workers', peasants' and soldiers' councils 1905–1921* (New York, 1958). More recent studies of particular provinces have given detailed accounts of regional soviet activity, in particular Raleigh, *Revolution on the Volga*; Michael C. Hickey, 'Local government and state authority in the provinces: Smolensk, February–June 1917', *Slavic Review* 55 (1996), 863–81.

participation for ordinary people in community decisions and representation. Though they were modified in the course of 1917, allowing, for
example, an equal voice for women, or the participation of soldiers on
leave, they proved to be durable organisations that functioned as effectively
in 1917 as they had before.[25] Other pre-revolutionary forms of rural organisation also mobilised in 1917, including peasant unions, co-operatives, artels
and so on, but none were so overarching or powerful as the communal and
village councils in Nizhegorod and Kazan. In the factories and garrisons on
the other hand, organisation and representation had been specifically prohibited by the tsarist administration. Pre-existing bodies including health
insurance organisations, artels, *zemliachestva* and shop committees provided the basis for worker mobilisation in 1917, but these organisations
were overlaid by specifically revolutionary committees, councils and soviets in the revolutionary year. While rural representation was certainly less
prominent at central levels, and there were fewer specifically revolutionary
organisations in the countryside, the countryside was organically organised,
and developed its structures in keeping with existing village organisations.

The Provisional Government's commissar system was dogged by association with the old regime and its system of local administration that was
formed from the ashes of the old *zemstva*. The soviets, on the other hand,
were untainted by any such associations and could invoke a pure revolutionary pedigree. Their apparent differences paled, however, before the
magnitude of governing the provinces. These two unrelated branches of
governance often worked in close co-operation, sharing leaders and facing
the ire of the population together when they were perceived to be failing in
their duties. The February revolution heralded significant changes, not only
in the mechanics of local administration, but also in popular expectations
of government. The rhetoric of revolution promised equality, freedom and
justice, while the practical and financial problems of providing material
support were actually increased by the massive tumult of revolution.

The ability of any administrative body, whether soviet or Provisional
Government sponsored, to build and sustain the trust (*doverie*) of the population was crucial if it was to have any chance of long-term success in
maintaining order among its constituency. Just what was required to win
such trust is elusive. 'Trust of the population' is an abstract concept, but it
was invoked as if it were a solid reality. Despite the diversity of administrative bodies that formed in the wake of the February revolution, none of

---

[25] V. V. Kabanov, 'Oktiabr'skaia revoliutsiia i krest'ianskaia obshchina', *Istoricheskii zapiski* 3 (1984),
106–50; John Channon, 'The peasantry in the revolutions of 1917', in J. Frankel, E. G. Frankel and
B. Knei-Paz (eds.), *Revolution in Russia: reassessments of 1917* (Cambridge, 1992), pp. 105–30.

them could claim to have the unreserved trust and support of the population. The enormously high popular expectations that burdened all administrative bodies in the post-February period were combined with a very provisional support for the new structures, in so far as they were perceived to be satisfying popular need. Where they did not, they were mercilessly cast aside by a population energised by popular political participation. The relationship between local leaders and their constituents is to be a theme of all the chapters that follow.

The new administrative structures shared the conceit that they represented and defended all sectors of the community. In the case of the soviet, this representation and defence was targeted specifically at all 'toiling and impoverished' (*trudiashchiesia i obezdolennyi*) people. The administration was under pressure to be formed either entirely from representatives elected by the local community, or at least for existing structures to be supplemented by such popularly elected representatives. A national report to the Provisional Government for the period March–May commented, 'Under the present system of popular elections, the idea of *appointment* did not fit in with national understanding. It suspected in this practice an encroachment upon its liberties.'[26] The Provisional Government's executives were particularly tormented by the question of how they were to be recognised as sufficiently democratic and revolutionary when their roots were in pre-revolutionary structures. The *zemstva* were all re-elected in 1917 on democratic bases, but in many areas these elections did not occur till September, and until then the *zemstva* could only make token concessions to popular representation.

The structures that developed for governance in Kazan and Nizhnii Novgorod towns were similar in the ways that they provided forums for co-ordinated administration between soviet and Provisional Government structures, but they varied in form according to local peculiarities. The peculiarities of regional administration become more marked when we look at administration at *uezd* and *volost* level. At these lower levels, forms of administration were extremely diverse and strongly reflected local conditions and personalities. Where the former head of the *zemstva* had been a popular figure, the Provisional Government-approved committee springing from the old *zemstva* was likely to endure through 1917. Where they were not popular, they were quickly superseded by a range of other individuals and

---

[26] Robert P. Browder and Alexander F. Kerensky, *The Russian Provisional Government of 1917: documents* (Stanford, 1961), vol. I, p. 247, doc. 226; taken from report of the Provincial Section of the Temporary Committee of the State Duma, based on reports of its field representatives for the first three months of the revolution. The original copy of this report is held in RGIA, f. 1278, op. 10, d. 4.

even organisations. Where there was community interest and active local leaders, soviets of workers', soldiers' and peasants' deputies were formed at local levels. More often, however, at *uezd* and *volost* levels no such soviets existed. The diversity of forms in low-level administration does not allow for broad generalisations on administrative structure.

We can draw a detailed picture of the shape of administrative bodies that formed in Nizhnii Novgorod and Kazan towns. Central administration was located in the capitals in both provinces, and was formed around the town administrative bodies. The Town Duma played a role in both towns, though it proved to be far more influential in Nizhnii Novgorod than in Kazan. In both Nizhnii Novgorod and Kazan there were close links in structure, policy and personnel between Provisional Government and soviet bodies. These links were less formally recognised in Nizhnii Novgorod than in Kazan. In Nizhnii, the senior executive body in the town was the provincial executive committee, headed by the provincial commissar, and formed from representatives of all the large public organisations in the province. It was also the executive organ of power for the province, with representatives from all the *uezds*.[27] It addressed the problem of 'democratisation' of its parts very specifically at its meeting on 8 May. This rather late date gives us a good idea of how slow the process of democratisation was in practice, as representatives had to be sought from Nizhegorod's far-flung *uezds*:

The provisional revolutionary assembly represents the organised public opinion of Nizhegorod province in questions of public political life, and exercises control over assemblies and representatives of government power, and also over *zemstvo*, town and peasant and other *soslovnyi* assemblies, if they are not reorganised on the basis of universal, equal, secret, direct voting.[28]

This (unelected) body aspired to co-ordinate the democratised parts of regional administration. Where democratisation had not taken place, it was to 'exercise control', even though it had no clear popular legitimacy itself. Not least because of its lack of close connection with its constituency, the provincial executive committee was regarded as rather toothless. Though in principle it had no clear links with the soviets, in practice it worked closely with them. The different branches of government in Nizhnii responded to crises like the July soldiers' rising harmoniously.[29] This indicates that despite

---

[27] GANO, f. 1887, op. 1, d. 11, ll. 58–9; meeting of Nizhegorod provincial executive committee, 25 July 1917.

[28] GANO, f. 1887, op. 1, d. 1, l. 5; meeting of Nizhnii Novgorod town executive committee, 8 May 1917.

[29] The July soldiers' rising is discussed in chapter 4.

the lack of formal links between soviet and executive bodies, the closeness of their membership and of their aspirations ensured that dual power existed more in principle than it did in practice. The pragmatic needs to administer the region won over any dogmatic considerations of separation of soviet and Provisional Government administration. The peasants' soviet complained that the work of the provincial executive committee was so insignificant that it wasted the time and energies of its two delegates.[30] Though the relationship between the provincial executive committee and the soviets was close and symbiotic, with two of the provincial commissar's closest advisers also members of the peasants' soviet, the connections between the two were much less clearly and closely delineated than in Kazan.[31]

In Kazan, the dual power model was irreparably breached at the outset by the close co-operation that developed between the Provisional Government-sponsored commissar organisation and the autonomously formed soviets of workers' and soldiers' deputies. These bodies worked in close co-operation in an enlarged committee of public safety, which throughout 1917 provided an administrative hub for the province. The Kazan committee of public safety, formed at the end of March, constituted the highest administrative organ of the province. The primary role of the committee of public safety was to co-ordinate regional power structures. From the outset, Kazan's executive power was broader and more inclusive than its comparable institution in Nizhnii Novgorod; it was also more active in addressing the problem of its inadequate 'democratisation'.

Though the committee was initially composed of former *zemstvo* members, it was quickly supplemented with representatives from a diverse range of other organisations including *uezd* commissars, all the main political parties, the soviet of soldiers and workers' deputies, the Latvian committee of refugees, various professional and co-operative unions, and national groups.[32] The committee of public safety was clearly regarded by the Provisional Government's appointed representatives as a legitimate holder of popular support and regional power. V. N. Chernyshev was appointed by the Provisional Government as provincial commissar in May, replacing the incumbent commissar A. N. Plotnikov who resigned on ill-health grounds.[33] Chernyshev refused to take up the post until it was ratified by the committee of public safety. A committee of public safety meeting,

---

[30] *Narod* 61, 3 September 1917, p. 4.   [31] *Narod* 61, 3 September 1917, p. 4.

[32] NART, f. 1353, op. 1, d. 1, l. 3; protocol of the meeting of the provincial committee of public safety, 10 April 1917.

[33] NART, f. 1353, op. 1, d. 1, l. 73; telegram from provincial commissar Plotnikov to Minister of Internal Affairs, 19 May 1917.

attended by ninety-five members, duly agreed his election with only four votes against him.[34]

The central question for its first meeting on 10 April was that, in its current incarnation, it could not utilise full authority among the population, and that it should accordingly be 'democratised'. There was an extensive discussion over what this democratisation should entail and, crucially, how it was to represent the majority of the population, who were peasants, but who had not yet formed into recognisable unions or affiliations.[35] This was a thorny problem for a group which sought 'democracy' when the reality was that democracy and representation could not be offered without preparatory work which would have been years in the making. Iu. P. Denike, a well-known Menshevik activist, came up with a compromise whereby representatives from the *uezds* and peasants' union would be added at a later stage. He stressed the need to keep the committee compact and workmanlike, as he was clearly aware of the dangerous impasses faced by excessively large committees.[36]

Although the committee's executive body was trimmed down from thirty members to fifteen, he was unable to control the burgeoning size of the committee. The committee, which aimed to 'embrace all sectors of public and political life in the town', quickly became unwieldy as an administrative organisation. By the end of April it had 260 members, including such notables as representatives of the beekeeping society. The committee's president, Denike, was forced to address the problem of non-attendance at the committee by some of these disparate groups, which made quorum difficult to reach. It was decided to reduce the quorum of the meeting by a third in order to keep the committee functioning.[37] This gives an indication of the clash between democratisation and efficient administration. It is not possible to assess with any accuracy the exact political make-up of the committee of public safety over the course of 1917, not least because political affiliations were not often attributed to members. Based on its leadership and its policies on key issues, however, we can be confident that it pursued moderate socialist politics in the course of 1917, keeping itself roughly in step with Provisional Government declarations.

Denike, its first president, declared boldly that 'the committee of public safety works in total harmony with the soviet of workers' and soldiers'

[34] *Kazanskaia rabochaia gazeta* 40, 30 May 1917, p. 3.
[35] NART, f. 1353, op. 1, d. 1, ll. 3–8; protocol of the meeting of the provincial committee of public safety, 10 April 1917.
[36] NART, f. 1353, op. 1, d. 1, l. 40b; from protocol of the meeting of the provincial committee of public safety, 10 April 1917.
[37] *Kazanskaia rabochaia gazeta* 17, 29 April 1917, p. 3.

deputies. There can be no question of dual power in Kazan.'[38] Though Denike's statement might be discounted as wishful thinking, Kazan's administration in fact bore out his claim. Joint meetings of the various branches of town and province power were common in Kazan and contributed to a more 'joined up' feeling in government.[39] A telling example of the unity of purpose shown by Kazan's disparate administration was in their response to a major crisis that overwhelmed the city in mid-August. In our efforts to evaluate the shape and co-ordination of local government, a crisis offers a good vantage point to oversee the balance of power in the town. The fire in Kazan town that occurred in mid-August offers us just such a vantage point. This report from the *Kazanskaia rabochaia gazeta* does it justice:

TO THE POPULATION OF THE TOWN. On the 14, 15 and 16 August in Kazan, unfortunate events for all our homeland occurred. At 3.30 pm at the Pokhorovnaia depot a small fire started without known cause, and caused some shells nearby to explode. This could be heard in all corners of the town. Then some sort of bombardment began as explosions went one after the other, from small to enormous. Panic spread in the town. Terrible rumours went round . . . when the explosions began there was a terrible scene as the townspeople just ran, forgetting their children and their loved ones, running onto the streets; but where, why? They ran to the villages, the villagers ran still further, and all waited for some sort of terrible explosion which would rent apart the whole country. The explosions were terrible. Whole wagons of shells exploded in the air . . . there were deaths not only in the districts closest to the fire – Admiratel′skoi, Pokhorova, Iagodnoi hamlets, but also up to three versts away . . . and still explosions came one after the other. Struggle with the fire began in Uskhov factory. By the evening there was a sea of fire. Fires started in separate towns and areas . . . for the whole of the 15 August the town was obscured with smoke . . . millions of state money has been lost. It was the panic that was really terrible and which overcame citizens, soldiers, officers, even the general staff. The citizens of the overwhelmed hamlets and soldiers of the 240th regiment are to be praised, as they sought to fight the blaze. But the other town citizens, especially men, soldiers, officers, evacuee military, George cavalry; they ran, and this only increased the panic of women and children. The shame of this flight was equal to the flight from the front before the face of the enemy for soldiers and officers.[40]

National attention was attracted by the magnitude of the fire; Kerensky himself sent a letter expressing his sorrow to Kazan,[41] and national as well as

---

[38] *Kazanskaia rabochaia gazeta* 17, 29 April 1917, p. 3.
[39] For example, the organisation of Iron Day in Kazan at the end of July, a process in which all branches of power in Kazan participated. *Kazanskaia rabochaia gazeta* 71, 7 July 1917, p. 3.
[40] *Kazanskaia rabochaia gazeta* 102, 16 August 1917, p. 1.
[41] Published in *Kazanskaia rabochaia gazeta* 111, 26 August 1917, p. 3.

local papers reported the events. A Nizhnii Novgorod newspaper devoted several hundred words to coverage of the event, which was described as a catastrophe for the whole country, as it impacted on the war effort by mass destruction of shells.[42] These extraordinary events brought many features of a frontline war zone absolutely without warning to this peaceful capital city. Hazy photographs taken at the time show the expanse of city shrouded by great plumes of smoke.[43] Fire spread rapidly, destroying homes and businesses. The explosions provoked a mass panic and exodus from the town and its environs. Panicking citizens and abandoned children fled not just to the surrounding countryside, but further afield on steamers along the Volga to Sviazhsk, Simbirsk and Chistopol.[44] One can speculate that the already heightened feelings provoked by the uncertainties of revolution made anything seem possible, so increasing the potency of rumours of imminent apocalypse that engulfed the population.

The ways in which the varied administrative strands of Kazan coped with this crisis are impressive and demonstrate the unity of purpose that Provisional Government and soviet bodies shared. Though soviet deputies led the efforts to restore order, the Town Duma and the provincial Executive committee all participated in the efforts:

> The soviet of soldiers' and workers' deputies remained at their place, heroically working around the smoke. Workers of Pokhorovo factory were also there, and trainee officers from the military college, both schools of young officers and artillery, and a command of the voluntary battalions, they all worked in defence of the town. Workers of the electric station carried out its defence, and all prepared to light the town that evening . . . automobiles with members of the executive committee ran around the town, and calmed the population. In the evening of 14 and 15 August the Duma gathered. A committee for the assistance of those whose homes had been destroyed by fire was organised at the meeting. Drinking points around the town and a financial committee to collect donations were organised. It was established through talks with the military authorities that the town was not in danger. The Duma made an appeal to citizens, calling for calm, and asking them to join in the common work with the military power, the soviet of workers', soldiers' and peasants' deputies, the town Duma and the committee of public safety . . .[45]

Not only fire-fighting and water points, but provisions, accommodation and general becalming and regrouping of the panicked town population went on at a prodigious rate. These were difficult tasks, and the general

---

[42] *Narod* 55, 20 August 1917, p. 4.
[43] Photos held in the National Museum of the Republic of Tatarstan, Kazan.
[44] *Kazanskaia rabochaia gazeta* 104, 18 August 1917, p. 2.
[45] *Kazanskaia rabochaia gazeta* 102, 16 August 1917, p. 1.

impression of the immediate aftermath of events was of total chaos. Military law was enforced, and all Russia's newly won freedoms of expression, meetings and publications were suspended, as attempts were made to quash dangerous rumours and public disorder. Consignments of bread were delivered by car to the most stricken areas, including the Pokhorovo hamlet, where the fire had initially broken out. The tone of the papers reporting these events was often highly charged in its public condemnations of those who did not do their duties, particularly men in uniform. In contrast to these sorry figures, the soviet deputies and other members of the town and regional administration were portrayed as the heroes of the moment, leading the efforts to put the town back onto a more normal footing. The Kazan fire confirms that pragmatism in facing the challenges of governing the city won out over dogmatic separation of the different branches of regional administration.

The positions held by the Town Dumas in 1917 are a good indication of the extent to which local factors defined the development of local government. In Kazan, the Town Duma was a largely irrelevant body, which contributed little to the governance of the town and was explicitly associated with the old regime. In Nizhnii Novgorod, on the other hand, the Duma became a rallying point for the moderate socialists that dominated the town's administration and played a pivotal role in governing the town. The chief difference between the two was that Nizhnii Novgorod's Duma was successful in disassociating itself with its past, and identifying with the new forces of democratisation, whereas in Kazan the Duma was out of step with democratisation. The date of re-elections was important; in Kazan they were not held till October, whereas in Nizhnii they were carried out in July. The Town Duma of Nizhnii Novgorod was established in 1781, and though its membership was transformed in 1917, the institution itself was to remain a significant uniting force for democratic elements in Nizhnii Novgorod town.

The Town Dumas were explicitly associated in popular consciousness with wealthy, old regime Russia. In a piece encouraging people to vote, the SR V. B. Libin declared, 'Up until now, citizens, the majority of us only knew this about the Town Duma, that it was located on such and such a street, and that the town mayor was so and so.'[46]

The challenge for the Town Duma in the wake of the February revolution was how to popularise and democratise itself. In Nizhnii Novgorod, as Libin proposed, ordinary people 'reclaimed' the Duma by voting in

[46] *Narod* 14, 17 May 1917, p. 2.

their own constituents. In Kazan, on the other hand, from the very outset the Duma was out of step with the 'democratisation' sweeping Kazan's
administration and failed to make an impact on governing the town. The
Kazan Duma initially proposed that its membership should be supplemented by a further forty-five representatives from 'democratic society',
including ten from the soviet of workers' and soldiers' deputies, thirty from
the non-propertied elements (*netsenzoviki*), and five from national minorities. Initially, re-elections were scheduled for 5 May, but this was opposed
by the soviet and committee of Public Safety because it was considered
insufficient time to prepare for the elections.[47] In the event, the elections
were not held until October. These late elections meant that the Duma
never established itself as part of the 'democratic' town administration and
was consequently marginalised.

A problem for the Duma's effectiveness in Kazan was that the Duma's
supplementary, 'democratic' membership was at absolute loggerheads with
the old Duma members. At its very first meeting with new members on 26
April, the Duma's membership was split right down the middle by a vote on
sending greetings to the Provisional Government. The new faction, headed
by the ubiquitous Denike, opposed the sending of greetings on the basis
of current disagreements with the government, and was narrowly outvoted
59–46 by the old members. The current of hostility between old and new
members was a discrete theme in the local press, as in the 10 May discussions in the Duma regarding the establishment of reconciliation chambers
to settle town employee demands, which 'provoked endless discussions
of a semi-principled character'.[48] Unsurprisingly given its limited impact,
and the draw of numerous other administrative organisations, the Duma's
sessions were poorly attended on the whole, a factor that was apparently
utilised by the Duma's non-democratic minority. There was a scandal in the
Duma meeting of 5 July, when an extraordinary meeting was called towards
the end of the day with only thirty-six deputies present, and all the soviet
deputies had left, to discuss the important question of whether the neighbouring hamlet of Pokhorovo should be incorporated into Kazan town.
This issue was politically sensitive because Pokhorovo was a predominantly
heavy industrial area with a large worker population, which meant it was a
potentially radicalising force in town politics. The Duma meeting, taking
advantage of sparse attendance, decreed that it should not be included in
the town, despite Denike's heated speech to the contrary.[49] Such polarised

[47] *Kazanskaia rabochaia gazeta* 2, 7 April 1917, p. 2.
[48] *Kazanskaia rabochaia gazeta* 27, 13 May 1917.
[49] *Kazanskaia rabochaia gazeta* 71, 7 July 1917, p. 3.

views in the Duma continued to be apparent throughout 1917: strikes and searches carried out by the soviets were condemned in October by old Duma deputies, but the soviet deputies, 'spelling out the facts', clarified their position.[50]

In Nizhnii Novgorod, the Town Duma played an integral role in town governance. While the Kazan Duma was regarded as a hangover from the old regime, in Nizhnii Novgorod the Duma effectively bridged the gulf between old and new. It acted as the town's administrator for much of 1917, but the most significant manifestation of this uniting role was its part in resisting the Bolshevik seizure of power.[51] From the very outset of the revolution, Nizhnii Novgorod's Duma sought to embrace the new 'democratic' organisations, and to offer them representation. This ensured that there was no clear distinction between the local state apparatus and 'revolutionary democracy'. The town Public Committee that the Duma established to 'promulgate the aims and orders of the State Duma' included representatives from a range of public organisations, including soviets, unions and *zemstva*.[52] On 10 April representatives of other public organisations were included in the constitution of the Town Duma, including delegates from the soviet of workers' deputies.[53] This declaration was extended to include representatives from the soviet of soldiers' deputies at the end of April.[54] This ensured that the Duma maintained some level of credence and authority despite its restricted franchise.

New elections were held in good time on 16 July. Their basis of four-tailed suffrage ensured that the Duma rightfully represented the town population. Though this date was later than some provincial towns managed, it was a good deal earlier than the October elections held in Kazan. The Duma became a genuine democratic authority in the town, and seemed to have some degree of popular support and authority. Results of the July elections demonstrated the authority enjoyed by the PSR. Of the 105 seats, they won 40. Note that in contrast to many other provincial cities, the PSR stood independently, rather than participating in a socialist bloc with Mensheviks and Popular Socialists (NS).[55]

---

[50] *Kazanskaia rabochaia gazeta* 143, 7 October 1917, p. 3.
[51] This role of co-ordinating resistance to the Bolshevik takeover was taken by city Dumas across the country. (See Vladimir N. Brovkin, *The Mensheviks after October: Socialist Opposition and the rise of the Bolshevik dictatorship* (Ithaca, NY, 1987), pp. 19–21.)
[52] GANO, f. 27, op. 1, d. 1, l. 59; from Town Duma records, 1 March 1917.
[53] GANO, f. 27, op. 1, d. 1, l. 191; from Town Duma records, 10 April 1917.
[54] GANO, f. 27, op. 1, d. 1, l. 287; from Town Duma records, 29 April 1917.
[55] GANO, f. 27, op. 1, d. 2, ll. 69–70; from Duma records, 28 July 1917. The PSR victory in Nizhnii Novgorod was exceeded in Moscow, where the PSR won some 50 per cent of the vote in the June

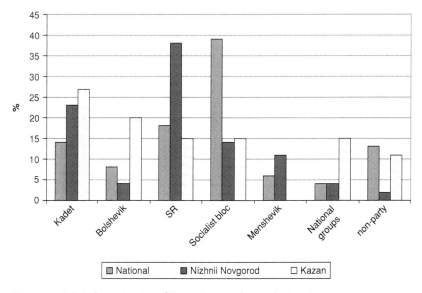

Figure 1.2. Political constitution of Town Dumas after re-elections in 1917
Source: National data from GANO, f. 1887, op. 1, d. 3, ll. 8–11; information on the course
of Town Duma elections, submitted to Nizhegorod provincial executive committee, 4
August 1917. Figures for Nizhnii Novgorod from GANO, f. 27, op. 1, d. 2, ll. 69–70;
report of the new elections at the Town Duma, 28 July 1917. Data for Kazan from
Kazanskaia rabochaia gazeta 147, 14 October 1917, p. 4.

When compared with national results, we can see that in Nizhnii Novgorod the PSR vote took the place of the socialist bloc in other areas,
which is a good indication of the strength and depth of the party's organisation and support in Nizhnii Novgorod. The situation was very different
in Kazan, where elections were not held until 8 October. The turnout was
lamentable, with less than 30 per cent of those eligible, 34,092, casting a
vote. This compared unfavourably with the national average of voting in
province town elections, which was 46 per cent.[56] The low turnout meant
that a seat could be won with only 310 votes. The Kadets were the largest
single group, winning 29 of the 105 seats available. As a glance at figure 1.2
shows, however, they were overwhelmed by the socialist blocs and parties,
and by ethnic and religious groups.

elections to the Moscow municipal town Duma. (For an analysis of these results, see Diane P.
Koenker, *Moscow workers and the 1917 revolution* (Princeton, 1981), pp. 196–208.) An analysis of
results of Duma elections of 1917 in other towns can be found in William G. Rosenberg, 'The
Russian Municipal Duma elections of 1917', *Soviet Studies* (1969), 131–63.

[56] GANO, f. 1886, op. 1, d. 3, ll. 8–11.

The results are interesting, particularly in the very strong showing made by the Kadet party. Given the low turnout, one can speculate that the Duma's status as a survivor institution caused it to draw support from the town's moderate and conservative forces. On the other hand, the elections also exposed the radicalism of Kazan's voting population by October. The 'Young SRs', led by Kolegaev, stood their own list, here represented in the 'SR' column, and were to the left of the SRs who remained allied to the Menshevik and soviet bloc. It was Kolegaev's 'Young SRs' who were to form the nucleus of Kazan's Left SR organisation after the party's formal split in November.

The Bolsheviks performed very strongly, and the Left SRs equalled the socialist bloc. It is difficult to make any comparisons between the party political climate of Kazan and Nizhnii Novgorod's Dumas, because the national political climate had swung hard to the left by October as compared with July. By October the political climate was transformed, and moderate socialists were increasingly being squeezed out of power. Some aspects of these voting patterns, in particular the strong showing of the Bolshevik party, can be explained by the lateness of the election. Others, however, offer some insight into more unique aspects of Kazan's political climate. The strong showing for national groups (of which fifteen were for Muslim groups, and three were Jewish) indicates the importance of national questions in this ethnically diverse province. Secondly, the weak showing of both the socialist bloc and the SRs is apparent. The splintering of the SR group may well have actually weakened both causes.[57]

This survey of executive power in Kazan and Nizhegorod shows that though the power structures that developed in Nizhegorod and Kazan were essentially similar in form, their interrelations and operations differed significantly according to local conditions. The Town Duma in Nizhnii Novgorod succeeded in meeting the need to democratise, and as a result formed a coherent part of the town's administration, whereas the Kazan Town Duma was dismissed as an irrelevancy. In both towns, there was close co-ordination and co-operation between soviet and Provisional Government bodies, though this co-ordination was more firmly structurally embedded in Kazan than in Nizhnii Novgorod. The ways in which the towns' diverse administrative forms responded to crisis, as with the Kazan fire, illustrated their common purpose and co-ordinated actions. The welter of challenges facing local government, along with the domination of moderate socialist personnel, masked to some extent the division of administrative

---

[57] GANO, f. 1887, op. 1, d. 3, ll. 8–11. See also Rosenberg, 'The Russian Municipal Duma'.

branches between the 'democratic' soviets and the 'bourgeois' Provisional
Government sponsored associations.

This book aims to address the failure of democratic party politics in Russia in 1917 from the perspective of ordinary people's experiences of the
revolution, and the political elite's attempts to communicate with them.
The book's chapters are organised thematically, and organised so that the
argument progresses from a discussion of those who 'control' power as traditionally defined (positions of state power) towards discussion of those who
held non-institutionalised power. Throughout, the argument is formed and
illustrated with examples from different parts of Nizhegorod and Kazan.
Because geographical specificity is an important part of this work's conclusions, all places are located where possible by their *uezd* location, as well as
by their province. As the agricultural and population profiles of different
uezds varied so widely, this level of detail is important in our attempts to
understand revolutionary events for ordinary people. Chapters 2, 7 and
8 make explicit comparisons between regions. Chapters 3, 4, 5 and 6 use
examples from Nizhegorod and Kazan in order to illustrate and explore
more general questions.

Chapter 2 assesses the spread of the news of the February revolution,
and the ways in which political elites tried, and often failed, to control
revolutionary discourse. Chapter 3 focuses on the Socialist Revolutionary
Party in order to assess the political party's role in 1917, how ordinary people
understood or related to political parties and how regional political activists
renegotiated their own positions in 1917. This discussion is important in
that it challenges what party political support actually involved, so that
other political processes in which political parties participated can be better
evaluated. Party politics did play a role in some aspects of provincial political
life, but they were not the only or the dominant force. Chapter 4 moves
on from parties to individuals, and evaluates the selection process and
social background of local leaders in 1917. This chapter confirms that party
political affiliations were less important than local affiliations and identities
in being chosen as a local leader. Chapter 5 focuses on the so called 'cultural
enlightenment programmes' that were promulgated in 1917, which allow
us to consider further the pitfalls and features of elite communication with
ordinary people.

Chapter 6 is the only one to focus on a particular social grouping, in this
case soldiers and their wives. These groups have received special attention

because of their size and importance in 1917, and because some aspects of their impact on the revolutionary process have been neglected. Local leaders among soldiers seemed to have very limited control and authority over their constituents, as independent initiative overwhelmed executive direction. We see that soldiers and their wives were a volatile and destabilising presence in both town and country, and that the sense of crisis that escalated through 1917 was predicated in part by their actions. Chapters 7 and 8 concentrate on ordinary people's actions in 1917 on the key issues of land and the provisions crisis, both of which help to elucidate the ways in which the political elite's messages and attempts at governance were received by ordinary people. These practical issues help to connect problems of communication with real local problems, and illuminate the fractured realities of provincial politics in 1917.

CHAPTER 2

The February revolution: whose story to believe?

> Filled with joyous feelings in this happy moment of my life, I one
> hundred times cry: Long live the toiling Russian people! Long live an
> everlasting century of the new way of life they have won! URA! URA!
> URA!
>
> (Letter from A. A. Ostafev, Gorbatovskii *uezd* commissar,
> 12 March 1917)[1]

Ostafev's words exemplify the joy with which news of the February revolution was received across provincial Russia. This chapter will tackle the ways
in which the political elite sought to control and define understandings
of the February revolution. Political power operated on a huge range of
levels in 1917. The holding of office, or direct control of political decisions,
were tangible indicators of political power. There were, however, other less-
obvious forums for the operation of political power. The transmission of
revolutionary news gives us our first glimpse of the political elite's anxiety
in trying to control the message of revolution. The February revolution
is often spoken of as if it were a single event, which was received by and
large uniformly, and which had an even ripple of response across Russia.
Closer investigation of local conditions, however, reveals that the February
revolution in Petrograd initiated a wave of localised revolutions all over
Russia, as local populations came to terms with the fall of the old regime,
and the establishment of a new order, in a multitude of different ways.[2]

---

[1] GANO, f. 2603, op. 1, d. 2, l. 2; letter from A. A. Ostafev, Gorbatovskii *uezd* commissar, to president
of the Gorbatovskii provisional *uezd* executive committee, Vasilii Pavlovich Shelamaev, 12 March 1917.

[2] Recent work that assesses the reception of the February revolution in the provinces includes Raleigh,
Revolution on the Volga, pp. 76–91; Hugh Phillips, '"A bad business" – The February revolution in Tver',
Soviet and Post Soviet Review 23 (1996), 120–41; Michael C. Hickey, 'Discourses of public identity and
liberalism in the February revolution: Smolensk, Spring 1917', *Russian Review* (1996), 615–37; Mark
Baker, 'Peasants, power and revolution in the village: A social history of Kharkiv province, 1914–1921',
unpublished PhD thesis, Harvard University (Cambridge, MA, 2001), chapter 2; A. Retish, 'Peasant
identities in Russia's turmoil: status, gender and ethnicity in Viatka province, 1914–1921', unpublished
PhD thesis, Ohio State University (Columbus, OH, 2003), pp. 100ff., pp. 105ff., pp. 118ff.

SPREADING THE NEWS

News of the February events in Petrograd was slowly and unevenly disseminated across the Russian empire. The difficulties of Russian communications were manifold. There were the usual problems of a vast, sparsely populated landmass with relatively slender infrastructure.[3] Telegraphs played
an important part in the dissemination of news. Railways were the most
important part of Russia's transport network, with three-fifths of all freight
moving by rail. Though the track network had expanded rapidly between
1900 and 1913, stock of engines and carriages was ageing and could not meet
the challenge of population and freight movement demanded by the First
World War.[4] Added to these physical problems of communications, there
was an acute shortage of educated people in rural regions to transmit the
political elite's versions of events. While these conditions afflicted urban as
well as rural areas, the problems of dissemination were far more acute in
rural areas. Not only were urban centres better serviced with both funds and
human resources, they were also more densely populated and had a higher
proportion of educated people.[5] This study of the February revolution in
Nizhegorod and Kazan highlights the shared experiences of the regions'
two capital cities, and the different problems that faced the dissemination
of revolutionary news in rural areas.

Funding for the distribution of pamphlets and leaflets announcing
the new revolutionary order was very limited, and rural areas suffered
more acutely than towns from these shortages of funds. Though Nizhnii
Novgorod Town Duma was able to allocate two thousand roubles for
brochures informing the population of revolutionary events,[6] such financial reserves were not available to hard-pressed *uezd* administrators. In
Semenovskii *uezd*, for example, the town committee was unable to spread
anything but the most elementary news of revolution. Though the new
Provisional Government decrees on the provisions question and regional
self-government were transferred to *volost* committees, they were unable to
publish many of their planned 'regional information leaflets', as they did not
have funds to buy paper. In Semenovskii *uezd*, only one hundred copies of a
report about the overthrow of the state were distributed. The Semenovskii

[3] See R. W. Pethybridge, 'The significance of communications in 1917', *Soviet Studies* 19 (1967), 109–14.
[4] See Gatrell, *Russia's first world war*, p. 5.
[5] Jeffrey Brooks, *When Russia learned to read: literacy and popular literature, 1861–1917* (Princeton, NJ, 1985), p. 33.
[6] GANO, f. 1887, op. 1, d. 17, l. 10; excerpt from protocols of the extraordinary meeting of Nizhnii Novgorod Town Duma, 3 March 1917.

uezd committee of public safety concluded its opening post-revolutionary statement with a warning that they were unable to distribute any proclamations, orders or appeals in future as they had no means available for printing.[7]

Commercially published newspapers played an important part in the spreading of news, but their circulation was concentrated in urban areas. These newspapers were an important forum for the political elite to present their visions of the February revolution. The newspapers with the largest circulation and most regular publication in both Nizhegorod and Kazan were those produced in association with the soviets of soldiers and workers' deputies and the soviets of peasants' deputies. In both Nizhnii Novgorod and Kazan, the newspapers published in association with the peasants' soviet had close associations with the PSR, while the newspapers published in association with the soviets of workers' and soldiers' deputies were dominated by Menshevik activists. Though these were the largest and most important newspapers in the region, there were a range of other publications produced, including continuations of pre-revolutionary publications, and some party and interest-based papers. These last usually had very small circulations and sporadic output. Newspapers that were associated with liberal or right-wing tendencies came under severe pressure in the course of 1917, and extreme right-wing papers were forcibly closed.[8]

News of the revolution reached major urban centres, and those areas in close proximity to the major rail networks, first. The dissemination of revolution in the provincial capitals of Kazan and Nizhnii Novgorod illuminates the advantages urban centres had in terms of speed and detail of news acquisition. In Nizhnii Novgorod and Kazan, the spread of news was facilitated and defined by politically well-developed groups within the local populations – Sormovo workers in Nizhnii Novgorod and students in Kazan. Studying the events surrounding February in Kazan and Nizhnii Novgorod shows three processes taking place: the spread of information, the semi-spontaneous mass actions co-ordinated by existing radical networks of workers in Nizhnii Novgorod and students in Kazan, and the rapid and almost unprotesting collapse of the old order.

Sources are patchy for the initial news of revolution in Kazan town, but all speak of bubbling excitement in the town and endless meetings: 'Kazan

[7] GANO, f. 1887, op. 1, d. 2, l. 22; report of the representative of Semenovskii *uezd* executive committee to the provincial meeting of executive committees in Nizhegorod province, 23 May 1917.

[8] In Kazan for example, the paper *Kazanskago telegrafa*, renamed as *Golosi Kazani* was stymied by the refusal of typesetters to work on the newspaper, which they alleged was 'black-hundredist' (*Kazanskaia rabochaia gazeta* 4, 13 April 1917, p. 1).

then was a time of meetings. In the streets, one demonstration replaced another. Orchestras rang out. People sang the "Marseillaise". Red bows flamed in the sun.'[9] On 28 February, demonstrators gathered just north of the city centre on Theatre Square and its nearby gardens and adjoining streets, though 'it is unknown, what gathered them there and who led them'.[10] Cossacks and policemen dispersed the crowds, who sang the 'Marseillaise' and 'Varshavianka', and continued to loiter.[11] K. Shnurovskii, a political exile who was in the small town of Chistopol, Kazan province, in February 1917, heard news of the old regime's collapse from the town's telegraphist late in the evening of 28 February. He and a comrade headed for Kazan early the next day: 'Everything was seething and in full swing there. Political parties were being formed. Never ending meetings went on.'[12] The university formed a hub for activities, with meetings going on in one of the lecture theatres 'from early morning till late at night, almost without a break'.[13] Kazan was a university town, and its student community was an important facilitator in the spread of revolutionary news.[14] Student circles that had worked in the underground quickly threw themselves into organisational work, forming close links with factory workers and, crucially, with the garrison and military colleges of Kazan.[15] Iakob Chanyshev, an officer who later joined the Bolsheviks, recalled how news of February was received in the officer training college in Kazan where he was stationed. The college's commanding officers tried to keep the news of revolution from subordinates, but students visited to tell the trainees, who demanded the news from their captain. Amid exultant shouts of 'URA!!', the trainee officers sent a delegation into Kazan town, to link with revolutionary organisations and to reassure the population that the military college backed the revolution.[16]

The spread of revolutionary news in Nizhnii Novgorod offers a good example of the ways in which a large and established worker community contributed to a full and rapid dissemination of news. Though a memoir

---

[9] Ia. Chanyshev, '1917 god v Kazani', *Druzhba Narodov* 5 (1957), 121–38.

[10] A. Zhakov, 'Nasha partiia v period ot fevralia do oktiabria v Kazani', *Kommunisticheskii put* 26 (1923), 86–92, p. 86.

[11] Zhakov, 'Nasha partiia', p. 86. This account is verified by N. Ezhov, *Voennaia Kazan v 1917 g.* (Kazan, 1957), p. 23.

[12] K. Shnurovskii, 'Vospominaniia o tovarishche Ol'kentskom', *Kommunisticheskii put* 11 (1922), 20–30.

[13] Zhakov, 'Nasha partiia', p. 86.

[14] On traditions of student radicalism, see Susan K. Morrisey, *Heralds of revolution: Russian students and the mythologies of radicalism* (Oxford, 1998).

[15] I. Volkov, 'Vania Volkov (Vospominaniia tovarishcha)', *Kommunisticheskii put* 11 (1922), 31–3, p. 32, on importance of student circles; Zhakov, 'Nasha partiia', p. 87, on worker links; Chanyshev, '1917 god', p. 121 on links with the soldiers.

[16] Chanyshev, '1917 god', p. 122.

of unknown provenance written by a fellow called Povarov suggested that revolution was received cautiously and without enthusiasm in Nizhnii Novgorod,[17] this assessment was contradicted by a number of other accounts. News of the revolution came to Nizhnii Novgorod town via the massive worker community of Sormovo on its outskirts. Eshchin, son of the editor of the newspaper *Nizhegorodskii listok*, heard news of revolutionary events and told some Sormovo workers in his acquaintance on 28 February.[18] The well-developed revolutionary underground in Sormovo ensured that this news was rapidly and extensively disseminated. News spread around the factory shops along with a strike.[19] The Sormovo PSR group printed leaflets overnight.[20] The next morning on 1 March, a cold and sunny day, more than 10,000 workers from the Sormovo factories left work to attend a meeting outside the factory.[21] Workers, joined by Sormovo locals, marched into Nizhnii Novgorod town, singing in 'a great choir of voices'.[22] Workers and townspeople from other parts of town joined the marchers as they progressed. Red fabric was commandeered from local shops to serve as flags, so that by the time the crowd reached town, ten red flags were displayed, emblazoned in white paint with 'LONG LIVE THE REVOLUTION'.[23] This was an enormously symbolic occasion, as more than 20,000 workers marched into town, under the very noses of the tsarist police. The crowd went to the Town Duma first, and was received cautiously by the town mayor Sirotkin. In the Duma itself, the mood became celebratory when Rodzianko's telegram confirming events was read out; 'Rodzianko's telegram was read. Deafening cries of "hurrah!" and loud applause drowned out the last words of the town mayor.'[24]

Memoirists describe how a 'sea of people' including workers, soldiers, townspeople, dockers and teenagers in their school uniforms congregated outside the Town Duma and then moved towards the town jail. A number of 'known revolutionaries' were being held there, including a Sormovo worker, Ivan Petrov. After some resistance from the town mayor, all the

[17] N. Povarov, *Revoliutsionnyi period v g. Nizhnem* (Nizhnii Novgorod, 1918).
[18] P. E. Shul'gin, *Za vlast sovetov: vspominaet uchastniki bor' bi za vlast v Nizhegorodskoi gubernii* (Gorky, 1967), p. 24; Ikonikov's memoir. Ikonikov was a Nizhnii Novgorod native, who had been exiled back to his home town for revolutionary activity in Petrograd.
[19] Shul'gin, *Za vlast sovetov*, p. 40; P. E. Vorobev's memoir. Vorobev was a Sormovo worker.
[20] RGASPI, f. 274, op. 1, d. 26, p. 103; excerpt from Zinovii Magergut's memoir, entitled 'writings-recollections of a member of the Sormovskii organisation of the PSR, from April 1916 to April 1917'.
[21] Shul'gin, *Za vlast sovetov*, p. 41; Vorobev's memoir.
[22] Shul'gin, *Za vlast sovetov*, p. 41; Vorobev's memoir.
[23] RGASPI, f. 274, op. 1, d. 26, l. 103; Magergut's memoir.
[24] GANO, f. 27, op. 1, d. 1, l. 59; from Town Duma records, 1 March 1917.

prisoners were freed. A number of Sormovo workers moved on to the barracks in order to secure the support of the garrison.[25] Large numbers of ad hoc meetings and speeches were held as the population came to terms with the momentous news.[26] Two memoirists described a terrific noise, as music thundered, revolutionary songs were sung, and a general carnival atmosphere pervaded.[27] Both Nizhnii Novgorod and Kazan experienced the February revolution as an event of great immediacy, with no mention of individuals supporting the old regime. In both towns, the presence of a well-developed and political active community contributed to the wholesale dissemination of revolutionary news.

Outside the big towns, the spread of revolutionary news was rather more haphazard. Sources on how revolution was received are dominated by the political elite, so that what we know of events must be seen as a reflection of the political elite's preoccupations, in particular that formal political organisation, in the form of unions or party cells, ought to accompany the spread of revolution. In some outlying areas, 'revolution came quickly', as a result of proximity to railroad telegraphs, postal telegraphs and army bases.[28] Where a garrison or sizeable worker community existed, dissemination of revolutionary news was more rapid, and was reported to be more 'ordered'. Factory workers in particular were credited with being the harbingers of political organisation. In the small factory complex of Tishinskii in Ardatov *uezd*, Nizhegorod province, all work stopped when news of the revolution was heard. There were meetings everywhere, and 'everyone hoped that life would become better'.[29] A correspondent to the Nizhegorod soviet newspaper in May, describing events in Balakhna, a small town in Nizhegorod province, revealed his concerns about maintaining perspectives on revolution that mirrored those of the political elite:

The great overthrow that has occurred in Russia began to be spoken of even in our backwater. Bars and billiard halls had become the only place where the people of Balakhna could gather. So far there are almost no organisations here. Thanks to the small number of workers the formation of professional organisations has been difficult. The organisation of a workers' union has been no less difficult. There are SD and SR groups, but to call them organisations is still difficult. They

---

[25] Shul'gin, *Za vlast sovetov*, p. 44; Vorobev's memoir.

[26] GANO, f. 1887, op. 1, d. 17, l. 10; excerpt from protocols of the extraordinary meeting of Nizhnii Novgorod Town Duma, 3 March 1917.

[27] Shul'gin, *Za vlast sovetov*, p. 42; Vorobev's memoir; p. 103, N.V. Demianov's memoir.

[28] See, for example, NART, f. 983, op. 1, d. 21, l. 35, anonymous report from Kukmor village, Kazan province, 26 May 1917.

[29] Shul'gin, *Za vlast sovetov*, p. 148; S. E. Musatov. Musatov was a factory worker in Tashinksii factory, Ardatov *uezd*.

are rapidly formed circles, forming around groups of initiative. On Thursday and Sunday there were meetings in the reading building, with the participation of a small number of regional intelligentsia.[30]

In Chistopol, a small town in Kazan province, 'The overthrow and the following days of freedom found our town in total disorganisation. There was no public life, and not a single workers' organisation or professional union existed. There is very little industrial development here, and no big factories.'[31] Comments on 'chaos' in non-worker areas should be read with extreme caution. They reveal that the political elite's revolutionary narrative was not being followed, and that the workers' unions and party cells that they recognised as legitimate agents of revolution were not present. Where there was no party-led or sanctioned worker community, the political elite reported confusion and disorder. Workers' organisations represented the 'orthodox' face of revolution, but their absence should not be interpreted as chaos, but rather a reflection of diverse responses to the news of revolution from the rural population.

The most serious impediment to the spread of revolutionary news outside urban centres, both in Kazan and Nizhegorod, was a shortage of literate personnel. The rural intelligentsia were called upon to help establish the new revolutionary regime, and in particular to take the news of revolution to the outlying areas. As we will discuss in chapter 4, the rural intelligentsia did not take on the role of local leaders that the political elite drew out for them. Clergy were not generally included in the category of rural intelligentsia, and the role of churchmen in spreading revolution was complicated. On the one hand, the church as an institution was intrinsically linked to the old regime.[32] On the other hand, many clergymen were closer to their parishioners than they were to the church's elite.[33] The church elite responded very cautiously to revolution, though priests quickly turned to the new temporal power.[34]

A Kazan archiepiscopal address to parishioners issued on 3 March used formal language, gave almost no information on what exactly had happened and provided no explanation regarding the abdication of the tsar. It noted only that the tsar had abdicated and, again without explanation,

---

[30] *Izvestiia sovetov rabochikh i soldatskikh deputatov* 15, 18 May 1917, p. 4.
[31] *Kazanskaia rabochaia gazeta* 7, 16 April 1917, p. 3.
[32] Boris I. Kolonitskii, 'The Russian idea and the ideology of the February revolution', in Teruyaki Hara and Kimitaka Matsuzato (eds.), *Empire and society: approaches to Russian history* (Sapporo, 1997), pp. 41–71, p. 44. 'Orthodoxy and the autocrat were connected institutionally and ideologically.'
[33] See Chris J. Chulos, *Converging worlds: religion and community in peasant Russia 1861–1917* (DeKalb, IL 2003), chapter 7.
[34] Kolonitskii, 'The Russian idea', p. 46.

exhorted parishioners to have faith in the Provisional Government, and to continue their lives peacefully.[35] A further Kazan archiepiscopal address intended for the clergy themselves was only slightly more enlightening. It commented on the clergy's historic position as leaders and spiritual leaders, especially in the villages. The role of the church in protecting the weak and bringing true salvation to believers was reiterated. Though the clergy were exhorted to 'raise your pastor's voice to the enlightening of the people in this historic moment', the only guidance given in terms of what exactly the clergy should be exhorting their parishioners to do was to give grain to the army, and to appeal for peace and order.[36] The cautious response of the church elite shows them caught adrift by events; they had little to say other than to appeal for submission to the Provisional Government as the new face of authority.

The factor that set rural Kazan apart from rural Nizhegorod in its reception of revolutionary news was Kazan's numerous ethnic minority communities. The foremost of these, Tatars, Cheremis (Marii) and Chuvash, did not share language, letters or religion with the Russians, which made attempts to spread news effectively particularly difficult.[37] A further complication was that ethnically divided communities were not united in the ways that they received and interpreted news of the revolution. Reception of the revolution in Kazan's non-Russian quarters was mixed. A peasant deputy from Tsarevokokshaiskii *uezd* stated in May that the local non-Russian population 'related to the current moment with total consciousness'[38] and that the local population was united in its response. By 'total consciousness', we can assume that our reporter referred to general public order and calm. Other areas witnessed population clashes based on ethnic divisions. In Kumor village, Kazan province, the village itself was populated predominantly by Russians. On the outskirts the population was an admix of ethnic groups, including Tatars, Cheremis, Votiaks and others, with Tatars numerically dominant. The reporter noted a 'general lack of trust towards the Russian population, as a result of dark forces and the adherents of reaction'. This mistrust manifested itself in profound splits

[35] NART, f. 1246, op. 1, d. 55, l. 222; archbishop's epistle to pastors caring for congregations in Kazan, 3 March 1917.

[36] NART, f. 1246, op. 1, d. 55, ll. 225–6; published declaration of the pastors of Kazan town to the pastors of Kazan diocese, undated.

[37] Aaron Retish's work on Viatka found similar problems for the elite in communicating with non-Russians (Retish, 'Peasant identities in Russia's turmoil', pp. 175–6).

[38] NART, f. 983, op. 1, d. 16, l. 122; report from E. N. Kovediaev, peasant deputy from Morsinskii *volost*, Tsarevokokshaiskii *uezd*, Kazan, to be given at the All-Russian Peasants' meeting in Petrograd, 10 May 1917.

in the revolutionary organisation that was set up in Kumor, the 'Kumor village union of workers and employees'.

Divisions in Kumor came to a head over the selection of a candidate to the Kazan soviet of workers' and soldiers' deputies, and the Muslims withdrew from the union and demanded a refund of their subscriptions. The 'mistrust' manifested towards the Russians from the Tatar population was such that the reporter appealed for a Muslim who spoke Tatar to come and adjudicate, since the Tatars did not even trust Russians who spoke Tatar.[39] As well as divisions between the Russian- and non-Russian-speaking communities in terms of receiving the revolution, there were divisions within the Muslim community itself, which manifested themselves at the very outset of revolution.[40] A socialist Muslim group formed in opposition to the 'bourgeois-nationalist' Muslim group backed by the Muslim clergy and some Muslim intelligentsia figures, which crystallised after a meeting of Muslims held on 8 March.[41] The sharp distinctions within the Muslim community only served to exacerbate the confusion of revolutionary events.

CREATING A REVOLUTIONARY NARRATIVE

Constructing narratives of the February events in Petrograd were the start of a struggle to define what the revolution meant in practical terms, and what its implications were. A rapid mythologisation of the February events themselves took place in the immediate aftermath of the revolution. Events were told and retold, with the State Duma, workers and soldiers variously taking leading roles. The apparently simple task of informing the population about Petrograd's revolution was racked with interpretative variation, not least because in the fall of the old regime, political activists sought to structure the shape and legitimacy of the new regime. Interpretations of the revolutionary events reflected the agendas of the narrators, whether these were defined by class, political or other personal interests. Fundamental disagreements existed over the direction in which the revolution was heading, from those who saw the events of February as encapsulating the whole revolution, to those who saw February as only the starting point of world revolution and a new international order.[42]

---

[39] NART, f. 983, op. 1, d. 21, l. 35; anonymous report from Kukmor village, Kazan province, 26 May 1917.

[40] Christian Noack, 'The Tataro-Bashkir Feud in 1917' (Conference paper given at Conference of the Study Group on the Russian Revolution, University of Durham, 2001).

[41] A. Rakhmatullin, 'Mulla-Nur Vakhitov', *Kommunisticheskii put* 11 (1922), 34–40, p. 35.

[42] Trotsky's writings on 1917 declared faith in the imminent wave of proletarian revolution to sweep over Europe and posited Russia's revolution firmly in this context. Russia's revolution was to be

When the story of the February revolution in Petrograd was told, its key components were why it happened, who initiated it, who was defending it, and where it was leading. The version of the February revolution propounded by moderate socialists was the most widespread and represents a starting point for the revolutionary orthodoxy propounded by the Provisional Committee of the State Duma, the Provisional Government and the moderate socialist-controlled soviets.[43] The information leaflets printed by educational and socialist presses provide a useful source for moderate socialists' narration of the February revolution. Workers and soldiers were placed in absolute centre stage as key revolutionary activists. Such leaflets' accounts of February events started with a dramatic presentation of the failings of the old regime, emphasising incompetent prosecution of the war and brutality of the old regime towards the people. The demands of the 'hungry and exhausted' striking workers were 'bread, only bread', and the brutality with which they were repressed was emphasised. One well-circulated report suggested a grossly inflated figure of nearly 800 citizens killed by police in the first four days of strikes.[44] The revolts of separate regiments were carefully documented, as was their defence of the Duma and later the Provisional Government.[45] Though the formation of the soviet was mentioned, it was not portrayed as central to revolutionary events, which were described in elemental terms, as absolutely justified and rational events, predicated primarily on inadequate prosecution of the war. Political agency was significantly downplayed, contributing to a sense of inevitability and absolute popular support.[46]

Provisional Government bodies put calls for peace and order at the forefront of their bulletins on the February revolution, and they emphasised above all else that Russia was still at war. The Provisional Government had an advantage over other competing sources in transmitting news of the revolution, as it had inherited the old regime's communication network. The first official news of the revolution came through the Provisional

permanent, as it would continuously apply its state power to the undoing of international capitalist exploitation. (See Leon Trotsky, *What next?: vital questions for the German proletariat* (New York, 1932), p. 8.) The Liberals that made up Russia's right in 1917, on the other hand, viewed the February revolution as a political revolution that was completed, not an on-going social revolution.

43 On the role played by the State Duma's Provisional Committee, see A. B. Nikolaev, *Gosudarstvennaia Duma i fevral'skoi revoliutsii: ocherki istorii* (Riazan, 2002), p. 248.

44 E. N. Medynskii, *Kak i pochemu narod unichtozhil staruiu vlast i za chto on boretsia* (Moscow, 1917), p. 10.

45 E. N. Medynskii, *Kak vesti besedi po politicheskam voprosam: metodicheskie ukazaniia, konspekti i spiski literaturi dlia lektorov, uchitelei i pr.* (Moscow, 1917), pp. 13–14.

46 The best recent discussion on the 'spontaneity' of the February revolution is Melancon, *Rethinking Russia's February revolution*.

Government's telegram to the head of the provincial *zemstva*, which passed on to the *uezd zemstva* chairmen, announcing the fall of the old regime and the shape of the new. The *uezd* and provincial *zemstva* were expected to form the foundations for the administration of the new regime.[47] The priorities of these first organisations at *uezd* and province level were unfailingly to preserve public order and calm, and to ensure smooth transference of the region's administration. This desire is reflected in the names of the first committees formed, which were usually known as 'committees of public safety', a name which of course recollected both the French revolution of 1789, and the European revolutions of 1848.

The public meeting in Iadrinskii *uezd*, Kazan province, called by Iadrinskii's new *uezd* commissar, the president of the *uezd zemstvo* A. F. Ashmarin, was held on 12 March in order to inform the population of events. It provides a useful source in identifying the ways in which revolutionary events were portrayed, and in particular the facets that were emphasised. The new *uezd* commissar, A. F. Ashmarin, made the opening speech, in which he announced the fall of the old regime in terms strongly reminiscent of those used by the Provisional Government. He announced that the State Duma was now administering the country, and dwelt on the evils of the old regime, which he emphasised had been corrupted by bureaucrats and Germans. He concluded with a reminder that Russia was at war, and that every effort needed to be made to pursue the war effort. The nature of the new regional administration was clarified.[48] Much of this echoed the position of the Constitutional Democrats (Kadets) on the revolution. An appeal to the population was drawn up, which was intended both to clarify the passing events, and to outline the shape of the new state structure. This appeal followed the rubric of other moderate socialist proclamations on revolution, though its language was particularly grandiose. We can see that at this early stage of revolution, liberal interpretations of the revolution's causes coexisted with the socialist rhetoric that was to predominate in 1917.

News of the revolution reached Semenov town, Semenovskii *uezd*, on 2 March, when the Nizhnii Novgorod executive committee forwarded the State Duma's telegram around the *uezds*. In response to this, the town mayor held an extraordinary meeting of the Town Duma on 3 March in

---

[47] Browder and Kerensky, *Russian Provisional Government*, vol. I, pp. 243–9, docs. 219–29; circulars from the Minister of the Interior regarding the organisation of the new administration.

[48] NART, f. 1246, op. 1, d. 46, ll. 132–3; journal of meeting called to discuss questions linked with recent events in state life and detailed acquaintance with them, with the aim of the widest possible acquaintance of them for the whole population of Iadrinskii *uezd*, 12 March 1917.

a hall 'filled with citizens'. Without any recorded debate or discord, the meeting declared itself to be in accord with the State Duma. The meeting organised an executive committee and announced that the committee's aim was 'to establish and strengthen the new, free life of the country, to defend the *uezd* from all risings and sad misunderstandings, and to prevent all disorder'.[49] This summary of the new regime's objectives emphasised the maintenance of order, and of some semblance of continuity in the midst of dislocation. Religion was often used to smooth these announcements of profound change, demonstrating the ways in which existing societal structures were utilised and melded into the new order. Aaron Retish, in his work on Viatka, described the use of religion in announcing the new regime as a sacralisation of the new order.[50] Prayer often played an integral part in announcements of the new order, which ensured that the church was involved, and offered the recipients of new and groundbreaking news a reassuringly familiar form. Nizhnii Novgorod's town university marked the opening of the new course for preparation of militia personnel with a prayer.[51] A 'ceremonial meeting' held by *zemstvo* employees in Spasskii *uezd* opened with a prayer to honour the memory of the victims of the struggle for freedom, and a thanksgiving for the new free Russia.[52]

The role played by the church in spreading the word of revolution shows the close allegiance between church and the Provisional Government, despite the Orthodox Church's conservative reputation.[53] An archiepiscopal address to the churchmen of Kazan illustrated the relative harmony of church and Provisional Government, although it also exposed some differences of emphasis. Its explanation of revolutionary events focused on hunger and the threat of an undernourished army as the main reason for public disorder leading to the abdication. The archbishop's address emphasised that public concern about inept prosecution of the war was the focal point for revolution, and the Duma was credited with the removal of the old government and the seizure of power. No mention whatsoever was made of the striking workers and mutinying soldiers who were commonly depicted as the heroes of February, and the overall impression was not so much of a revolution as of a manoeuvre of power into the hands of Duma deputies in order to save the nation from humiliation and defeat at

---

[49] GANO, f. 815, op. 1, d. 15, l. 1; first protocol of Semenovskii *uezd* executive committee, undated.
[50] Retish, 'Peasant identities in Russia's turmoil', pp. 109–10.
[51] GANO, f. 1887, op. 1, d. 28, l. 5; note from director of Nizhegorod town public university to Nizhegorod town executive committee, 15 March 1917.
[52] NART, f. 1352, op. 1, d. 3, l. 11; journal of the meeting of *zemstvo* employees, 19 March 1917.
[53] For a more detailed look at the relations of the church with revolution, see Kolonitskii, 'The Russian idea', pp. 46ff.

war.[54] This emphasis on continuity was an important theme of conservative interpretations, which saw the February revolution as the end of revolution, rather than the beginning. Statements from rural communities indicated that some villages accepted the story of the February revolution starring the Duma. A meeting of Kstovskoi *volost* peasants, held on 7 March 1917, resolved to:

warmly greet the heroic victory of the State Duma in the business of overthrowing the government, saving our dear homeland from the unavoidable enemy. In this highest victory, all help will be given to the State Duma to save and successfully bring this holy affair to a final end.[55]

This statement suggests that these peasants had understood the narrative of February as a story featuring the State Duma as their primary defender, as we would expect given that it was issued in the first days of revolution. Michael Melancon's work, however, indicates that over the first few months of 1917, the State Duma's role as figurehead was quickly superseded by the Provisional Government and the Petrograd Soviet.[56]

The dissemination of revolution was not simply a matter of presenting a narrative of revolution. The bringers of news also sought to countermand 'false' versions of revolution that were disseminated by opponents and by that trickiest of agents, rumour. These attempts to counter 'false' revolution illustrate that the spread of news was actually about the early fight to define the revolutionary narrative. Makar'evskii *uezd*, in Nizhegorod province, actually formed two *uezd* committees, one representing the mountainous part of the *uezd*, and the other representing the lowlands. The 'mountainous' *uezd* committee, which formed on 18 April, declared in a telegram to the provincial commissar that it strove to 'establish the correct course of life in the *uezd*, changing and clarifying the incorrect declarations of *volost* committees regarding right of ownership, land rental and the insatiability of the peasant population regarding the property of the state and private owners'.[57] But these so-called 'incorrect' declarations of *volost* committees were in fact just alternative interpretations of what

---

[54] NART, f. 1246, op. 1, d. 55, ll. 225–6; published declaration of the pastors of Kazan town to the pastors of Kazan diocese, undated.

[55] GANO, f. 830, op. 1, d. 5, l. 103; declaration from elected representatives of Kstovskoi *volost* to captain of Nizhegorod *uezd*, A. A. Ostafev, 7 March 1917.

[56] Michael Melancon, 'The syntax of Soviet power: the resolutions of local soviets and other institutions, March–October 1917', *Russian Review* 52 (1993), 486–505.

[57] GANO, f. 715, op. 1, d. 7, l. 36; report from Lyskovo to *zemstvo* administration in response to telegram of 1 April 1917, undated.

the revolution meant and implied. The resolution passed by the 'working peasantry' of Saralovskii *volost*, Laishevskii *uezd*, Kazan, in May is a good example of differing interpretations of revolution:

'We declare that we have long awaited and long hoped for the current state revolution. We, all the working peasantry of Saralovskii *volost*, decree:

1) to defend with all the strength and means in our possession the freedom obtained by us in all its fullness, in particular: freedom of speech, freedom of faith, freedom of self-determination and freedom of self-government.

2) conscious, that we are all descended from the one man made by God, but that this man has been given by God all the land made by him in full use, by his order, that we gathered here, on the basis of this declaration of God – we demand, that all this land with all its water, woods and with all its riches within, in order that it be transferred in full from private ownership without any compensation, to the total possession of all the labouring people, that is all those who will work it with their own hands . . .'[58]

The second clause of this statement echoed SR rhetoric on the land question, and all socialist parties shared these peasants' general sentiments. The crucial difference between the socialist political elite and these working peasants was not of principles but of timescale and actions. The Saralovskii peasants used their statement to explain their decision to seize privately owned land, something that both Provisional Government and soviets condemned. The revolution was understood by these peasants to have offered them freedom and justice, as so many of the official proclamations declared. Their conceptions of what the revolution was, and what freedom and justice entailed, may have accorded with the Provisional Government's. Their actions substantiating these beliefs, however, placed them in opposition to the political elite.[59]

Rumour was an unseen but powerful dynamo in the spread of revolution. Lynne Viola and Sheila Fitzpatrick both regard the role of rumour in the Russian countryside as an important 'way into' peasant understandings and feelings.[60] The unofficial news that passed from place to place offered a powerful challenge to the narrative of revolution offered by the political elite. Rumours ranged from the mundane, that all savings in the bank would be lost, to the supernatural, that the Antichrist had risen. The Antichrist rumour came from a sermon given by a preacher in Tsivilskii *uezd*, Kazan

---

[58] NART, f. 983, op. 1, d. 16, l. 23; resolution agreed by all the working peasantry of Saralovskii *volost*, Laishevskii *uezd*, 11 May 1917.

[59] Steinberg, *Voices of revolution*, pp. 8–17; presents an excellent analysis of the different meanings allotted freedom and justice by lower-class Russians.

[60] Viola, *Peasant rebels*; Fitzpatrick, *Stalin's peasants*.

province, which initiated mass unrest by declaring that Kerensky was in fact
the Antichrist.[61] Lynne Viola argues that the apocalyptic rumours circulating in the 1920s were used as political metaphor and parable and portended
the end of traditional ways of life.[62] This interpretation makes sense for
Russia's rural dwellers in 1917, who had to interpret and live through fundamental social and political change.

The political elite published rebuttals of more inflammatory rumours
in a desperate attempt to direct revolutionary understanding and to protect public order. Ironically, in rebutting the rumours, official sources may
well have bolstered them, by repeating them. Lysovskii public committee
produced a leaflet, appealing to the population in highly emotive terms to
leave their savings in the bank, and to ignore rumours that the money was
under threat:

> In recent times dark, malicious people have spread rumours that the savings fund
> will be dissolved and the money will vanish. Don't, citizens, listen to these people
> and these rumours, as they are spread only in order to breach the calm of the people,
> calm which is so necessary for Russia at the current time. These dark people are
> adherents to the old regime, and are united in their aim, which is to undermine
> the new government.[63]

Semenovskii *uezd* committee devoted some of their very limited printing
budget to 1,500 copies of a leaflet appealing to the population not to pay
attention to orators who claimed that the fall of the tsar made churches
superfluous.[64] The *uezd* committee feared that such orators would stir up
hostility to the new regime. Reports of 'dark rumours' spread by 'hirelings
of the old government'[65] were widespread in official reports, but the verac-
ity of such reports needs to be questioned. It is very rare indeed to come
across evidence of truly counter-revolutionary activity, that is, concerted
monarchist activities. The situation in Kazan and Nizhegorod confirms
Rex Wade's assertion that the February revolution consigned the old right
wing of Russia's political scene to oblivion.[66] It is more likely that official
warnings of bands of counter-revolutionary plotters roaming the countryside reflected genuine but misplaced fears on the part of the political elite,
who sought to alert the population of the dangers they faced, and the need

[61] *Kazanskaia rabochaia gazeta*, 135, 28 September 1917, p. 3.
[62] Viola, *Peasant rebels*, pp. 46–8, and Fitzpatrick, *Stalin's peasants*, pp. 45–7.
[63] GANO, f. 715, op. 1, d. 8a, l. 33; leaflet published by Lysovskii public committee, undated.
[64] GANO, f. 1887, op. 1, d. 2, l. 22; report of the representative of Semenovskii *uezd* executive committee
to the provincial meeting of executive committees in Nizhegorod province, 23 May 1917.
[65] NART, f. 1246, op. 1, d. 46, ll. 132–3; journal of public meeting held in Iadrinskii *uezd*, 12 March
1917.
[66] Wade, *The Russian revolution*, p. 53.

to support their 'orthodox' view of revolution.[67] Anyone who countered their version was labelled as 'counter-revolutionary'.[68] Again, we see parallels of these figurative dark forces in the early Soviet period, when rumours were blamed on 'kulaks and priests', in order to focus the impact of such rumours onto 'official enemies'.[69]

Kazan's new provincial commissar wrote to the archdeacon of Kazan's diocese on 8 March, appealing for the assistance of the clergy in spreading revolutionary news. In doing so, he utilised the often-repeated tropes of 'dark people' and 'ignorant peasants':

> Your Grace, the village population in their masses cannot comprehend the current events and are led only by rumours, often of the most unfounded kind, current events are being interpreted differently. As a result of this risings are beginning among the population, developing into pogroms in some regions. In order to avert dangerous complications in public life, it is necessary to quickly announce the emperor's renunciation of the throne and the refusal of Grand Prince Mikhail Aleksandrovich to take the throne in all churches, and for the clergy to make any necessary clarifications, and also to make pastoral calls to the population to defend order and calm and continue usual peaceful labour for the good of the motherland . . . I humbly ask you to make an urgent order without delay about the reading in church pulpits the memorised manifesto to the population and about the call to the population to total order before the clergy. Don't fail to inform me about this.[70]

The appeal is revealing in the ways that news of revolution was being received and promulgated in the regions. Despite the best efforts of the Provisional Government, rumour and hearsay were powerful dynamos, which led to understandings and interpretations of revolution that countered the 'official' position. The Provisional Government, the soviets and the church all shared the desire to maintain calm and order in Russian public life and to continue the war effort. Their promulgation of revolutionary news reflected these desires, as did their attempts to rebut the diverse interpretations of the revolutionary situation which emerged, and which challenged their desire to maintain order.

---

[67] Gabor Rittersporn's analysis of the 'omnipresent conspiracy' in social and political relations in the Stalin period is a useful point of comparison here (Rittersporn, 'The omnipresent conspiracy: on Soviet imagery of politics and social relations in the 1930s', in J. A. Getty and Roberta Manning (eds.), *Stalinist terror: new perspectives* (Cambridge, 1993), pp. 99–115).

[68] See Boris I. Kolonitskii, 'Antibourgeois propaganda and anti-"Burzhui" conciousness in 1917', *Russian Review* 53 (1994), 183–96, for the ways in which labelling was used to great effect but without much accuracy in 1917, though Kolonitskii does not suggest it was used as a conscious tool.

[69] Viola, *Peasant rebels*, p. 62.

[70] NART, f. 1246, op. 1, d. 55, l. 102; letter from Kazan provincial commissar to the archbishop of Kazan diocese, 8 March 1917.

HOW TO RESPOND?

The responses of ordinary people to the political elite's attempts to define a revolutionary narrative and 'orthodox' revolutionary position were not straightforward. Different individuals and key societal groups reacted to the news in very different ways, but three themes emerge in the ways that ordinary people responded to the revolutionary news. All three show the ways in which the narrative presented by the political elite was interpreted and contested by ordinary people. These three themes can be characterised as the hunt for heroes, the hunt for villains and the search for something new. These themes show how the news of February transmogrified in different directions that may have been initiated by the political elite, but could not be controlled by them.

The heroes of the revolution, those who had been imprisoned, exiled or killed for devotion to the revolutionary cause, became an immediate focal point for public attention and sympathy. On this question, the political elite's narrative combined with popular sentiment. Interest in the fate of revolutionaries was not a new phenomenon. Both Maria Spiridonova and Ekaterina Breshko-Breshkovskaia, for example, caught the attention of the national press and were portrayed even by the moderate press as 'martyrs to the cause'.[71] They were mythologised, Spiridonova as a young warrior for justice and Breshkovskaia as the 'grandmother of the revolution'.[72] The work of Sally Boniece shows how Spiridonova exemplified the myth of the revolutionary-martyr-heroine, and how both Spiridonova and the Tambov PSR organisation actively manipulated this image.[73]

The PSR had emphasised the importance of 'suffering for the cause' in the pre-revolutionary period, and this tendency towards the glorification of the party's martyrs found full expression in 1917. There were distinct religious overtones in the new revolutionary narrative, particularly

---

[71] See A. Rabinowitch, 'Spiridonova', in Edward Acton, V. U. Cherniaev and William G. Rosenberg (eds.), *Critical companion to the Russian revolution* (Bloomington, IN, 1997), pp. 182–7, p. 182. For further evidence of Spiridonova receiving public sympathy, see V. Vladimirov, *Maria Spiridonova* (Moscow, 1906).

[72] Breshkovskaia was described as such by V. P. Antonov-Saratovski, *Pod stiagom proletarskoi bor' by: otryvki iz vospominanii o rabote v Saratove za vremia s 1915g. do 1918g.* (Moscow and Leningrad, 1925), p. 92. On Breshkovskaia's iconic status in Russia and abroad by 1917, see J. E. Good and D. R. Jones, *Babushka: the life of the Russian revolutionary E. K. Breshko-Breshkovskaia* (Newtonville, MA, 1991). Evidence of Spiridonova's lasting reputation as icon and martyr of the revolution was the warnings Lenin received that her imprisonment could provoke a European national scandal, and his decision to release her from prison in 1921. (See 'Ob osvobozhdenii M. A. Spiridonovoi', *Izvestiia TsK KPSS* (1991), 178–80.)

[73] A fascinating exploration of the creation of Spiridonova's 'myth' can be found in Sally Boniece, 'The Spiridonova case, 1906: terror, myth and martyrdom', *Kritika* 4 (2003), 571–606.

in the use of martyrdom and familiar ethical and religious concepts.[74] To have been exiled or imprisoned for the revolutionary cause lent individuals significant cachet, and massive public sympathy. The physical distress of released political prisoners offered a real physical manifestation of the evil oppressions of tsarism and had clear religious overtones. It was not only the 'celebrities' of the revolutionary world, like Spiridonova, that attracted public sympathy and interest in the post-revolutionary months. Zinovii Magergut, a PSR activist from Sormovo, wrote a pathos-ridden description of released prisoners in Nizhnii Novgorod in April 1917, which offers a good example of the sort of sympathy and interest expressed to all political prisoners:

The comrades from katorga (hard labour) arrived. Their bodies were still stung by chains. But they did not feel it. They fixed their eyes on the red flag, on the clear sun, the bright sky. They were carried aloft by the crowd, threw up their arrested caps, echoing the people 'LONG LIVE THE REVOLUTION'. And then one comrade arrived, bending under the burden of a long imprisonment. He moved slowly, his feet covered with wounds, eyes that could not get accustomed to the blue light, ears could not carry the roar (*shum*) of the rejoicing crowd. For almost ten years he had been oppressed in solitary. He said: 'Comrades, thank you, I am glad that I lived to witness liberty . . . take me away, I need to calm down . . .' His voice trembled and his feet did not hold even his decrepit body. The years forced, they did their business . . .[75]

The political prisoners freed at the start of March attended the first meeting of the Nizhnii Novgorod soviet of workers and soldiers' deputies. When they entered the hall, all those present rose to their feet in silent acclaim, and the speech of one of their number was received rapturously. Many of those present in the stalls were only there to catch a glimpse of the freed political prisoners.[76] The greeting these men received reflected their high status in the new revolutionary climate. Provisional Government and soviet sources stressed the importance of the revolution's heroes in immediate responses to the February revolution. Returnees from political exile were reported triumphantly in the local press.[77] The lead article in *Kazanskaia rabochaia gazeta* on 16 April was devoted to a discussion of the importance of the return of émigrés and expressed gratitude to the British Government for facilitating returns.[78] Special committees were set up to

---

[74] Kolonitskii, 'The Russian idea', p. 52.
[75] RGASPI, f. 274, op. 1, d. 26, l. 104; Magergut's memoir.
[76] Shul'gin, *Za vlast sovetov*, p. 31; Ikonikov's memoir.
[77] For example, *Izvestiia soveta rabochikh i soldatskikh deputatov* 6, 9 April 1917, p. 4.
[78] *Kazanskaia rabochaia gazeta* 7, 16 April 1917, p. 1.

assist Russia's returning exiles,[79] and numerous appeal funds were set up for the families of 'victims of the revolution' and for exiles and political prisoners.

At the first post-revolution meetings in towns and villages across the provinces, there were often prayers spoken, songs sung and collections taken in the name of the revolution's victims. Iadrinksii *uezd*'s first revolutionary meeting on 12 March, for example, included an interlude when all stood in memory of Russia's glorious freedom fighters, and '*Vechnaia pamiat*' (Let their memory be eternal) was sung.[80] While many of these meetings and written reports were orchestrated by the national or local political elites, the level of support shown by ordinary people for collections and at meetings indicate that the search for heroes struck a popular chord. There was a special meeting in Kniagininskii town, Nizhegorod province, on 15 March to 'commemorate those who had fallen in the struggle for freedom'. A requiem was held, and numerous speeches made in memorial of events. More than 246 roubles were collected at the close of the meeting specifically for these 'victims of revolution'.[81]

The size of public donations to these specific causes is remarkable, in a period when the giving public were inundated with demands for money. We can view the act of donating money more generally as a means to participate in the civic sphere, and the donation to funds for former political prisoners as a means of publicly identifying with the revolutionary struggle. Yet even given the symbolic resonance in donations to the revolutionary cause generally, ordinary people had a choice of causes they could donate to, and many chose to donate their money to the 'victims of the revolution'.[82] As of 16 March, the Nizhnii Novgorod soviet of workers' deputies had received donations of 7,462 roubles, the vast majority of which, 6,114 roubles, had been given to the 'fund for the assistance of freed political prisoners'. The second most heavily supported fund that the soviet ran was the fund for the assistance of victims of the revolution, which attracted donations totalling 709 roubles.[83] Soviet records show that this level of support continued; in the period 20 March–8 April, the soviet received 6,352 roubles, of which

[79] GARF, f. P-3349, op. 1, 72 dela; *Society for the assistance of freed political prisoners (1917–1918)*.
[80] NART, f. 1246, op. 1, d. 46, l. 133; journal of public meeting chaired by Iadrinskii *uezd* commissar, 12 March 1917.
[81] GANO, f. 1887, op. 1, d. 28, l. 7; letter from Kniagininskii *uezd* commissar to Nizhegorod province executive committee, 23 March 1917.
[82] Diane Koenker argued that workers' contributions to political causes were more telling indicators of their political attitudes than resolutions passed. In her assessment of Moscow workers' donations to political causes, the fund for victims of the revolution was one of the best supported (Koenker, *Moscow workers*, chapter 7, esp. pp. 274, 286).
[83] *Izvestiia soveta rabochikh i soldatskikh deputatov* 3, 19 March 1917, p. 2.

almost half was donated to revolutionary heroes (1,604 roubles was donated to the fund for the assistance of freed politicals, and 1,493 roubles to the fund for victims of the revolution).[84] These donations give a clear indication that the narrative glorifying the revolution's heroes was taken up with enthusiasm by ordinary people.

Alongside the glorification of the revolution's heroes came the hunt for the revolution's villains. This was another theme dominating the political elite's narrative of the revolution that had significant popular resonance. The most conspicuous villains of the revolution were former police and secret agents, prominent old-regime figures, especially those in military positions, and alleged grain hoarders. The much hated tsarist police force was disarmed, disempowered and sometimes attacked or imprisoned in villages and towns. Though no particular distinctions were drawn in my sources, recent work by Michael Hickey indicates that a distinction was drawn between gendarmes and the police cadres.[85] In Nizhnii Novgorod, Sormovo workers arrested the gendarmes, who had tried to destroy their own records.[86] In Semenovskii *uezd*, the regional police were 'relieved of their duties' as soon as news of the revolution broke by the newly formed Semenov town executive committee, on 3 March. Various senior figures in town were arrested, including the military captain. These arrests were carried out by the Semenov town executive committee to prevent violence against the old-regime figures, especially the military captain, who was a recognised agent of suppression. When passions were considered to have died down five days later, he was released to return to his own flat.[87]

In Iurino village, Nizhegorod province, the Nizhegorod soviet newspaper reported that as soon as news of the revolution was heard, the police were disarmed and the militia and guard arrested. The senior police officer was clearly a particularly unpopular figure, who had spoken against the Provisional Government and the revolution. His liberation provoked 'pogroms' in a neighbouring village,[88] and he was rearrested in order to maintain public order. The term 'pogrom' was not always used to describe the anti-Semitic violence we associate with it. In Russian, 'pogrom' translates more generally as 'massacre'. The use of the term in the sources considered here

[84] *Izvestiia soveta rabochikh i soldatskikh deputatov* 9, 25 April 1917, p. 4.
[85] Michael C. Hickey, 'Moderate socialists and the politics of crime in revolutionary Smolensk', *Canadian-American Slavic Studies* 35 (2001), 189–218, p. 194.
[86] Shul'gin, *Za vlast sovetov*, p. 44; Vorobev's memoirs.
[87] GANO, f. 1887, op. 1, d. 2, l. 21; report of the representative of Semenovskii *uezd* executive committee to the provincial meeting of executive committees in Nizhegorod province, 23 May 1917.
[88] *Izvestiia soveta rabochikh deputatov* 17, 25 May 1917, 'News from the *uezds*', p. 4.

supports Gerald Surh's interpretation, that 'pogroms' could involve hetero-geneous motives and individuals.[89] In this context, the political elite may have used the term to describe general rioting or violent crowd behaviour. In Kazan town, the unpopular captain of the regional armed forces, General Sandetskii, along with many commanding officers, was arrested. The Provisional Government ordered that Sandetskii be sent to Petrograd without military convoy, but the mood of the town would not tolerate such an 'escape', and he was accordingly transferred to the town guardhouse.[90]

Former secret police agents took their places with the 'popular villains' of revolution. Secret police records were published in the socialist papers by local political elites to expose police agents and anyone who was alleged to have collaborated with the regime. In some cases, the unfortunates who were accused denied these collaborations, but denials counted for little in the climate of exposure and revenge. Lists of local individuals were circulated around regional committees and were published, ensuring maximum naming and shaming.[91] In connection with such revelations, the accused individuals were usually barred from office or lost their jobs. More than a hundred police informers were arrested in Nizhnii Novgorod.[92] Chistopolskii *uezd* executive committee passed a decree excluding all former secret police (*okhrana*) members from committee membership.[93] A village teacher in Kozmodem'ianskii *uezd*, for example, was declared to have been a secret police employee and was dismissed from her post.[94]

Another group identified as popular villains was those people believed to be hoarding grain or other products. The new captain of Kazan town militia, M. Bukhov, in early April appealed specifically to the public to report those suspected of hoarding foodstuffs.[95] This encouragement of an 'informing mentality' was an early indicator of attempts to polarise society between those 'parasites', often described as 'spiders' (*pauki*) who ignored national needs, and those who supported the state and by implication the

---

[89] Gerald D. Surh, 'The Russian pogroms of October 1905' (Conference paper given at Labour History of Russia and the Soviet Union: Work in Progress, Amsterdam, 2005). See also John Klier, 'The pogrom paradigm in Russian history', in John Klier and S. Lambroza (eds.), *Pogroms* (Cambridge, 1992), pp. 13–38, pp. 34–5.

[90] Ezhov, *Voennaia Kazan*, pp. 28–9.

[91] See, for example, NART, f. 1246, op. 1, d. 44, ll. 1–143; minutes of Iadrinskii *uezd* soviet of peasants' deputies, 8 August 1917; NART, f. 1246, op. 1, d. 42, l. 125; letter from secretary of Akulevskii *volost* committee, Cheboksarskii *uezd*, to Kazan provincial commissar, 17 June 1917.

[92] Shul'gin, *Za vlast sovetov*, p. 44; Vorobev's memoirs.

[93] NART, f. 1246, op. 1, d. 53, ll. 113–15; minutes from the meetings of Chistopol *uezd* committee of public safety, 8–10 May 1917.

[94] NART, f. 1246, op. 1, d. 48, l. 48; handwritten note from provincial commissar, 24 April 1917.

[95] *Kazanskaia rabochaia gazeta* 4, 13 April 1917, p. 3.

February revolution. It was also an indication of a much deeper level of revolution that was taking place: market activities were often equated with criminal 'hoarding', and attacks on capitalism were meted out in the name of protecting the war effort, or, more fundamentally, in the name of social justice.[96] The 'bourgeoisie' was a label used for any 'enemy of the revolution'.[97] The political elite's adoption of an 'informing mentality' was intended to involve ordinary people in the work of defending the revolution. By defining a small group of 'parasites' and counter-revolutionaries, a broader popular sense of revolutionary identity was encouraged, and reinforced the idea that state needs were above personal and class interests. The meeting of Lysovskii town residents' committee on 4 March focused predominantly on the 'search for villains'. In addition to organising a new voluntary militia, they appealed to the population to report any suspected grain hoarders, and announced that searches would be made of all those holding or suspected of holding grain reserves.[98] These measures were based on rumours of large grain reserves held by speculators, which searches revealed were absolutely unfounded.[99]

Both the Provisional Government and the soviets at national and local levels sought above all else to prevent outbreaks of violence, and to protect the personal safety of all citizens. The heightened passions and opportunities provoked by the hunt for villains made this maintenance of order difficult to achieve. Threatened violence in some places spilled over into actual violence, and at times was indistinguishable from more traditional violent modes of behaviour.[100] Frequent appeals from *uezd* commissars for soldiers to be sent to defend public order are a reflection both of the fears of the administration, and the tenuous nature of the existing order. The hunt for villains was encouraged so long as it remained within boundaries defined by the political elite, and at the targets authorised by them. The danger was that once popular anger and resentment was unleashed, these

[96] Peter Holquist describes the events of 1917 in relation to the food crisis as demonstrating 'overarching antimarket consensus' (Holquist, *Making war, forging revolution*, p. 44).

[97] On this, see Hiroaki Kuromiya, *Freedom and terror in the Donbas: a Ukrainian-Russian borderland, 1870s–1990s* (Cambridge, 1998), pp. 84–5, and Kolonitskii, 'Antibourgeois propaganda'.

[98] GANO, f. 715, op. 1, d. 7, l. 5; protocol no. 1 from meeting of Lyskovskii residents' committee, 4 March 1917.

[99] GANO, f. 715, op. 1, d. 7, l. 7; protocol no. 3 of Lyskovskii residents' committee, 6 March 1917.

[100] Cathy A. Frierson, 'Crime and punishment in the Russian village: rural concepts of criminality at the end of the nineteenth century', *Slavic Review* 46 (1987), 55–69; descriptions of *samosud* and peasant behaviour contained here include fearsome displays of violence; J. Neuberger, *Hooliganism. Crime, culture and power in St. Petersburg, 1900–1914* (London, 1993); on the performance of *samosud* in 1917, see Tsuyoshi Hasegawa, 'Crime, police and mob justice in Petrograd during the Russian revolutions of 1917', in Rex A. Wade (ed.), *Revolutionary Russia: new approaches* (New York, 2004), pp. 46–72, pp. 61–3;.

official targets and boundaries could easily be transgressed or forgotten. In Kazan province, Spasskii *uezd*'s commissar Vedeniapin appealed on 13 March for one hundred soldiers to be sent to the *uezd* 'for the defence of *zemstva* stores, state property and the defence of order'.[101] This suggests that popular resentment and violence had spilled over into attacks on areas that had not been condoned by the elite.

The 'spilling over' of popular resentment and violence highlighted divergences between the discourses of the political elite, and the discourses of ordinary people. Scapegoating and popular violence had been a feature of Russian provincial life before the 1917 revolution, when Jewish people were the pariahs of choice.[102] In 1917, anti-Semitism persisted, but the list of villains, or pariahs, was appended with other categories including former policemen, spies and grain hoarders. The need for scapegoats was intensified by the tumult and uncertainties of the revolutionary period. While the elite discourse sought above all else to maintain order and to prevent violence and arbitrary actions, popular discourse did not preclude and even encouraged violence and acts of revenge. The emotive hunt for villains was the ideal forum for such differences to become apparent.

The revolution's administrators both initiated and restrained the disempowerment of harmful forces, as they tried to capitalise on resentment towards old-regime figures while maintaining at least a semblance of a legally ordered state. Eric Lohr has shown how the state failed to exercise its monopoly on violence in relation to the 1915 anti-German riots in Moscow.[103] Joshua Sanborn's work on the army shows how Russia's Bolshevik leaders in the early civil war period exploited and encouraged popular violence but were rather less successful in containing it.[104] Provincial administrators in 1917 were far less explicit and enthusiastic than their Bolshevik successors in encouraging violence but were absolutely unable to contain violence. Searches and arrests took place without the backing of local authority, but at the initiative of 'spontaneous revolutionaries', that is, individuals working outside the remit of Provisional Government and soviet organisations. The government's struggle in containing such actions

---

[101] NART, f. 1246, op. 1, d. 41, l. 9; telephonogram from Spasskii *uezd* commissar Vedeniapin to commander of Kazan military region, 13 March 1917.

[102] Sanborn, *Drafting the Russian nation*, pp. 114ff., discusses the utilisation of deep personal anxieties and angers through national channels to strengthen the sense of 'nation'. For detailed case studies of how and why Jews were pariahs, see R. Weinberg, 'Workers, pogroms and the 1905 revolution in Odessa', *Russian Review* 46 (1987), 53–75, pp. 55–7; R. Weinberg, *The revolution of 1905 in Odessa: blood on the steps* (Bloomington, IN, 1993), pp. 15–19; Charters Wynn, *Workers, strikes and pogroms: the Donbas-Dnepr bend in late imperial Russia, 1870–1905* (Princeton, NJ, 1992), esp. pp. 65, 68.

[103] Eric Lohr, 'Patriotic violence and the state: the Moscow riots of May 1915', *Kritika* 4 (2003), 607–26.

[104] Sanborn, *Drafting the Russian nation*, pp. 174–8.

is apparent. On taking over his new role on 9 March, the Kazan provincial commissar reiterated that searches and arrests in Kazan town could take place only when backed with a written order signed by him or the president of the executive committee. He concluded that

[a]ll searches and arrests carried out without legal authorisation are illegal, and those individuals initiating such actions must understand that their illegal actions only discredit the Provisional Government. Once again I call on the population to submit to the legal organs of the new government, to the preservation of order and the peaceful continuation of peaceful labour.[105]

This appeal encapsulates the problems the new regime faced; the commissar appealed to legality, and called on citizens to submit, but had no clear grounds for his own authority, and no means of coercion available. Even though his announcement came only days after news of the revolution broke, it demonstrated the weakness of his position and hinted at unmanageable disorder. The political elite fostered a mentality of scapegoating and informing but were unable to contain the popular hostility that scapegoats attracted. The parameters of state-controlled violence were transgressed in 1917 by popular involvement in the cause of hunting out enemies.

Popular hostility and violence in 1917 spilled over from officially sanctioned targets onto local administrators established with Provisional Government authority. The local administration established by the Provisional Government was not immune to the climate of change and challenge to the establishment heralded by the February revolution. The collapse of the old regime was almost uncontested, but the form that the new regime was to take highlighted some acute differences between the elite and ordinary people. The *zemstvo* administration that was authorised by the Provisional Government to take over administration of the *uezd* was not always a popular body. In Spasskii *uezd*, for example, 'an exchange of public opinion' at a public meeting attended by more than 400 people on 16 March established that the new *uezd* commissar Vedeniapin and the members of the *zemstvo* administration 'did not answer to the demands of the current time'. Vedeniapin was slow to remove the old police force, and his actions, along with those of his administration, were 'enervating the population'. The unpopularity of Vedeniapin was not tolerated for long, however. The society of *zemstvo* employees deposed his administration on 12 March, considering that such a move was necessary 'for the good of peace and order in the *uezd*'. The deposition was administered peacefully; Vedeniapin resigned

---

[105] NART, f. 1246, op. 1, d. 55, l. 182; decree of Simbirsk provincial executive committee, 14 June 1917.

his post and was replaced by 'an individual enjoying the trust of the population'.[106] The change of administration in Spasskii *uezd* showed that unpopular administrators were not tolerated, but replaced.

Cheboksary provides an extreme example of such conflicts and mistrust within local administration. Cheboksary, the small and unremarkable capital of Cheboksarskii *uezd* in Kazan province, was the scene of intense power struggle right from the outset of 1917, not least because of the strong characters that vied for revolutionary power and authority there.[107] The conflict in Cheboksary was atypical, in that it was highly politicised and openly expressed, but is useful as an example of conflicting visions for revolution. An unnamed correspondent to the Menshevik edited soviet newspaper *Kazanskaia rabochaia gazeta* remarked in April on events in Cheboksary that

[t]he revolutionary People must take power away from the bureaucrats and deliver the country from disorder. We need to move away from the former situation. We must have regional government of the moment, elected by four-tailed suffrage, otherwise the government will be regarded by the people as 'decorations'.[108]

Karl Grasis, a radical who later led the Kazan Bolsheviks, pressed for violent overthrow of the Provisional Government's incumbents at his first public uttering in April, and for ousting of former *zemstvo* workers. The worker-backed soviet that Grasis initiated and headed was openly hostile to other elements of the town administration. A meeting formed in one of Cheboksary's parks on 8 March, attended by peasants from neighbouring villages, gives some indication of the rawness of the conflict that developed between Grasis and the town administration. The *uezd* commissar Ennatskii reportedly tried to incite the crowd against Grasis, and called on them to 'Beat the swindler!' A group of armed soldiers and workers protected Grasis, and in the confrontation that followed Ennatskii was forced to sign a paper standing down from the commissariat.[109] The ferocity and politicisation of the conflict over control of power in Cheboksary is exceptional at such early stages of 1917, but similar open conflict and contestation over local power occurred all over Kazan and Nizhegorod towards the summer of 1917. Visions of what the revolution was to entail became

---

[106] NART, f. 1352, op. 1, d. 3, l. 157; journal of the meeting of Spasskii *uezd* committee of public safety, 16 March 1917.

[107] See Sarah Badcock, 'From saviour to pariah: a study of the role of Karl Ianovich Grasis in Cheboksary during 1917', *Revolutionary Russia* 15 (2002), 69–96.

[108] *Kazanskaia rabochaia gazeta* 13, 25 April, p. 3.

[109] V. K. Kirillov, *Karl Ianovich Grasis* (Cheboksary, 1969), p. 26.

increasingly disparate from April onwards, as ordinary people's high expectations of what the revolution was to mean to them personally translated into enthusiasm for changes of personnel and even regime changes in local government. The political elites failed to control visions of the revolution, and their control of political power at local level was repeatedly challenged.

CONCLUSIONS

For ordinary people, the February revolution offered great hopes, and the promise of profound social and political change. In this climate of tumultuous emotions and profound uncertainties, ordinary people were quick to adapt to the new regime, but often used known and well-trodden discourses to frame their responses. The support shown for the 'victims of the revolution' and for political prisoners had a religious feel, with its focus on martyrs and on suffering for the cause. The scapegoating of those perceived to be 'against the people', and thus against the revolution, was manifested initially in popular hostility and even violence against police and old-regime administrators. This popular feeling was capitalised on by the Provisional Government and soviets, who actively demonised the old regime and its figureheads. The net of counter-revolution was widened however, in popular imagination and actions, to include those believed to be profiting from the war, like traders and speculators, and increasingly to the Provisional Government's own administrators. The Provisional Government and soviets were unable to prevent this extension of popular enemies to include their own supporters. We can detect the seeds of the subsequent breakdown of local government in the initial challenges posed by the February revolution.

Interpreting what the February revolution meant in real terms to ordinary people is an important starting point to understanding ordinary people's experiences of the revolution. The political elite sought to control the ways in which the February revolution was spread and tried to create a 'revolutionary orthodoxy' of what the revolution signified. Even in the first weeks after February, they struggled to maintain their vision of revolutionary orthodoxy. The ways in which ordinary people responded to the revolutionary news demonstrates just how complex the dynamic of power and authority was. While the Provisional Government, and to some extent the Petrograd Soviet, held power in principle, in practice they were not able to control either the ways in which the revolution was understood, or the responses of ordinary people.

CHAPTER 3

The Socialist Revolutionary Party and the place of party politics

The newly democratised political system placed party politics at the very heart of political debate and discourse. The new political elite presented political parties as the vehicles by which ordinary people could participate in political life and shape Russia's future. If we move away from elite politics, however, political parties often played a very low-key role in grass-roots politics and in people's daily life. In order to understand the role of political parties, we must try to establish how ordinary people related to political parties. Support for a political party was the most widely recognised way for individuals to express political will, and this support is often used as an indicator for the opinions, moods, feelings and motivations of the population. It is relatively straightforward to estimate support for political parties using voting statistics and membership figures. What this support, manifested in voting and party membership, might actually signify about the political attitudes of those offering it has not been adequately explored.

This chapter will tackle the difficult problem of popular understandings by focusing on the Socialist Revolutionary Party (PSR). The PSR cannot be used to represent the experiences of all political parties. As we will see from this study of the PSR's foundations and support, the genesis of party political support was caught up in a complex network of social, historical and psychological factors, which were particular to the party. By looking at one party in detail, we are able to unpick the various factors that contribute to its support, and this process sheds some light on questions of party political support more generally in 1917. So while this chapter is concerned exclusively with the PSR, its conclusions shed some light more generally on the nature of popular support. Most importantly, this more focused study offers some explanation of the apparent paradox inherent in party politics of 1917, that while party politics saturated political discourse, parties were often absent from the mechanisms of grass-roots politics.

The PSR was Russia's largest political party in 1917, and its failure to capitalise on its apparently enormous support base is emblematic both of the failure of moderate socialists to put up a challenge to the Bolsheviks, and of the apparent irrelevance of popular support to the ultimate winners and losers of 1917. Despite its majority support, the PSR was unable to make a positive impact on Russia's power struggle as it descended into civil war. As one of the PSR's leading chroniclers Michael Melancon put it, the PSR 'experienced defeat in full measure', both in its defeat by the Bolsheviks and in its exclusion from the historiography of the revolution.[1] The PSR helps us to re-evaluate our understandings of what it meant to support a political party in 1917. The PSR provided little more than an umbrella of widely recognised party image, and a loosely constructed theoretical framework for its members and supporters. Though in principle the party's ideology and leadership defined party identity, in practice members and supporters themselves redefined what it meant to be a member of or to support the PSR. Understandings of 'loyalty' to a given political party need to be reconsidered in this light. The failure of the democratic party political system in Russia was predicated in part on the ways in which support for political parties were understood by ordinary people in 1917.

THE PLACE OF THE PARTY IN 1917

The collapse of the tsarist regime heralded an explosion of pluralism in Russia's political life and pushed Russia's nascent political parties into the forefront. Both established and newly formed political parties were able to organise and campaign freely, and to set out their programmatic alternatives for Russia's future development. The relationship of political parties with the broader public was transformed by the February revolution. Whereas in the pre-revolutionary period, revolutionary parties had focused their activities among key activist groups, now they sought to attract and represent mass support. Political parties also had to engage in open political competition. This drive to popularise political parties was successful to some extent. Ordinary people participated in party-based elections, joined parties, especially the PSR and Bolsheviks,[2] and were subject to intense political

---

[1] Melancon, 'The Neopopulist experience', p. 195.

[2] Though the socialist parties, in particular the PSR, and as 1917 wore on, the Bolsheviks, saw large influxes of new members in 1917, providing figures of membership is problematic, not least because the party organisations themselves were in the dark as to the size of their new mass membership. A tentative figure of some 1 million can be estimated for PSR membership, based on known figures of members in the provinces and the active army, though this is certainly below the number describing themselves as PSR members in 1917. Membership figures from *Partiniia izvestiia* 1, 28 September 1917, pp. 18ff.; 2, 5 October 1917, pp. 49–50; 3, 19 October 1917, pp. 35ff.; 5, 20 January 1918, pp. 56, 59–60. Estimates for Bolshevik party membership in 1917 are also approximate. Rigby suggests figures of 24,000 at the start of 1917, and by October 1917, figures of between 115,000 and 400,000 members (T. H. Rigby, *Communist Party membership in the USSR, 1917–1967* (Princeton, NJ, 1968), p. 59, p. 61).

education campaigns. It is beyond question that the political party as an institution was utilised by the electorate in 1917. This does not necessarily tell us much, however, about what ordinary people thought they were supporting.

The political elite portrayed political parties as the mechanism by which ordinary people could express their political interests and become involved in political life. There were a succession of elections in 1917 to choose local administration at a range of levels, and these elections culminated in the Constituent Assembly elections, finally held at the beginning of November. The structure of voting systems for local elections varied and often offered blocs of candidates from different party affiliations standing for one list, or lists of individuals without party political affiliations. In the Constituent Assembly elections, however, the electorate were offered choices between party lists rather than individuals, which meant that the political party had to be both understood and embraced by the electorate if the election was to have any democratic meaning. An article in the peasant-oriented *Simbirskaia narodnaia gazeta* at the beginning of June put the importance of the party in the new state structure succinctly: 'It is necessary not only to become acquainted with political parties and their demands, but to enter into their life, and to form them yourselves, to select and put forward your own candidates; otherwise the Constituent Assembly and *volost zemstva* will not represent all the living desires of the peasantry.'[3]

Ordinary people had experienced some degree of party political contestation both in 1905 and in the elections to the State Duma, but the socialist press sought to clarify the nature and role of political parties. Articles with titles like 'What Is a Party, and Why Do We Need Them?' appeared in local newspapers, and sought to clarify what a party was, emphasising the political party's importance and central role in the formation of Russia's new state structure. Political parties were presented as mass movements that would unite people with common class interests and fulfil their demands in changing the political and economic life of the country. The description of parties offered in the socialist press often started with an essentially Marxist discussion of class divisions produced by the control of capital, and the exploitation of working people particularly.[4] The socialist press made no attempt to engage with the ideas of non-socialist parties, who were brusquely consigned to irrelevancy. The differences between political parties were often drawn out in broad brush strokes in the first instance,

[3] *Simbirskaia narodnaia gazeta* 17, 7 June 1917, p. 3.
[4] Even the PSR, an avowedly non-Marxist party, used Marxist terminology when describing basic models of exploitation.

separating socialist parties from their 'bourgeois' rivals without internal distinctions. Again from the June *Simbirskaia narodnaia gazeta* article:

All parties may be divided into two distinct categories: one strives to build in our future life a situation where there will be no rich and no poor, and every member of the community can receive all that he needs in life through his own labour – these are the socialist parties. The other category of party considers such a future to be an impossible dream, that it is impossible to abolish property and capitalist gains from waged labour – they consider only certain improvements possible. Socialist parties call such parties bourgeois, since they defend the inescapable interests of the bourgeoisie – the wealthy and not the working class of the population.[5]

In order to impart understanding of party political activity to the population, the socialist press described party political action in the same terms as those used to describe the operation of traditional peasant institutions. The political party was presented as a form of national commune (*obshchina*).[6] The socialist press struck an uneasy balance between the need for unanimity of action, which harked back to traditions of unanimous voting within peasant organisations, and the significance of ordinary people's views and wishes. Overall, the need for collective unity outweighed individualism. An article in the newspaper *Zemlia i volia* in August, published by the Nizhegorod soviet of peasants' deputies, stressed the need for unity of action:

Alone it is impossible to achieve anything, as an individual will not be considered at any time in any place . . . A united political party, on the other hand, which can count in its ranks tens of thousands of united people, achieving as one, and acting to one plan by identical means . . . for such a party, of course, there will be strength, and it can achieve all and everything in life.[7]

These contemporary definitions perceived political parties as mass movements that embodied the views of their mass membership, and used the power that they gleaned from such support to carry out their programme in public life. In this they resembled pre-revolutionary party cultures, which

[5] *Simbirskaia narodnaia gazeta* 17, 7 June 1917, p. 3.
[6] Teodor Shanin, *The awkward class – Political sociology of peasantry in a developing society: Russia 1910–25* (Oxford, 1972), esp. p. 34, discusses the form of peasant politics prior to 1917: 'The wide functions of the commune made the gathering into a most powerful body, at least potentially. The actual process of decision making, however, was far removed from the formally democratic procedures laid down by the law. The decisions were typically unanimous.' Christine D. Worobec, *Peasant Russia: family and community in the post emancipation period* (Princeton, NJ, 1991), highlights the central role the peasant commune took in regulating and maintaining peasant society.
[7] '*Zemlia i volia*', *krest'ianskaia gazeta (Izvestiia Nizhegorodskago guberniia sovet krest'ianskikh deputatov)* 22, 15 August 1917, p. 1.

tended towards democratic centralisation. The party elites did not practically embrace this model in 1917 and sought to define and control members' behaviour, rather than to be defined by it. At grass-roots level, however, in the villages and factory shop floors of provincial Russia, far from the centres of political power, the party elite was unable to exert significant influence, and the PSR's supporters reshaped and redefined the party's local policy and character. Why was the PSR elite unable to prescribe the party's public face? The transformation for all the revolutionary parties from revolutionary underground to open politics was problematic. Such a transformation required that the PSR clarify what its message was, and develop lines of communication with the electorate, in order to present the ideology and character of the party, primarily through the political mechanisms of electoral campaigns, but also through newspapers, associations, propaganda and education. In the pre-revolutionary period, the PSR could be categorised as a thoroughly radical revolutionary party, whose attitude towards the state was essentially antagonistic. The party's leaders dramatically shifted party attitudes towards the state in the post-February days. Its decision to support the Provisional Government and to work within the new administration established by the February revolution was a significant retrenching for what was an inherently radical party.[8]

The PSR appealed to the electorate in 1917 by building on their historical associations, and on the symbolic representations of the party as martyrs and stalwart fighters for 'land and freedom'. A popular misconception of the PSR is that it was a predominantly agrarian party. Whilst the vast majority of its electoral support in 1917 came from the countryside, this should not devalue its significant followings among soldiers and urban workers. The party programme, drawn up by Victor Chernov, had clear Marxist influences both in its exploitation models and the relations of capital but embraced a much broader view of the working classes, including peasants, industrial workers and the working intelligentsia. This harmony of broad working-class interests is a central part of PSR doctrine. In fact, as a result of practical constraints, the PSR in the 1905–17 period focused its activism first on the urban working class, then on the military and then on the peasants.[9] Though the party's campaigns in the garrisons and on the shop floor did refer to peasant-oriented themes, they also appealed to issues that

---

[8] Michael Melancon, 'The Left Socialist Revolutionaries and the Bolshevik uprising', in Vladimir N. Brovkin (ed.), *The Bolsheviks in Russian society* (New Haven, CT, 1997), pp. 59–82, p. 60. 'Chernov's new, unwonted moderation was also a factor (in the party's shift to the centre) . . . Chernov never explained this deviation from his accustomed path.'

[9] M. I. Leonov, *PSR v 1907–1914 gg.* (Moscow, 1997), pp. 456–90.

addressed workers and soldiers specifically.[10] The PSR won widespread support in the factories and garrisons in 1917, though this support was reduced by the autumn of 1917, and fragmented by the split of the Left SRs away from the PSR after the Bolshevik seizure of power. Michael Melancon suggests that the party's loss of worker and soldier support in 1917 came from the move of the PSR Central Committee to the right, particularly in terms of supporting the war, when the party's cadres and mass support were inherently radical.[11]

Melancon's explanation of the PSR's falling support among workers and soldiers is compelling and fits in well with the strength of the Left SR group in that period. What then galvanised PSR support in the country-side, where the PSR was absolutely dominant? Melancon's work in identifying the PSR's non-peasant grass-roots has provided a vital corrective to assumptions that the PSR was a peasants' party, but we cannot discount its rural constituency altogether. The founding tenets of the PSR's political programme intermingled references to age-old peasant grievances. The basis for the party's practical political programme was land socialisation, whereby land could not be private property but would be reapportioned on an egalitarian basis, and its produce would belong to those who worked it. Land socialisation envisaged a strengthening of the commune as the organising force in rural life, and through it the establishment of social equality and justice. This was the bedrock of the PSR programme, and it appealed to peasant conceptions of justice. We cannot discount this fundamental appeal to social justice from the party's appeal to workers and soldiers as well, many of whom continued to maintain close links with rural Russia.[12]

Although the PSR's agitation work in the pre-revolutionary period focused on workers and soldiers, the party's support base was founded around the peasant milieu. PSR policies and its presence and recognition in the countryside explain its appeal to the peasant milieu. The PSR was the only radical revolutionary party to address the issues of ordinary peasant Russians and was the only party with a history of agitation in the villages, particularly in the first revolution of 1905–7, but also in the 1907–14

---

[10] Michael Melancon, *The Socialist Revolutionaries and the Russian anti-war movement, 1914–17* (Columbus, OH, 1990), p. 2.

[11] Melancon, *The Socialist Revolutionaries and the Russian anti-war movement*, p. 282.

[12] The majority of the army was of course made up of peasant recruits. A number of studies have considered the links between worker behaviour and peasant mentality. Among the most recent is Nikolai V. Mikhailov, 'The collective psychology of Russian workers and workplace: self-organisation in the early twentieth century', in Michael Melancon and Alice K. Pate (eds.), *New labor history: worker identity and experience in Russia, 1840–1918* (Bloomington, IN, 2002), pp. 77–94.

period. Its support from the rural intelligentsia of teachers, co-operators, *zemstvo* activists and so on provided the party with a crucial direct link into rural life.[13] The PSR's associations were not just with given policies, but with the peasant way of life. The milieu concept, used by Karl Rohe and other German historians to explain patterns of voting behaviour, and more generally to explain the support offered to political parties, is useful in understanding Russian voting behaviour, though it cannot be applied wholesale, not least because the model requires voters to have developed a long-standing loyalty to a party, expressed in the voting act. Milieu voting suggests that voters operate in groups which are defined culturally, and which eschew the narrower and more proscriptive delineations of class or religion. Rather, a party's support base can be seen as a 'political expression of complex constellations of social, religious and regional factors, which then merge into comparatively stable social-cultural milieus'.[14] We can account for the PSR's breadth and depth of support in its attraction to the peasant milieu.

WHO WERE THE SOCIALIST REVOLUTIONARIES?

The PSR's support base, centred on the peasant milieu, was broadly defined and indistinct. It is worth exploring what people thought they were supporting. One way of getting at this question is to look at the ways in which the party defined itself, not just nationally, but regionally. The PSR's heterogeneity was not just an incidental feature of a party that lacked a strong organisational framework but was one of the party's key programmatic bases. The PSR did not have a clearly defined programme that constituted an 'orthodox' party line. The lack of any clear PSR 'orthodoxy' fundamentally undermines many of our notions about the nature of the political party, emphasising regional variation rather than national homogeneity, and close responsiveness to its milieu of support rather than rigidity of party doctrine. This flexibility allowed the party to appeal to a broad range of people, and to win and maintain an enormous support base. It also undermined the party's ability to act as a unified political body. The party's failure to form a unified and coherent political force in 1917 was based on its programmatic ideological basis, which was committed to heterogeneity

---

[13] Scott J. Seregny, 'Revolutionary strategies in the Russian countryside: rural teachers and the SR party on the eve of 1905', *Russian Review* 44 (1985), 221–38; See also Scott J. Seregny, *Russian teachers and peasant revolution: the politics of education in 1905* (Bloomington, IN, 1989), pp. 88–97.

[14] Karl Rohe, *Elections, parties and political traditions: social foundations of German parties and party systems, 1861–1917* (Oxford, 1990), p. 1.

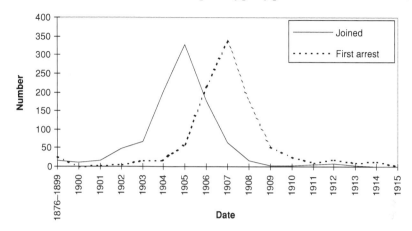

Figure 3.1. Dates of membership and first arrest of PSR members
Note: Data is based on 999 PSR members included in M. M. Konstantinov and F. M. Tochilin, *Politicheskaia katorga i ssylka: biograficheskii spravochnik chlenov obshchestva politkatorzhan i ssyl'no-poselentsev* (Moscow, 1934). See also Maureen Perrie, 'The social composition and the structure of the Socialist Revolutionary Party before 1917', *Soviet Studies* 24 (1972), 223–50, pp. 225–7.

within the party. The very real problems for the party in leadership, lack of membership commitment and organisational and financial problems were overshadowed by the party's commitment to heterogeneity.

In the pre-revolutionary period, the PSR was predominantly an underground party, whose members faced police surveillance and repression. The party's close association with terrorist activity caused its members to be particularly targeted by the tsarist secret police. Sources for the evaluation of the party's activities in Russia before the revolution come from the PSR's organisations outside Russia, conferences, letters, reports and the memoirs of party leadership on the one hand, and police records on the other. These are useful, but tell us about the activities of the party elite, mainly in exile overseas, and the party cells inside Russia that the police were aware of, but not the more successful underground organisations. The figures quoted in figure 3.1 on party recruitment and arrest are based on the 999 former PSR members of the Society for Political Prisoners and Exiles. These members were not necessarily 'typical', in that they reflected those former SRs who chose to join a soviet-sponsored association. That said, they do offer useful indications of membership patterns. On the basis of these 999 members, party recruitment hit a peak just before 1905 and was high between 1903 and 1906. Date of members' first arrests show that police activity kept up with this growth in the party – arrests peaked in 1907, and were high between 1906 and 1908.[15]

The average pre-revolutionary member from this source collection was active in the party for around two years before trial. Trials were almost inevitably followed by either Siberian exile, or a spell in a hard-labour prison followed by Siberian exile. Almost all of the individuals whose arrest history is tabulated were not able to return to European Russia until after the February revolution. In May 1909 the PSR's central committee, from its place of exile in Paris, sent a number of party members back to Russia to try and establish the state of the party after the post-1905 repressions.[16] One of these scouts, the prominent SR Vladimir Zenzinov, reported that the party organisation was shattered by 1909, and that former party activists refused to come forward for their party.[17] The historian Chris Rice profiled the activities of the PSR in five different regions and found that by 1907 party activities in all but the Urals had entered 'painful and inexorable decline' as a result of state oppression.[18] Spiridovich, a police officer who published a survey of the PSR in 1916, commented that 'By the beginning of 1914 there was no party organisation operating within Russia in the stricter sense of the word. There were only socialist revolutionaries scattered around different towns, dreaming of such organisations and of party work.'[19]

At the beginning of 1917, as far as the party's central committee knew, the PSR's grass-roots organisation had been reduced to a skeletal organisation of illegal groups, with no links to the centre, and an inert constituency. Most of its workers had been exiled, imprisoned or had moved into 'legal' political work, in people's universities, insurance funds, co-operatives and journalism. It is difficult to be sure of just how accurate this picture was, as some underground party organisations operated without the knowledge of the party leadership, and if effective they went undetected by the police, and so left little trace of their existence. Michael Melancon has found that though

---

[15] The date of members' 'first' arrests are rather difficult to ascertain, since most of the individuals were arrested on a number of occasions prior to being tried for their revolutionary activity. The date taken here corresponds with the members' first arrests that resulted in a trial.

[16] V. V. Shelokhaev, *Politicheskii partii Rossii, konets 19– pervaia tret 20 veka. Entsiklopediia* (Moscow, 1996), p. 216; from biography of Zenzinov, written by N. Erofeev.

[17] Oliver H. Radkey, *The agrarian foes of Bolshevism: promise and default of the Russian Socialist Revolutionaries, February to October 1917* (New York, 1958), p. 80. Radkey based this on a personal interview with Zenzinov.

[18] C. Rice, *Russian workers and the SR Party through the revolution of 1905–7* (Basingstoke, 1988), pp. 129–76.

[19] A. E. Spiridovich, *Partiia sotsialistov revoliutsionerov i ee predshestvenniki, 1886–1916* (Petrograd, 1916), p. 495. Note that the Bolsheviks were also crushed as a result of police surveillance by 1916 (E. H. Carr, *The Bolshevik revolution 1917–1923* (Harmondsworth, 1983), p. 79).

the 1908–10 period was characterised by intense repression, some revival of PSR organisations was notable in some factories and garrisons by 1910, and in the countryside by 1912.[20] The records of Sormovo's underground PSR group collected by one of its members, Zinovii Magergut, provides a fascinating snapshot of the activities of these unseen party cells. Police activity necessitated small, secret, underground organisations, which were frequently harried or halted by searches and arrests.[21] Sviatitskii's account of his tour of the Urals and the Volga in Spring 1916 showed no trace of SR agitation,[22] indicating that the remaining party activists were forced into inactivity, or into highly surreptitious work by police surveillance.

The PSR came through the challenge of its underground existence and became recognised as a political party with nationally recognised aims and objectives. Its underground networks, however enfeebled, enabled it to build its membership rapidly after the February revolution. Its new membership was expected to carry a membership card, abide by the party's regulations and pay regular sums to party funds.[23] The party strove to build a committed, educated and diligent membership. The PSR did not address the issues of control over its membership or of strengthening party discipline in 1917, either in the party's centre or in the regional organisations. An indication of the inability of the PSR to summon or control its membership was the party's serious financial difficulties in 1917. The provincial organisations levied 10 per cent of their subsidiary organisations' income, and the Central Committee in its turn levied 10 per cent from the provincial organisations, but little of this money filtered back to the Central Committee. Oliver Radkey remarked that only 3 per cent of the party's money came from the party organisation itself, and that the remainder was furnished from bank loans.[24]

Practical difficulties inhibited the development of effective party discipline in 1917. The party lacked the existing infrastructure required to coordinate its new-found mass membership. This does not in itself explain the party's organisational failings; all socialist political parties whose activities

---

[20] Melancon, *The Socialist Revolutionaries and the Russian anti-war movement*, pp. 13–14.
[21] RGASPI, f. 274, op. 1, d. 26, ll. 84–113; Magergut's memoir.
[22] 'Voina i predfevrale', *Katorga i ssylka* 75.2 (1931), 32–3.
[23] GARF, f. 9591c, op. 1, d. 31, ll. 24–8: membership card for the Moscow-Zastovskii region, with detailed party regulations, and section for party stamps to be inserted with each monthly payment, filled in by one Ivan Starakov, a soldier, on 25 September 1917. Membership procedures varied considerably from region to region, however; see Sarah Badcock, '"We're for the muzhiks' party!" Peasant support for the Socialist Revolutionary Party during 1917', *Europe Asia Studies* 53 (2001), 133–50. See also *Narod* 10, 7 May 1917.
[24] Oliver H. Radkey, *The sickle under the hammer: the Russian Socialist Revolutionaries in the early months of Soviet rule* (New York, 1963), p. 200.

had been illegal in the tsarist period faced such difficulties. The PSR's difficulties were enhanced by three factors. First, the size and speed of growth of their mass membership was exceptionally large and fast, and far outpaced other political parties. Secondly, the PSR won the bulk of its new support in the countryside, where it was more difficult than in urban areas to establish organisational networks. Finally, the party's inherently loose philosophy allowed and even encouraged the proliferation of opinions within the party. This encouraged factionalism and blurred understandings of what being a member of the PSR entailed.

Any one province was enmeshed in an array of PSR organisations of varying levels and densities that even the provincial PSR committee struggled to track and maintain links with. Geographically based groups formed in villages, *volosts*, small towns and *uezds*, supplemented by interest-based groups of peasants, workers and soldiers. These groups often formed at the initiative of individuals who did not have any connection with the provincial organisation, far less with the Central Committee. Further, they formed and expanded at a speed that the provincial organisations were unable to keep up with. The physical distances separating these groups, and the difficulties of travel and communications,[25] particularly within rural areas, enhanced their isolation. An infrastructure that could adequately maintain such a web of organisations effectively required a durability that could only have come from sustained operation. The makeshift structures established in 1917 were inadequate to this mighty task. While all political parties faced this problem of getting information and controlling their regional party, the size of the PSR's membership, and its geographical spread across rural as well as urban areas, made its problems far more acute than, for example, the predominantly urban Bolsheviks and Mensheviks.

It is estimated that in 1917 there were 436 regional PSR organisations, 312 committees and 124 groups,[26] though this is almost certainly below the true number of groups describing themselves as 'PSR'. The party lacked basic information about its new mass membership and regional organisations. The issue for the Central Committee in the first instance was not in ensuring party discipline among these regional groups, many of which were new, but just of finding out how many and how strong they were. The Bolshevik party's Central Committee faced similar problems and received little statistical information from local party groups.[27] The

[25] On the problems of communication generally, and more particularly the difficulty of spanning Russia's vast geographical distances, see Pethybridge, 'The significance of communications'.

[26] Figures from Shelokhaev, *Politicheskii partii Rossii*, p. 440.

[27] Rigby, *Communist Party membership*, p. 61.

PSR's Central Committee sent out a detailed questionnaire to provincial organisations in an attempt to establish information about the state of the party.[28] This questionnaire enquired of the form and amount of party work going on in factories, villages and garrisons; the structure and hierarchy of the regional party organisation; and participation in organs of regional self-government. Only 123 of 426 regional organisations submitted responses.[29] The PSR group in Petrograd was among those who did not submit a response, indicating the laxity of organisation even in large central party organisations. These requests for information from the PSR's regional organisations were repeated throughout 1917, especially before the fourth party congress held between 26 November and 4 December. The party leaders were largely ignorant of the size and political mood of the party's regional groups.

While these organisational questions impeded the formation of a coherent party, the core reason for the party's lack of discipline can be found in the party's uniquely liberal attitude towards the question of party discipline. An article published in the national PSR newspaper, representing the views of the Central Committee, entitled 'Freedom of Thought and Unity of Action',[30] emphasised that differences among the party's membership were not only accepted, but welcomed. The anonymous author emphasised that the party's programme and resolutions were sufficiently broad to be acceptable to a wide range of comrades of different temperaments, types and characters. John Stuart Mill was quoted to accentuate the importance of the PSR membership's broad political views; 'If all mankind was of one opinion, and only one person held another view, then all mankind has to stand by the rights of that one individual, since to stifle one man is to stifle all of mankind.'[31]

Having established the right and even the desirability for party members to express a range of discordant political views, the author went on to state that unity was necessary both for party work and for party existence. To suggest that personal freedom of political opinion and such wide scope of political difference and discordance was in any way compatible with the construction of a coherent and unified political party was surely naïve. The party's theoretical basis was unsuited to the demands of constructing a

---

[28] RGASPI, f. 274, op. 1, d. 2, ll. 112–13; form sent to regional organisations by the commission on the formation of the third PSR party meeting, undated.

[29] *Partiniia izvestiia* 3, 19 October 1917, pp. 20–4, in section 'Party life'.

[30] *Delo naroda* 78, 18 June 1917, p. 1.

[31] *Delo naroda* 78, 18 June 1917, p. 1. Such an opinion from Mill can be found in his discussion of representative government, in chapter 7, on 'true and false democracy'; J. S. Mill, *Utilitarianism, liberty, representative government* (London, 1960), pp. 256–62.

coherent mass party. As early as 1901, Chernov spelt out the heterogeneity that the PSR embraced:

Every vital developing social movement, which comprehends reality according to local conditions of strength, cannot expand without certain programmatic and tactical disagreements. Moreover, these disagreements may rightly be called the moving force to develop a party programme. A party must be able to guarantee to its members in each given moment freedom of opinion, full freedom of speech in defining their tactics [while] uniting with this full discipline to act in the completion of those tasks accepted by majority decision. The party must be organised democratically.[32]

Though the Bolsheviks also had factions, Chernov's enthusiasm for democracy and disagreement within the party structure placed him in stark contrast with the party philosophy developed by Lenin.[33] Chernov's philosophical position inevitably led to a degree of woolliness in any attempts to define party policy; a definition too rigid would have excluded parts of the PSR's membership. There was not only a precedent, but actually a programmatic commitment to the profound discord and disunity that finally tore the party apart in 1917. Dissent within the party was so widespread that it was the norm, rather than the exception; almost any single element of party programme was not unanimously supported. Before 1917, when the PSR operated predominantly in the underground, this dissent produced distinct party factions but did little to affect party activities, which were after all very restricted.

In 1917, however, the party had to transform from its patchwork of underground cells to a national party that could wield significant political power. Its inability to act in a coherent way explains the party's mass support, as ordinary people supported the party on the grounds of what it meant to them. This loose support and lack of coherence also prevented the PSR from mobilising its mass support. The variations between local party organisations and representatives ensured that voters could identify with the policies they preferred from the PSR's political programme. Support for the PSR from a particular group within the population did not imply anything about their approval of central party policy, but only approval of the PSR policy selected by them, as presented by their local leaders. This offers an explanation for their mass membership's failure to win political clout for the party.

---

[32] Victor Chernov [under pseudonym O.], 'Bibliografia', *Nakanune* 3, 28 (1901), 343–4.
[33] See Robert Service, *Lenin: a biography* (Basingstoke, 2000), pp. 138–46, on the genesis of 'What is to be done?', Lenin's thesis on the necessary organisation of the revolutionary party.

The freedom of political opinion within the party was reflected by the myriad of positions taken by regional PSR organisations in 1917, most notably on the war, land question and attitudes to the Provisional Government. Despite its position as the single most popular political party of 1917, and its status as Russia's 'organic' socialist party, the political programme of the PSR was shrouded in uncertainty. Beyond vague assertions of the party's connections with 'land and freedom', and its links with the peasantry, only the resolutions of the third party congress in May 1917 offered a clear guide to party programme. This uncertainty was an accurate reflection of the PSR's essentially vague programme.[34] The best-known and most completely worked out aspect of its programme was socialisation of land, a draft for which was formulated in October 1917 by Semion Maslov. This programme was later adopted by Lenin as a basis for the redistribution of land that was authorised in November 1917.

Though Chernov was the party's leading theorist, the PSR, like the Mensheviks, never had a single, clearly expressed leader.[35] A number of figures were dominant in party leadership, and though Chernov was an active party spokesperson and provided often telling theoretical analysis of the situation in 1917, he was not the dominant influence on party policy in 1917. Abram Gotz and Vladimir Zenzinov were among the most influential figures in keeping the party allied with the Provisional Government for much of 1917, and in maintaining an irreconcilable pro-war stance, both positions which countered Chernov's left centrist views. Oliver Radkey's work blames failures of the PSR's leadership for the party's inability to respond adequately to the challenges of 1917.[36] While Radkey makes the failings of the PSR's leading figures clear, it is misguided to blame the party's incoherence on individual leaders. The party's founding tenets embraced a heterogeneity that was at odds with the demands of wielding power, especially in war-torn revolutionary Russia.

The resolutions of the third party congress, which opened on 25 May 1917 and closed on 4 June 1917, served as the basis for the formation of party orthodoxy by the centre. The resolutions passed there, on the war, on land and on the question of future governmental forms, were to be quoted by regional groups as the official party programme for much of 1917, even

[34] See the PSR first party programme agreed at the first party congress held in Imatra, Finland, from December 1905 to January 1906, in V. V. Shelokhaev, O. V. Volobuer, M. K. Gorshkov et al., *Programmi politicheskikh partii Rossii konets XIX–XX veka* (Moscow, 1995), pp. 139–46.

[35] See K. N. Morozov, *Partiia sotsialistov-revoliutsionerov v 1907–1914gg.* (Moscow, 1998), p. 109.

[36] The failure of PSR leadership to respond adequately to the challenges of 1917 and instead to depend on Menshevik and Kadet initiative is a running theme of both Radkey's major works on the PSR in 1917. See Radkey, *The agrarian foes of Bolshevism*; Radkey, *The sickle under the hammer*.

when their sentiment and content had been overwhelmed by the changing political climate. Though its resolutions clarified party policy, the congress also served to confirm the irreconcilable differences between members on a range of key issues. Right, left and centre all vied for political dominance, and while the centre dominated the Central Committee, which controlled official party policy, both right and left threatened factionalism at the outset of 1917.

The right had been an identifiable force in the party since 1909[37] and was close to forming a separate party prior to the third congress in May.[38] It published its own national paper, *Volia naroda*. The right failed to make a final break from the party, as a result both of lingering loyalty to and nostalgia for the PSR, and its heavy representation and influence in the party's Central Committee. The left, however, with the figureheads of Maria Spiridonova and Mark Natanson, and led by Boris Kamkov and Alexander Kolegaev, was from the outset a dangerous group within the party, since it was largely disenfranchised by the Central Committee and by the PSR's policy direction in 1917.[39] The PSR's left faction had existed semi-independently from the official party since 1909, though its final break from the party can be dated to its members' expulsion from the party conference at the end of October 1917. The Central Committee of the party itself was almost evenly split between two essentially irreconcilable groups. Spiridonova's comments on central party policy made in the leftist newspaper *Nash put* highlight the extent of party divisions, 'The PSR is under the influence of the right wing of the party, which is filled with narrow-mindedness, and does not have any elements in common with socialism. They stray further and further from the true path – close links and unbreakable unity with the people.'[40]

These factions polarised around the war question, which accentuated existing rifts within the party. The defencist group within the Central Committee, which supported the belief that Russia had to defend herself against Imperial Germany, however unpalatable the roots of the conflict, had a majority of one and thus dominated party policy. Their domination

---

[37] See Melancon, *The Socialist Revolutionaries and the Russian anti-war movement*, p. 12.
[38] See Radkey, *The agrarian foes of Bolshevism*, p. 188.
[39] Radkey did not credit Spiridonova with much political credibility. A more positive view of her role in the Left PSR is put by S. V. Bezberezh'ev, 'Mariia Aleksandrovna Spiridonova', in A. G. Golikov and A. P. Korelin, *Rossiia na rubezhe XIX–XX vekov: materialy nauchnikh chtenii* (Moscow, 1999), pp. 335–55. See also Sally Boniece, 'Mariia Spiridonova, 1884–1918: feminine martyrdom and revolutionary mythmaking', unpublished PhD thesis, Indiana University (Bloomington, IN, 1996).
[40] Maria Spiridonova, 'O zadachi revoliutsii', *Nash put* 1. This article may well have been considered a significant turning point in the crystallisation of the rift within the party. It was published in the Kazan newspaper *Za zemliu i voliu* 5, 11 October 1917.

could not, however, conceal the large and increasingly vocal minority of the left.[41] The Central Committee managed to hold the central party together till November, but in the provinces party factions competed openly and formed separate 'Left' and 'Right' SR groups from spring 1917. The profound divisions within the party centre enabled provincial organisations to define their own versions of what it meant to be an SR. In effect, the PSR offered a nationally recognised party umbrella to a diverse array of different mini-parties.

Party orthodoxy in the regions was defined by the actions and persuasions of the local group, or of its most vocal local leaders. In some cases, these local definitions of party orthodoxy bore little resemblance to the party programme agreed at the third congress. In practice, party orthodoxy was very flexible, and this undermines any preconceptions we may have of the political party as a monolithic entity. Individual party members themselves redefined the party's political position locally, and prevented the formation of a nationally accepted standard PSR programme.[42] On the question of socialist participation in the Provisional Government, for example, some provincial organisations condemned coalition with the Kadets as early as May and declared that only an all-socialist administration would be acceptable, despite the central party policy of accepting the coalition.[43] The radicalism of SR-led soldiers' committees and the soviets of peasants' deputies significantly overstepped the policy lines set out by the party's Central Committee.[44]

The freedom for local activists to interpret the ill-defined PSR policy as they chose shows how the PSR retained and developed its milieu support but was unable as an organisation to have significant influence in grass-roots politics. The PSR umbrella was used freely by ordinary peasants, as well as by party activists, to legitimise and justify their interpretations of the meaning of revolution. A letter received by the Nizhegorod province PSR committee from PSR sympathisers in Apraksina village typifies the problems faced by the party's Central Committee in establishing an 'orthodox' national policy.

---

[41] Radkey, *The agrarian foes of Bolshevism*, chapter 6, entitled 'The third party congress', discusses the rifts within the Central Committee of the party in detail; see particularly pp. 187–233.

[42] See Badcock, 'Saviour to pariah', on the potential significance of individuals within local politics.

[43] *Narod* 18, 26 May 1917, p. 3, as reported in the second Nizhegorod province PSR conference, 21 May 1917, and continued in *Narod* 19, 28 May 1917, p. 3.

[44] For discussion of the activities of the SR-led soldiers' committees and Petrograd soviet of peasants' deputies, see Michael Melancon, 'Soldiers, peasant-soldiers, and peasant-workers and their organisations in Petrograd: ground-level revolution during the early months of 1917', *Soviet and Post Soviet Review* 23 (1996), 161–90, For the radicalism of peasant committees, see chapter 7 of this work, and Michael C. Hickey, 'Urban *zemliachestva* and rural revolution: Petrograd and the Smolensk countryside in 1917', *Soviet and Post Soviet Review* 23 (1996), 142–60.

This letter was published in the regional PSR newspaper at the beginning of July:

Comrades! We have many people in our village who sympathise completely with the PSR programme, and in the near future will certainly form a PSR *volost* organisation. But recent events have been difficult to explain. People, purportedly SRs, came to the village, and persuaded the peasants that they should quickly take over for the common need buildings, inventory (living and dead) and grain owned by landowners. The landowners, of course, would not voluntarily agree to this, and they declared that they only left their property because of pressure from the peasants. This 'SR' propaganda has, of course, strongly agitated the local population. As a result of these events, we urgently wish to know how the PSR looks on this rapid seizure of landowners' property, even where this property is to be used to fulfil the needs of all the commune, and for every member of the commune separately, and even if it was made with the agreement (in truth forced) of the landowners.

We wish to know if the party considers such tactics and propaganda necessary and expedient, or if it considers them bad, since they decide questions prematurely, which must be decided only by the Constituent Assembly. We, for our part, sympathise with the PSR programme, do not trust such propaganda and are convinced that such actions harm the most important affair in the current time for the future – the organisation of the peasantry and the preparation for Constituent Assembly elections. We ask the party to give us some explanation of this question and to clarify directly the views of the party on such seizure of property of landowners, since we need to know if these agitators act in the name of the PSR, or if they only protect themselves with the name of the party. (Signed by 'sympathisers of the party')[45]

The party's Central Committee might have drafted the second paragraph of this letter, so closely did it echo the official PSR position on the land question. As such it does not really ring true, but nevertheless the letter gives a good example of cavalier usage of PSR identification. If local activists declared that PSR policy supported seizure of privately owned land, why would ordinary people challenge them? There were real grounds for confusion on the question of privately held land since Chernov, the PSR's titular leader, had circulated a telegram around land committees in his status as minister of agriculture giving them authority to control land stocks. Though this order was later rescinded under pressure from the rest of the Provisional Government, it is easy to see how rumours of 'PSR' policy could circulate. Political thought and action could not be simply defined and controlled by the centre.

[45] *Narod* 34, 2 July 1917, p. 4.

The PSR organisation in Kazan shows how practical dislocations and confusions manifested themselves among party activists in the provinces. The splits in the Kazan PSR group exposed the profound disunity of the PSR at regional as well as national level, and to some extent mirrored the schism of right and left groups from the central party organisation that occurred later in 1917. Splits in the Kazan group show how factionalism manifested itself and demonstrate the intransigence of the factions despite their substantial common ground. The PSR organisation in Kazan was a stronghold of the Left SRs,[46] whose strength seems to have predated a strong showing of the left in the party's central committee. The party organisations that formed in Kazan were profoundly divided from the very inception of revolution. Alexander Kolegaev played an important role in the politics of the region and was an important influence in the radicalism of the Kazan SRs.

Three identifiable factions emerged in Kazan, formed from clashes of personalities and generation as well as of political ideology. The proto-internationalist 'Left' SRs described themselves both as the 'Young PSR Committee' and the 'SR Internationalists', and were often referred to by their opponents within the party as 'SR Bolsheviks'. The 'Old Committee', which supported the centre-right policies pursued by the PSR's Central Committee in 1917 was recognised by the Central Committee as the orthodox and legitimate PSR organ in Kazan. A breakaway rightist group emerged after the unification of these two groups in mid-September, calling itself the 'Kazan PSR Elders' Committee'. The PSR Central Committee took an active role throughout 1917 in the verification of party orthodoxy and the reconciliation of these groups. Central Committee member Vasilii Gavrilovich Arkhangel'skii attended the Kazan PSR provincial conference held on 6–7 August and confirmed that the Old Committee was recognised by the Central Committee, as it upheld the decrees of the third party congress.[47]

The origins and development of these splits are unclear, though two PSR committees and newspapers existed in Kazan almost from the beginnings of revolution in mid-April.[48] This level of organisation and differentiation within the regional party was unusual so early in 1917. The SR Internationalists published their own newspaper, *Sotsialist revoliutsioner*. Surprisingly,

---

[46] NART, f. 983, op. 1, d. 21, l. 221; letter from delegate N. Ulanov, at the All-Russian Peasants' Union, held in Petrograd, to the executive committee of the Kazan soviet of workers and soldiers' deputies, dated 7 May 1917. Ulanov stated with shame that the delegates from Kazan were alone in their refusal to accept the Provisional Government's authority.

[47] *Golos truda* 29, 14 August 1917, pp. 3–4, in section 'Party life'.

[48] *Za zemliu i voliu* 1, 29 September 1917, p. 1, editorial.

this newspaper did not represent the extreme left of the party – it repeated faithfully much of the party line from the Central Committee in Petrograd. Its main point of departure from its competitor newspaper published by the 'Old Committee', *Golos truda*, was the prominence given to reporting of the Zimmerwaldist conference, and its internationalist stance on the war.[49] Attitudes towards the war were without doubt the most important issue in defining party splits.[50] A general meeting of the Old Committee held on 11 June discussed their competitor group and its newspaper and, not acknowledging their apparent common ground, declared the group to be in cohort with anarchists and Bolsheviks. All relations were broken off with the Internationalist group, and an appeal was made to any individuals who had joined the group in good faith as SRs to leave at once and instead join the Kazan (Old) Party Committee.[51] This split within the local party was clearly a focal point of discussion for the Old Committee, although curiously the Internationalist SR's newspaper *Sotsialist revoliutsioner* never referred to internecine party strife.

Despite the June resolution to break off relations with the SR Internationalists, the Old Committee resumed talks with them in July over elections to the Town Duma. Disagreements between the groups continued to hinder attempts at co-operation; the Old Committee's references to the Internationalist group as 'SR Bolsheviks' are a fair indicator of its tone towards them. The SR Internationalists opposed the June offensive, considering it a 'stab in the back of the revolution', and refused to form a bloc either with the Peasants' Union or with the Mensheviks. The Old Committee refused to relinquish the bloc they had already formed with the Mensheviks and confirmed their support for the offensive.[52] Negotiations were broken off abruptly. The situation was clearly very confusing for the party's potential supporters in the factories, garrisons and villages. There was a scuffle between the opposing SR sides at a soldiers' meeting on 20 July 1917. A representative from the Internationalist group asserted that there was only one PSR committee, the Internationalists. This reportedly provoked outcry from the assembled soldiers, who demanded a return to the podium of Old Committee representatives.[53] This was no doubt rather sanguine reporting by the Old Committee's newspaper; a later report from the

---

[49] The Zimmerwaldists were a group of anti-war internationalist socialists named after their first meeting in Zimmerwald, near Berne, 5–12 September 1915. A second conference was held in Kienthal in 1916 and a third in Stockholm in 1917.

[50] Melancon, *The Socialist Revolutionaries and the Russian anti-war movement*, pp. 55ff.

[51] *Golos truda* 20, 13 July 1917, p. 1.   [52] *Golos truda* 20, 13 July 1917, p. 3, in section 'Party life'.

[53] *Golos truda* 22, 20 July 1917, p. 4, in section 'Party life'.

PSR military organisation reported that merging with the Internationalist group was desirable for 'more intensive and productive work'.[54] The rift within the Kazan party organisation adversely affected the party's recruitment and support. The PSR factions in Kazan showed themselves unable to consolidate their considerable common ground for the greater good of the party.

The PSR Central Committee recognised the dangers of this schism, and again sent one of their members, this time Dmitrii Rakov, to Kazan for a resolution of the issue. Rakov arranged a town PSR conference for 12 September, and a provincial conference the following day. He supervised the election of committees for both with representatives from both party factions, which according to the new united PSR newspaper *Za zemliu i voliu* liquidated the rift between the groups:

Now all the strength of the party is again united and directed along the same channel. It is unnecessary to speak of the massive work that lies before the party prior to the elections for the Constituent Assembly, unnecessary to speak about this because the difficulties of party work have been reflected in organisational divisions. Now we are again united, no two different individually named committees, no two party newspapers . . . Let there be differences of opinion between us – this is necessary in a party that is growing and broadening, but now after the liquidation of divisions all strength of the Kazan PSR goes on one path of revolutionary activity. And so, in Kazan one united PSR organisation will act. A long and persistent struggle lies ahead in continuation of which the flag of revolutionary socialism cannot be for one minute lowered. All strength of the party must be returned to the great struggle for land and freedom.[55]

This optimistic report reaffirmed Chernov's vision of a broad and all-inclusive party and glossed over the serious issues that had divided the Kazan group so acutely in 1917. Unsurprisingly, a group splintered from the new united organisation within days. This was the rightist Kazan PSR Elders' Committee, which disagreed with the Central Committee-commissioned Kazan organisation enough to run a separate list for the Constituent Assembly elections.[56] The Kazan PSR Elders' Group continued to publish *Golos truda* in the name of their faction and regarded themselves as representatives of Central Committee policy, even though they had formed in opposition to the express wishes of the Central Committee. The PSR's philosophy, embracing a range of opinions within the forum of the party, proved to be impracticable in real political life. When the policies loosely formulated

[54] *Golos truda* 37, 14 September 1917, p. 4, in section 'Party life'.
[55] *Za zemliu i voliu* 1, 29 September 1917, p. 1 editorial.
[56] *Za zemliu i voliu* 3, 6 October 1917, p. 1 editorial.

prior to 1917 were faced with practical applications in the year of revolution, key irreconcilable differences inevitably emerged among members
who had been drawn to the party with different agendas, and the disparate groups were unable to coexist successfully. The party's philosophy
explicitly embraced heterodoxy, which terminally wounded party unity and
discipline in 1917.

PARTY LOYALTIES

The atmosphere of open political competition after the February revolution made distinctions between party programmes clearer, even though
differences in the parties' programmes were not always recognised by the
electorate.[57] Rex Wade describes the grouping of political parties in three
blocs, the 'new right' formed by the Liberals, the moderate left and the
extreme left.[58] These categories were clearly important for the electorate in
making political choices, but we should not overstate them. Party political activity and understandings were to a great extent defined by local
conditions and personalities. The extent to which the heightened hostility
between socialist parties transferred to the way ordinary people understood and offered support for political parties is difficult to gauge, not least
because of the distinction that needs to be drawn between party activists
and those people who offered passive support for the party. Party activists
were those who may have been a party member in the pre-revolutionary
period, and who were engaged in active work on behalf of the party. 'Passive'
supporters, on the other hand, may have expressed support for the party in
the act of voting or in donating funds but did not engage actively in party
work.

  Relationships between party activists of different party political persuasions were often close and convoluted in the pre-revolutionary period.
As Melancon has found in his work on Petrograd, the pressure of work
underground prior to the revolution encouraged many local groups into
close co-operation.[59] After February 1917, however, this togetherness among
the socialist parties, engendered by the solidarity of an oppressed minority, quickly eroded, allowing the harsh inter-party conflict that had always

---

[57] Koenker, *Moscow workers*, pp. 190–3, discusses the low levels of partisan awareness of the Moscow workers in 1917.
[58] Wade, *The Russian revolution*, pp. 53–76.
[59] Melancon commented of pre-1917 that 'Russian political parties had not yet achieved a high degree of definition; they were movements, operating in daunting circumstances, rather than parties.' Michael Melancon, '"Marching together!" Left bloc activities in the Russian revolutionary movement, 1900-February 1917', *Slavic Review* 49 (1990), 239–52, pp. 251–2.

existed between party leaders to permeate down to local activists. It is much more difficult to make generalisations about the political clarity of 'passive' supporters. On the one hand, the real political issues facing voters in 1917, such as participation in the war, the form of Russia's government and policies on land, offered voters clear choices between the political solutions offered by the different parties. On the other hand, the use of socialist blocs in election lists militated against this sharpening of boundaries between parties for ordinary voters.[60] Some people chose to support non-party local-interest groups, eschewing the party system. Disillusion about the political process and rising voter apathy resulted in some ordinary people withdrawing from the party political arena.

There are numerous examples of solidarity among socialist activists generally prior to 1917, and more specific examples of individuals who moved relatively fluidly between party affiliations. Melancon has argued convincingly that socialist parties' activists in Petrograd, especially the Bolsheviks and PSR, worked in relative harmony on a practical level prior to the February revolution.[61] The war, in particular, was an important factor in drawing socialists together on the grounds of their position on war rather than on their party political affiliation.[62] Anna Geifman's work offered evidence of extensive co-operation among terrorist groups of varying political affiliation,[63] and Maureen Perrie's study of the PSR membership in the 1905–7 period found that 16.1 per cent had at some time changed or shared party allegiance.[64] This considerable degree of mobility amongst the revolutionary parties was offered by Perrie as confirmation of David Lane's thesis that 'the rank and file membership of the revolutionary groups might for many purposes be regarded as one group, the members having "revolution" as the common goal and showing little awareness of the details of policies'.[65] Yet who was this rank and file? Party activists and passive supporters need to be distinguished clearly if we are to make sense of party political affiliations.

The idea of the revolutionary parties being 'more together than apart' is an important tool in understanding pre-revolutionary socialist party organisations, but it should not be overstated. Even before the revolution, party activists maintained a barbed hostility in their relations at local and national

---

[60] Wade, *The Russian revolution*, pp. 53ff.   [61] Melancon, '"Marching together!"'
[62] Melancon, *The Socialist Revolutionaries and the Russian anti-war movement*, p. 3.
[63] Anna Geifman, *Thou shalt kill: revolutionary terrorism in Russia, 1894–1917* (Princeton, NJ, 1993), chapter 6, pp. 181–206, and pp. 182–6 on PSR collaboration with other radical groups.
[64] Perrie, 'The social composition', p. 229.
[65] D. Lane, *The roots of Russian communism: a social and historical study of Russian Social-Democracy, 1898–1907* (Assen, 1969), pp. 116–17.

level, despite willingness to collaborate on practical issues. When activists
were described in biographies, the socialist press or when participating in
regional government, party identifications were usually given. The use of
party political 'labels' when describing activists in itself demonstrated a clear
awareness of and affinities with separate political parties. Maureen Perrie
pointed to the fluidity of party affiliations in the members of the society
for political prisoners and exiles.[66] This fluidity was clearly an important
feature of political behaviour but did not devalue the importance of political affiliations altogether. Political affiliation was clearly stated and each
change of party carefully noted down by party members. This is indicative
of the importance placed by activists on party affiliation. Activists may
have changed parties as situations altered, or worked in relative harmony
with other groups underground or during terrorist campaigns, but these
changes were considered important – their exact dates are noted down.
The inter-party divisions among pre-revolutionary political prisoners were
so passionately held that in some cases different party groups were barely
on speaking terms, despite the pressures drawing political prisoners into
close association.[67]

The February revolution required that political parties win support from
ordinary people as well as from party activists. Political parties now had to
compete for members, votes and financial support. Their differences of
ideology and image became crucial. Parties published their own newspapers and ran propaganda campaigns in which they attempted to both set
out their own position and criticise that of their rivals. Where clear party
delineation and definition had existed prior to the revolution, namely in
communities with high-profile party political activity, party political identities quickly polarised. In areas where such party political delineation had
not existed prior to the revolution, the polarisation of party political identities operated at a much lower level or was altogether absent.

Despite the saturation of press and elite discourses of 1917 with party
political conflict, party politics was generally very low-key or even absent in
provincial grass-roots political participation. In the vast majority of sources,
no reference whatsoever was made to political affiliations when discussing
representatives to councils, soviets and assemblies at village and town level,
beyond the occasional cursory nod to the PSR. Local and occupational
identities were more important than identification with particular political

---

[66] Perrie, 'The social composition', pp. 227–9.
[67] Lydiia Dan recalls that the Social Democrat prisoners refused to call PSR and Bundist prisoners
'comrade', but referred to them as 'mister', which caused a lot of hostility (Leopold J. Haimson, *The
making of three Russian revolutionaries* (Cambridge, 1987), pp. 164–6).

parties, particularly in the early months of 1917.[68] This lack of evident party affiliations in the countryside does not indicate that ordinary rural people had not engaged with the political issues of 1917. It does, however, indicate that political parties were not the primary means by which individuals expressed themselves politically. Peasants voted in the various elections of 1917, often by party list, usually for the PSR, and they joined the PSR in large numbers. Political parties were increasingly recognised and utilised as political tools in 1917 in the countryside but did not penetrate daily life in the villages. This supports the idea that the PSR's mass 'passive' support was defined more by peasant milieu voting than by more closely defined party politics.

The exception to this lack of sharp party political delineation was in traditionally politicised environments like large skilled worker communities.[69] In 1917, provincial-level soviets of workers' deputies unfailingly operated on party political lines. Workers' soviets tended to be by far the best delineated of any public body in terms of political affiliations. While a whole range of committees and organisations across the province often offered very little information on their members' political affiliations, workers' soviets at provincial level were meticulous in both listing party political affiliations and in apportioning representation on executive bodies by party affiliation. This makes them an interesting thermometer of political affiliation, even though, as elsewhere in Russia, their make-up did not change rapidly and frequently enough to reflect the political desires of their constituents. Nizhnii Novgorod's workers' and soldiers' soviets were first formed in early March 1917 and were re-elected in August and in November. The PSR and Mensheviks dominated the March and August incarnations of the soviet.[70] Moderate socialist dominance is reflected in their politics, which consistently supported Provisional Government policies and viewed the Bolsheviks as a dangerous counter-revolutionary force.[71] The factory complex of

[68] See Badcock '"We're for the Muzhiks' party"', which discusses this with reference to PSR support in the villages.

[69] See Koenker, *Moscow workers*; Steve A. Smith, *Red Petrograd: revolution in the factories 1917–18* (Cambridge, 1983). Kevin Murphy's assessment of a Moscow metalworking factory suggests that workers did not distinguish between different socialist parties in the first months after the revolution, but his analysis includes clear party political delineations (Kevin Murphy, *Revolution and counterrevolution: class struggle in a Moscow metal factory* (New York, 2005), chapter 2).

[70] *Izvestiia soveta rabochikh i soldatskikh deputatov* 36, 6 August 1917, p. 2.

[71] GANO, f. 1100, op. 1, d. 1, ll. 7–9; discusses impermissibility of Bolshevik-inspired demonstration in Molitov factory in June. GANO, f. 1102, op. 1, d. 7, l. 25; example of Menshevik resolution passed which supported new coalition government on 26 May. *Narod* 41, 19 July 1917, p. 1; editorial reporting on united meeting of soviets of workers, soldiers and peasants' deputies, condemning Bolshevik policies, which are 'pushing the country to civil war'.

Sormovo on the outskirts of Nizhnii Novgorod provides a valuable example of a highly party political environment. Around 25,000 workers were employed there in 1917.[72] Its main manufacturing products were ironwork, steel and mechanical parts, and for the duration of the war its production was almost entirely military.[73] The organisations representing Sormovo workers had clearly delineated party political lines. The main socialist parties were represented in various factory committees, and individuals were referred to by their party political affiliation.

The political climate in Sormovo, both in 1905 and in 1917, was dominated by the PSR, which had the largest support base and most deep-rooted organisation. By June 1917, one-fifth of the Sormovo workers were members of the Sormovo PSR organisation.[74] Sormovo provides an illuminating case study of PSR support among workers in 1917.[75] Bolshevik support rose significantly in the build up to October but did not produce a collapse of the PSR's core support. The PSR continued to play a leading role in Sormovo during 1918, and Sormovo was a 'hotbed of opposition to Bolshevik rule' throughout 1918.[76] The Sormovo PSR group was the strongest single PSR organisation in Nizhegorod province[77] and was one of the largest party groups in the country.[78] An unusual and exciting memoir written by a Sormovo PSR member in 1917 provides a wealth of information on the party's extensive pre-revolutionary activity in Sormovo.[79] The Sormovo PSR group had worked closely with Sormovo Bolsheviks in 1916; they

---

[72] GANO, f. 442, op. 1, d. 5, l. 69; telegram to the minister of labour from the director of Sormovo factories, 26 July 1917, cites 25,000 workers.

[73] GANO, f. 442, op. 1, d. 22, l. 318; letter from central administration of Sormovo factories in Petrograd, to the director of Sormovo factories, 23 May 1917. GANO f. 442, op. 1, d. 5, l. 69; telegram to the minister of labour from the director of Sormovo factories, 26 July 1917.

[74] This calculation is based upon an estimate of 5,000 workers being members in June 1917, out of an estimated worker population of 25,000 (M. D. Smuchebnikov, D. A. Chugaev, D. A. Kovalenko, G. E. Reuzhberg and E. N. Vladimitsev, *Revoliutsionnoe dvizhenie v Rossii v mai–iiune 1917g.: Iiunskaia demonstratsiia* (Moscow, 1959), p. 119).

[75] Hildermeier, Melancon, Perrie and Rice have assessed PSR support within worker circles prior to 1917; M. Hildermeier, *Die Sozialrevolutonare partei Russlands: Agrarosozialismus und Modernisierung in Zarenreich (1900–1914)* (Cologne, 1978), esp. chapter 9, pp. 281–304; Michael Melancon, 'The Socialist Revolutionaries from 1902 to 1907: peasant and workers' party', *Russian History-Histoire Russe* 12 (1985), 2–47; Perrie, 'The social composition'; Rice, *Russian workers*. For analysis of the strength of PSR support among Petrograd workers in the early months of 1917, see Melancon, 'Soldiers, peasant-soldiers'.

[76] Vladimir N. Brovkin, *Behind the front lines of the civil war* (Princeton, NJ, 1994), p. 77.

[77] GARF, f. 9591c, op. 1, d. 11, ll. 3–4; protocols of the first Nizhegorod province PSR conference, 23–24 April 1917 (incomplete).

[78] *Partiniia izvestiia* 3, 19 October 1917, p. 54: central party records of contributions to the party coffers from regional organisations include an entry on Sormovo, which in July gave the largest sum of any of the contributors, which included province organisations and even Moscow.

[79] RGASPI, f. 274, op. 1, d. 26, l. 112; Magergut's memoir.

collaborated in planning a strike,[80] and Tiurikov, their leading member, composed a proclamation for the Bolshevik group.[81] After the February revolution, however, the suppressed hostility between the two groups was openly expressed. Both groups were vying for the votes and support of the Sormovo workers, and they attacked one another's policies and personalities vehemently.

The PSR's work in the underground and notoriety among Sormovo workers in 1916 enabled them to build their membership rapidly in 1917, rising from 1,500 by April 1917, to 3,000 in May and 5,000 in June. The PSR's political dominance in Sormovo was acknowledged even by Soviet accounts that generally preferred to discount PSR support altogether.[82] The Sormovo PSR group's financial records confirm its massive support and authority in 1917. For the months March–September 1917, the group had an income of some 25,000 roubles, a sum equivalent to more than a third of the Sormovo soviet's income for the same period, and which dwarfed the funds collected by the Moscow PSR group.[83] The Bolsheviks, on the other hand, despite significant gains in the latter part of 1917, still had only 950 members by January 1918, and total funds of around 5,000 roubles.[84] The PSR retained significant support levels in Sormovo into 1918 despite the drop off of their political power.[85]

The Sormovo PSR group was arrayed towards the left of the national SR organisation. The Mensheviks accused Sormovo's PSR of 'tagging on the tails of the regional Bolsheviks',[86] though given the strength of personnel and support the PSR enjoyed, this is unlikely. An indication of the radicalism of Sormovo's SRs, however, is offered by the attitude taken regarding the July days. A meeting on the crisis of power called by Mensheviks just after the July days attracted more than 2,000 people. The SRs and Bolsheviks present walked out of the meeting in protest at the meeting's refusal to hear any resolutions other than those condemning Bolshevik actions

[80] RGASPI, f. 274, op. 1, d. 26, l. 88. Magergut's memoir.
[81] RGASPI, f. 274, op. 1, d. 26, l. 97. Magergut's memoir.
[82] Smuchebnikov et al., *Revoliutsionnoe dvizhenie v Rossii v mai–iiune 1917g.*, p. 119. The report of the Bolshevik Vorobev at the plenary meeting of Moscow Oblast RSDRP (b) 28–29 June, acknowledged that the SRs were by far the strongest organisation in Sormovo, with some 5,000 members. This contrasted with Bolshevik party membership of around 900.
[83] Diane P. Koenker, 'The evolution of party consciousness in 1917: the case of the Moscow workers', *Soviet Studies* 30 (1978), 38–62, p. 60; the Moscow PSR workers' group collected 1,922 roubles in August 1917, and nothing thereafter.
[84] *Krasnoe znamia* 46, 18 January 1918, p. 3.
[85] RGASPI, f. 274, op. 1, d. 5, l. 33; report of Nizhegorod province PSR group, undated, but definitely written after the Brest-Litovsk agreement. Proclaims continuing strong support for the PSR in Sormovo, with nineteen of the thirty-eight soviet places going to the PSR.
[86] *Izvestiia soveta rabochikh i soldatskikh deputatov* 30, 16 July 1917, p. 2.

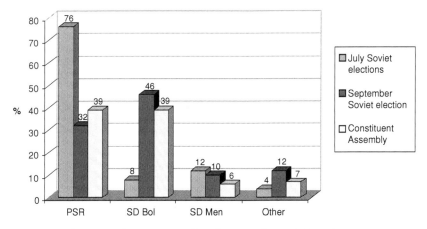

Figure 3.2. Election results in Sormovo for July, September and November 1917.

in the July days.[87] Like the national PSR, Sormovo SRs were riven with dissent throughout 1917, as the moderates and radicals within the organisation solidified their position. The organisation finally split on 8 December, when part of the SRs, led by O. F. Fillipov, broke away from the main group and formed an independent Left SR group that agreed to co-operate with the Bolsheviks.[88] This followed the pattern of Left SR participation in the Bolshevik-led government at national level, and in other regions.

Indications of changing party support levels in 1917 can be found in elections, party membership and attendance at party political meetings.[89] These are, however, only indicators of party loyalties that shifted extensively and quickly. Figure 3.2 compares results of Sormovo elections in July, September and November. Although the Constituent Assembly elections are not directly comparable with the soviet elections of July and September, they nevertheless give an indication of political affiliations in November. These indicators of relative support for different parties does not, however, equate to the parties' relative power. Though the Bolsheviks were the most numerous party in the Sormovo soviet after the September elections, the SRs continued to wield significant authority in the soviet. In a soviet meeting on 11 November, voting for membership of the soviet's commissions

[87] *Izvestiia soveta rabochikh i soldatskikh deputatov* 30, 16 July 1917, p. 2.

[88] *Krasnoe znamia* 17, 9 December 1917, p. 3.

[89] Statistics on election results come from the following sources: July elections, *Narod* 45, 28 July 1917, p. 4, in section 'Sormovo life'; September elections, GANO, f. 442, op. 1, d. 7, l. 166; list of members of the Sormovo soviet of workers' deputies, undated but included in September documents; Constituent Assembly elections, *Krasnoe znamia* 3, 19 November 1917, p. 4.

of provisions and control gave unanimous support to the PSR candidates, but only partial support for the Bolshevik candidates.[90]

After the October seizure of power, the PSR and Menshevik factions in Sormovo abstained from soviet voting and refused to participate in the presidium and executive committee. Had they continued to participate in the soviets, the Bolsheviks would have been forced either into actions against the soviets, or complicity in 'anti-soviet' administration. The usual Bolshevik tactic was to form a 'military revolutionary committee' and disband the soviet.[91] As it was, the general factory meeting (*obshchezavodskii sobranie*) voted on 26 October to accept the Bolshevik revolution. The soviets struggled to function without SR and Menshevik support and accused them of sabotage in December.[92]

The strength of party politics in Sormovo was exceptional, even among worker communities. Away from the intense political atmosphere of Sormovo, party political conflict was much less prominent. Across the provincial workers' soviets in Nizhegorod province, political apathy and low party membership were reported. In a number of regions, there were no party political groups, while in others, like Vysunskii, of 7,000 workers only 350 were members of a political party. In Lukoianovskii *uezd*, less than 100 of over 1,000 workers had joined the small SR and SD groups there, and there was no formal worker organisation.[93]

Support for political parties was extremely dynamic, and subject to change, even in areas like Sormovo that had high levels of party political awareness. As the summer of 1917 wore on, attitudes towards party politics both in the towns and the countryside were suffused with apathy and disenchantment. In charged party political environments like Sormovo, the failure of party political activity to achieve any real improvements in conditions resulted in a more general disenchantment with party politics. Michael Hickey's work on Smolensk, and Diane Koenker's work on Moscow, found similar patterns of disenchantment by the summer of 1917.[94] Splits within the socialist camp also encouraged increased ambivalence towards

---

[90] *Krasnoe znamia* 10, 30 November 1917, p. 3.

[91] *Narod* 102, 15 November 1917, l. 3; offers an excellent example of the problems that the PSR could have posed the Bolsheviks but did not. In a meeting of the Sormovo office of soviet of workers' deputies, on 9 November 1917, of the thirty-eight members who attended, twenty-two abstained, leaving the Bolsheviks in a definite minority.

[92] *Krasnoe znamia* 26, 20 December 1917, p. 4; protocol of the general meeting of the soviet of workers and soldiers' deputies, 15 December 1917.

[93] *Izvestiia soveta rabochikh i soldatskikh deputatov* 56, 22 September 1917, pp. 2–3.

[94] Koenker, *Moscow workers*, pp. 172ff.; Michael C. Hickey, 'The rise and fall of Smolensk's moderate socialists: the politics of class and the rhetoric of crisis in 1917', in Donald J. Raleigh (ed.), *Provincial landscapes: local dimensions of Soviet power, 1917–1953* (Pittsburg, 2001), pp. 14–35.

identification with a particular political party.[95] This is particularly apparent when looking at candidates put forward for local elections and the emergence of 'independent socialists', who sought to bypass the confusions of warring socialist factions.[96] In Kazan, for example, a 'People's Republican (Independent Socialist) Party' was formed.[97] Even within highly partisan urban environments, some parts of the population preferred to avoid party politics. Non-partisan groups stood for the Town Duma elections in Nizhnii Novgorod and in Kazan. Employees and workers from the Kazan town administration, for example, put forward their own list in the Kazan Town Duma elections.[98] Such groups represented platforms for local interests. Their formation is a clear indication that party politics did not embrace all ordinary people, even in urban areas that had greater exposure to party political contestation.

A number of commentators remarked that the soldiers in Nizhnii Novgorod garrison did not subscribe to any specific political party's view or programme, even after the Bolshevik seizure of power, an event that might have been expected to polarise their political positions. This letter published in *Narod* in mid-November 1917 exemplifies some people's unwillingness to engage with party political discourse. This may have been particularly the case in the wake of the Bolsheviks' cavalier treatment of the soviets in Nizhegorod province:

In view of the prevailing mood, I consider it necessary to clarify the following. I am a member of the executive committee of the soldiers' section of the soviet of workers' and soldiers' deputies, and from the very first days of revolution I have not and do not stand with any one party, and not now or before have I ever stood with the Bolshevik party, though all the time I have sympathised with the Social Democrats, and only a month ago at a general meeting I declared that I sympathised with the ideas of the Bolsheviks. But that was a month ago. I now remain without party affiliation (*bezpartiinyi*). I ask comrades not to consider me in any other way. I do not hold any political responsibilities but remain a member of the soviet of workers' and soldiers' deputies. M. L. Dun.[99]

The first months of 1917 saw a rise in the clarity of political affiliations for party activists, and offered the political parties a platform to share their

---

[95] Koenker remarks on the support within Moscow workers for solidarity among revolutionary socialist parties (Koenker, *Moscow workers*, p. 227).

[96] *Kazanskaia rabochaia gazeta* 133, 24 September 1917, pp. 1–2. In list no. 3, the socialist bloc list for Kazan's Duma elections, Ia. Antropov listed himself as an independent socialist.

[97] *Kazanskaia rabochaia gazeta*, 17, 29 April 1917, p. 3; report on this group's meeting.

[98] NART, f. 1246, op. 1, d. 102, l. 1750b; list of candidates to the Town Duma elections, for the elections on 8 October 1917.

[99] *Narod* 101, 14 November 1917, p. 4. Koenker comments that *bezpartiinyi* when used later in 1917 may have been a euphemism for those individuals who had defected from the PSR and Mensheviks, but were unwilling to join the Bolsheviks (Koenker, 'Party consciousness in 1917', p. 61).

image and their programmes with the population at large. This clarity for party activists inevitably led to a break up of many of the socialist parties' collaborative efforts in the years prior to the February revolution, when the threat of tsarism had been of greater importance to local party activists than the threat of socialist competition. The population at large engaged with political parties by voting for them and registering support for their programmes, but party politics did not become particularly significant for the day-to-day life of many. Party politics did become an important factor in a few key areas, such as the Sormovo works in Nizhnii Novgorod, but even there party politics were fast moving. There was disenchantment with participation in and affiliation with political parties from the early summer onwards even in party politically active communities. Confusion and disillusion with the political situation caused some groups to eschew party politics altogether.[100] This disenchantment was dangerous, since the rejection of party political identifications signified a broader failure of the political party system to incorporate itself successfully into Russia's emerging political culture.

CONCLUSIONS

Political parties were portrayed by the political elite as a lynchpin for the new regime's construction and the fulfilling of national will. Russia's newly fledged electorate chose among them as they exercised their political choices. We should not, however, overstate the extent to which party politics permeated ordinary Russian life. The front-line garrisons and some urban environments were the exception rather than the rule in their operation of partisan party politics. Outside these highly politicised environments, party politics played a low-key role.

The PSR had national recognition and developed mass popular support from workers, soldiers and peasants. Its support among workers and soldiers dropped off somewhat, particularly after August 1917, and was fragmented by the party's split in November 1917, but its support among peasants remained solid. Though the party's pre-war campaigning efforts had focused on workers and soldiers, the party's appeal was primarily to the peasant milieu. The party's programmatic disunity allowed it to shelter a large spectrum of groups that described themselves as 'SRs'. While all political parties faced organisational problems in 1917, the PSR was faced with a large and rapidly growing membership and a large rural constituency,

---

[100] This was Koenker's conclusions based on her detailed study of Moscow workers' voting patterns (Koenker, 'Party consciousness in 1917', p. 52, p. 61).

alongside its programmatic commitment to heterogeneity. In Kazan, local PSR leaders were unable to reconcile themselves to one another's programmatic differences and expressed extreme hostility towards one another. One can speculate here that clashes of personalities and histories of personal disagreement may have played a role in the Kazan PSR's splits, alongside the evident programmatic discord.

The question of party loyalty is a difficult and an important one. Though bloc voting by faction rather than by party is an important feature of 1917's voting patterns, we need to look more closely at party loyalties as well. There needs to be a distinction drawn between party activists, who were most likely to polarise their political positions in 1917, and ordinary people in areas without a tradition of party political competition, where there was more likelihood of broad voting blocs. From the summer onwards, many ordinary people became disenchanted and frustrated with the party political system. Sormovo offers an example of a highly politicised environment, in which the PSR had strong and vibrant support that was eroded but not overwhelmed by Bolshevik advances in 1917.

The role of party politics in 1917 needs to be recast. Looking at political parties' central leadership in 1917, we see that the leadership retained their ideological platform largely unchanged, and largely stuck to their original party programmes regardless of popular desire, to an extent that was remarkable. Away from the political centre, however, this clear adherence to party ideology was lost. This study of the PSR from a regional perspective shows that the party's programmatic position was in practice redefined by the political attitudes and actions of its supporters and local leaders. The political parties lost the battle to maintain hegemony over ordinary Russians. Rather than the parties leading and defining political behaviour, the parties themselves were manipulated at local level to be vehicles for local interests and aspirations. The lack of national party political loyalty contributed significantly to the failure of the democratic party political system in Russia.

CHAPTER 4

Choosing local leaders

The personalities and political persuasions of those local people who led grass-roots politics played an important part in determining the climate and policies of local politics. This chapter will concentrate on the most tangible section of local leadership, those who were elected into positions of authority and representation for the community. These elected leaders formed an important conduit between local people and the various organs of power that developed in 1917. Those individuals selected by their communities to represent them at every level, from the Constituent Assembly right down to village committees, were invested with authority that came from their direct selection and were a significant influence on the climate of local politics. Though these local leaders cannot be considered to represent all local leaders, many of whom did not participate in any electoral process, they can at least offer us a starting point. This chapter will develop our understanding of the grounds on which elected leaders were selected, who they were and the multiple pressures that they faced.

A profound dichotomy developed for local leaders in the course of 1917. They were selected, generally speaking, because they were seen to be able to reflect specifically local demands and concerns, yet their very participation in the structures of power implicitly moved them away from these local concerns and towards the agendas set at national level by political parties, the Petrograd Soviet and the Provisional Government. As Michael Hickey has shown for Smolensk, local leaders selected at the outset of 1917 in many cases alienated the very people who had selected them.[1] This chapter brings the problem of distinctions and overlaps between 'political elite' and 'ordinary people' to the forefront. At grass-roots level, local leaders came from the ranks of their constituents, as ordinary people, but their very participation in administration moved them towards categorisation as political elite. This confusion between ordinary people and political elite is

[1] Hickey, 'The rise and fall'.

unavoidable and brings to a head the ways in which participation in formal political processes could challenge and re-form ordinary people's identities and priorities.

WHO WERE LOCAL LEADERS?

In this assessment of local leadership, material has been included from *volost* and *uezd* land committees, candidates to Town Dumas, Constituent Assembly candidates and soviet members. Urban and rural leaders have been considered together, to help distinguish commonalities and differences between them. We can establish confidently that local leaders were most often local, working men. Beyond this, there is often very little biographical information available about them. For the historian, their voices seem almost lost. Before the February revolution, the administrators and public figures of regional life in the *uezds* and provinces were to some extent traceable. Those with suspect political connections were meticulously tracked by the secret police (*okhrana*),[2] and the relatively restricted access to local administrative roles meant personnel remained fairly constant. There was a dramatic shift in administrators' social background from the pre-revolutionary intelligentsia and nobles to the ordinary working men that dominated 1917. The local leaders and activists of 1917 rarely left much written record.[3] Attempts to establish the backgrounds of lower-level local leaders rely upon extremely fragmentary evidence. This study has collected available information to form a picture of the backgrounds of local leaders. The fluidity of the political scene at local level gave individuals more scope to play a significant role, as they were less constrained by the framework of administration around them.

Information about 680 individuals who participated in local administration and the electoral process at a range of levels has been collated to provide some quantitative backing to these conclusions (see figures 4.1 and 4.2). The regional soviets did not, unfortunately, leave any detailed information about their membership, so it has not been possible to include them in

---

[2] See RGIA, f. 1278, op. 9, for a list of individual files on State Duma members, for example of information available on State Duma deputies. GARF holds a huge collection of pre-revolutionary political surveillance material. The enormous f. 102, with its 265 *opisi*, holds the former tsarist police records.

[3] The exception to this rule of anonymity is the memoirs of Bolsheviks produced in the Soviet period, of which there are many collections. An example of such material is S. E. Mukhamedov and V. P. Timofeev, *Za vlast sovetov: sbornik vospominanii uchastnikov revoliutsionnikh sobytii v Tatarii* (Kazan, 1960). These memoirs, with notable exceptions, are a problematic source on 1917, as their ideological zeal often overwhelms historical accuracy.

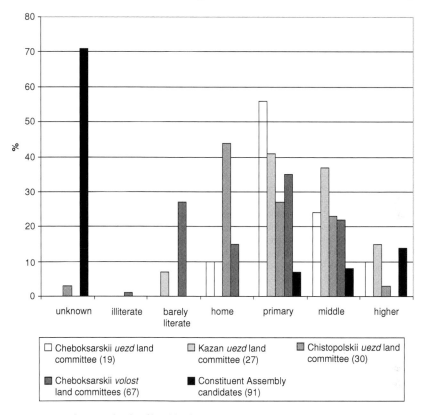

Figure 4.1. Education levels of local leaders in 1917

these statistics. There are, however, rich non-statistical sources on soviet membership, which this chapter draws on to get an impression of their make-up and membership problems. The statistical information presented here comes from lists describing 145 members elected onto *volost* and *uezd* land committees, lists describing 444 candidates in the elections to the Kazan and Nizhnii Novgorod Town Dumas and lists describing 91 candidates for the PSR lists to the Constituent Assembly elections. Though the level of information about individuals varies, levels of education and occupations have been particularly noted, as these were the two categories that were most often mentioned in information about individuals. The individual voices of these leaders are heard only in exceptional cases, but some broad trends emerge in the backgrounds of those individuals chosen to represent their communities.

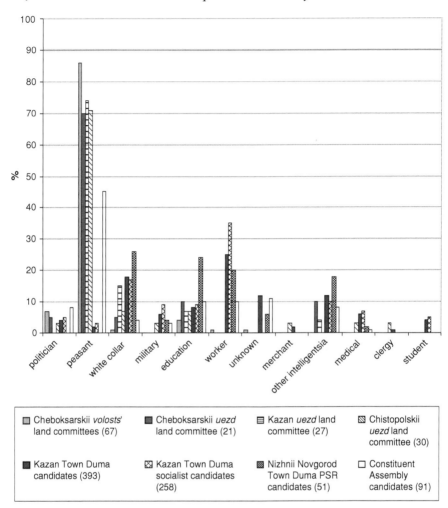

Figure 4.2. Occupations of local leaders in 1917

Individuals' education and occupation have been grouped into categories, a process that involves generalisations and inevitably loses something
of the individual along the way. Levels of education are not an obviously
contentious area of classification but do raise some problems. The category 'home' education reveals little about the standard of education the
individual attained. For the peasants in this sample, it probably indicated
that he was self-taught, or that a literate member of the family taught
the pupil his letters and maybe some basic arithmetic. For those with

better-off backgrounds, it could mean private tuition and a high level of literacy. 'Middle' education included the diverse categories of technical schools, teacher training colleges, seminaries and the classical gymnasia. There is no way of verifying the educational levels these individuals ascribed to themselves, and more importantly, these education levels do not tell us much about the active literacy levels of the sample.[4] Some patterns emerge from the data presented in figure 4.1. *Volost* committee members had low levels of education, and we can speculate that they may not have been actively literate. The profile of *uezd* land committees is essentially very similar to that of *volost* land committees, except that those with middle education make up a high proportion – around 20 per cent. Kazan *uezd* land committee had a noticeably higher proportion of members with higher levels of education – this may be a reflection of its proximity to Kazan town, the most literate area in the province. The Constituent Assembly candidates are not a particularly helpful sample for education, as most did not state their educational level. Even with the limited figures shown, however, it is clear that this group included a far higher proportion of individuals with middle or higher education levels.

Categorisation of occupations is a particularly thorny task.[5] Dividing such a diversity of occupations into a handful of categories inevitably leads to questionable value judgements. The main problem for classification of occupation was in the designation of 'peasant', particularly with regard to Constituent Assembly candidates where little biographical information was offered. The designation 'peasant' did not necessarily refer to the individual's occupation; it could have been a reference to the person's origins or their estate (*soslovie*). In rural constituencies, those drawing up such lists were clearly keen to identify their candidates as labouring (*trudiashchiesia*), and may well have stretched the term to include those who may have been of peasant stock, or had worked in agriculture at one time, but were no longer making a living from agriculture. Also, many individuals had split occupations; some peasants worked in factories for part of the year, and artisan peasants supplemented their peasant income by plying an additional trade, as a carpenter, blacksmith or tailor. These occupational categories did not of course proscribe the identity of the individual concerned. This is exemplified by the transience of some individuals' occupational activities, particularly for those who had been party activists in the pre-revolutionary

[4] Ben Eklof, *Russian peasant schools: officialdom, village culture, and popular pedagogy, 1861–1914* (Berkeley, 1983), chapter 13, pp. 389–418.
[5] M. B. Katz, 'Occupational classification in history', *Journal of Interdisciplinary History* (1972), 63–88, p. 64, on the universality of these problems.

period, and whose lives involved repeated enforced relocation. The biography of D. P. Petrov, a Constituent Assembly candidate for Simbirsk, provides an exceptionally good illustration of the problem:

D. P. Petrov, a peasant from Biurgan village, Buinskii *uezd*, 32 years old. Born in a poor, land-deprived family. Lived and grew up in the country. Between the ages of 10 and 22, he worked on the land. Afterwards he trained and became a village teacher. In 1905 he organised a teachers' union in Buinskii *uezd*, establishing the famous section of the All-Russian Union of Teachers and Participants in Popular Education. Simultaneously, he organised cells of the All-Russian Peasants' Union among the peasants. On leaving school, he travelled around villages and explained the meaning of the events of that time to the *skhods*. When agrarian unrest began in the *uezd*, the landowners laid all blame on him and several of his colleagues. Persecution began. In fifteen months he was forced to relocate three times. At last on 15 December 1906 he was forced to leave teaching and go into hiding. Members of the administration and local landowners were especially strongly up in arms against him, and he gave them no peace, with exposures of their local 'activities' in the pages of *Simbirskii vesti*. Meanwhile he began work in the Chuvash PSR organisation, as a member of the Kazan *Oblast* committee. A police inquiry was raised against him. For six and a half years he was under unremitting police observation. After the destruction of the party organisation, he moved into newspaper work, collaborating in local and metropolitan newspapers. He spent the years 1908–9 in Kazan, where he played a significant part in the exposure of the commissariat's embezzling of public funds. In 1910 he was arrested in Kazan and sent home. At the beginning of the war, he went to Moscow, where he took the school leaving certificate at Shaniavskii popular university; he then became a student in the former imperial university, but he did not finish [that course]; he was called up for military service and became an ensign. At the start of the revolution, he took a lively part in the organisation of Simbirsk province peasantry. He was secretary for the first provincial peasants' meeting on 20–21 March, and president of the second and third meetings, on 15–20 July, and 25–27 September. He took part in several *uezd* meetings, and in the production of several leaflets and editorials of *Izvestiia Simbirskago gubernskago soveta krest'ianskikh deputatov*. He is president of the provincial soviet of peasants' deputies, a member of the provincial land committee, and of other public-political organisations.[6]

How is one to categorise such a life neatly? Though I would categorise him as a professional revolutionary, Petrov, who was only thirty-two years old in 1917, had been through at least five recognisable career moves.[7] It is only by closer investigation of individuals' lives that these categories really

---

[6] *Zemlia i volia* 1, 6 October 1917.
[7] The term 'professional revolutionary' is used here in the Leninist sense, of professionals in that they both relied on party support for their livelihoods, and were trained and proficient underground political operators. (See V. I. Lenin, *What is to be done?* (Peking, 1973), pp. 122–56.)

mean anything. Occupations of leaders in *volost* and *uezd* land committees were predominantly peasant, as one would expect, as were a significant proportion of Constituent Assembly candidates. It is noticeable that there was little distinction in terms of occupational background between socialists and all other candidates for the Kazan Duma. In towns, workers made up a significant proportion of candidates.

Intelligentsia participation in these forms of local leadership is notably low and requires some further exploration. The rural intelligentsia were specifically targeted in appeals from Provisional Government and soviet publications in 1917 to get involved in public political life. Numerous reports were published in the local press complaining about the reluctance of rural intelligentsia to get involved.[8] Broadly speaking, the term 'rural intelligentsia' was used to describe any individual based in the villages who had a professional role and a middle level of education. The vast majority of the rural intelligentsia was employed by the rural *zemstva*. These *zemstva* provided the first major network for the conveyance of new ideas from the towns into the villages, and their staff were accordingly very important in 1917. The main occupational categories encompassed by rural intelligentsia were doctors, teachers, medical assistants (*feldshery*), agronomists and veterinarians. Though the clergy were not a part of the so-called 'third element', their literacy and their role as educators in the villages merit their inclusion. Clergy and teachers were the most important groups in the rural intelligentsia as both had fixed audiences with villagers and an ideal platform from which to disseminate news.

We can establish that generally speaking the rural intelligentsia did not meet expectations laid on them by the political elite to take a pre-eminent role in village life. Though there are plenty of instances of the rural intelligentsia playing a role as leaders and educators in the villages, their failings in these respects were frequently noted by local government and press reports. From the evidence available, we can conclude that where the rural intelligentsia did not take a leading role, this was due to a combination of reluctance on their part, and their exclusion from village life by peasant society. Sources are conflicting on the willingness of the village intelligentsia to inform the village population. Both peasants and the local administration complained that the intelligentsia were not taking the hoped-for vanguard role in the villages. In Studenets village, Nizhegorod province, peasants complained that the intelligentsia had been excluded from village

[8] For example, *Kazanskaia rabochaia gazeta* 26, 11 May 1917, p. 4; *Izvestiia Kazanskago gubernskago soveta krest'ianskikh deputatov* 17, 27 August 1917, p. 4; *Izvestiia soveta rabochikh i soldatskikh deputatov* 47, 21 September 1917, p. 4; *Krasnoe znamia* 7, 25 November 1917, p. 3.

life because they did not tell the villagers anything.[9] In Chernukha village, Arzamasskii *uezd*, Nizhegorod province, the agitator sent by the soviet to travel around the region in April commented that despite the six teachers in residence there, not a single lecture had been held, and not even a library had been organised.[10] On the one hand, this was blamed on the refusal of the intelligentsia to participate in and assist the development of the new democratic path, and on the other, it was blamed on the villagers' rejection of intelligentsia figures. A discussion of the problem of intelligentsia involvement in village life by Lukoianovskii *uezd* executive committee at the end of May exposed both the reluctance of the intelligentsia to get involved, and the hostility of villagers towards intelligentsia figures:

The intelligentsia in the first days of revolution were boors, and that is why the mistrust (between the intelligentsia and the peasantry) remains unresolved. The *volost* committee invited the intelligentsia to take part in their work, but they did not answer the call of the committee. Irsetskii proposed that the old scores be forgotten, and that in future work they should go hand in hand . . . The reporter Balashov gave his conclusion, and highlighted the confusion of everyone in the first days of revolution. A resolution was passed: 'Hearing the report of Balashov, and taking into account, that the toiling intelligentsia are necessary in the building of a new life, but that they cannot work in an atmosphere of peasant mistrust, that is why it is declared: to clarify to all the population that the toiling intelligentsia are necessary elements in our life, all toilers must unite in the current moment, that is why there is absolutely no basis or sense in rejection and hatred of the intelligentsia. (From Lukoianovskii *uezd* executive committee journal, 27 May 1917)[11]

This statement recognised high levels of hostility towards intelligentsia figures from villagers. Other evidence confirms that the rural intelligentsia could face hostility ranging from passive indifference to physical violence. There were numerous reports of the village intelligentsia failing to become involved in village life and propaganda work. G. A. Barkhatov, a co-operative instructor in Vasilsurskii *uezd*, Nizhegorod province, commented in August that intelligentsia figures were denied a role in village life, and that this inhibited the development of the co-operative movement.[12]

Those occupied in education form around 10 per cent in most of the samples and outnumber other intelligentsia occupations significantly. This

[9] GARF, f. 9591, op. 1, d. 19, l. 11; report on the 1 May celebrations, published in *Narod*, nos. 5–6.
[10] GANO, f. 1887, op. 1, d. 3, l. 2; list of individuals attending the meeting of provincial commissars and representatives of provincial united committees of public organisations in Petrograd, 4 August 1917.
[11] GANO, f. 1887, op. 1, d. 18, l. 300b; protocol of general meeting of Lukoianovskii *uezd* executive committee, 27–28 May 1917.
[12] *Nizhegorodskaia zemskaia gazeta* 31/32, 10 August 1917, pp. 12–13; report about the state of co-operation in the area.

proportion is lower than one might expect and is a good indication that teachers, along with the rest of the rural intelligentsia, did not take the pre-eminent role as local leaders projected for them by the political elite. We cannot come to a definitive conclusion as to the causes of their failings; in some instances, individual intelligentsia figures were reluctant to get involved in public life, while in other instances, popular hostility to the rural intelligentsia precluded their involvement. Clergymen are largely absent from these figures. The role of the clergy as local leaders is problematical. Though the institution of the church was innately conservative, and some individual clergymen had lost the respect of their parishioners as a result of improper conduct, still many priests and clergymen commanded the respect and affection of local people.[13] Their absence on this graph may be a reflection of their resistance to involvement in political structures and highlights the reality that local leadership was not restricted to the committee membership, but that it could operate in alternative social spheres as well.

In the graphs, the military was notably under-represented in all the bodies considered. This is surprising given the prevalence of soldiers across the range of local government organisations. We can explain this in a number of ways. First, it reflects the absence of urban soviets from these figures, where soldiers were most prevalent. Secondly, it may be that many soldiers preferred to categorise themselves in the local context as peasants, workers or teachers. This is an interesting reflection of the multifaceted identities adopted by individuals in this revolutionary period. In 1917 soldiers in the rear all over Russia regarded themselves as revolution's guardians, reflecting the glory won by the Petrograd garrison's perceived role in liberating the nation from tsarism.[14] That some local leaders may have chosen to eschew this positive identity in favour of their local identities as peasants or workers indicates the importance of local identities in determining local leadership.

Though the figures offered in figure 4.2 do not reflect this, mainly because they do not include soviet bodies, soldiers played a prominent role in regional administration. The status of those local leaders who were also in active military service was a real headache for short-staffed local administration. Sergei Il'in's petition to the Kazan provincial commissar personifies

---

[13] On the role of the clergy in the villages, see Chulos, *Converging worlds*, especially chapter 7.

[14] Alan Wildman, *The old army and the soldiers' revolt (March–April 1917)*, vol. I of *The end of the Russian Imperial army* (Princeton, NJ, 1980), p. 159; 'The soldiers quickly developed a sense of their historic role and inherent power. The further course of events served to entrench this consciousness ever more firmly, as the various competitors for power entreated, flattered, cajoled and sought to overawe them in order to harness this new force for their own political designs.'

the problems of sending soldiers to the front whose skills and experience made them particularly valuable in local organisations. Il'in, a peasant from Iadrinskii *uezd*, was a Chuvash, and when on short leave from his reserve regiment he had quickly become involved in local administration, from the peasants' union to the *volost* land committee. His request to be freed from military service in order to pursue local affairs was accompanied by a petition from the citizens of the *volost*.[15] Some of the most important and active figures in the soviets and even in the Provisional Government administration were serving soldiers. The tone taken by the *Kazanskaia rabochaia gazeta* in its report on the departure of a soviet member for the front in May was typical, demonstrating both the willingness of the soldier to fight, and the reluctance of the civilian authorities to let him go:

> The soviet was concerned to hear that comrade Poplavskii was going to the front with his battery. Poplavskii has been the soviet's president and a leading figure in the soviet, but he was determined to go to the front and do his citizens' duty. He was closely and warmly linked to the soviet of course, and to his battery, but in the end his battery and his duty came first. They hope that their first president will return to them![16]

The Provisional Government was forced to clarify the position of such men. What was to come first – their role in administration, or their military duties? This was particularly pertinent given the irregularity and large size of many soviets, which involved significant numbers of military personnel. The General Staff had decreed that executive committee members were to be directed to the front along with their regiments. A whole range of administrative organisations challenged this decision on the grounds of staff shortages. The first meeting of *uezd* commissars in Nizhegorod province held in May resolved to petition the Provisional Government regarding 'the right of public organisations to retain those military members who work for organisation and whose work is considered necessary'.[17] In July, the regional Military Committee appealed to the war minister to exempt the presidium of *volost* executive committees, *volost*, *uezd* and provincial executive committee of peasants' deputies, the presidiums of land and provisions committees, and members of *zemstvo* and town administration.[18]

[15] NART, f. 1246, op. 1, d. 46, l. 247; handwritten petition from Il'in to Kazan provincial commissar, undated.
[16] *Kazanskaia rabochaia gazeta* 34, 21 May 1917, p. 4.
[17] GANO, f. 1887, op. 1, d. 2, l. 7; resolution of the meeting of the provincial and *uezd* commissars' meeting of Nizhegorod province, 23–25 May 1917.
[18] *Izvestiia Kazanskago gubernskago soveta krest'ianskikh deputatov* 5, 22 July 1917, p. 4.

The problem of military personnel in civilian administration was discussed at length by the Kazan soviet of workers, soldiers and peasants' deputies at the beginning of August, when troop movements resulted in a number of senior soviet figures being sent to the front. The focus of the discussion was on the disorganisation caused by personnel losses. After heated debate, the meeting decided to send a telegram to Kerensky asking that all executive committee members be exempted from active military service.[19] Those speaking in favour of exemptions were actually workers, while those soldiers called to the front declared that fighting the disorganisation sown by the German foe was more important than disorganisation in local government.

Numerous requests were made from local administrators to the military command for soldiers to be exempt from active service in order to continue their administrative role.[20] These requests often contained information that helps us evaluate the qualities that were most highly prized in local leaders. The soviet of peasants' deputies in Iadrinskii *uezd*, for example, requested that ensign Ivan Stepanovich Iukhtanov be exempted from military service, as he had been elected president of the *uezd zemstvo* administration:

Ensign Iukhtanov is a member of Iadrinskii *uezd* soviet of workers and peasants deputies, he took active part in the formation of this soviet, he was a member of the presidium of the first *uezd* meeting of peasants' deputies, and was a candidate for the post of *uezd* commissar, but withdrew his candidacy. Ensign Iukhtanov, regional resident and former public teacher, is well known by the *uezd* population and has great authority as a former worker in the liberation movement. Ensign Iukhtanov has mastered Chuvash language, which further confirms the significance his presence in Iadrinskii *uezd* has for the Chuvash population, and in particular the credence he gives to the *zemstvo* meeting.[21]

There was considerable confusion about the status of those who continued their work in administration even when they were in theory committed to active military service. Nikolai Sukhanov, for example, a candidate to the Constituent Assembly elections for the Kazan soviet of peasants' deputies, was threatened with court martial by the Black Sea military authorities for desertion. Kazan's provincial commissar defended Sukhanov, stating

---

[19] *Kazanskaia rabochaia gazeta* 93, 4 August 1917, pp. 3–4.
[20] See the collection of requests for soldiers to be commandeered by various local administrative organs in NART, f. 983, op. 1, d. 21, ll. 7, 8, 10, 60, 73, 104.
[21] NART, f. 983, op. 1, d. 21, l. 59; letter from executive committee of soviet of peasants' deputies, Iadrinskii *uezd*, to executive committee of the Kazan province soviet of peasants' deputies, 29 June 1917.

that he 'would return to his place of military service at a later date'.[22] Not all such requests were genuine or supported by the local population. Despite his apparent inability to fulfil any useful role, the captain of militia in Mariiskii village, Zaikin, repeatedly applied for exemption from military service 'not having the shame and patriotism of a true citizen', according to Cheboksary's captain of militia. Despite having his petitions rejected, Zaikin continued to act as militia captain and entered active service.[23]

Vladimir Genrikhovich Ganchel

Voices and personalities of local leaders are rarely heard in the sources left to us for 1917. An exception to this was Vladimir Ganchel, a leading soldier-politician of 1917. A more detailed evaluation of Ganchel offers us a rare insight into the personality and motivations of an influential local leader in 1917. As president of the Town Duma's executive committee and town mayor, Ganchel was among Nizhnii Novgorod's most influential figures during 1917. He was a member of the PSR, and a soldier in the 185th Infantry Reserve regiment, stationed in Nizhnii Novgorod. His father was a Polish accountant, and his mother was Ukrainian. Ganchel had been brought up in Kiev, where he had completed a teaching course and attended the Kiev Commercial Institute, until it was evacuated from Kiev in 1914, and Ganchel himself called up for military duty in 1916. He had been president of the *zemstvo* employees' society in Kiev, written for illegal and legal newspapers, and had been an active PSR member since 1906.[24] This political experience made him a valuable commodity within the Nizhnii Novgorod soldier body after the February revolution. He was elected first president of the Nizhegorod soviet of soldiers' deputies. Ganchel's nomination for presidency of the town administration provoked protest from the Kadets. His nomination, and indeed his legitimacy as a Duma member,

---

[22] NART, f. 983, op. 1, d. 36, l. 46; letter from commissar of western region of the Black Sea, to Kazan *uezd* committee of soviets of workers' and soldiers' deputies, 9 October 1917, p. 48; letter from Kazan province soviet of peasants' deputies to commissar of western region of Black Sea, 18 November 1917.

[23] See NART, f. 1246, op. 1, d. 42, l. 238; letter to provincial commissar from captain of Cheboksary *uezd* militia, 13 September 1917. Note however, the fierce political infighting going on in Cheboksarskii *uezd*, and speculate that the charges against Zaikin may have been jumped up; he was accused of being an illiterate, but a neat handwritten letter, apparently by Zaikin, regarding his dismissal, turned up in NART, f. 1246, op. 1, d. 183, l. 240.

[24] F. Seleznev, 'Our Town Mayor in 1917', *Nizhegorodskii rabochii*, June 1999, p. 6. His background, of middle education, teaching background and public activities, was typical of the PSR's urban activists.

was challenged, because he was a soldier, because he was not a resident of Nizhnii Novgorod and because his mother was Ukrainian. The socialist majority of the Town Duma ignored these objections, and he was voted in regardless on 1 August. 'Ganchel already takes on the responsibilities of the post, and though he is not a regional resident, and is a soldier, above all else he is a citizen, and that is why he will carry out his duties for all the working population of Russia.'[25]

Recognising that Ganchel's role as soldier theoretically precluded him from such political participation, the leaders of the Town Duma sent a letter directly to the Minister of War Kerensky, requesting that Ganchel, and another soldier elected to the Duma, A. Ivanov, be released from military service.[26] Ganchel's political tenor, broadly speaking, corresponded with the policies championed by the PSR's Central Committee. His acceptance speech of the mayorship provides ample evidence both of his use of SR rhetoric, and his starkly realistic view of the tasks faced by the Duma; he emphasised the need for continuation of the war, preservation of revolutionary victories and for all classes of the population to combine in order to combat the grievous economic crisis besetting Russia.[27] Ganchel provides a rare example of a model party worker – educated, informed, but aware of and in agreement with central party policy. This is in marked contrast to other major figures within the Nizhnii Novgorod PSR group.[28]

Ganchel's moderation and support for the Provisional Government defined Duma policies. Given his generally moderate position, his response to the Bolshevik seizure of power in October was surprisingly vehement, and set him apart from his cautious moderate socialist colleagues. He was the central figure in the Duma's special 'committee for the defence of the revolution' and repeatedly asserted his determination to oppose the Bolsheviks with all means including force. His arrest by the Bolsheviks on 27 November allows us to get an impression of the breadth of his support. Ganchel's arrest provoked protest from a diverse range of bodies, including the Sormovo workers, peasant assemblies, Nizhnii Novgorod students residing in Moscow and the PSR provincial committee.[29] On 7 December,

---

[25] GANO, f. 27, op. 1, d. 2, l. 84; from the speech of S. S. Vekslerchik (PSR) in the Town Duma, 1 August 1917.

[26] GANO, f. 27, op. 1, d. 2, l. 105; letter to Kerensky, in Duma records, 4 August 1917.

[27] GANO, f. 27, op. 1, d. 2, l. 85; Ganchel's acceptance speech in Duma records, 1 August 1917.

[28] For example, Dmitrii Tiurikov, the leading figure in the Sormovo PSR group promulgated policy which was to the left of the PSR's Central Committee.

[29] Reported in *Narod* 113, 30 November, p. 1 (PSR Provincial committee), *Narod* 114, 1 December, p. 4 (students), *Narod* 117, 5 December, p. 4 (Sormovo workers), *Narod* 129, 20 December, p. 4 (peasants of Revezen village, Kniagininskii *uezd*).

Ganchel's release was secured, on the basis of a report by a member of the Nizhnii Novgorod soviet of workers' and soldiers' deputies reiterating the soviet's support for him.[30] Ganchel returned to the Duma on 19 December and gave a defiant speech calling for struggle with the Bolsheviks till the bitter end.[31] Vladimir Ganchel's political position in 1917 situated him in the camp of the moderate socialists, but there was nothing moderate about his passionate and whole-hearted participation in public life. His ability to attract support from across the political spectrum in Nizhnii Novgorod is testament to his success as a public figure, despite the defeat of his moderate socialist position. This snippet of Ganchel's political life gives us a rare insight into the character and personality of one of 1917's mostly anonymous local leaders.

CAREER POLITICS IN 1917

While pre-revolutionary Russia had a paid civil service and political administration, popular representation was limited to the *zemstva* and the Duma. Those who participated often continued to earn their livings through their habitual occupations. The year 1917 witnessed the development of a corps of local leaders, many selected by popular consent, who laid aside their usual occupations and devoted their time entirely to paid public service. Alan Wildman identified the creation of a 'committee class' in the army during 1917, and Steve Smith considered the extent to which Petrograd factory organisation was 'bureaucratised' in the course of 1917. The new occupational category of committee membership has not, however, attracted significant attention in civilian political life.[32] Figure 4.2 shows that a small but growing percentage of local leaders were 'politicians', who became full-time political actors and were paid for their labours.

This new category cannot necessarily be considered to be a profession, in the self-aware, collective sense required by those looking for the development of civil society. It is, however, important in understanding 1917's political climate, and the ways in which participation in the political process itself could lead to the alienation of local leaders from their constituents. Those who became involved in professional politics in 1917 were forcibly divorced from their constituents, forswearing their usual occupations for a life of committee participation and public involvement. The shortage of suitable personnel for such roles heightened the pressure on those involved

[30] GANO, f. 27, op. 1, d. 6, l. 13, Duma records, 7 December 1917.
[31] GANO, f. 27, op. 1, d. 6, l. 45, Duma records, 19 December 1917.
[32] Wildman, *The old army*, p. 248; Smith, *Red Petrograd*, pp. 202ff.

in politics and administration to work exclusively in politics. Study of the selection process and the demographics of local leaders shows that local affiliations and identity with local interests were the most important factors in their selection. Several features of 1917's political life, however, combined to move local leaders away from their constituents and into the more insular world of committees and meetings as a career.

There were chronic shortages of personnel for the multiplicity of local government and administrative organisations that flourished in 1917. The Provisional Government struggled to establish a working bureaucracy to replace the discredited, fragmented or dismantled tsarist structures. The committees and organisations that they either initiated or authorised seemed to multiply almost exponentially in the early months of 1917. Discussions at the Nizhegorod provincial meeting of *uezd* executive committees, held on 23 May 1917, gives an insight into the practicalities of prolific committees:

Semenovskii town executive committee reported that they met eleven times between 3–26 March, but that in addition to these meetings there were also meetings of the different commissions of the committee; the commission for the organisation of *volost* executive committees, the commission for the organisation of *volost* provisions committees, the commission for the investigation of means of the material condition of Semenov town's *soldatki*, the commission for the working out a project of defence for the town and instructions to the militia, and the commission for the organisation of the affairs of acquainting the *uezd* population with the decrees of the Provisional Government.[33]

Those individuals with skills of literacy and numeracy were in great demand, and those with administrative experience or specialist skills even more so. There were simply not enough of these experienced individuals to fill places on the different administrative and representative bodies that emerged in 1917. This had serious implications for the operation of local administration. Right through 1917, appeals were heard from all sides for people to come forward and serve in the administration. These appeals had limited success, as we see from the laments regarding chronic shortages of personnel. Kozmodem'ianskii *uezd*'s administration complained in August that the drawing up of electoral lists went extremely slowly, as the *volost* secretaries and their assistants worked on this task without any help. The regional village intelligentsia (teachers are specifically noted) could not assist as they were occupied with the agricultural census. This report was

---

[33] GANO, f. 1887, op. 1, d. 2, l. 20; report of the representative of Semenovskii *uezd* executive committee at the provincial meeting of representatives of *uezd* executive committees, 23 May 1917.

concluded with a desperate request for an instructor to be sent to the *uezd* to direct *volost zemstvo* elections.[34] In Mamadyshskii *uezd*, a general meeting of *volost* secretaries formed on 18 June reported that the various committees that had been formed in the *uezd* at the instigation of the Provisional Government were run almost entirely by the *volost* scribes, because there were no other literate and experienced individuals available. The meeting went on to clarify that it was actually impossible for the *volost* scribes to execute such 'massive and complex work' accurately and in good time, not least because they had no assistants, and because 'the population was not restrained in placing demands upon them'.[35]

Tetiushskii *uezd* commissar reported to the Kazan provincial commissar on 3 October that he was unable to carry out provincial orders as a result of shortages of personnel, and that 'All *uezd* establishments, that is, the administration of the militia, sections of the captain of the militia, and *zemstvo* and *volost* establishments are all in the same condition regarding shortage of working hands; there is no-one to do anything, there are no people.'[36] One important implication of this shortage of personnel was that those individuals who did participate in local government often took on multiple roles. This pluralism (*sovmestitel'stvo*) was something that raised some very particular problems. It allowed some individuals to have inordinate levels of influence in local politics. There was also the problem of remuneration. As an increasingly large number of posts carried with them significant responsibilities, some also attracted full-time salaries. If one man was being paid to be occupied full time in one committee, how could this be reconciled with his payment for other occupations? During a Lukoianovskii *uezd* executive committee meeting on 24–25 June 1917 there was a long and heated discussion about the permissibility of such pluralism. One committee member, Burov, bluntly accused those who held more than one post of trying to seize power, and of avariciousness.[37] This accusation provoked a rash of resignations from the committee from those members who held dual posts. But as the discussion showed, though pluralism had the potential to allow multiple wages and inordinate power in the hands of a few key individuals, it was unavoidable. As Karegin, a member of Lukoianovskii

[34] NART, f. 1246, op. 1, d. 102, ll. 17–18; letter from Kazan province *zemstvo* administration to provincial commissar, 14 August 1917.
[35] NART, f. 983, op. 1, d. 21, l. 260; protocol of the general meeting of *volost* secretaries of Mamadyshskii *uezd*, 18 May 1917.
[36] NART, f. 1246, op. 1, d. 70, l. 140; letter from Tetiushskii *uezd* commissar to provincial commissar, 3 October 1917.
[37] GANO, f. 1887, op. 1, d. 17, l. 79; protocol of the meeting of Lukoianovskii *uezd* executive committee, 24–25 June 1917.

uezd executive committee said in retort to Burov, 'Pluralism occurred as a result of worker shortage, not because of power seizures and greed.'[38] Another committee member, Kudel'kin, said that in a range of the *uezd*'s committees and commissions, including the committee for refugees and the commission for the distribution of allowance to soldiers' families, there were absolutely no members.[39]

Absenteeism was commonplace across the plethora of committees and councils.[40] At the Nizhegorod provincial executive committee on 25 July 1917, specific measures were proposed to combat the high levels of absenteeism, including declaring a quorum if only 25 per cent of members were present, excluding members who missed three meetings without good cause, and improving publicity for the meetings.[41] *Uezd* level committees adopted such measures as well.[42] The problem of staff shortage was only heightened by the October revolution. At a meeting of provincial soviets held between 25 and 30 November 1917, the soviet executive committee explained that the Nizhegorod soviet's decrees were carried out very slowly because there were insufficient soviet workers.[43] A frantic appeal made in Semenov town on 1 November blamed the town's grain shortages not on lack of money or available grain for sale elsewhere, but on staff shortages, 'we will remain hungry because actually in all of Semenov there is not a single competent or honourable individual who can be commissioned for this affair. What shame! What disgrace!'[44]

The shortage of personnel was particularly notable where more specialist skills were required. In Kazan province, for example, the administration was desperately short of people who were literate in the ethnic languages of the region, especially Tatar and Chuvash. Ethnic Russians, even in areas where the majority of the population were non-Russian, dominated governance and administration. This can be explained predominantly because

[38] GANO, f. 1887, op. 1, d. 17, l. 79; protocol of the meeting of Lukoianovskii *uezd* executive committee, 24–25 June 1917.

[39] GANO, f. 1887, op. 1, d. 17, l. 79; protocol of the meeting of Lukoianovskii *uezd* executive committee, 24–25 June 1917.

[40] Report that Kazan Town Duma had very few members attending on 30 June (*Kazanskaia rabochaia gazeta* 67, 2 June 1917, p. 3). At the Nizhegorod soviet of workers' deputies general meeting, 31 May 1917, because of the small numbers of members attending, it was declared a private meeting (GANO, f. 1102, op. 1, d. 7, ll. 33–4).

[41] GANO, f. 1887, op. 1, d. 11, ll. 58–9; protocol of the meeting of the Nizhegorod province executive committee, 25 July 1917.

[42] GANO, f. 851, op. 1, d. 2, l. 199; journal of the general meeting of Makar'evskii *uezd* executive committee, 3 July 1917.

[43] *Krasnoe znamia* 18, 10 December 1917, pp. 3–4.

[44] GANO, f. 815, op. 1, d. 13, l. 33; poster, undated, signed 'Member of the verifying soviet of the savings and loan society. K. F. Kulakov.'

such organisations were town-based, and the towns were disproportionately ethnically Russian in make up (see figure 1.1, p. 7). Soldiers with middle education, experience as teachers, or knowledge of an ethnic language were particularly sought after.[45] The Chuvash military organisation in Kazan, meanwhile, appealed to the soviet of peasants' deputies for assistance in agitating among the Chuvash population of the province.[46] This only highlights the problems even exclusively Chuvash organisations faced in finding individuals suitable for agitation.

Payments offered for participation in committee work varied enormously. The Provisional Government struggled to keep a cap on local government budgets, and salaries for the newly burgeoning administration were a significant outlay. As Russia's financial crisis intensified, and inflation escalated, payment for an expanded administration was low priority. Who was to be paid, and how much, does not seem to have been standardised. Rather, wages were locally defined and decided. While the payment of Duma members had already been established in the pre-revolutionary period, and the executive provincial administration could be confident of payment, payment became more arbitrary further down the administrative chain. In Semenovskii *uezd*, only the presidium of the *uezd*'s executive committee was to be paid. This payment was to come from 'state means and regional institutions – the *zemstvo* and the town'. At the meeting of Nizhegorod *uezd* commissars in May, the representative from Semenovskii *uezd* commented that the question of means for the committee had been one that had occupied the committee from the first days of its existence.[47]

The amount paid also varied significantly. Lukoianovskii *uezd* established that the presidium would be limited to five, and each would be paid 180 roubles per month, with extra allowances for travel and accommodation.[48] What these figures actually indicated are difficult to judge because inflation in 1917, estimated by Kokhn to be running at 230 per cent, meant that wages and prices rose at a rapid rate.[49] One way to evaluate the comparative size of this wage is to compare with factory workers' wages in June. An unskilled worker earned on average 122 roubles in June, and a Petrograd metal worker

[45] See, for example, the appeal in *Izvestiia soveta rabochikh i soldatskikh deputatov* 26, 29 June 1917.

[46] NART, f. 983, op. 1, d. 13, l. 38; from a handwritten report on the meeting of the soviet of peasants' deputies executive committee, 13 July 1917.

[47] GANO, f. 1887, op. 1, d. 2, l. 26; report of the representative of Semenovskii *uezd* executive committee at the provincial meeting of representatives of *uezd* executive committees, 23 May 1917.

[48] GANO, f. 1887, op. 1, d. 17, l. 79; protocol of the meeting of Lukoianovskii *uezd* executive committee, 24–25 June 1917.

[49] See Kokhn, *Russkie indeksi tsen*, p. 18; also Gatrell, *Russia's first world war*, p. 52.

between 282 and 319 roubles.[50] These figures indicate that 180 roubles was probably enough to live on, but was by no means a large stipend.

Within the soviets, there was dispute over who was authorised to receive payment, and at what level this payment should be made. Each peasant delegate in the Kazan soviet of peasants' deputies received a daily sum of three roubles and free lunch when attending congresses or conferences.[51] The size of the sums involved here was considerable; for the period 27 June–8 July, for example, 23,282 roubles were spent on soviet members' daily payments, and 5,708 roubles on dinner money for delegates.[52] In the executive committee of the Kazan provincial soviet of peasants' deputies on the 16 September, it was proposed that members of the PSR committee be co-opted for unpaid agitation work in the garrison. A committee member, Sukhanov, responded dryly that not all members were wealthy and able to work without pay. Despite this, the PSR co-opted five unpaid members. The soldiers who were delegated for agitation work agreed to work for three roubles per day, plus the ubiquitous free lunch.[53]

WOMEN: THE QUIET MAJORITY

Women were by and large absent from all levels of administration, from the village *skhod* up to the Constituent Assembly. While some women played leading roles in their communities and even in political life, they did not usually figure among those who stood as candidates or were elected to local administrative posts. There were so few women in the ranks of the local leaders assessed here that they have not been given a separate categorisation. At lower levels of organisation, on *volost* and *uezd* executive committees, delegates were almost exclusively male. If a woman did have a place, it was usually the place allotted to a teacher's representative. A cursory examination of lists of soviet deputies demonstrates that women were very rarely elected as deputies to the soviet, and correspondingly very rarely participated in the soviet's higher committees. This is because local working men and soldiers dominated electoral politics, particularly at grass-roots level. The course of democratisation appealed explicitly to the electorate in 1917, and the electorate responded by returning almost entirely male

---

[50] Figures on workers' wages come from Smith, *Red Petrograd*, p. 117.

[51] NART, f. 983, op. 1, d. 13, l. 3; meeting of the commission on private means and finance, executive committee of Kazan provincial soviet of peasants' deputies, 14 May 1917.

[52] NART, f. 983, op. 1, d. 12, ll. 1–2; reports on the financial situation of the Kazan soviet of peasants' deputies, 8 July 1917, 15 August 1917.

[53] NART, f. 983, op. 1, d. 13, l. 50; protocol of the meeting of Kazan provincial soviet of peasants' deputies executive committee, 19 September 1917.

representation on the democratised bodies of 1917. Despite the fact that
women made up around 47 per cent of the total factory workforce, men
dominated the factory committees and soviets in 1917. Diane Koenker has
described the factory shop-floor as a 'gender battleground', where misogyny
was ubiquitous in the pre-revolutionary period. Shop-floor culture was
inherently masculine, and women were regarded as 'intruders into the male
club'.[54] Even the labour activists who paid lip-service to gender equality
made little effort to include women in labour organisations.[55] In the 1920s,
women were not usually elected onto factory committees and had to be
allocated a place by the elite.[56]

Of the ninety-two PSR candidates to the Constituent Assembly from the
provinces of Nizhegorod, Tambov, Penza, Kazan and Simbirsk, only three
were women.[57] Ekaterina Breshkovskaia, who was something of a national
icon, stood as candidate for the Simbirsk PSR Elder-defencists' list. Victor
Chernov's wife, A. N. Chernova Sletova, stood alongside her husband on
the Tambov list. Vera F. Vasileva, a weaver from the Alafuzovskii factory
in Kazan, was the only local woman to stand in the Constituent Assembly
lists. She was a member of the Alafuzovskii factory committee and also
ran as PSR candidate for the Kazan Town Duma elections. The Duma
election was conducted on the basis of proportional representation, so that
the higher a candidate was placed on a party list, the more likely they
were to be actually elected. Vasileva was listed at no. 11, a high place that
would ensure her a seat in the Duma. Most other women candidates were
positioned very low on the lists, which smacked of tokenism, as they were
very unlikely to win a place. Candidates to the Nizhnii Novgorod Town
Duma included four women out of fifty-one candidates, three of whom
were teachers, and the last a clerk. All these were placed very low down the
electoral list, at numbers thirty-five, thirty-nine, forty-eight and forty-nine,
so that despite the fact the forty PSR delegates were elected to the Duma,
only two women took a seat.

Peasant committees at every level from village to province in Kazan and
Nizhegorod provinces were almost exclusively male. Aaron Retish found

---

[54] Diane P. Koenker, 'Men against women on the shop floor in early Soviet Russia: gender and class in the socialist workplace', *American Historical Review* 100 (1995), 1438–64, p. 1439, p. 1497.

[55] R. L. Glickman, *Russian factory women* (Berkeley, CA, 1984), p. 203, pp. 276–7.

[56] Koenker, 'Men against women', p. 1446.

[57] These lists were collated from various local newspapers, namely, *Narod* (Nizhegorodskaia PSR/soviet of peasants' deputies list), *Za zemliu i voliu* (Kazan PSR/soviet of peasants' deputies list), *Golos truda* (Kazan Elders' PSR list), *Delo derevnia* (Tambov PSR/soviet of peasants' deputies list), *Chernozem, Sotsialist revoliutsioner* (Penza PSR/soviet of peasants' deputies list), *Zemlia i volia* (Simbirsk PSR/soviet of peasants' deputies list), *Simbirsk narodnaia gazeta* (Simbirsk PSR Elders-defencists).

a similar absence of women in peasant representative bodies in Viatka.[58] Where there was any female participation in *volost-* and *uezd*-level committees, it was always a teacher's representative. So, for example, of the eleven members of Naletskii *volost* executive committee, the only woman was Lydia Snezhevskaia, a teacher's representative.[59] Of the thirty-seven members of the Silibeiskoi *volost* provisional administration, Nizhegorodskoi *uezd*, there was only one woman. At thirty-five, she was also by far the youngest member of the committee, which was dominated by men in their late forties and fifties.[60] Bogiavlenskii *volost* provisional executive committee had one woman of its twenty-one members, and she was the representative from the regional teachers.[61] The Iurasovskii *volost* executive committee, Semenovskii *uezd*, had fifty-two members, all of whom were men working in agriculture except two female teachers, Natalia Andreeva Ul'ianicheva and Natalia Alekseevna Nishchenuova. A third woman, Olga Krylova, was in the unusual position of being vice-president of the committee, and a male teacher, Ivan Kulakov, served as secretary.[62] Since guidelines issued from the centre specified the need to include a teacher's representative, these women's presence in the committees does not indicate that their standing in the village was established. Indeed, Ben Eklof's work indicates that women teachers enjoyed very low status in the villages, based on their youth, unmarried status and lack of established household.[63]

How are we to explain the absence of women from positions of power? The provincial section of the temporary committee of the State Duma made an interesting observation about women's participation in grass-roots politics in its April report:

There is opposition from workers and peasants to the participation of women in elections. Nothing is said to women, and in places they not only do not participate in the building of public life, but also often don't know about their rights that they received in the course of the revolution. When delegates tried to clarify the situation they said that up until this time they didn't know anything and thanks to this they didn't understand anything. Greeting similar conversations, the peasants

---

[58] Retish, 'Peasant identities in Russia's turmoil', p. 140.

[59] GANO, f. 830, op. 1, d. 5, l. 39; list of members of Naletskii *volost* executive committee, undated. Other examples of this are numerous and are found predominantly in records of *uezd* commissars, which held lists of members of *volost* committees.

[60] GANO, f. 830, op. 1, d. 5, l. 97; list of individuals forming the provisional administration of Silibeiskoi *volost*, Nizhegorod *uezd*, undated.

[61] GANO, f. 815, op. 1, d. 18, l. 8; list of members of the Bogiavlenskii *volost* provisional executive committee, undated.

[62] GANO, f. 815, op. 1, d. 17, l. 35; list of members of the Iurasovskii *volost* executive committee, undated.

[63] Eklof, *Russian peasant schools*, pp. 188ff.

with resentment observed 'You stir up our women, then they will not go into the shafts.' [*i.e. will not get to work. SB*] And there are almost no cases of women being elected in the village.[64]

Such a comment offers some explanation for the lack of ordinary peasant women among local leaders. It does not, however, explain the low participation even of women who had been very active in the pre-revolutionary political underground. The ranks of PSR activists prior to the revolution were heavily stocked with committed young women. Why were these women not prominent in revolutionary politics? One possible explanation is that women activists moved to support and non-elected roles in 1917. Barbara Clements Evans's study of Bolshevik women showed that they took on the technical and propaganda roles they had fulfilled prior to the revolution, as well as engaging in public speaking.[65] Technical and propaganda work, though important to party activity, did not have a high profile in the press, which would account for the PSR activists' apparent absence in political life. Clements Evans comments of the Bolshevik party that 'The party proved more hospitable to women than other political institutions of the new Russian democracy.'[66] This was no doubt true of the PSR party organisation as well.

Prior to the February revolution, women had operated within the party cocoon, which was inhabited predominantly by educated individuals who treated men and women as equals. This sheltered environment allowed women to take up the prominent positions within party organisations that their varied talents deserved. With the February revolution, however, the nature of the party was altered significantly as it was subjected to mass democratic will. The realities of Russian political life in 1917 showed that the electorate largely speaking wanted to vote for local working men, and not women, to be their political representatives in 1917. Men dominated political decision making in village life, and though women were enfranchised in this period, it is difficult to judge the extent to which they utilised their voting rights.[67] In the factories, where women made up an absolute majority of the workforce in 1917, although some women workers mobilised and demonstrated political awareness, men dominated the political scene.[68]

[64] RGIA, f. 1278, op. 10, d. 4, l. 248; from report on the situation in Russia in the first three months after revolution, made by the provincial section of the temporary committee of the State Duma.
[65] Barbara Clements Evans, *Bolshevik women* (Cambridge, 1997), pp. 125–30.
[66] Clements Evans, *Bolshevik women*, p. 135.
[67] Orlando Figes, *Peasant Russia, civil war: the Volga countryside in revolution* (Oxford, 1989), pp. 37–8; suggests that women lacked the education or political understanding to use their vote independently.
[68] Koenker, *Moscow workers*, p. 207.

Maria Kashmenskaia

Maria Kashmenskaia is an example of the sort of woman that one might have expected to participate in the administrative structures of 1917, but did not. Kashmenskaia's activities within the Sormovo PSR group in the pre-revolutionary period demonstrate the pivotal role that women could take on within local revolutionary groups in the underground. Kashmenskaia, twenty-three years old in 1917, worked as a clerk but was an initiator and founder member of the influential Sormovo PSR group, and the only woman on its Central Committee.[69] She initiated the creation of a workers' circle in Nizhnii Novgorod town and was entrusted by the group to arrange the purchase of typography.

Kashmenskaia did not fit the stereotype of a revolutionary woman pre-disposed towards terrorist activity as a result of her emotional inadequacies, as put forward in an article by Amy Knight.[70] She did not involve herself in the group's terrorist undertakings and established her rational and non-violent stance in her opposition to expropriation activity pro-posed by the group in September 1916. Her opinions and judgements were clearly valued by her male comrades, and she was able to speak out on a range of issues. At a mass meeting in September 1916, she gave a report on the attitude of German Social Democrats towards the war that accord-ing to one of the listeners, Zinovii Magergut, was 'interesting and rich in content'.[71] The Sormovo group sent Kashmenskaia, along with the group's most experienced member, Dmitrii Tiurikov, to Voronezh to establish links with other PSR organisations in the Volga region in December 1916, and to discuss the formation of a party conference. This was a delicate and dangerous commission, and the hopes of the Sormovo group rested on her.[72] Forced to leave Sormovo in January 1917 as a result of police surveil-lance, Kashmenskaia returned to Sormovo in April 1917. Kashmenskaia's record in the Sormovo PSR group may be exceptional but is testament to the active and full role women could play in party organisations prior to 1917.

---

[69] Biographical information from her entry in GANO, f. 27, op. 638a, d. 94, l. 11; list of candidates to Nizhegorod Town Duma.

[70] Knight says 'their intense emotional faith in the cause and their will to heroic martyrdom prevented them from analysing their terrorist activities in terms of rational objective politics' (A. Knight, 'Female terrorists in the Russian Socialist Revolutionary Party', *Russian Review* 38 (1979), 139–59, p. 157).

[71] RGASPI, f. 274, op. 1, d. 26, l. 93; Magergut's memoir.

[72] RGASPI, f. 274, op. 1, d. 26, l. 97; Magergut's memoir.

How did the likes of Maria Kashmenskaia respond to the climate of the PSR after the February revolution? She was put forward as a candidate for Nizhnii Novgorod Town Duma, but she was placed right down the list, at number forty-eight, and subsequently withdrew her candidacy. The only other trace of her existence to be found in the local press was a letter she wrote to the PSR newspaper *Narod*, which was published in December 1917:

In view of the written inquiry from comrade Valinchevskii,[73] I wish to place on the pages of *Narod* my explanation of the following incident. In private conversation in a break of the Town Duma meeting, occurring in the theatre on 28 November, I asked comrade Valinchevskii why he was a member of the Duma but sat apart from them, in the balcony. He responded that the tactics of the faction shamed him – I abruptly replied that I consider such a position dishonourable, since if he considers their tactics unworthy, he must openly declare it and leave the faction, but not disgrace it behind its back. Such attacks in private I consider unworthy of a true SR, therefore on the rights of an old party comrade I take on myself the courage to loudly repeat this accusation.[74]

Based on this letter, we can infer that Kashmenskaia continued to be active in the party, and to take a passionate interest in the politics of the moment, as one would have expected her to based on what is known of her underground activities. Kashmenskaia's conspicuous absence, however, from reports of party activity in the local press, and indeed in the lists of contributors to the local paper, suggests that she did not play the role her political experience and ability merited. This is in contrast to the other main protagonists of the Sormovo PSR group of which she was a part, many of whom were regularly mentioned by the party press in various party and public capacities. The PSR women activists can be regarded as among the party's foot soldiers in 1917. The non-participation of women in the elected bodies of 1917 cannot be pinned on a lack of politically committed and experienced women who could become involved in these organisations. Kashmenskaia had exactly the sort of skills that were so sorely required in 1917's administration, and yet she did not play an active public role. Despite their abilities and experience in the political and organisational spheres, women were relegated to backroom positions by the needs of mass democratic politics. This was to deprive the new administration of some if its most experienced workers, and only accentuated the shortage of personnel that was faced.

---

[73] Valinchevskii was a PSR deputy in Nizhnii Novgorod Town Duma.
[74] *Narod* 114, 1 December 1917; letter signed by Kashmenskaia and dated 29 November 1917.

ELECTIONS

Why were political candidates chosen, and what were the priorities of the electorate in making their selections? The process of candidate selection gives us some insight into these questions and helps us to evaluate the importance of party political affiliations and 'personality politics' in ordinary people's political choices. There is evidence that the electorate engaged with the selection process. This is not surprising given that the process of selection often utilised collective gatherings and general voicing of opinions, which reflected traditional peasant methods of representation. The importance of party political affiliations is difficult to pinpoint with any certainty, since party politics were not often discussed explicitly. There is, however, evidence that a broad affiliation with the PSR was an important foundation for the selection of rural candidates.

Selection of candidates for the Constituent Assembly elections was the best-documented among local electoral processes and provoked heated debate among local communities, who recognised that the selection of their representatives to Russia's first democratically elected national assembly was a serious business.[75] The records for the selection of candidates for the Constituent Assembly in Makar'evskii *uezd*, Nizhegorod province, are particularly rich, but the solemnity of the selection process there was seen across Nizhegorod and Kazan in the selection of candidates for a range of bodies. The qualities local people valued in their leaders are suggested by the summary of candidates offered in the accounts accompanying the election of representatives to the regional *volost* committees in April in Makar'evskii *uezd*. Each candidate was summarised pithily in a sentence, with reference to his sobriety and 'good living', as well as occasional references to his political experience:

at the village *skhod*, in the presence of the village elder Fedor Nalornov, peasants from 75 households, in number 60 people, many of whom had an opinion about the election of a candidate to the regional *volost* committee, it was decided to elect a peasant of our commune, Aleksandr Petrovich Kornilov, aged 45, literate, and more experienced in village economic affairs . . .[76]

---

[75] *Delo derevnia* 5, 26 August 1917, p. 4. This 'seriousness' is reflected in the thoroughness with which the Tambov province peasants' meeting drew up their list of candidates to the Constituent Assembly. A list of fifteen candidates was drawn up, but a member of the executive committee claimed he had not been consulted, which led to a further two-hour discussion of the list. Finally, several of the former candidates were replaced, and the order of the candidates altered altogether (*Delo derevnia* 14, 22 September 1917, p. 1).

[76] GANO, f. 851, op. 1, d. 1, l. 43; decree of Kirikova village *skhod*, Lyskovskii *volost*, Makar'evskii *uezd*, 8 April 1917.

Presnetsov village *skhod* gathered, and elected Grigorii Egorov Moiveev, 'this person has good behaviour, a sober life, no (bad) reports existed or exist about him.[77]

These reports effectively condensed the factors that the electorate considered important in its selection of local leaders and are very similar in form to those from peasants in Viatka province.[78] Party politics did not at first glance seem to play a part. Candidate selection for *uezd zemstvo* elections in Voskresenskoe village, Makar'evskii *uezd*, was rigorous and again did not feature party politics. Candidates were chosen at the *uezd* soviet of peasants' deputies meeting at the end of August. Of the fifty candidates who presented themselves for selection, seventeen were chosen. Each of the candidates had to present his biography to the meeting and explain how he would act in the *zemstvo*, and what interests he intended to defend. He was cross-examined by those present at the meeting, to test the strength of his convictions and his sincerity. The candidates were then sent out of the room for a final decision to be made. A regional correspondent to the SR newspaper *Narod* described the candidates' loose political sympathies: 'Many of the candidates declared, "I don't know a party programme, but I will say only this, that I will with all my strength strive, that all the freedom goes to all the people, and that all the land goes to all the labourers without any compensation."'[79]

Superficially expressed as a statement of individuality, this sentiment actually reflected a broad summary of PSR political identity and showed the PSR's close affinity with its peasant milieu. Though the candidate declared ignorance of political programmes, the declaration included a succinct summary of the PSR's abiding slogan, 'Land and Freedom!' The avowedly non-party attitude declared by these local candidates can safely be projected onto those individuals who offered passive support to the PSR, perhaps voting for the party without taking further interest in party politics, or joining the party in a communal gathering without taking further interest in the party. Although party politics were not prominent in the selection of local leaders, loose affiliations with the PSR existed nevertheless.

A further indication of the PSR's associations with broadly defined peasant interests lies in its close association with the soviet of peasants' deputies, with whom it stood on a joint platform for the Constituent Assembly

---

[77] GANO, f. 851, op. 1, d. 1, l. 45; decree of Presnetsov village *skhod*, Lyskovskii *volost*, Makar'evskii *uezd*, 1 April 1917.

[78] Retish, 'Peasant identities in Russia's turmoil', p. 162.

[79] *Narod* 66, 17 September, p. 4.

elections in Kazan and Nizhegorod.[80] The connection between the peasants' soviet list and the PSR was a key area for dispute. A debate provoked by the selection of a Constituent Assembly candidate for Makar'evskii *uezd* highlighted the troubled question of party affiliations specifically. A meeting of the *uezd* soviet of peasants' deputies jointly with the *uezd* executive committee on 6 August discussed candidates to the Constituent Assembly. As well as the executive committee members, delegates from the *volosts* attended, making up a total of eighty-two people at the meeting. Two leading SRs from Nizhnii Novgorod, Kaliuzhnov and Tiapkin, attended the meeting. Tiapkin attended in the capacity of delegate from the province soviet of peasants' deputies and had a deciding vote, while Kaliuzhnov was present as the formal advocate for the electoral list of the peasants' soviet and of the PSR for the Constituent Assembly election. Both men gave heated speeches supporting the PSR, 'true fighters for land and freedom'. The president of the *uezd* soviet of peasants' deputies, Baranov, outlined SD and SR policies and dwelled on the question of land reform. One Bolshevik, Gagarin, spoke and claimed that Baranov had misrepresented Bolshevik land policies, but even he concluded with a call for unity of all peasants to the list of the PSR and the provincial peasants' soviet.

The meeting unanimously supported the list of seven SR candidates that had already been chosen and selected a candidate from the *uezd* to join the list. Zelenov, the candidate chosen by the meeting, was unusual in that he laid out his political affiliations and stated clearly that while 'his sympathies lay with the PSR' he did not support several points of their programme and would not join the party. Zelenov also stated firmly that the peasants' soviet should not be affiliated to any one party, and that the platform of the PSR did not represent the platform of Nizhegorod peasants. He wanted to represent a peasant mandate, not a party mandate. After a long and heated discussion, and despite protests from Kaliuzhnov and Tiapkin, the meeting continued to support Zelenov, whose concluding words were 'I am ready to serve the peasantry.'[81] The continued support for Zelenov despite his open defiance of the regional PSR leaders shows that his selection reflected his personal popularity, not just generic support for the PSR.

The information provided about candidates for the Constituent Assembly elections offers a useful source in evaluating the sorts of individuals that were chosen to stand. They also give us an idea of the factors that

[80] There was a joint PSR/peasant soviet list in Viatka as well (Retish, 'Peasant identities in Russia's turmoil', p. 170).
[81] GANO, f. 851, op. 1, d. 2, ll. 293–6; journal of united meeting of members of Makar'evskii *uezd* soviet of peasants' deputies and the *uezd* executive committee, 6 August 1917. Quote from p. 296.

those publishing the lists thought were important to the electorate, and that might help attract electoral support. PSR Constituent Assembly candidates in Kazan and Nizhegorod have been assessed alongside candidates for the neighbouring provinces of Penza, Tambov and Simbirsk, in order to present a slightly broader picture.[82] The lists show conclusively that PSR candidates were predominantly local working peasants. This conclusion contradicts the received wisdom that the PSR's Constituent Assembly candidates were largely rural intelligentsia and right-oriented peasants.[83] The information not given about candidates is particularly revealing. Nowhere on the electoral lists studied, even in those offering detailed information, did the candidate express any political intentions beyond the omnipresent slogan 'land and freedom!' There is no evidence that the candidate was recognised and voted for as a political entity. Local working men were popular candidates because they were 'one of us'.[84] Regional and local politics took precedence over national concerns.

The PSR's Central Committee was usually allotted the first one or two places on the list. In theory the regional leadership was compelled to accept the first Central Committee candidate, though in practice their acceptance was hotly debated by the provincial organisations.[85] Of the eventual 325 PSR delegates to the Constituent Assembly from these five lists, fifty were nominated from the centre.[86] Efforts were made by the Central Committee to place their candidates in areas where they had existing connections. Victor Chernov was placed in Tambov province, where he had worked as an activist in 1898. Martiushin, the Central Committee candidate in Kazan, was of local peasant stock, and Avksentev, who was one of the Central Committee candidates for Penza, was a native of the region. Local roots were an important factor in placing candidates. Acceptance of these Central

[82] These lists were collated from local newspapers including *Narod* (Nizhegorodskaia PSR/soviet of peasants' deputies list), *Za zemliu i voliu* (Kazan PSR/soviet of peasants' deputies list), *Golos truda* (Kazan Elders' PSR list), *Delo derevnia* (Tambov PSR/soviet of peasants' deputies list), *Chernozem, Sotsialist revoliutsioner* (Penza PSR/soviet of peasants' deputies list), *Zemlia i volia* (Simbirsk PSR/soviet of peasants' deputies list), *Simbirsk narodnaia gazeta* (Simbirsk PSR Elders-defencists).

[83] This position was put forward by Oliver Radkey in his canonical work on the PSR. Radkey, *The sickle under the hammer*, p. 290.

[84] Koenker, *Moscow workers*, pp. 222–5, assessed the candidates put forward by the Menshevik and Bolshevik parties as candidates to the city and local Dumas and concluded that Bolshevik success came down to 'them and us' mentality; the Bolsheviks fielded more candidates who were themselves workers, and these were the candidates most likely to be voted in.

[85] For a discussion of the wrangles within the Central Committee of the party over candidate nominations, see Radkey, *The sickle under the hammer*, pp. 285ff. Kazan, Nizhegorod, Simbirsk and Tambov all stood one Central Committee candidate, while only Penza stood two Central Committee candidates.

[86] Radkey, *The sickle under the hammer*, p. 288.

Committee candidates was a matter that was given serious consideration by the regional electoral boards set up by the province party organisation. The candidates proposed by the Central Committee for Kazan, Vera Figner and G. A. Martiushin, were discussed at length at the PSR provincial conference, and it was concluded that since both candidates had strong local connections, they would be accepted.[87]

Information offered about electoral candidates was generally dominated by the occupation and local background of the candidate. Their poverty, devotion to the party and spells in prison and exile were other factors that were emphasised. The Nizhegorod PSR/soviet of peasants' deputies' list offered almost no information about its candidates. The list put forward by the Kazan PSR and the soviet of peasants' deputies was also sparse – the only biographical information offered was the candidates' occupation and his birthplace.[88] Ten of the twelve candidates were listed as peasants, and the remaining two industrial workers. Eleven of the twelve were local people. The compilers of these lists regarded candidates' local associations and working origins as the most important factors.

Other lists did offer more information and give some indicators of other factors considered significant by compilers of such lists. Both Kazan and Simbirsk had two separate PSR lists in the Constituent Assembly elections, as a result of conflicts within their regional organisations. The list which can be likened to regional PSR lists in other provinces, in so far as it included candidates from the soviet of peasants' deputies, in both Simbirsk and Kazan was pitted against a second SR list of similar name in both cases – in Kazan, it was the 'Kazan Elders' PSR', and in Simbirsk the 'Simbirsk PSR Elder-defencists'. The Kazan Elders' PSR list offered very detailed biographies of its members,[89] who were all well educated. With the exception of Firsov, an eminent professor of history at Kazan University, the candidates on this list had all been long-term PSR members, and had lengthy prison, hard labour and exile sentences to their names. Each candidate's biography emphasised that 'All his life has been a struggle for freedom, land and freedom.'[90] The list offered by the Simbirsk provincial PSR and the soviet of peasants' deputies offered detail on their candidates that in some cases defies classification – the occupations of the eleven candidates, for example, in eight cases changed at least three times. Like the Kazan list, though, eight of the eleven candidates were from peasant families. The working, poor peasant background of these candidates was emphasised. Also, like

[87] *Golos truda* 30, 21 August 1917, p. 4.   [88] *Za zemliu i voliu* 8, 23 October 1917.
[89] *Golos truda* 43, 20 November 1917.   [90] *Golos truda* 43, 20 November 1917.

Kazan, emphasis was placed on their local origins – ten of the eleven candidates came from Simbirsk province. The Constituent Assembly electoral list of the Vologda PSR group even included the candidates' addresses, emphasising the importance of local origin and residence in selection of candidates.[91]

Overall, elections in Nizhegorod and Kazan provinces went well. Elections were widely held, and though there were breaches in electoral procedure, they were relatively few and far between. The most significant elections at village level were the *volost* committee elections, which ran from April onwards, the *volost zemstvo* elections that did not take place until August onwards, and of course the Constituent Assembly elections, which got under way on 12 November. The Constituent Assembly elections, in particular, enjoyed respectable turnout and largely followed electoral procedure. The high level of public consciousness and participation indicates that ordinary people recognised the importance of elections and chose to participate in the electoral process. This section will, however, focus on the fierce resistance to elections in some areas, which serves to confuse our impression of the course of elections, and the ways in which local leaders were selected.

The rural intelligentsia were expected to play multifaceted roles in the various elections of 1917, but especially the Constituent Assembly elections. They were to explain the significance and importance of voting, and the differences between the main political parties. As organisers, they were to carry out the pre-electoral work of compiling electoral lists, collecting information for the demarcation of electoral boundaries and preparing electoral materials (boxes, papers and so on). The intelligentsia were regarded as of key importance in specific political parties' campaigns, spreading propaganda and explaining various party programmes. Finally, they were expected to stand as candidates. As has already been discussed, their marginal position in village society meant that these roles were ambitious and difficult to fulfil effectively, and the burden of work placed upon the literate in the villages was very great. There were reports from parts of Nizhegorod and Kazan provinces that elections were postponed for long periods because there were insufficient literate people to run them.[92] The problem of personnel shortage was accentuated by the timing of the elections; they coincided with

[91] *Partiniia izvestiia* 3, pp. 31–4.
[92] *Nizhegorodskaia zemskaia gazeta* 36, 7 September 1917, pp. 7–8; NART, f. 1246, op. 1, d. 102, ll. 17–18; letter from Kazan provincial *zemstvo* administration to provincial commissar, 14 August 1917, letter from Kozmodem'ianskii *uezd zemstvo* administration to Kazan province *zemstvo* administration, 9 August 1917.

the summer, when many teachers and *zemstvo* employees were on holiday away from the villages.[93]

Electoral fairness and comprehensiveness is difficult to judge effectively, not least because there was an enormous range of response in terms of interest, consciousness and turnout from one village to the next, and because popular interest in elections seems to have waned over the course of 1917. There are numerous reports that the *volost zemstvo* elections attracted little attention or enthusiasm and were poorly attended, reflecting these institutions' lack of prestige and significance among the rural population. The Constituent Assembly elections, however, enjoyed satisfactory turnout in the villages.[94] Indifference was the most dangerous foe of elections and was reported in varying degrees all over the place in a population whose initial intoxication with democracy apparently gave way to disinterest over the course of the summer. There were frequent complaints in the press that preparation for elections was inadequate, and that political parties were not presenting their programmes, in the towns as well as in the villages.[95] A rather desperate appeal from the Presidium of the Nizhnii Novgorod soviet of peasants' deputies that was sent around the *volosts* in July warned:

Comrade citizens, we are not ready for the elections. Our peasants' organisations are not prepared, and when the day of elections comes, whom will we send when we have not named candidates, those candidates that will stand for peasants' rights of land and freedom ... We must show ourselves worthy of the title 'free citizens'.[96]

In some areas, elections provoked little interest. In Chebaksa village in Kazan province, despite lively agitation carried out by a range of groups regarding the importance of the September *volost* elections, 'villagers showed very little interest' in the course of *volost* elections. This disinterest was reflected in the woeful turnout, where only 69 of the 500 eligible voters cast a vote.[97]

---

[93] GANO, f. 830, op. 1, d. 7, l. 5; report from Nizhegorod *uezd* commissar to the *uezd* administrative court, November 1917.

[94] L. G. Protasov, *Vserossiskoe uchreditel'noe sobranie: istoriia rozhdeniia i gibeli* (Moscow, 1997), pp. 193–204.

[95] *Kazanskaia rabochaia gazeta* 119, 6 September 1917, p. 2, regarding lack of preparation for the Town Duma elections; *Nizhegorodskaia zemskaia gazeta* 38, 21 September 1917, p. 5, reports that citizens in Semenovskii *uezd* were 'in general unprepared or simply unenlightened'; *Krasnoe znamia* 5, 23 November 1917, p. 4, noted that in Sormovo and Lukoianovskii *uezds* there was very little pre-electoral campaigning from any party other than the PSR, and that this was reflected in the voting (though this source is dubious, as it seeks to legitimise Bolshevik seizure of power, and to suggest that had they campaigned, the Bolsheviks would have won).

[96] GANO, f. 851, op. 1, d. 2, l. 236; letter from presidium of Makar'evskii *uezd* soviet of peasants' deputies to Lysovskii *volost* executive committee, 22 July 1917.

[97] *Kazanskaia rabochaia gazeta* 132, 23 September 1917, p. 4.

Russia was to use a direct, secret, equal, universal voting system, often referred to as four-tailed suffrage, in its forthcoming elections. This system differed significantly from the indirect voting methods used for the State Duma elections and had to be clarified to the newly fledged electorate. Some aspects of the new electoral laws provoked resistance, particularly in the villages. Secret voting, in particular, was the aspect of four-tailed suffrage most alien to traditional peasant voting practices that involved communal and often unanimous voting through a show of hands. Reports in the socialist newspapers blamed resistance on ignorance, but it can just as easily be explained by a knowing refusal to accept externally imposed regulations.

In Pokrovskoe village, Semenovskii *uezd*, local people complained bitterly about the secrecy of the *volost* elections, as an open vote was perceived as fairer.[98] In Khomutov village, also in Semenovskii *uezd*, the men refused to allow their wives to go into the voting booths without them; 'Are you saying I'm not the master of my woman, are you soft in the head?! What could my woman keep secret from me? Anyone would tell you that husband and wife are one; it says so in the scriptures!'[99] In Semenovskii *uezd*, though women did vote in *volost zemstvo* elections, their participation was not that of conscious citizens: 'Regional public activists carried out agitation – they wrote leaflets for the illiterate or barely literate citizens and declared, "bring the women quickly or you won't get bread!" and the women (*babi*) were brought, not wasting a minute.'[100] Particular problems were raised by the women's vote among Muslim communities, especially in rural regions. In Mamadyshskii *uezd*, the residents in two largely Muslim *volosts* refused to include women on electoral lists, and would not submit women's names.[101] In one *volost*, a partial solution was offered to the problem of women voting by stating that in Muslim electoral regions, women would vote separately from men, at stated times, and that in areas where there was a mixture of Muslims and non-Muslims, electoral officials would be sent who corresponded to the ethnic mix of the region.[102]

Administrators of Kazan's non-Russian communities faced the fiercest and most sustained resistance to elections. The administrators of

---

[98] *Nizhegorodskaia zemskaia gazeta* 38, 21 September 1917, p. 5.
[99] *Nizhegorodskaia zemskaia gazeta* 38, 21 September 1917, p. 5.
[100] *Nizhegorodskaia zemskaia gazeta* 38, 21 September 1917, p. 5.
[101] NART, f. 1246, op. 1, d. 102, l. 11; from Mamadyshskii *uezd zemstvo* administration to the provincial commissar, 4 August 1917.
[102] NART, f. 983, op. 1, d. 21, l. 57; protocol of Staro-Moshinksii *volost* committee of public safety, 2 June 1917.

non-Russian communities in Viatka faced similar problems.[103] Whole villages in rural Kazan refused to be entered onto the electoral roll. Some of this resistance can be explained by the population's suspicion of external forces, and fears that any listing of individuals in the village was associated with the grain monopoly. In other cases, the resistance was very specifically directed against the process of the elections themselves. In two Muslim-dominated *volosts* of Kazan *uezd*, formal decrees were sent to the *uezd* commissar in September from two *volost* committees stating their refusal to carry out elections.[104] In some places, resistance spilled over into violence. In Kozmodem'ianskii *uezd*, there was widespread resistance to the *volost zemstvo* elections. In Bolsheiunginskii *volost*, the situation was particularly grave:

> The electoral lists have not been drawn up as a result of agitation, the *volost* executive committee has been disbanded, the *volost* commissar removed, the treasurer is under arrest and the *volost* administration's building was burnt down on 5 August. It is only a matter of time before life is taken in this *volost*.[105]

The province's administrators were unsure what provoked resistance to elections among the non-Russian community and were unable to pin blame on anyone but the 'regional population'. Kazan's provincial *zemstvo* administration asked the provincial commissar to explain why elections faced such resistance, whether through 'unculturedness, the backwardness of the population, or the instigation of separate individuals'.[106] Hard-pressed administrators tended to favour the explanation that the trouble was caused by counter-revolutionary individuals. This blaming of an external enemy for the problems was understandable, as it offered the administration a convenient scapegoat. A better explanation for the resistance put up by rural non-Russians, however, was the lack of information they were offered regarding the shape of the new regime and the importance of elections, and the inherently alien nature of the electoral systems imposed upon them. For Tatar communities, religious missionaries' attempts to convert the population

---

[103] Retish, 'Peasant identities in Russia's turmoil'; non-Russians refuse the census, pp. 147–8; non-Russian resistance to elections, pp. 154ff.

[104] NART, f. 1246, op. 1, d. 102, l. 131; report from Kazan *uezd* commissar to Kazan provincial commissar, 22 September 1917.

[105] NART, f. 1246, op. 1, d. 102, l. 20; from Kozmodem'ianskii *uezd zemstvo* administration to the provincial commissar, regarding problems in carrying out elections, 14 August 1917. A report about the same situation can be found in NART, f. 1246, op. 1, d. 102, l. 18.

[106] NART, f. 1246, op. 1, d. 102, l. 17; report marked 'very urgent' from Kazan provincial *zemstvo* administration to provincial commissar, 14 August 1917.

from Islam left a legacy of fear and hostility to Russian intervention in their communities.[107]

Kazan's administrators faced formidable problems in trying to find individuals with skills in the various non-Russian languages who could explain the new political processes to the locals, and in finding the funds and expertise to have official proclamations and educational pamphlets translated and printed in other languages. Kozmodem'ianskii *uezd*'s *zemstvo* administration sent a 'humble request' to the provincial *zemstvo* administration for funds and for two instructors who could oversee electoral affairs.[108] There were instances where the mainly Russian administrators of the province failed to recognise the sensitivity of the non-Russian question. In Kazan *uezd*, the *uezd* committee informed the provincial commissar that they had appointed two *uezd* assistant commissars, even though only one was provided for. This second assistant, a student named Latyf Mustafin, was commissioned specifically to assist with the *uezd*'s Muslim community:

In Kazan *uezd* nearly half of the population is Muslim, and it is predominantly this Muslim population, as a result of their darkness, which opposes the Provisional Government's undertakings, including the grain monopoly and the *volost zemstva* elections. We wish to have on the commissariat a person who has the faith of the Muslim population and who knows the Tatar language.[109]

The provincial commissar, however, refused to authorise the appointment of Mustafin, as funds were not available for two assistant commissars.[110] This myopic response failed to respond to local needs and provides some explanation for the problems faced with the non-Russian communities. In non-Russian areas, the local administration seemed largely unable to tap into a source of locally esteemed and recognised leaders through whom they could implement policy. Without the participation of local leaders, regional administrators were unable to mobilise or to control the population. Despite resistance from the centre, Kazan *uezd*'s committee employed Mustafin anyway, and he was sent around the *volost*s trying to combat anti-election feeling.[111] The short-sighted response from the central provincial administration failed to respond to local needs and helps to

---

[107] Geraci, *Window on the east*, p. 37, p. 39.
[108] NART, f. 1246, op. 1, d. 102, l. 18; report from Kozmodem'ianskii *uezd zemstvo* administration to Kazan provincial *zemstvo* administration, 9 August 1917.
[109] NART, f. 1246, op. 1, d. 75, l. 148; letter from Kazan *uezd* commissar to Kazan provincial commissar, August 1917.
[110] NART, f. 1246, op. 1, d. 75, l. 149; letter from Kazan provincial commissar to Kazan *uezd* commissar, 24 August 1917.
[111] NART, f. 1246, op. 1, d. 102, l. 131; supplementary report from Kazan *uezd* commissar to Kazan provincial commissar, 22 September 1917.

explain why the administration experienced difficulties when dealing with Kazan's ethnic minorities.

From this study we can establish the obvious first, that local working men predominated in the ranks of local leaders. The rural intelligentsia did not play the prominent role in local leadership that the political elite hoped that they would, and this made it more difficult for the political elite to gain hegemony among rural communities. Soldiers were in a particularly awkward position as local leaders, since they were subject to competing demands from military obligations and from understaffed local administration. Women were largely excluded from the democratic process. Quite apart from the implications of this for the shape of political life, the exclusion of women heightened the problem of personnel shortages, as many highly suitable and qualified women did not participate in the public political sphere.

The shortage of suitable and willing people to serve in the proliferation of committees that emerged in 1917 rather changes our perspectives of 'committee crazy' 1917. A small group of local leaders were effectively forced into full-time political and administrative service, and this new occupation divorced many local leaders from their grass-roots constituents. The problem of absenteeism is helpful in undermining any romantic notion of general popular commitment to self-government. Democratisation and popular control of government may well have been popular concepts, but remuneration for committee work was clearly not sufficient to induce members to attend regularly. Based on these personnel shortages, we can assert that popular participation in local government was not as popular in practice as it was in principle.

The choice of electoral candidates brings us back to chapter 3, and the place of political parties in local politics. Party politics was often not particularly significant in the choice of local leadership, but this was partly because the peasant milieu was so closely tied to the PSR that there was often no question of choice. In many peasant discussions of political affiliations, support for the PSR was virtually a given. The general demands and aspirations of the peasant milieu tied in closely with the PSR and offer a strong explanation for that party's rural support. In the Constituent Assembly elections, where voting was by party list, the information offered about candidates further confirms that local affiliations and occupation were predominant in the factors that determined selection.

The progress of the elections themselves offers us a context for how leaders were chosen. Resistance to elections from parts of the Russian population, especially the non-Russian community, did not demonstrate ignorance. It displayed instead a determination to be self-directed and autonomous in political life. The non-Russian community was not well served by local government; in fact it could be identified as a part of Kazan's population whose local leaders were largely unable to tap into the democratic process, because of the language barrier, and because they were predominantly rural.

CHAPTER 5

Talking to the people and shaping revolution

Comrades! Public teachers! You gave the people literacy, now you must
give them development! Make free Russia's conscious citizens out of
yesterday's village philistines!

(From educational pamphlet, 1917)[1]

This chapter looks at the methods used by the political elite to communicate with ordinary people and offers some explanations for the problems
that they faced. Russia's political elite sought to educate ordinary people,
and to transform their cultural lives, in the pre-revolutionary period. These
attempts to communicate with and to educate ordinary people were intensified in 1917. So-called 'cultural-enlightenment campaigns' were high on
the agenda of public life in the course of 1917. Correspondingly, ordinary
people sought out and utilised information on the nature of the revolution,
and of how they were to participate in the revolution. The Provisional Government and soviets, and educated society in general, sought to orchestrate
popular education. For the Provisional Government, popular education
had to be a success, as they relied on popular understanding and participation in the administration. Without popular support, their stated goals of
overseeing democratic elections, keeping Russia in the war and preventing
civic disorder were unachievable.

Educational campaigns were undertaken with heartfelt faith from Russia's political elite that education could 'transform' Russia's citizens into
newly fledged democratic citizens, who could participate in the building
of an egalitarian, even utopian, state. This emphasis on 'transformation'
lies at the heart of the problems for Russia's political elite in 1917; the new
revolutionary regime required conscious citizens, but the political elite did

---

[1] Medynskii, *Kak vesti besedi*, p. 3. Medynskii was an educationalist, who wrote prolific educational
literature in the revolutionary period and went on to be a leading educational theorist in the Soviet
period. See also T. Iu. Krasovitskaia, *Rossiiskoe obrazovanie mezhdu reformatorstvom i revoliutsionerizmom, fevral 1917–1920 god* (Moscow, 2002), p. 15.

123

not recognise the majority of Russia's ordinary people as conscious citizens. Contemporaries interpreted the failure of some aspects of the elite's education programmes as evidence of the ignorance and unculturedness of the Russian population. The 'dark', 'uncultured', 'ignorant' nature of ordinary people, particularly in the villages, were consistent tropes used by the political elite. These tropes help us understand the attitudes the political elites took towards those they sought to educate. The challenge for the historian is to look beyond such clichés of Russian rural life, and evaluate what ordinary people really understood and thought.

The revolution provoked a range of creative responses and interpretations among ordinary people that were not always in accord with the visions of revolution espoused by the elite.[2] Chapters 7 and 8, looking at land and provisions, explore in more detail the ways in which ordinary people interpreted communications from the centre and made conscious and informed political choices that often did not accord with the views and aspirations of the political elite. This chapter will focus on the ways that the political elite tried to communicate their messages; it will argue that the old tropes of 'dark' and 'ignorant' ordinary people are misleading and attempted to depoliticise ordinary people's alternative responses to revolution. Ordinary people were astute and selective in their acceptance of educational programmes, but they did not accept the projections of others wholesale.

Cultural enlightenment campaigns went on across Russia, in towns, villages and factories. The Provisional Government addressed cultural and educational issues from its inception. It sought to decentralise and secularise education but essentially did no more than encourage and expand the pre-revolutionary educational efforts of the *zemstva* in village primary education. Its goals, of general education and literacy, were very much in the pre-revolutionary liberal tradition and did not envisage a profound transformation of cultural models.[3] The activities that went on at local level in some respects reflected the Provisional Government's attempts but were more concerted and more diverse. A whole spectrum of groups involved in popular organisation played a part, running courses, meetings, literacy programmes and spectacles.

There are no clear distinctions between the problems and features faced by Nizhegorod and Kazan generally, but there are clear distinctions between

---

[2] Aaron Retish's work comes to similar conclusions based on Viatka's peasantry (Retish, 'Peasant identities in Russia's turmoil', p. 180).

[3] Daniel T. Orlovsky, 'The Provisional Government and its cultural work', in A. Gleason, Peter Kenez and Richard Stites (eds.), *Bolshevik culture: experiment and order in the Russian revolution* (Bloomington, IN, 1985), pp. 39–56, pp. 44–5. This article presents a detailed analysis of the Provisional Government's cultural policies.

the problems and features faced by urban enlightenment campaigns on the one hand, and rural enlightenment campaigns on the other. In towns, the political elite who orchestrated education campaigns drew on a pool of educated people and an existing network of cultural facilities such as theatres, public spaces and concert halls. Urban dwellers were liable to be better educated as a group, more culturally aware and more amenable to education programmes.[4] The process of enlightenment in rural areas raised specific problems. The rural population was geographically dispersed, which made it more difficult to reach, and were generally less cosmopolitan and had lower levels of formal education. To compound matters, there was a dearth of educated people to initiate such programmes in rural areas.

The enlightenment campaigns of 1917 in many respects built on pre-revolutionary developments. The work of Stephen Frank on elite attitudes towards ordinary people helps us understand that elite obsessions with the drive for enlightenment among the village population in 1917 were not new but were a heightened version of the activities and priorities of educated society before the revolution, and reflected a wider culture of learning that was slowly infiltrating the countryside as well as the towns.[5] Recent work has shown that by the turn of the century the villages were increasingly 'opened' to outside influences and peasants were drawn into the public sphere.[6] The spread of literacy and education was an important facilitator for these processes. Scott Seregny commented that from the 1890s onwards, schooling 'assumed the intensity and scale of a religious crusade'.[7] Village connections with the outside world were intensified by military conscription, which exposed a significant proportion of young men to the wider world and heightened their literacy levels.[8] The outbreak of the First World War and accompanying mass mobilisation gave the village population a new incentive to engage with the world around them. The war and mass mobilisation transformed national politics into a sphere

[4] Brooks, *When Russia learned to read*, p. 33.
[5] See Stephen P. Frank, 'Confronting the domestic Other: rural popular culture and its enemies in fin de siècle Russia', in Frank and Steinberg, *Cultures in flux*, pp. 74–107. On the difficulties of defining this 'educated society' or *obshchestvennost*, and the challenging concept of 'civil society', see Samuel D. Kassow, James L. West and Edith W. Clowes, 'The problem of the middle in late Imperial Russian society', in Samuel D. Kassow, James L. West and Edith W. Clowes (eds.), *Educated society and the quest for public identity in late Imperial Russia* (Princeton, NJ, 1991), pp. 3–14, p. 3. See also Cathy A. Frierson, *Peasant icons: representations of rural people in late nineteenth century Russia* (Oxford, 1993).
[6] Andrew Verner, 'Discursive strategies in the 1905 Revolution: peasant petitions from Vladimir province', *Russian Review* 54 (1995), 65–90, esp. pp. 72–3; Jeffrey Burds, *Peasant dreams and market politics: labour migration and the Russian village, 1861–1905* (Pittsburgh, 1998).
[7] Scott J. Seregny, 'Power and discourse in Russian elementary education: the school inspectorate, 1869–1917', *Jahrbucher für Geschichte Osteuropas* 47 (1999), 161–86, p. 167.
[8] Sanborn, *Drafting the Russian nation*, p. 19.

intricately associated with peasants' daily lives. The *zemstva* set up a range of adult education programmes to fill this need and established educational links with ordinary people that were to be further developed in 1917.[9]

A wide range of different organisations and institutions threw themselves into cultural-enlightenment work in 1917. Though these groups all purportedly pursued the same general goal of bringing literacy and political education to ordinary people, they harboured very different aspirations regarding the outcome and content of their contributions. The soviet-led 'committees of cultural-enlightenment' were the most prominent and provided an umbrella for a diverse range of other public organisations that sought to become involved in cultural-enlightenment work. Other governmental and non-governmental bodies also participated to some extent in the work of public education and enlightenment. To give an example of the range involved, at its founding, eighteen different public organisations and political parties delegated representatives to the Kazan soviet's cultural-enlightenment section. These included the Society of Public Universities, the Society of Young Teachers, Bolsheviks, Mensheviks, Socialist Revolutionaries, the Party of Independent Socialists, the Workers' Club, the Polish Democratic Organisation, the Socialist Committee of Muslims, the Peasant Group, the Student Co-operative, the Union of Teachers, the Union of Military Medical Assistants, the Union of Zemstvo Employees, the Society of Volga Minority Nationalities, the Organisation of Evacuated Military in Kazan town, Kazan University and the Women in Higher Education group.[10]

The success of cultural-enlightenment campaigns cannot be evaluated objectively. Many of the goals espoused by cultural-enlightenment campaigns were indefinite, and concerned more general aims of political and social progress. This makes any assessment of their success impressionistic. Most of the available sources – newspaper reports, educational literature and local government and soviet reports – deal with the promulgation, but not the reception or impact of cultural-enlightenment campaigns. In his work on the popular press, Daniel Brower acknowledged the difficulty of evaluating reception of newspapers by their readers and tackled it by effectively 'constructing' his reader from the forms of the material that was presented to them.[11] This is more difficult to do with the educational

9 Scott J. Seregny, 'Zemstvos, peasants, and citizenship: the Russian adult education movement and World War I', *Slavic Review* 59 (2000), 290–315, esp. p. 312.

10 NART, f. 1246, op. 1, d. 72, l. 83; list of public organisations and parties delegating their representatives to the cultural enlightenment section of the soviet of workers and soldiers' deputies, undated.

11 Daniel R. Brower, 'The Penny Press and its readers', in Frank and Steinberg, *Cultures in flux*, pp. 147–67, p. 148, p. 153.

campaigns of 1917, as they were mostly non-commercial ventures, which did not have the same requirement as the popular press to be responsive to its readers. The extent of popular engagement with these campaigns will be evaluated here, and the commercial 'enlightening' entertainment that was a feature of 1917 will be discussed. This chapter will offer some explanations for the purported 'failure' of the enlightenment campaigns by evaluating the range of different approaches taken by the political elite, and popular involvement in cultural-enlightenment events.

AIMS OF EDUCATIONAL PROGRAMMES

The political elite's aims in conducting cultural-enlightenment programmes were diverse and far-reaching but showed common emphases on literacy, political education and citizens' education (*grazhdanskoe vospitanie*). The basic aims were to increase levels of literacy and literate activity among ordinary people. Political dictionaries were written in 1917 that sought to explain political terminology, and to ease the assimilation of political language into mass consciousness.[12] The broader goals of educational campaigns were extraordinarily ambitious. The Kazan soviet of workers, soldiers and peasants' deputies' cultural-enlightenment section offers a typical expression of the desire to instil political literacy among ordinary people: 'Democracy will only be invincible when it is formed from itself, and organised into one united army. For this it is necessary that all the labouring masses (*trudiashchiesia massa*) are deeply inspired by conscious public interests and have fixed ideas about their aims.'[13] The language of this statement is combative and determined, demanding as it does that ordinary people consciously embrace 'public interests', to be defined no doubt by the soviet itself.

Cultural-enlightenment campaigns sought to inform ordinary people about their best interests, and through this to set the course of the revolution. Educational literature recognised that mass political literacy could not be achieved in the short term but nevertheless sought to spread political understanding as much as possible. The elections for the Constituent Assembly, to be held before the year was out, required that ordinary people understand the rudimentaries of political life. Basic literacy was regarded as an essential foundation stone for public consciousness, but only the beginning of the task that lay ahead. The establishment and reinforcement of public literacy had to go alongside campaigns to heighten public awareness.

[12] Kolonitskii, '"Democracy" as identification', p. 165.
[13] NART, f. 1246, op. 1, d. 72, l. 82; outline of programme for soviet of workers' and soldiers' deputies cultural-enlightenment section, undated.

The political elite's first and most basic aim was to bring literacy to the illiterate and to improve the literacy levels of those who already had some degree of education. This aspect of the campaigns built on pre-revolutionary activities like workers' schools and societies for adult education, and the formation of 'popular universities' in the pre-revolutionary period.[14] In an educational leaflet written by E. N. Medynskii, who produced a number of educational pamphlets in 1917 and went on to be a leading authority on education in the Soviet regime, the importance of keeping adult education entirely separate from children's education, and of keeping reading material and study subjects as interesting and as relevant as possible, was stressed.[15] Medynskii emphasised that literacy should not be exclusively Great Russian literacy, but should embrace Russian ethnic diversity. There is evidence that this call for education in native tongues was met in 1917. For Kazan, with its amalgam of different ethnic minority groups, this was a sensitive and difficult task, particularly as Tatars had been denied the opportunity to publish in Tatar in the pre-revolutionary period.[16]

Real efforts were made in 1917 to educate and communicate with non-Russians. In the literacy school set up by the soviet's cultural-enlightenment committee and officers and soldiers of the 94th regiment stationed in Kazan town, for example, four schools were opened for the regiment, divided by nationality – Russian, Tatar, Ukrainian and Chuvash. Of the 557 identified illiterates in the regiment, 227 enrolled in the schools, while the school's teachers came from the ranks of the officers and soldiers themselves. The groups met in the soldiers' club for their study sessions.[17] The ethnic divisions here reflect an important aspect of cultural enlightenment activities in Kazan. This example also blurs the distinction between educators and pupils, as teachers and pupils lived and worked together.

The second, closely related aim was to increase the opportunities for reading and learning available to Russia's working population, urban and rural. Not content with the reading of folk stories and tales, cultural-enlightenment literature stressed that books would not only improve the practical environment of readers, by teaching about improved agricultural methods and so on, but would change the world-view of those that perused them, and cause the newly awakened minds to ask challenging questions

[14] On the development of 'people's universities', which were particularly notable in the post-1905 period, see David Wartenweiler, *Civil society and academic debate in Russia, 1905–1914* (Oxford, 1999), chapter 5, pp. 165–215.
[15] E. N. Medynskii, *Ot temy k svetu! Nashe neumyn'e i nasha bednota. Nasha temnota. Kak borot'sia s nashei temnotoi* (Nizhnii Novgorod, 1917), p. 26; E. N. Medynskii, *Kak organizovat i vesti selskie prosvetitel'nye obshchestva i kruzhki* (Nizhnii Novgorod, 1918), pp. 31–3.
[16] Geraci, *Window on the east*, p. 26.   [17] *Kazanskaia rabochaia gazeta* 45, 4 June 1917, p. 3.

about the natural world around them.[18] The main facilitator for such enhanced learning was considered to be the establishment of libraries and 'people's houses' (*narodnyi dom*) in towns, and reading rooms in villages.[19] The importance of such establishments was not just as a place to access books, but also as an environment for learning, and as a social space to interact with other conscious citizens. We can see the aims of educational campaigns in the broadest of senses here, as bringing ordinary people into the sphere of civil life. The instilling of citizens' values was almost insepara-ble from the more clearly stated aim of improving literacy levels and access to books. Public libraries and spaces were to provide a new forum for con-scious, civilised Russia. Existing public gathering spaces of bars and taverns were explicitly challenged by these new, more worthy meeting places:

> There must be a tearoom in the *narodnyi dom*, where local residents can go to sit in their spare time, have a chat with one another. At the moment, people go to the tavern or the teashop, which is like a tavern; the cursing in such teashops is heard ceaselessly, it's dirty all around, vodka or spirit is often drunk there. The tearoom in a *narodnyi dom* is not like that at all; it's clean, bright and comfortable, there are no drunkards, no swearing; there are newspapers and journals on the table. There one is enticed to rest and to peacefully chat with one another . . .[20]

This statement of aspiration for the *narodnyi dom* reveals much of what the cultural-enlightenment campaigns sought to address. Swearing, dirt and alcohol were all implicitly identified as undesirable aspects of Russian life that needed to be reformed. This was not a matter of giving skills of literacy in order that people could form their own ideas and make their own political decisions. The aim was rather a total transformation of societal norms and behaviour. In this, one can again trace clear continuity from the pre-revolutionary aspirations of educators, who sought not just to impart literacy but also to transform society.[21] Conduct manuals became increasingly popular in late Imperial Russia. Some conduct manuals were targeted at ordinary people, instructing them on how to behave and conduct themselves, propagandised self-education and training in the pursuit of

---

[18] Medynskii, *Ot temy k svetu!*, p. 24, for example, suggested that a discussion could be instigated on what day and night were.

[19] Charles Clark offers a detailed assessment of the use and pitfalls of the Bolsheviks' use of peasant reading rooms in the early Soviet period (Charles Clark, 'Uprooting otherness: Bolshevik attempts to refashion rural Russia via the reading rooms', *Canadian Slavonic Papers* 38 (1996), 305–30).

[20] Medynskii, *Ot temy k svetu!*, pp. 29–30.

[21] Brooks, *When Russia learned to read*, p. 51; Gary Thurston, 'The impact of Russian popular theatre, 1886–1915', *Journal of Modern History* 55 (1983), 237–67, p. 240; Anthony E. Swift, 'Workers' theater and "proletarian culture" in prerevolutionary Russia, 1905–1917', in Reginald E. Zelnik (ed.), *Workers and intelligentsia in late Imperial Russia: realities, representations, reflections* (Berkeley, CA, 1999), pp. 260–91, p. 278.

civic virtue.[22] As Stephen Frank put it when describing the efforts of pre-revolutionary educators, 'Activists engaged in these diverse attempts to transform popular culture repeatedly revealed that their ultimate goal was the creation of a new peasant class capable of filling what they saw as the moral and cultural vacuum of Russia's dangerous countryside.'[23] The establishment of *narodnyi dom* at *volost* and *uezd* levels usually by the newly formed committees of public safety can be seen in this context as attempts to shape the peasant class anew. It is hard to envisage them living up to their lofty ambitions.[24]

TALKING TO THE PEOPLE

The political elite perceived that they faced serious barriers in communicating their message to ordinary people, especially in the countryside. Much of 1917's educational literature focused on the means that could be used to communicate with the rural population, and to bridge the gulf between the language of the villages and the language of the revolution, which often utilised abstract or foreign terminology. Orlando Figes wrote about the purported gulf between peasant understandings of the revolution and the world around them, and the understandings and expectations of their would-be educators. This issue of communication with ordinary people is an important one, which requires further exploration. Figes used a number of anecdotes taken from educational literature of peasant ignorance about key revolutionary words and concepts, alongside the reports of State Duma deputies visiting the countryside in the first three months after the February revolution.[25] If we look more carefully at the content

---

[22] Catriona Kelly, *Refining Russia: advice literature, polite culture, and gender from Catherine to Yeltsin* (Oxford, 2001), esp. pp. 189–229, on advice manuals directed towards ordinary people.

[23] Frank, 'Confronting the domestic Other', p. 103.

[24] A *narodnyi dom* was set up in Lysovskii *uezd* in commemoration of the events of 27 February, which was funded in the first instance by a private donation of 5,000 roubles (GANO, f. 715, op. 1, d. 7, p. 8; protocol no. 4 of Lyskovskii residents committee, 7 March 1917). A *narodnyi dom* was similarly established by Sarleiskii *volost*, 'to commemorate free Russia' (GANO, f. 830, op. 1, d. 5, p. 120; declaration of Sarleiskoi *volost* citizens, 15 March 1917).

[25] Orlando Figes, 'The Russian revolution and its language in the villages', *Russian Review* 56 (1997), 323–45. Figes utilises a single educational pamphlet written by Medynskii, and the reports submitted to the Temporary Committee of the State Duma, which have been published in a number of forms, but which are currently held in RGIA. These reports, while a rich and lively source on the state of the countryside in 1917, are not definitive, as reporters' views of rural life did not necessarily reflect 'objective reality' (RGIA, f. 1278, op. 1, d. 4, ll. 240–56; report on the situation of Russia for three months of revolution by the current section of relations with the provinces of the Provisional Committee of the State Duma). On the need to treat outsider sources on peasant life with caution, see Verner, 'Discursive strategies', p. 65.

of educational literature, however, it contains genuine and well-grounded attempts to conduct educational activity in language and in forms that would be understood and accepted in the villages. Educational literature was explicit in pointing out the limitations and desires of their audience and offered diverse alternatives of how best to communicate with them. Cultural-enlightenment events were held regularly and enjoyed enormous popularity in towns and countryside. The funds that they generated alone indicate the success of such efforts.

Educational literature stressed the need to adopt emotional, localist and non-conceptual arguments when addressing a peasant audience. The examples given in the educational literature and used by Figes of how peasants misunderstood foreign words and concepts were given specifically so that such pitfalls could be avoided. Lecturers were beseeched to speak in a way that was both accessible and engaging:

You must force your listeners not only to listen, but also to experience everything you speak about, not just to understand, but also to feel. For this, your exposition must be clear and simple; the argument must occupy a lesser place in your words as far as is possible, attention must be paid predominantly to examples, and especially examples from regional life.[26]

Lecturers were warned specifically not to use foreign or unfamiliar terms in their speeches, to illustrate them profusely with living examples from Russian peasant life, and to engage not so much in lectures as in conversation with the listeners. Questions from the audience were answered in an informal way, by 'going down into the crowd of listeners, and when receiving a question from an individual, answer very loudly, so that the answer could be heard by other people around'.[27] Cultural enlightenment literature left nothing to chance. Specific examples were given of how to respond to common questions, and how to explain abstract concepts in terms that peasants would understand.

Language was certainly an important factor in the ways that educational campaigns were conducted and received, but it was not an insuperable barrier for educators in the countryside. The negative attitudes of the political elite towards the rural population offer a more pervasive explanation for the problems educators faced in taking their message to the countryside. One can draw some useful parallels between the 1873–4 'Going to the people' (*khozhdenie v narod*) and the renewed drive for enlightenment witnessed in 1917. The 'Going to the people' movement describes the actions of some thousands of intelligentsia, mainly students, who went to live and

[26] Medynskii, *Kak vesti besedi*, p. 4.   [27] Medynskii, *Kak vesti besedi*, p. 8.

work in the countryside in order to propagandise among peasants, and to
spread the gospel of revolution. The source of the movement was imprecise
but was nourished by twenty years of preparatory work by Populists. It
was grounded in a desire to pay back the 'debt' owed to the peasantry. One
contemporary, Stepniak-Kravchinsky, described the movement as more religious than political.[28] Both in the 1870s and in 1917, enlighteners aimed
for a utopian transformation of the state, and attempted to bridge the gulf
between educated society and ordinary people.[29] But whereas Populism
sought to resolve the conflict between state and society by using the might
of the peasantry to transform the state through revolution, in 1917 the political elite sought to draw the peasantry into the sphere of civil society to
solidify the revolutionary transformation of the state.[30]

Though by 1917 there were significant developments away from the perceptions of the 1870s, many underlying assumptions continued to reflect
much older ideas about the nature of the peasantry, and on essentially
hierarchical understandings of culture.[31] The most important of these was
the idea that the peasantry was essentially 'dark', unable to escape from
their poverty with their own intellectual resources, and that they required
external agents to lead them out of their benighted position.[32] The role
of educators in 1917 was conceptualised by the political elite as an external influence, moulding and leading the so-called 'dark people' (*temnyi
narod*). Both Provisional Government and soviet sources demonstrate this
attitude towards the enlightenment of the countryside. The political elite
perceived the drive for enlightenment in the countryside as an alien imposition, and in no way an organic development. Dan Orlovsky commented
that enlightenment in the countryside retained an abstract flavour for Provisional Government intellectuals, 'the imposition of an alien world upon
little-understood peasants'.[33] The countryside was perceived as an alien and

[28] F. Venturi, *Roots of revolution: a history of the populist and socialist movements in nineteenth-century
Russia* (London, 1960), pp. 503–5.
[29] See A. Gleason, 'The terms of Russian social history', in Kassow, West and Clowes, *Educated society*,
pp. 15–27, p. 18.
[30] On the 'Going to the people' movement, see Venturi, *Roots of revolution*, chapter 18, and Daniel
Field, *Rebels in the name of the tsar* (Boston, 1989). C. Pape, 'On the margins of utopia? Zemstvo
liberals and the peasant commune', *Russian History-Histoire Russe* 11 (1984), p. 224, provides a detailed
analysis of the utopian goals of the *zemstvo* liberals, which has been instrumental in forming this
conception of 1917 utopianism.
[31] On the significance of cultural hierarchies, see Neuberger, *Hooliganism*, pp. 10–11; Frank, 'Confronting the domestic Other'; Thurston, 'The impact of Russian popular theatre', p. 251.
[32] Judy Pallot, 'Imagining the rational landscape in late Imperial Russia', *Journal of Historical Geography*
26 (2000), 273–91, pp. 273–5, addresses this idea in relation to government involvement in land
reform.
[33] Orlovsky, 'The Provisional Government', p. 43.

benighted place by the 'democratic' soviets as well as by the more distant Provisional Government bodies. The cultural-enlightenment commission of the soviets of workers' and soldiers' deputies in Nizhnii Novgorod published a frantic appeal in August for assistance in the task of 'bringing light to the darkness':

Working intelligentsia of Nizhnii Novgorod! If you have free time, and you want to use it in the struggle with darkness, take part in the work of the enlightenment commission of Nizhegorod soviet of workers and soldiers' deputies. In this terrible hour, the living word of enlightenment can carry out true struggle with the darkness that is our bitterest enemy.[34]

The soviet's appeal has an apocalyptic and evangelical feel, of enlightenment as an externally led crusade against the forces of darkness within village life, which corresponded with the views expressed by the Provisional Government-led bodies. The soviet's barely veiled fear and suspicion of the countryside offers an insight into the ever-present tension between town and country.[35] Enlightenment campaigns usually originated in town-based organisations. The tensions in the campaign for enlightenment were not just between educated society and the countryside, but also the oft-frequented line of contestation between town and country. Much of the contemporary debate centred around why the intelligentsia did not participate more fully in village life, and how the enlightenment campaigns were to penetrate the villages more successfully, but the very positioning of the enlightenment as an external force offers one powerful explanation. The outsider bringing knowledge and light into the benighted villages was not a model that lent itself well to engaging with rural people.

The drive for enlightenment was not a one-way process. Though educators cast themselves as external agents, much of what they offered was actively sought out by some parts of the rural community. Village society had become increasingly aware of the benefits wrought by education,[36] and the tumult of written material generated by the democratisation process of 1917 only heightened the premium put on literacy in the villages. A prominent feature of reports and documentation from the villages was the appeals and comments from the peasants themselves commenting on

---

[34] *Izvestiia soveta rabochikh deputatov* 41, 24 August 1917, p. 3.
[35] The conflict between town and countryside during 1917 occurred on a range of levels from macro, as in the problems of food supplies, down to micro, in personal hostilities between, for example, peasants and workers.
[36] Eklof notes that 'Peasants recognised that their children had to learn to read, write and count in order to survive in a world increasingly crowded with written documents, but they had no use for the cultural baggage that accompanied basic instruction' (Eklof, *Russian peasant schools*, p. 476).

their 'darkness' and ignorance of current affairs, and their requests for assistance in understanding current events. Such self-descriptions of 'darkness' from the villagers must be treated with caution. Peasants themselves utilised stereotypes of the 'dark peasantry' in their discourse with educated society, but we cannot impute from this that the peasantry were actually ignorant and childlike. Rather, they were utilising understood tropes as the most effective means of communication.[37] Despite this caveat, reports from the villages repeatedly stressed the need for educated people to come to the assistance of the rural population. Soldier deputies from the Nizhegorod soviet of workers' deputies travelled around Sergachskii *uezd* in May. Their reports in the soviet newspaper described the archetypal 'dark' countryside:

Peasants complained that they were forgotten by the town and didn't know anything; wanted to know everything about past and forthcoming events. Newspapers and leaflets are needed. Among listeners were eighty-year-olds as well as seventy-year-olds. In general one has to say that there was virtually no youth in the countryside and in the villages youth was not seen at all.[38]

In conscripting young men, wartime mobilisation removed the most literate segment of the village community.[39] This meant that those literates remaining in the villages were of particular value. The 1897 census gives some indications of the weighting of literacy according to age. Women over thirty had literacy levels of less than 20 per cent, though literacy increased significantly among those under thirty.[40] There was an urgent need for literate administrators to fathom out the vast array of commands, appeals and imprecations coming from central and regional government. The skills of literacy held by the rural intelligentsia gave them special significance in the context of the shortage of literate people in the villages. The rural intelligentsia was specifically targeted in appeals from villagers

---

[37] E. E. Pyle, 'Peasant strategies for obtaining state aid: a study of petitions during World War One', *Russian History-Histoire Russe* 24 (1997), 41–64; on the formulaic ways in which soldiers' families presented themselves in petitions to the state. Verner, 'Discursive strategies', offers a detailed analysis of peasant petitions in Vladimir province and suggests that peasants 'consciously manipulated' language (p. 70). Scott J. Seregny 'Peasants, nation, and local government in wartime Russia', *Slavic Review* 59 (2000), 336–342, p. 340, comments on the way in which peasants subscribed to official discourses.

[38] *Izvestiia soveta rabochikh deputatov* 19, 1 June 1917, p. 2.

[39] See Seregny, 'Zemstvos, peasants, and citizenship'. In Ufa, an official commented, 'the war has now removed nearly all literate males' (p. 310). In addition to the loss of the young men, there is evidence that teachers left their posts in wartime as a result of the rising costs of products of the first necessity (p. 312).

[40] Figures taken from U. A. Poliakov, *Naselenie Rossii v XX veke: istoricheskie ocherki. vol. I.* (Moscow, 2000), p. 23.

to help them understand current events. The elder of Khvostikovskii *volost* executive committee, Semenovskii *uezd*, appealed specifically to those individuals who lived in the *volost* but were not strictly members of the commune, such as priests, teachers and shop managers, to take part in a meeting held on 14 March to form the *volost* executive committee and the *volost* militia.[41] Despite this appeal, of the twenty-three members of the Khvostikovskii *volost* executive committee subsequently formed, all but two (the *volost* scribe and a housekeeper) were peasants. All were men.[42] Local male peasants dominated the village's formal political power structures in 1917. Despite an apparent awareness from peasants of the need for rural intelligentsia involvement, the domination of the new administrative structures by male peasants perpetuated traditional village power structures and produced an extra barrier for the political elite in communicating with the rural population.

The role that partisan politics played in educational programmes caused some problems for the political elite. Educational literature stressed that cultural-enlightenment programmes should be non-partisan in their treatment of political issues. Medynskii even suggested that political struggle was the worst possible form of political education.[43] In practice, party political activity played an important role in educational campaigns, and educational programmes presented an exclusively socialist perspective. Party politics saturated the political elite in 1917, and this was reflected in cultural-enlightenment campaigns. Some educational literature emanated directly from party political sources, leaving one in little doubt as to its political persuasions. Tellingly though, even the literature which professed to be non-partisan was itself highly partial. It is a reflection of the mood of 1917 that this literature was exclusively socialist and assumed socialist development as both necessary and beneficial. None of the mainstream cultural-enlightenment material propounded a liberal-capitalist perspective. This reflects the hijacking of 'democracy' by socialist parties, and the ways in which democracy was increasingly associated only with socialism.[44]

All the political parties that participated in the Constituent Assembly elections needed to make ordinary people aware of their programmes and conscious enough that they would vote. The main socialist parties all

[41] GANO, f. 815, op. 1, d. 19, l. 1; report from Khvostikovskii *volost* elder, early March 1917.
[42] GANO, f. 815, op. 1, d. 19, l. 2; list of members of Khvostikovskii *volost* executive committee, undated.
[43] E. N. Medynskii, *Revoliutsiia i vneshkol' noe obrazovanie. S prilozheniem konspektov besed s krest' ianami na temy, sviazannym s revoliutsiei* (Moscow, 1917) p. 15.
[44] Kolonitskii, '"Democracy" as identification', p. 161.

affiliated with the soviet's cultural enlightenment section in Kazan and Nizhegorod, and some of them operated very effectively as educators, particularly when they utilised existing networks of support. A survey of meetings held by the PSR in Nizhegorod province during 1917 reveals that although the PSR programme was the most frequently discussed topic, the topics covered were wide-ranging and reflected the topics covered by cultural-enlightenment literature. The PSR activists embraced a wider mandate and did not work solely in narrow party propaganda.[45]

The Provisional Government and other organisations demonstrated their commitment to public education by pouring money into cultural enlightenment campaigns. The bulk of the money for campaigns came from central funds, though large sums were raised by various non-government organisations. Kazan Town Duma allocated 19,500 roubles 'for the enlightenment of the population and cultural needs, in terms of literacy and improved library facilities'.[46] Nizhegorod provincial *zemstvo* allocated 5,000 roubles in March and April alone for the organisation of lectures and discussions. These sums pale, however, compared to the astonishing expenditure of Perm provincial *zemstvo*, which allocated 50,000 roubles, and Saratov provincial *zemstvo*, which reportedly allocated 260,000 roubles.[47] The allegedly non-political nature of cultural enlightenment led to real problems in terms of funding allocation. The financial crisis of 1917 did not lend itself well to massive spending on public education anyway, but this was further complicated by the Provisional Government's reluctance to fund the class-based soviets. The soviets relied on popular support for their funding and made frequent appeals for donations to education funds, while more specific organisations like the Sormovo workers' organisation regularly spent significant sums sending delegates out to the countryside.[48]

One of Medynskii's educational leaflets, 'How to Organise and Run Village Enlightenment Societies and Circles', recognised the problems of funding and suggested that for the best results educational campaigns had to rely on organic growth and the possibility of self-sufficiency if they were to take root and flourish in the community.[49] Medynskii reiterated that *zemstva* did not have the funds available to finance local cultural-enlightenment activities, and that for such circles to be successful, they had

[45] Survey of thirty-two PSR propaganda meetings reported in *Narod*, newspaper of the Nizhegorod PSR and provincial soviet of peasants' deputies.

[46] *Kazanskaia rabochaia gazeta* 45, 4 June 1917, p. 3.

[47] Medynskii, *Revoliutsiia i vneshkol'noe obrazovanie*, p. 7.

[48] See Sormovo financial records, in particular *Izvestiia soveta rabochikh i soldatskikh deputatov* 54, 14 October, p. 4.

[49] Medynskii, *Kak organizovat i vesti*, p. 10, p. 32.

to find the necessary means from donations and dues of local people.[50] Despite this advice, the press resonated with complaints and appeals for money from those who led educational campaigns.

The material difficulties faced by cultural-enlightenment campaigns were not just in shortage of money, but shortage of materials. One of the most frequent complaints from the soviet's enlightenment commission and from local political elites was of a shortage of books. There was a chronic shortfall in literature to feed the new needs of the public, and soviet and government sources repeatedly requested that books and reading matter be donated so that they could be distributed to libraries and reading rooms.[51] There was even explicit competition among the various cultural-enlightenment organisations operating in this quest for written material.[52] Not only was there a shortage of written materials, there was also a crisis in paper supply that attracted some attention from the socialist press. A writer on Nizhegorod's *Izvestiia* adopted a hilariously moralistic tone when he called for a boycott of the low-quality semi-pornographic material that was sold on the streets and the trams by young boys, since the paper used would be better utilised by the socialist press.[53] Materials shortage added to the sense of urgency and moral fervour that accompanied the campaigns.

SWEETENING THE MESSAGE

The discussion so far has focused on the aims of the political elite's educational campaigns, and the barriers they faced in communicating with ordinary people. If we conceptualise the elite's educational campaigns as attempts to engage ordinary people in civil society and not just to establish basic literacy, we can look at a broader range of media than the traditional means of speeches, written material and general haranguing. A range of other media was adopted by the political elite to communicate political and social messages to the population. These included theatre, songs and spectacles. As with other fields of activity, these activities were continuations of pre-revolutionary elite activities.[54] By 1903, there was a 'dense

[50] E. N. Medynskii, *Kak organizovat i vesti*, p. 10.
[51] For example, *Kazanskaia rabochaia gazeta* 13, 25 April 1917, p. 2; *Kazanskaia rabochaia gazeta* 27, 13 May 1917, p. 2; *Izvestiia Soveta rabochikh i soldatskikh deputatov* 38, 13 August 1917, p. 2.
[52] See, for example, the three separate appeals from the soviet of workers' deputies, soviet of soldiers' deputies and the soviet of peasants' deputies in Nizhnii Novgorod, all requesting book donations (*Izvestiia soveta rabochikh i soldatskikh deputatov* 38, 13 August, p. 4).
[53] *Izvestiia soveta rabochikh i soldatskikh deputatov* 22, 11 June 1917, p. 3.
[54] Frank, 'Confronting the domestic Other', pp. 95ff. Thurston, 'The impact of Russian popular theatre'.

network' of popular theatre groups operating across Russia that could serve as a basis for the sort of educational campaigning conducted in 1917.[55] After 1905, discontent with the status quo was increasingly evident in popular cultural forms, and urban culture expanded very rapidly between 1905 and 1917.[56] The more elaborate media of spectacle and theatre were most frequently seen in urban settings, since towns provided a larger audience and more amenable environment for such activities. In urban settings, there were a range of commercial entertainments on offer whose outputs overlapped with the explicitly cultural-enlightenment activities organised by the political elite. In the villages and countryside, more limited avenues of enlightenment were utilised, but they were varied none the less.

A striking feature of cultural-enlightenment work was the way in which the wholesome messages it wished to convey were sweetened with music and simple joys. Singing, theatre, public spectacles and funfairs were all regarded as important vehicles for the enlightenment process. These forms of entertainment tell us about how ordinary people used familiar, symbolic and entertaining forms of expression, as well as about how the political elite sought to construct these forms. The celebrations held by the 164th regiment in Kazan in commemoration of the revolution used colour, song, music and group activities to engage with its audience. For the occasion, on 9 April, the barracks were carefully decorated with pictures, placards and flags. General Myshlaevskii, commander of the region, watched the regiment perform manoeuvres, then the band played the Marseillaise. There was a succession of speeches, and the regiment shouted 'URA!' repeatedly together. In the evening, there was a 'diversion', with music, songs and verses, and the evening was ended with a display of fireworks.[57] Events like this engaged the interest of ordinary people with entertaining pursuits, but also provided them with information about and interpretation of revolutionary events.

Among the most frequent events held in the towns were general spectacles, variously called 'funfair-lottery-concerts' (*narodnoe gulian'e-loteriia-kontserti*). In Nizhnii Novgorod, for example, the soviet of workers' and soldiers' deputies organised a 'grand funfair-lottery-concert' to raise funds for the soviet, held in the gardens of the Kremlin (renamed the 'Gardens of Freedom') on the last Sunday in May. This started with a morning of 'children's events', then progressed to a lottery, cinematograph, buffet, and concluded with 'grandiose fireworks'.[58] The entrance fee raised significant

[55] Thurston, 'The impact of Russian popular theatre', p. 238.
[56] Von Geldern, *Entertaining tsarist Russia* (Bloomington, IN, 2000), pp. 275–6.
[57] *Kazanskaia rabochaia gazeta* 13, 25 April 1917.
[58] *Izvestiia Soveta rabochikh i soldatskikh deputatov* 18, 28 May 1917, p. 1.

funds for the soviet. Spectacles of this nature were features of Kazan's cultural life too. The Kazan soviet's cultural-enlightenment section held a fund-raising day for the soviet on 10 September that involved a succession of concerts, spectacles, bazaars and lotteries. An orchestra played military music all day long, which 'was a great success', and the halls were decorated with flowers, greenery and coloured lights.[59] These spectacles were not just fund-raising events. By engaging with the population in this way, campaigners sought to create an alternative set of rituals, and to establish a fresh cultural environment that could move ordinary people away from the dirty, 'uncultured' tea shops and taverns that were the alternative focuses of Russia's popular cultural life.

The efforts of the soviet's cultural-enlightenment section were supplemented by events organised by a whole range of other groups. In Kazan, for example, the 'old PSR group' organised a number of grand 'revolutionary evenings' that offer some indication both of the diversity and the popularity of these events. The 'revolution evening' held on 26 April was extensively advertised, and boasted a guest appearance from the revered revolutionary icon Ekaterina Breshkovskaia, as well as a 'no-loss' lottery, two orchestras, a theatre of miniatures, a 'cloth village', drama, comedy, cabaret, diversions and pictures.[60] The tickets were all sold by 13 April, and a second showing was offered for the 27 April in response to demand.[61] The day after the event, a fiercely critical letter about the event was printed in the local soviet newspaper *Kazanskaia rabochaia gazeta*. Breshkovskaia had not attended, there had been extensive speeches from senior regional SRs, and the character of the evening had been a political propaganda opportunity rather than an evening's light entertainment. As if that were not enough, it was alleged that the verses recited were pre-revolutionary and praised Nicholas II! The organisers were forced to address the discontented audience directly, and rather provocatively suggested that 'if you don't like it, you can leave'.[62] This is an illuminating exchange and offers rare feedback on the reception of such events. The hostile response of the public leaves no doubt that they were a highly critical and aware audience, who had high expectations and were not fobbed off with thinly veiled educational material, but demanded enjoyable entertainment.

Concerts and theatrical performances were frequent in Nizhnii Novgorod and Kazan towns and were enthusiastically attended by the town's population. Some of these were commercial ventures, and some were put

[59] *Kazanskaia rabochaia gazeta* 123, 12 September 1917, p. 3.
[60] *Kazanskaia rabochaia gazeta* 12, 23 April 1917, p. 1.
[61] *Kazanskaia rabochaia gazeta* 13, 25 April 1917, p. 2.
[62] *Kazanskaia rabochaia gazeta* 16, 28 April 1917, p. 3.

on by the soviet. Such performances attracted daily reviews in the socialist press.[63] There were precedents in the pre-revolutionary period of high cultural fare as vehicles for political education,[64] and the relationship between popular opinion and commercial culture became more intense through 1917.[65] Educational literature was very specific in its suggestions of how to stage plays as part of cultural-enlightenment programmes. Ostrovskii was the most popular choice, followed by Chekhov and Gogol.[66] The idea was to make these cultural experiences as accessible as possible for audiences not necessarily familiar with theatre. Plays were to be amusing, not too long and sufficiently simple that they could be effectively staged with a small cast, and without expensive and complicated props.

Theatre became increasingly politicised, and scenes from the young revolution were added to new productions.[67] There were even plays written especially for revolutionary events that recounted the events of revolution in dramatic form, and that cast Kerensky in the leading role.[68] These revolutionary diversions were not always very professional, but this only emphasised their 'democratic' nature. They also reiterate that these events were not always orchestrated by the political elite, but could reflect ordinary people's involvement in cultural enlightenment. At a soviet-organised 'soldiers' evening' held in Nizhnii Novgorod to celebrate the first day of Easter, a play was staged along with singing and dancing. Workers as well as soldiers attended. A reviewer noted charitably that the first performers were 'not at all bad', and that with 'only a small effort' they became quite good. One of the performers, a chemist called Roznatovskii, was commended specially for his free and simple speech in his roles as Fedor Dan and Vasilii Shulgin.[69] Such amateur efforts are strong indications that some aspects of the cultural-enlightenment literature were being observed; this was 'people's theatre', speaking to ordinary people in language they understood.[70] These enlightening performances were a very prominent feature of city life.

[63] *Kazanskaia rabochaia gazeta* had a regular reviews column, no. 133, 24 September 1917, just as an example.

[64] See Thurston, 'The impact of Russian popular theatre'; Swift, 'Workers' theater', p. 275.

[65] Von Geldern, *Entertaining tsarist Russia*, p. 276.

[66] On the importance of Ostrovsky to popular theatre, and the choice of repertoires, see Thurston, 'The impact of Russian popular theatre', pp. 245ff.

[67] Orlando Figes and Boris I. Kolonitskii, *Interpreting the Russian revolution: the language and symbols of 1917* (New Haven, CT, 1999), p. 46.

[68] *Izvestiia Tambovskago soveta rabochikh, soldatskikh i krest'ianskikh deputatov* 119, 24 August 1917.

[69] *Izvestiia soveta rabochikh i soldatskikh deputatov* 6, 9 April 1917, p. 4. Fedor Dan was one of the leading Mensheviks on the presidium of the Petrograd Soviet in 1917. Vasilii Shul'gin was a right-wing Duma deputy.

[70] See Swift, 'Workers' theater', p. 280; he comments that amateur performance was less important than worker involvement: 'For both actors and audiences, the performances were an affirmation of their identity as cultivated people who appreciated drama.'

A glance at newspaper advertising shows that hardly a day went by without a performance of some description.

The use of music as a means to engage ordinary people in educational efforts was well established. Listening to and participating in sung prayers was an integral part of the Orthodox faith, and a part that many ordinary people enjoyed best.[71] Medynskii's guide to establishing village cultural enlightenment activities proposed that any efforts should commence with the establishment of a village choir, and most programmes of entertainment and education involved music as well.[72] The memoirs of N. Sukhanov, a deserter in 1917, describe how he organised a demonstration in Saralovskii *volost*, Laishevskii *uezd*, Kazan. He wanted the Marseillaise to be sung, but realised that no one knew the words![73]

There were also touring musical performances, which were hugely popular. The Volynskii regiment's orchestra, of which more than half the members had higher musical education, for example, visited Nizhnii Novgorod twice in the course of its national tour and was enthusiastically welcomed. Their performance was supplemented by a meeting, at which political themes were addressed.[74] Even without the addition of political meetings, these musical evenings carried political and ideological significance. Iakov Posen, the director of Kazan's town orchestra, had a letter published in the local soviet newspaper responding to criticisms he faced from unnamed persons about his choice of music, which was allegedly aimed at the 'clean public', meaning educated society, and not at ordinary people. What this accusation inferred was that Posen's programme was too highbrow. Posen appealed to the newspaper's readers to tell him what was wrong with his musical programme, which included Robespierre's revolutionary overture, Chopin's funeral march and pieces from Glazunov, Rimsky-Korsakov and Kochetov.[75] Literary-musical evenings were popular. Cultural-enlightenment literature suggested that they be organised to coincide with the birth or death of a particular writer. These interspersed readings from well-known authors with lectures, songs and dancing. Such themed evenings were held, with some success. The workers' club in Nizhnii Novgorod organised a Chekhov evening, for example, on 15 August.[76]

---

[71] Page Herrlinger, 'Orthodoxy and the experience of factory life in St Petersburg, 1881–1905', in Melancon and Pate, *New Labor History*, pp. 35–64, p. 50.

[72] Medynskii, *Kak organizovat i vesti*, esp. pp. 6–8.

[73] N. N. Sukhanov, 'Iz proshlogo: etiudi fevralskoi revoliutsii', *Kommunisticheskii put* 2 (1923), 61–65, p. 62.

[74] *Izvestiia soveta rabochikh i soldatskikh deputatov* 48, 24 September 1917, pp. 2–3.

[75] *Kazanskaia rabochaia gazeta* 26, 11 May 1917, p. 4; letter from Posen defending his musical programme.

[76] *Izvestiia soveta rabochikh i soldatskikh deputatov* 38, 13 August 1917, p. 1.

The sometimes elaborate manifestations described above were predominantly city-based events. Events were organised in the countryside, but they tended to be much simpler in form, reflecting the practical difficulties of organising in the villages. They did, however, share features with the more sophisticated city events, utilising music, colour, entertainment and group activities to mobilise participants. Demonstrations and celebrations of freedom and the revolution were often held in the villages. They might involve a march around the streets of the village carrying coloured flags and placards, and conclude with speeches from prominent locals and outside agitators. The village priest frequently played an important role in such procedures, saying a prayer to open events.[77] In Bolshe Akhmutov village, Sergachskii *uezd*, Nizhegorod province, the priest even blessed the red flag with holy water in preparation for a visit by soldier deputies from the soviet.[78] The participation of the priest offered villagers a reassuring air of continuity; just as he had led and participated in pre-revolutionary festivals and events, so his role in the revolutionary proceedings lent an air of normality to the new era.[79]

The most important, and most widely advertised, public holiday of 1917 was that called to celebrate May Day. This socialist holiday provided an opportunity for a wide range of public consciousness-raising activities. The socialist parties, alongside the soviet's cultural-enlightenment section, played the most prominent role in bringing the celebrations to fruition. May Day, held on 18 April to coincide with the Julian calendar, was widely advertised and reported in the socialist press. Reports came in from towns and villages on the size and success of the May Day holidays. The holiday was imbued with different meanings according to the agenda of the organisers. Most widely, it was used to celebrate Russia's new-found political freedom, and to herald the unity of working peoples. At the celebrations held by the Sormovo and Kanavin factories in Nizhnii Novgorod, around 80,000 people attended, carrying 150 flags.[80] These banners defined the procession of the demonstration, and the banners denoted a range of different affiliations, with party devices an important feature of affairs:

[77] For example, Sukhanov, 'Iz proshlogo', p. 62: Sukhanov was a deserting soldier who was based in Saralovskii *volost*, Laishevskii *uezd*, Kazan province, and he described the demonstration arranged by him and some visiting student agitators.

[78] *Izvestiia soveta soldatskikh i rabochikh deputatov* 19, 1 June 1917, p. 1; report from soviet deputies' journey around the *uezds*.

[79] For similar events in Viatka, see Retish, 'Peasant identities in Russia's turmoil', pp. 123–4.

[80] RGASPI, f. 274, op. 1, d. 26, l. 112; Magergut's memoir.

Slowly and solemnly, in immaculate order, the dense columns of workers and citizens advanced. Every factory shop came forward separately with their banners, and every party section under the leadership of its representatives. The PSR's workers' and peasants' organisations presented their own especially beautiful picture. The whole banner was embroidered and painted with loving care with the party's devices and slogans – 'In struggle you will get your rights', 'Land and freedom' and others – these swayed over harmonious columns of thousands of organised comrades. In every hand, on every breast, in every buttonhole, were red bands, bows, ribbons with party initials and divisions.[81]

In Kazan, the dominant Menshevik group tried to harness the goodwill generated by the event to solder over the factions in the Social Democratic Party.[82] The Kazan celebrations included a procession around town. The town's different party groups all formed, and were greeted with varying degrees of enthusiasm by the procession of workers and soldiers.[83] As well as events organised by the soviet, political parties took advantage of the heightened political mood to hold meetings throughout the day. This was a forum for political competition as well as for working solidarity. There was hostility, for example, between the 'bourgeois' 'Ittifaku-Musilmin' (Tatar nationalist party) and the Muslim socialist committee, which held competing meetings throughout the day.[84] In Balakhna, Nizhegorod province, the May Day celebrations were reported to have been a great success, and raised 147 roubles. The organisers of the Balakhna festivities included the presidents of the town's SR and SD organisations.[85] It was remarked that the demonstration and meeting held that day were 'impressive for Balakhna', and suggested that they constituted a revolutionary awakening for the town.[86]

CONCLUSIONS

The first and most important question to ask is to what extent 1917 represented a continuity of pre-1917 educational efforts. The efforts of campaigners built on the activities of pre-revolutionary educational activists and were able to tap into increasing societal interest in education. The drive for

[81] GARF, f. 9591c., op. 1, d. 11, l. 13; xeroxed three-page leaflet, first page missing, signed by Tiurikov, undated.

[82] There were a number of well-known Mensheviks in Kazan, including Iu. P. Denike, who worked for unity of the Social Democrats (Z. Galili, *The Menshevik leaders in the Russian revolution: social realities and political strategies* (Princeton, NJ, and Guildford, 1989), pp. 196–7).

[83] K. Magnov, 'Dni Oktiabria', *Kommunisticheskii put* 12 (1922), 98–117, p. 99.

[84] Rakhmatullin, 'Mulla-Nur Vakhitov', p. 37.

[85] *Izvestiia soveta rabochikh i soldatskikh deputatov* 11, 13 May 1917, p. 4.

[86] *Izvestiia soveta rabochikh i soldatskikh deputatov* 15, 18 May 1917, p. 4.

enlightenment witnessed in 1917 was, however, on an entirely different scale to the educational campaigns that had preceded it. It involved all sectors of educated society and utilised an incredibly diverse array of means to forward its aims. Crucially, the 1917 campaign was imbued with fresh urgency, as it was apparent both to Russia's political elite and to her grass-roots activists that if their vision of a democratic, ordered, egalitarian Russia was to be implemented, and civil war avoided, their education campaigns had to succeed in enlightening the population. While cultural-enlightenment campaigns were posited as non-partisan, they actually reflected the specifically socialist climate of revolutionary Russia and acted as a forum for political competition and for partisan political activities.

The aims of cultural-enlightenment campaigners were far-reaching and ambitious. They sought to engender a fundamental transformation of Russian socio-political life, using the gains of the February revolution as a starting point, and education as the lynchpin of their efforts. Their campaigns sought to bridge the gap between the perceptions of educated society, and those of 'the people'. The campaigners of 1917, though they may have presented their vision of revolution in a partial way, never contemplated violent means of enforcing it. Their naïve faith in the power of education was striking but misplaced, and is reflected in the general feeling that the failure of these campaigns to realise their lofty ambitions was predicated on the inability of Russia's dark population to understand their message. Communication and alien language between educators and villagers was not, however, the fundamental problem that educators faced. A diverse range of educational forms were utilised in cultural-enlightenment activities, a major feature of which was the sweetening of educational material with music, theatre and diversions. Public holidays, especially May Day, provided a major forum for cultural-enlightenment campaigners. It is nonsense to blame the failure of the political elite's programmes to be adopted by Russia's ordinary people on questions of communication. Cultural-enlightenment programmes were stymied not by the language used, but by the content of their messages. This becomes apparent when we study the problems of land and food supplies in chapters 7 and 8.

CHAPTER 6

Soldiers and their wives

In 1917, Russian soldiers and their wives demanded that the revolution represent and reflect their interests and concerns. Their actions and demands shaped the revolution and contributed to the confusion and sense of disorder that were defining features of 1917. The actions and impact of the unarmed soldiers' wives alongside the actions and impact of their armed and mobilised husbands demonstrates the commonality of the experience of war and highlights that troop mobilisation was perhaps the single most important factor in shaping experiences of the revolution. The recent work of Joshua Sanborn explored the role of military conscription in forming national identities and in transmitting the violence of war to civilian Russia in the course of the civil war.[1] This chapter explores the role played by soldiers and their wives and illustrates in part Sanborn's thesis of conscripted soldiers as the source of escalating violence and collapsing authority in provincial life. Whether deserters, members of reserve regiments, prisoners of war, on leave or invalids, soldiers played a highly vocal and visible role in political life. This was partly because they were armed, and had clear and easily identifiable group identity. Regional power structures depended on soldier support, both for their own safety and for the maintenance of their orders. When force or violence occurred in civilian life, it almost invariably included soldier participants. Soldiers' wives were a less visible group, but this study of their actions shows that like their soldier husbands, they sought to be recognised as citizens, to have their grievances addressed and to have their voices heard in local politics. In so doing they, like their husbands, contributed to a rising sense of crisis and the collapse of formal authority.

The sheer numbers of soldiers stationed in the provincial capitals demands that they be paid particular attention. Both Kazan and Nizhnii Novgorod were hosts to garrisons, Nizhnii Novgorod housing a garrison of

---

[1] Sanborn, *Drafting the Russian nation.*

145

some 40,000, and Kazan a garrison of around 50,000. Nizhnii Novgorod's garrison was made up predominantly of reserve infantry regiments and numerically approached workers as a force in the town.[2] A further 12,000 men from the front arrived in Nizhnii Novgorod in June 1917. Most of the troops, some 40,000 men, were situated in Nizhnii Novgorod town itself, with small but significant military units stationed in the *uezd* capital towns.[3] The pattern of distribution was similar in Kazan, with most troops based in Kazan town itself. The logistical problems of providing living space and provisions for such large numbers of men were supplemented by the demands of newly fledged 'citizen soldiers' to take a role in the governance of the province and to decide their own fates. While chapter 4 has shown that soldiers played an important role as local leaders and administrators, this chapter will highlight their more pernicious implications. Soldier presence heightened violence, pressure on transport and recreation facilities, and increased anti-social behaviour.

WHO WERE THE SOLDIERS?

The social revolution experienced in 1917 produced dramatic changes for ordinary working people both in their perceived status and in their expectations of the state. These changes were felt especially keenly in the army. Some aspects of 1917's social revolution fundamentally undermined what would normally be considered to be essential features of soldiers' lives. In the act of mobilisation, the state called upon men to give their liberty and if necessary their lives in defence of the state. All modern armies to some extent dehumanised and denied individualism to the men who entered their ranks. In order to be part of the military machine, men had to submit to orders unquestioningly, and they had to value the collective will above individualism. It was this submission to the collective, and to all higher authority, that allowed armies to function, and that allowed the seeming absurdity of mass slaughter in the name of a greater cause.[4]

Soldiers, along with the rest of the population, adopted with ardour the exercise of individual freedoms and 'rights'. In place of 'soldier slaves', Russia now boasted soldier-citizens, whose rights when not on duty to all

---

[2] Golub, et al., *Entsiklopediia*, pp. 214–15, p. 336.
[3] *Izvestiia soveta rabochikh i soldatskikh deputatov* 16, 22 May 1917, p. 4; location and numbers of troops in Nizhnii garrison, with 40,000 in the town itself and between 25 and 400 scattered around each of the eleven *uezd* towns.
[4] See Sanborn, *Drafting the Russian nation*, p. 10.

the freedoms accorded to other citizens were loudly proclaimed.[5] The reality of this situation was harsh for Russia's administrators. They were faced with a mass of armed men who no longer felt obliged to submit to the orders of the state, and who took upon themselves citizens' rights and dues. Soldier-citizen was widely used and accepted within 1917's popular revolutionary discourse, but in real terms it was something of a contradiction. Soldiers could not be soldiers when they were accorded the same rights as other citizens. The state was obliged to request, rather than to order, and the fate of the state was left to the goodwill of soldiers. This assessment of soldiers in the rear illustrates the problem of soldier-citizen.

The phrase 'peasants in greatcoats' has often been coined to describe soldiers in 1917. Such broad and undifferentiated descriptions helped observers try to comprehend and interpret complex and rapidly changing political situations, but they are unhelpful in understanding the complexity and diversity of soldiers' social identities. While mobilisation and conditions of service were significant in providing common grievances for the soldier body, soldiers encompassed a diverse array of competing and conflicting identities. For some soldiers, peasant identity carried equal or even greater weight than any distinct soldier identity. Soldier-peasant soviets and executive committees formed in Petrograd and Kharkiv during 1917.[6] Similar bodies emerged in Nizhegorod and Kazan at levels from division up to garrison. At the first regional meeting of soldiers' soviets held in Kazan on 29 July, one delegate provoked rapturous applause when he declared; 'I, as a villager, wish to say that orators speak, but that they did not learn. Our wish is to obtain land and freedom, and as you soldiers are by a large part also peasants, then you understand, that only through unity can our wish be fulfilled.'[7]

In Kazan, soldier-peasant soviets were formed in several units, on the general principle of defence of peasant interests. The soldiers' soviet was hostile to soldier-peasant soviets, as its leaders recognised that peasant organisations in their midst threatened to undermine a united and distinctive soldier identity.[8] For other soldiers, ethnic, religious or national identities divided them from their fellow soldiers. The tsarist government had allowed the

---

[5] As laid out in order no. 1. Issued by the Petrograd Soviet, and intended only for the Petrograd garrison, this order quickly spread across the army (Browder and Kerensky, *Russian Provisional Government*, vol. III, documents 744–7).

[6] Melancon, 'Soldiers, peasant-soldiers'; Baker, 'Peasants, power and revolution', chapter 2.

[7] *Kazanskaia rabochaia gazeta* 95, 6 August 1917, p. 4.

[8] *Izvestiia Kazanskago gubernskago soveta krest'ianskikh deputatov* 18, 1 October 1917, p. 3. See also NART f. 983, op. 1, d. 23, l. 208; meeting of divisional soviet of soldier-peasants, 6 May 1917.

formation of some ethnic units in August 1914,[9] and the differentiation of ethnicity continued in 1917, despite resistance from the political elite.[10] Ukrainians petitioned successfully to form their own independent divisions. The Ukrainians that formed part of the mutinous 62nd regiment in Nizhnii Novgorod later formed their own national brigade.[11] Muslim soldiers, who formed an important minority in the army, increasingly sought to identify themselves religiously rather than ethnically. There were some one and a half million Muslim soldiers serving in 1917,[12] and as the new rights and freedoms of citizen-soldiers filtered down through the ranks, so Muslim soldiers increasingly sought to assert their own specific identity. Salavat Iskhakov considered that the most significant and the most widely spread of the Muslim movements in 1917 was among soldiers. Iskhakov suggests that the need to take religious and national interests of soldiers into account made itself felt increasingly strongly.[13] The soviet of workers and soldiers' deputies in Nizhnii Novgorod agreed to send out literature in Arabic for front-line soldiers.[14] The first attempted formation of a Muslim regiment was in Kazan's 95th reserve regiment, in May, and Muslims made repeated requests to have their own regiment in the active army.[15]

Muslim soldiers rarely succeeded in forcing the authorities to recognise their interests. The proposal to have two extra Muslim representatives for soldiers on the Kazan peasants' soviet executive committee was refused.[16] Muslim soldiers petitioned, usually without success, for various concessions to be made to them on the basis of their religion. While the Kazan military region decreed in mid-June that Muslims would be freed from active service on Fridays, a similar request from Muslim soldiers in Nizhnii Novgorod garrison was turned down, as 'holidays cannot be granted separately from Orthodox holidays'.[17] This willingness to accommodate Muslim soldiers in Kazan but not Nizhnii Novgorod may reflect the large numbers of Muslims in both the local population and the reserve regiments

[9] Sanborn, *Drafting the Russian nation*, p. 76.

[10] Salavat Iskhakov, *Rossiiskie musul'mane i revoliutsiia* (Moscow, 2004), p. 223; the question of national regiments was discussed by the Petrograd Soviet on 9 May, and it was decided not to offer support for these regiments on practical grounds.

[11] *Izvestiia soveta rabochikh i soldatskikh deputatov* 25, 25 June 1917, pp. 1, 4. On the problems of separate Ukrainian divisions, see Sanborn, *Drafting the Russian nation*, p. 81.

[12] *Kazanskaia rabochaia gazeta* 95, 6 August 1917, p. 4; from report of first regional Muslim soldiers' meeting.

[13] Iskhakov, *Rossiiskie musul'mane*, p. 222, p. 224.

[14] *Izvestiia soveta rabochikh i soldatskikh deputatov* 40, 20 August 1917, p. 4.

[15] Iskhakov, *Rossiiskie musul'mane*, p. 225.

[16] NART, f. 983, op. 1, d. 13, l. 50; protocol of the meeting of Kazan provincial soviet of peasants' deputies, 19 September 1917.

[17] *Izvestiia soveta rabochikh i soldatskikh deputatov* 45, 14 September 1917, p. 2.

in Kazan. Kazan was the venue for the first meeting of Muslim military personnel, though the commander of the Kazan military region, P. A. Kovichenko, refused to attend. He offended the organisers of the meeting by declaring that 'now, when blood is being spilt at the front, is not the time to chat'.[18] Kovichenko's attitude indicates that the military elite was reluctant to acknowledge Muslim soldiers' attempts to assert their religious identity.

Even within those seeing themselves first and foremost as soldiers, loyalties and self-definitions were sharply divided. The loyalty to one's own division or regiment could be compelling. Evacuees from the front were a complex group, who in some cases identified themselves as distinct from the active army and formed their own subset. Invalids and war-wounded in some cases identified themselves as such and organised on these terms. The war invalids of two *volosts* in Nizhnii Novgorod province met formally and demanded from the provincial executive committee that committees be formed for invalids at local (*raion*) level, and that *uezd* and provincial committees should be formed. A number of other invalid demands were made.[19] The soldiers' greatcoats encompassed a range of identities and agendas, not just peasants.

RAISING HELL IN TOWN AND COUNTRY

Soldiers' impact on day-to-day life in Nizhegorod and Kazan provinces is not quantifiable. We cannot state with precision what proportion of soldiers were disorderly, or exactly what the implications of their actions were, but a broad reading of archival sources and local newspapers suggests that soldiers contributed significantly to the sense of crisis that pervaded 1917. The transformation of soldiers into soldier-citizens in 1917 made them an imposing presence in civilian life. They participated in the meetings and public events that characterised the revolution. In their free time, soldiers strolled around town, went to tea shops, bars, cinemas and theatres. Their position as part-time civilians was one that could be, and was, abused. Soldiers on duty were reported wandering around town without convoy or uniform.[20] Hooliganism, illicit trade, pressure on public services and particularly pressure on the transport system all made soldier presence in the towns very noticeable. Finally, the presence of soldiers in town raised the crime rate,

[18] Iskhakov, *Rossiiskie musul' mane*, p. 233.
[19] GANO, f. 1887, op. 1, d. 20, l. 26; decree from invalids of Elkhovskii and Borisopol'skii *volosts* to provincial executive committee, 23 April 1917.
[20] *Izvestiia soveta rabochikh i soldatskikh deputatov* 44, 10 September 1917, p. 1.

and crime and public fear of crime were highly charged political issues.[21] A letter to the local newspaper *Kazanskaia rabochaia gazeta* in April from 'comrade soldier Solov'ev' appealed to Kazan soldiers to 'behave appropriately' in town, as they were behaving 'too freely and wilfully' (*slishkom uzhe razviazno i vol'no*), without concern for who was around them.[22] Even without disorderly behaviour, the very presence of soldiers in the town placed pressure on town amenities. Housing shortages in urban areas were accentuated by the need to house soldiers. The town bathhouses were inundated with tens of thousands of dirty soldiers as well as the townspeople they had been meant for, with the result that prices rose, standards fell and establishments closed.[23]

The overstretched transport system often provided a flashpoint for pressure on amenities and soldier-civilian tensions. The Nizhnii Novgorod town administration reported cases of armed soldiers stopping the trams, filling them, refusing to pay and preventing other passengers from alighting. The soviet of soldiers' deputies was asked 'in the most respectful terms' to do something about this and issued a gently worded appeal accordingly.[24] A declaration was made in the Kazan newspapers in April reiterating that soldiers without tickets and proper documents did not have the right to travel on railways, and that class restrictions were maintained.[25] Such appeals did not resolve these problems. In September in Kazan, a group of soldiers demanded tickets without queuing and eventually beat up their own soviet deputy who was sent to negotiate with them.[26] Soldiers' elected representatives were subject to the same scrutiny and outright hostility as any other part of the community who presented a challenge to what soldiers perceived as their interests.

The presence of soldiers in civilian settings had a significant impact on the civilian community, even where soldiers were not behaving unlawfully. A reader's letter to the Kazan soviet newspaper in April complained that

[S]oldiers on the street often badgered women . . . women say, 'its impossible to go past the barracks, and one doesn't know where to turn for shame'. Many argue that these tricks are carried out by hooligans on leave, saying that 'no family is without a monster', and so on. Even soldiers on patrol are accused.[27]

---

[21] See Hickey, 'Moderate socialists', p. 189.   [22] *Kazanskaia rabochaia gazeta* 6, 15 April 1917, p. 4.

[23] *Kazanskaia rabochaia gazeta* 13, 25 April 1917, p. 2. The price for bathing rose by 100 per cent on 7 July (*Kazanskaia rabochaia gazeta* 71, 7 July 1917, p. 1).

[24] *Izvestiia soveta rabochikh i soldatskikh deputatov* 24, 22 June 1917, p. 4.

[25] *Kazanskaia rabochaia gazeta* 6, 15 April 1917, p. 4.

[26] *Kazanskaia rabochaia gazeta* 148, 13 September 1917, p. 3.

[27] *Kazanskaia rabochaia gazeta* 5, 14 April 1917, p. 4.

The writer went on to say that she and her mother were addressed in foul language as they passed a mounted patrol of two soldiers. She concluded with the stark warning that many people considered the old regime to be better. People had been able to go about their business quietly and were not permitted to offend others: 'freedom is one thing, and hooliganism another'.[28] What might seem to be innocent boisterousness on the part of soldiers had a real impact on the local community and heightened the sense of crisis and dissatisfaction with the new regime. In Nizhnii Novgorod the *zemstvo* administration filed a special report in September about the activities of the soldiers of the 183rd and 185th regiments who went into Kuznochikha, the village adjoining their billets, on their holidays. It was reported that these soldiers 'drank there, bothered the women with filthy proposals, sang incorrect songs, offered to sell state property, and in general comported themselves not as soldiers of a free republic, but soldiers not fit even for the old regime'.[29]

Soldiers contributed to a lively black market in their kit and weapons, which further heightened this sense of disorder and lawlessness. Even before the February revolution, the commander of the Kazan military region requested that measures be taken to halt soldiers' extensive trade in illegally brewed alcohol.[30] Soldiers' goods were sold in the ubiquitous street side-stalls and found their way into local shops. Galoshes were apparently a particularly popular item of sale. In Nizhnii Novgorod, the executive committee was forced to intervene and control the sale of all galoshes, as large quantities of army supplies were appearing in local shops.[31] Extra patrols were established on one Nizhnii Novgorod street to try and control soldier-traders, but such measures were of limited impact.[32] This trade continued unabated through 1917. In November, the soviet of soldiers' deputies announced that anyone caught buying or selling state property would be arrested.[33] In the scavenge for cash and goods, soldiers even sold their own labour. A decree published in Nizhnii Novgorod specifically forbade the employment of soldiers in private enterprises.[34]

Trading and petty rabble-rousing heightened a sense of crisis in provincial urban life, but the soldiers' most significant contribution to civilian life

---

[28] *Kazanskaia rabochaia gazeta* 5, 14 April 1917, p. 4.
[29] *Nizhegorodskaia zemskaia gazeta* 39, 28 September 1917, p. 6.
[30] NART, f. 1246, op. 1, d. 17, ll. 165–9; letters dated 18 February 1917.
[31] *Izvestiia soveta rabochikh i soldatskikh deputatov* 45, 14 September 1917, p. 2.
[32] *Izvestiia soveta rabochikh i soldatskikh deputatov* 24, 22 June 1917, p. 4.
[33] *Krasnoe znamia* 4, 21 November 1917, p. 4.
[34] GANO, f. 1887, op. 1, d. 3, l. 79; compulsory decree of Nizhegorod province executive committee, 4 August 1917.

was their import of military violence into civilian life.[35] The presence of soldiers raised the likelihood of violence and correspondingly reduced the administration's chances of doing much to restrict violence and disorder. In Tsivilsk town, Kazan province, the soldiers stationed there demanded that they be sold wine and beer. When they were refused, they seized the cellar key and started to drink the beer reserves. The garrison was very drunk for a couple of days, until at last the *uezd* executive committee resolved the crisis by adding kerosene to the beer to spoil it.[36] The *uezd* administration was exposed as powerless in real terms against the soldiers in their midst. There were no means available for administrators to control their supposed protectors, apart from to wait for a punitive expedition from a neighbouring barracks. Such alcohol-related problems were replicated elsewhere and can be compared to traditional forms of peasant and worker violence. The *uezd* commissar of Spasskii *uezd*, Kazan province, noted that soldier disorders often flared up after alcohol seizures had been made in the town.[37] As well as alcohol-fuelled violence, arbitrary violence was increased by the presence of armed men on the streets. The papers reported such incidents, like the shopkeeper murdered by two soldiers for just ten roubles,[38] or the bloody retribution exacted on a soldier accused of shoplifting by fellow soldiers in Kazan town.[39]

Finally, some soldier disorders were not such general and disarrayed hooliganism, but trenchant political gestures that challenged town administration directly. One such example was the attack on the retired tsarist General Sanetskii in Kazan. This event was described in the local press as 'an illegal rising of an active armed force'.[40] A small group of soldiers disobeyed their commanders and went to the Red Cross station with the intention of seizing Sanetskii. They were joined en route by an 'imposing crowd' of soldiers, and despite the interventions of the town commander and soviet members, the general was seized and forcibly removed to the guardhouse. In Nizhnii Novgorod, soldiers guarding trainee officers

[35] Graham Tan noted a strong correlation between violence and soldier presence in Ukraine during 1917, though the area in question was close to battle lines, which may have heightened soldiers' violent behaviour (Graham Tan, 'Village social organisation and peasant action: right bank Ukraine during the revolution, 1917–1923', unpublished PhD thesis, School of Slavonic and East European Studies, University of London (1999), p. 68).

[36] NART, f. 1246, op. 1, d. 49, l. 11; letter from Tsivilskii *uezd* commissar to provincial commissar, 30 June 1917.

[37] NART, f. 1246, op. 1, d. 41, l. 134; report from Spasskii *uezd* commissar to Kazan provincial commissar, 28 April 1917.

[38] *Kazanskaia rabochaia gazeta* 95, 6 August 1917, p. 3.

[39] *Kazanskaia rabochaia gazeta* 35, 24 May 1917, p. 3.

[40] *Kazanskaia rabochaia gazeta* 28, 14 May 1917, p. 4.

who had been captured during the garrison's revolt in July were themselves threatened by large groups of off-duty soldiers, who subjected them to threats and abuse, as they were intent on carrying out *samosud* against the captured officers.[41] Such events point up the problems of soldier 'leadership'. Citizen-soldiers proved to be fickle in their submission to their elected leaders, and when a group embarked on a course of action contrary to the position taken by their leaders, there was little short of brute force that could restrain them.

The role of soldiers in Cheboksary town, Kazan province, was directly and unambiguously political. Cheboksary was the scene of confrontational and violent political squabbling from the outset in 1917, predicated partly by a young student-activist Karl Grasis. Grasis was only able to cause such a stir in local politics because he won the backing of a cohort of soldier and sailor supporters, who backed the prognostications of Grasis with threats and violence. The State Duma deputy, Rossolovskii, was called in to resolve the power crisis, but when he denounced Grasis at a public meeting, he was beaten and imprisoned by a crowd of soldiers and sailors. Five hundred soldiers who were freed from active service for summer fieldwork proved to be fertile ground for Grasis' supporters, and many refused to leave the town, adding to the sense of crisis and violence that pervaded Cheboksary.[42]

The heavy concentration of soldiers in Kazan and Nizhnii Novgorod towns accentuated their profile, and the soldiers' rising in Nizhnii Novgorod on 4–5 July exposed the power of garrison soldiers, the impotence of their military and political leaders; it also revealed something of the political climate of the garrison. The causes for the rising were complex but included evacuees' resistance to being sent to the front, hostility to workers and a total loss of the military subordination necessary in mobilised men. It revealed the lack of authority soldiers' leaders felt, and the authorities' difficulties in dealing with recalcitrant soldiers. The core of the rising was formed by the 62nd reserve regiment, which included a large number of convalescing soldiers. F. E. Golov was one of these evacuees. Golov was a peasant who had entered the army in 1912 and was wounded in the leg during front-line battle during 1917. He was sent to the rear for three months to recuperate with the 62nd reserve regiment. Golov claims that there was a 'revolutionary mood' in the 62nd regiment, with thirteen active Bolsheviks counted among its numbers.[43] Evacuees threatened the established soviet and Provisional

---

[41] Shul′gin, *Za vlast sovetov*, p. 117; recollections of F. E. Golov, a soldier in the 62nd reserve regiment.
[42] For a more detailed discussion of the situation in Cheboksary, see Badcock, 'Saviour to pariah'.
[43] Shul′gin, *Za vlast sovetov*, pp. 114–15; Golov's recollections.

Government administrations from as early as the beginning of May, when they formed a separate organisation.[44] There was an acceleration of tension in the garrison in June, when some reserve regiments were sent to the front to support the June offensive. Some of the garrison's evacuees campaigned against the offensive, going round the barracks and holding demonstrations in town.

A key element of the evacuees' complaints was that all semi-specialist and unspecialised workers should be sent to the front in their place. They even threatened to storm the factories and seize workers to satisfy themselves that workers hiding from military service had been rooted out.[45] The soviet and soldier leaders tried to reassure soldiers that appropriate measures were being taken. 'Complaints from the trenches' led to close searches being made of the Sormovo factory complex at the end of May, and more than 1,000 draft-evaders were found.[46] The Nizhnii Novgorod soviet of soldiers' deputies received so many tip-offs about draft-dodgers that they were unable to act on all of them, and warned that if sent anonymously such tip-offs would be discarded.[47] The level of hostility to workers displayed by soldiers in Nizhnii Novgorod was not just a reflection of popular hostility towards 'bourgeois' draft-dodgers but reflected a deeper discomfort in relations between workers and soldiers, which did not accord with Soviet memoirists' claims of close links between Sormovo workers and the 62nd regiment.[48] Though soldiers and workers in many respects displayed unity in their political actions, these assaults on workers indicate that worker–soldier harmony was not absolute.

Sources are hazy as to the exact causes and events of the soldiers' rising. Local newspapers elaborate very little, due no doubt to a reluctance on their part to report events that so harshly contravened the political elite's ideals of revolutionary consciousness. From archival, newspaper and memoir accounts, we can, however, piece events together. Archival and newspaper sources suggest that the 62nd regiment's dispatch to the front provided the spark for soldier resentments. The 62nd Infantry reserve regiment was escorted by a group of trainee officers to the station on 4 July, where several of the 62nd regiment escaped. They returned to the barracks to ask for help from their comrades, and several soldiers were killed in a bloody

---

[44] *Izvestiia soveta rabochikh i soldatskikh deputatov* 12, 7 May 1917, p. 1; 13, 11 May 1917, p. 4.

[45] *Izvestiia soveta rabochikh i soldatskikh deputatov* 24, 22 June 1917, p. 1.

[46] *Izvestiia soveta rabochikh i soldatskikh deputatov* 20, 4 June 1917, p. 4.

[47] *Izvestiia soveta rabochikh i soldatskikh deputatov* 21, 8 June 1917, p. 4.

[48] Golov's memoirs claimed that the regiment's Bolsheviks had links with the Sormovo workers, one of whom was Golov's brother (Shul'gin, *Za vlast sovetov*, pp. 114–15).

conflict between trainee officers and garrison members at the station on the night of 4 July. The trainee officers were arrested, along with other loyal elements in the garrison, and the evacuees freed. By this stage the soldiers' volition accelerated way beyond the reach of their elected soviet deputies. The mutinous soldiers disbanded the soviet of soldiers' deputies.

The political elite of the town responded by trying to wrest control of the rising into their hands. A 'New Provisional executive committee' (NPEC) was formed, with two representatives each from PSR, Bolshevik and Menshevik factions, and five representatives from the soviet of workers' deputies and professional unions. The NPEC formed an armed militia, to defend public order by protecting the factories and key points around the town. The night of the 5 July saw a culmination of the threat to public order, with numerous reports of robberies and attempts on alcohol stores. Our Soviet memoirist Golov recalls that there were incidents of severe drunkenness among soldiers but put this down to rather far-fetched deliberate sabotage by 'counter-revolutionary forces'.[49] The NPEC responded by sending out their members, accompanied by loyal soldiers, for the defence of alcohol stores and other parts of the town. Their success in this defence was limited, because they had no cars for rapid response to the outbreaks of disorder around the town.[50] The soviet of workers' deputies also distributed arms to workers, soldiers and private individuals, for self-defence and the formation of militias.

Troops from Moscow military region, led by General Verkhovskii, the head of the region, were sent by the Provisional Government to control the situation in the town. Despite appeals by the soviet of workers' deputies to these troops to stay outside the town in order to avoid bloodshed, they entered the town on 6 July and re-established order. A Soviet memoirist recalls that the mood among soldiers and workers was combative.[51] After 'two days of fierce terror in the town', with Cossacks and armoured cars patrolling to restore order, Verkhovskii succeeded in disarming the soldiers.[52] The 62nd, and also the most active elements of the 182nd and 185th regiments were sent to the front on 7 July. More than two hundred soldiers were arrested, though all but nine were freed soon afterwards.[53] The NPEC, although ostensibly the leaders of this 'rising', actually sought to control the

[49] Shul'gin, *Za vlast sovetov*, pp. 116–17; Golov's memoir.
[50] D. A. Chugaev, L. S. Gaponenko, M. D. Smuchebnikov, I. U. Tomashevich, A. V. Chernov, and L. E. Iakovlev, *Revoliutsionnoe dvizhenie v Rossii v iiule 1917g. Iiulskii krizis* (Moscow, 1959), doc. 110, pp. 133–4, from the newspaper *International* (Nizhnii Novgorod, 12 July 1917).
[51] Shul'gin, *Za vlast sovetov*, p. 47; memoirs of Sormovo worker P. E. Vorobev.
[52] Shul'gin, *Za vlast sovetov*, p. 117; Golov's memoir.
[53] Shul'gin, *Za vlast sovetov*, p. 118; Golov's memoir.

garrison's actions and prevent further bloodshed. The obduracy between the Bolsheviks and other socialist parties was forgotten in the struggle to establish order in the garrison and prevent a total collapse of public order. Lenin subsequently remarked that the suppression of the rising was one of the first signs of factual transfer of state power to the hands of counter-revolutionaries.[54] Local Bolsheviks did not share this position even after their October seizure of power. In an editorial at the end of November, the Bolshevik paper *Krasnoe znamia* described the July rising as an elemental rising, provoked by 'Kerensky's provocateurs and the clumsy tactics of the Menshevik soviet'.[55] It was careful to deny rumours that the Bolsheviks had played any part in the rising's instigation. This version was to change in the stories of subsequent Soviet memoirists.

A commentary in a soviet newspaper in Moscow noted that the tactics of the Nizhnii Novgorod evacuees were similar to those of Moscow evacuees; in both cities evacuees shared the aim of ending the war and demonstrated a lack of consciousness, which meant they were unable to recognise their sense of duty.[56] Though there was clearly common ground between the evacuees in Nizhnii Novgorod and Moscow, not all evacuees shared these aims. Though Kazan's evacuees had, like Nizhnii's evacuees, a clear self-awareness, met regularly as a group and formed their own association, they stood far to the right of the Nizhnii group. The Kazan union of evacuated military was 16,000 strong at the end of April and delegated their representatives to the soviet of workers, soldiers and peasants' deputies. The political tone of this union was extremely moderate. Their declarations expressed a complete and unwavering faith in the Provisional Government that was at odds with most of the press.[57] Its appeals for organisation and unity were frequently published in the socialist press and carried an exceptionally moderate and upbeat tone.[58] They were described as 'weak in body, but strong in spirit, deriving great joy that they could continue to work for the good of the country',[59] and participated in a range of fund-raising and cultural-enlightenment activities. They established an office to supply the town with brochures on contemporary themes, for example.[60] Even in October, when the political climate was swinging firmly to the left, the evacuees' union continued to be active, creating a fund to finance the building of an evacuee

[54] V. I. Lenin, *Polnoe sobranie sochinenii* (Moscow, 1977), vol. XXXIV, p. 1.
[55] *Krasnoe znamia* 8, 26 November 1917, p. 1.
[56] *Izvestiia soveta rabochikh i soldatskikh deputatov* 29, 13 July 1917, p. 2.
[57] *Kazanskaia rabochaia gazeta* 26, 11 May 1917, p. 4; *Kazanskaia rabochaia gazeta* 73, 11 July 1917, p. 3.
[58] See, for example, *Kazanskaia rabochaia gazeta* 45, 4 June 1917, p. 4.
[59] *Kazanskaia rabochaia gazeta* 71, 7 July 1917, p. 4.
[60] *Kazanskaia rabochaia gazeta* 89, 30 July 1917, p. 3.

hostel.[61] The moderation of the Kazan evacuees indicates that evacuees as a group were not inevitably predisposed to radicalism and disorder. Harder to define internal features such as particularly influential grass-roots leaders, the background of the particular evacuees involved, and the reasons for their evacuation, clearly played an important part in the formation of their political attitudes.

Ultimately, such risings threatened the hegemony of the soviets, as well as disrupting public order. The soviets, popularly elected, self-proclaimed representatives of working and toiling people, were forced to take stern measures against their own constituents in order to maintain public order. In the aftermath of the rising, alternative explanations of the events were mooted, which allowed the soviet to present itself as continuing to defend and represent its constituents. Some clearly pointed the finger at the Bolsheviks.[62] At a pre-electoral meeting for the soviet of soldiers' deputies on 27 July, a report given by a member of the executive committee Malafeev related the soldiers' rising directly to a counter-revolutionary movement sweeping across Russia, initiated by black hundreds conspirators and Guchkov among others.[63] In this way the rising was rebranded as something emanating from dangerous counter-revolutionary forces.

A longer-term problem provoked by the rising was the general arming of the population, which was to prove difficult to rescind once the crisis had abated. The united presidium of the provincial executive committee, in an extraordinary meeting on 7 July, appealed to the regional military commissar to assist in general disarmament of the population, particularly of the workers of Sormovo and the other big factory complexes. It also attempted to have firearms held only by permit, and to regulate the new militias that had formed.[64] The sense of crisis initiated by the soldiers' rising proved difficult to abate, not least because it instigated a more general arming of the population.

In the towns, as we have seen from events in Nizhnii Novgorod, reserve and evacuee soldiers contributed to a sense of disorder and of crisis. In the countryside, the profile of soldiers differed significantly, though they too contributed to a general sense of disorder and of crisis. Relatively small

---

[61] *Kazanskaia rabochaia gazeta* 147, 12 October 1917, p. 1.

[62] *Izvestiia soveta rabochikh i soldatskikh deputatov* 30, 16 July 1917, p. 3; all three soviets met to discuss the 5 July events, and a resolution was passed which 'refused to apportion any blame on individuals or organisations before the investigative enquiry meets'. This to me indicates that some had accused particular parties of instigating the events.

[63] *Izvestiia soveta rabochikh i soldatskikh deputatov* 34, 30 July 1917, p. 3.

[64] GANO, f. 1887, op. 1, d. 33, l. 77; writings from the journal of the extraordinary meeting of the united presidium of Nizhegorod province executive committee, 7 July 1917.

numbers of soldiers, in the hundreds, were stationed permanently outside the provincial capital. Where active soldiers were present, they were usually there at the request of the *uezd* commissar, to help maintain order, support the militia, or to assist in the management of the provisions crisis. The focus of this section will not be these active soldiers, but those whose role in the countryside was most conspicuous; agitators, deserters, soldiers on leave and prisoners of war.

A whirl of professional soldier-agitators moved through the villages from the capitals, the front and the fleet. Some of these agitators worked for official soviet 'cultural-enlightenment' programmes. The content and tone of their delivery was, however, difficult to vet, and those with other agendas swelled the numbers of officially sanctioned soldier-agitators. Kronstadt soldiers were particularly notorious for their radical politics. A rather histrionic report in the moderate socialist Kazan soviet paper headlined 'Bolsheviks in the countryside' declared that soldiers and sailors from Petrograd and Kronstadt had been 'moving round the villages, giving provocative speeches, inciting peasants to rise against landowners'.[65] In Nizhnii Novgorod, the provincial commissar warned darkly in May of soldiers describing themselves as empowered delegates from the front or the soviets, circulating the countryside and making 'provocative speeches . . . to seize private property and not to submit to the orders of the Provisional Government'.[66] In Kazanskii *uezd*, two soldier-agitators ordered the population in July not to participate in the grain monopoly, as 'this would allow the war to continue'.[67] Some of these 'outside agitators without proper validation' were deserters.[68]

The impact of soldiers sent specifically to the countryside as agitators paled into insignificance when compared with the impact of soldiers on leave and deserters in the countryside.[69] The numbers of deserting soldiers nationally is impossible to estimate with any accuracy, though Golovine offered an estimate that Wildman concluded was excessively high of some 1,900,000 men.[70] Soldiers on leave included those being given holiday from

[65] *Kazanskaia rabochaia gazeta* 68, 4 June 1917, p. 4.
[66] GANO, f. 733, op. 1, d. 1, l. 161; from Nizhegorod provincial commissar to all *uezd* commissars and *uezd* and *volost* committees, 12 May 1917.
[67] NART, f. 1246, op. 1, d. 75, ll. 111–13; from Kazan *uezd* provisions administration to provincial commissar, 29 July 1917.
[68] NART, f. 983, op. 1, d. 21, l. 541; decree of Marasinskii *volost* meeting, Spasskii *uezd*, 5 September 1917.
[69] This is comparable to the situation in right-bank Ukraine during 1917, when soldiers were often seen to incite peasant action and violence (Tan, 'Village social organisation', p. 74).
[70] N. N. Golovine, *The Russian army in the World War* (New Haven, CT, 1931), p. 124. This figure is rather high, and includes those soldiers who 'deserted' for a short time, then subsequently returned to the ranks. For a discussion of the problems of estimating desertion rates, see Wildman, *The old army*, pp. 362–72.

the front or active regiments, and those given summer leave for working the fields. Kerensky had given soldiers over the age of forty-three leave for field-work in July.[71] The authorities were inundated with requests from soldiers asking to return home for fieldwork throughout the spring and summer. In Nizhnii Novgorod, so many requests came in that the soviet of soldiers' deputies asked *volost* committees to screen the requests first.[72] There were numerous reports of soldiers on leave inciting violence and disobedience to government orders.[73] Mamadyshskii *uezd*'s commissar reported that sol-diers on leave provoked incidents of disorder, most often land seizure, and that all excesses, the term usually coined for violent incidents, were perpe-trated by soldiers on leave.[74] Another report from this area confirmed that large numbers of deserters lived in the area, and that soldiers on leave were a thoroughly pernicious influence.[75]

Where force or violence was involved in local conflicts, soldiers were invariably involved. Rydnovskii, a member of the old State Duma, was fiercely beaten along with his wife by a gang of fifteen armed soldiers who searched his Kazan estate and threatened his children with revolvers.[76] A group of thirty-five soldiers, either on leave or deserters, took wine and weapons from the estate of another Kazan landowner, Olga Elend, and behaved in a threatening fashion.[77] In some cases, soldiers acted not just against unpopular individual landowners but threatened the village com-munity more generally. Soldiers on leave stole horses in Zhediaevskii *volost*, Spasskii *uezd*, threatened the village committee and forced them to accept the theft.[78] In other cases, however, the local community actively colluded

[71] Alan Wildman, *The road to Soviet power and peace*, vol. II of *The end of the Russian Imperial army* (Princeton, NJ, 1987), p. 367.

[72] *Izvestiia soveta rabochikh i soldatskikh deputatov* 24, 22 June 1917, p. 1.

[73] NART, f. 1246, op. 1, d. 73, l. 146: telefonogram from Tsarevokokshaisk to Kazan provincial com-missar, undated; NART, f. 1246, op. 1, d. 45, l. 212: verdict of citizens of Varvarshskii commune, Ten'kovskii *volost*, Sviazhskii *uezd*, Kazan province, 28 May 1917; NART, f. 1246, op. 1, d. 73, l. 146: report from Sotnurskaia *volost* provisions administration to Tsarevokokshaiskii *uezd* provi-sions administration, 1 September 1917.

[74] NART, f. 1246, op. 1, d. 51, l. 207; report written by instructor of the office of petty credit of the provincial *zemstva* M. Sermets, 23 May 1917.

[75] NART, f. 1246, op. 1, d. 43, l. 179; report from instructor of the office of petty credit of the provincial *zemstva*, M. Sermets, 23 May 1917.

[76] NART, f. 1246, op. 1, d. 54, l. 416; telefonogram to president of State Duma Rodzianko, from Rydnovskii, 20 May 1917.

[77] NART, f. 1246, op. 1, d. 41, l. 435; statement of Olga Sergeevna Yelend to the Kazan soviet of agriculturalists, 2 June 1917.

[78] NART, f. 1246, op. 1, d. 41, l. 413; letter from Zhediavskii *volost* committee, Spasskii *uezd*, to Kazan provincial commissar, 10 July 1917. On the harsh treatment usually accorded horse thieves by village communities, see Frierson, 'Crime and punishment', pp. 62–5; Stephen P. Frank, 'Popular justice, community and culture among the Russian peasantry, 1870–1900', *Russian Review* 46 (1987), 239–65, pp. 257–9.

in soldier violence. The Kazan landowner Natalia Neratova, for example, was forced to leave her property after a crowd of soldiers accompanied by local women and their children made repeated threats.[79] The manager of a forest in Kozmodem'ianskii *uezd*, Kazan province, was forced to sign a paper resigning his post by a group of soldiers on leave accompanied by 'quite small children'.[80] These examples show that in some cases, soldier-deserters acted against local communities, but that in other cases, they colluded with or led the local community.

Local government records catalogue a losing battle in controlling deserters in the countryside, in both Nizhegorod and Kazan provinces. Deserters brought the problem of soldier-citizen to its apex; deserters had cast away the last bounds of their soldier service and submission to the state as they exercised their individual freedom, yet their position as outside the law and yet still armed and potentially violent made them uniquely volatile. Regional administration lacked the armed force to tackle deserters and their lawlessness, which left the rural population exposed. The task of tracking down deserters, even with the best efforts of the local population and militia, was a difficult one. This is reflected in the paltry 270 deserters captured in Nizhegorod province by September.[81] Administrative disorder made documentation difficult to verify, and escape and evasion relatively straightforward. The Kazan committee of public safety issued a decree warning about the arrival of deserters in the region, and asking village committees to verify all documentation.[82] Even when deserters were found, strong policing was required to apprehend deserters, many of whom were armed. Calls for military assistance in dealing with desertion were made repeatedly but were often not satisfied by the overstretched provincial commissar.[83]

Deserters played an active role in inciting the population against the grain monopoly in Kazan,[84] and in some areas made important contributions to the power structures. A gang of deserter-soldiers, led by a 'clear supporter of

[79] NART, f. 1246, op. 1, d. 54, ll. 331–2; letter from landowner of Laishevskii *uezd*, Natalia Vasil'evna Neratova, to Kazan provincial commissar, 27 May 1917.

[80] NART, f. 1246, op. 1, d. 48, l. 133; report from the manager of Ilinskii woodland, P. Terent'eva, to the captain of Kazan land affairs and state property, 2 May 1917.

[81] *Izvestiia soveta rabochikh i soldatskikh deputatov* 45, 14 September 1917, p. 2.

[82] NART, f. 1246, op. 1, d. 69, l. 48; published decree from the Kazan provincial committee of public safety, undated.

[83] For example, *Narod* 31, 25 June 1917, p. 4, where the militia was powerless against the mass of deserters reportedly living in Sormovo raion. See also NART, f. 1246, op. 1, d. 75, ll. 53, 60; request from Kazan *uezd* for half a regiment of reliable soldiers to capture deserters.

[84] This is discussed at length in chapter 8. A specific example is NART, f. 1246, op. 1, d. 75, l. 295; report of provincial commissar, September 1917.

the old regime', for example, disrupted the elected committee of Chernyshevskii *volost*, and the president of the meeting was forced to run away and hide for fear of being killed.[85] A gang of soldiers drank and protected illicit stills (*kumishkovareniiu*) and removed the village committee in the hamlet of Arkhangel'skii, Chistopolskii *uezd*, Kazan province.[86] In Mamadyshskii *uezd*, Kazan province, it was reported that there were large numbers of deserters, who were the mainstay of provisions resistance and committed many other crimes. Large numbers of soldiers from the town were requested to deal with the disorders.[87] A number of soldiers suspected of robberies and without documentation lived in Rozhnovskii *volost*, Semenovskii *uezd*, Nizhegorod province. The *uezd* administration had no means at its immediate disposal to apprehend these scoundrels, and requested five armed soldiers from the province executive committee in March to capture them.[88] Forty-five deserters led a group of peasants in seizing a flour mill in Arskoi *volost*, and the weak local militia were unable to prevent them.[89]

Public attitudes towards deserters in the countryside varied significantly, reflecting the fact that some deserters had returned home to their families, who protected and supported them, while others roamed through the countryside as strangers to the local population. Many villages passed fiery decrees condemning deserters and pledging their utmost assistance in capturing absconders. The very first decree of Tepelovo village's meeting was that measures must be taken to bring deserters to justice.[90] This public face against desertion was clearly not uniform or complete. Some deserters were protected by their families or their communities. In Mamadyshskii *uezd*, the total number of deserters was listed at 104, but the *uezd* commissar declared that this was way below the real figure, as many were in hiding, often in the non-Russian hill villages that were particularly difficult

[85] NART, f. 1246, op. 1, d. 54, l. 387; letter from Cheremishskii *volost* committee to provincial commissar, 26 May 1917.
[86] NART, f. 983, op. 1, d. 16, l. 106; protocol of the meeting of Chistopolskii *uezd* committee of public safety, the soviet of peasants' deputies, *volost* commissars, soviet of workers' and soldiers' deputies and representatives of the town committee of public safety, 26 June 1917.
[87] NART, f. 1246, op. 1, d. 43, ll. 86–7; letter from Mamadyshskii *uezd* commissar to Kazan provincial commissar, 18 July 1917; telegram, to captain of Kazan military region staff, from provincial commissar, dated 26 July 1917.
[88] GANO, f. 815, op. 1, d. 17, l. 4; protocol no. 1 of Rozhnovskii *volost* committee, 6 March 1917.
[89] NART, f. 1246, op. 1, d. 75, l. 163; letter from Kazanskii *uezd* commissar to provincial commissar, 2 September 1917.
[90] GANO, f. 1887, op. 1, d. 3, l. 2; report of the member of the executive committee of the Soviet of soldiers' deputies Alexander Kuprianov, about his journey around Arzamasskii and Nizhegorodskii *uezds*. He visited Tepelovo on 2 April 1917.

to search.[91] There were reports of the unsavoury influence of soldiers 'who cannot be counted among the active army' in village decisions, though nothing I came across in the archives made reference to this specifically.[92] Nizhegorod's provincial commissar reported to the *uezd* commissars in May that complaints had flooded in regarding disorder carried out by deserters, and asked that all areas should take 'the most energetic measures'.[93]

Prisoners of war formed a significant presence in the provincial countryside. The new fashions of freedom, democracy and representation were hard to equate with their position as captives of the state, and this was reflected in their sometimes erratic treatment. Their numbers were estimated at some 2 million nationally,[94] and many were stationed in rural areas, either on work details or in makeshift camps. More than half of these prisoners of war were employed in agriculture, and in many areas they were seized from private estates by peasants in the course of 1917 to work on peasant land.[95] Such seizures were not a feature of Kazan and Nizhegorod, however, a reflection of the low level of waged labour there. Some historians have suggested that Russia's treatment of prisoners of war during the First World War were 'prototypes' of communist gulags and Nazi concentration camps.[96] The experience of prisoners of war in Nizhegorod and Kazan provinces does not support this but confirms the thesis put forward by Alon Rachami-mov that conditions for prisoners of war were locally defined rather than centrally ordained.[97] Though the living conditions for prisoners of war in Kazan and Nizhegorod were often very poor, so were the conditions of Russian soldiers and civilians in some areas.

Many prisoners of war had a surprising degree of personal freedom in 1917, not least because their position as captives of a state at war was blurred by the revolutionary rhetoric of proletarian solidarity and civil rights for all. The Minster of War Guchkov sent a circular round the provinces on 16 April 1917 that reiterated the appalling conditions of Russian prisoners

[91] NART, f. 1246, op. 1, d. 43, ll. 264–5; protocol of Mamadyshskii *uezd* committee of public safety, 14 August 1917.

[92] *Nizhegorodskaia zemskaia gazeta* 36, 7 September 1917, p. 14.

[93] GANO, f. 733, op. 1, d. 1, l. 161; letter from Nizhegorod provincial commissar, to *uezd* commissars and to all *uezd* and *volost* committees, 12 May 1917.

[94] Alon Rachamimov, *POWs and the Great War* (Oxford, 2002), pp. 34–44.

[95] A. D. Maliavskii, *Krest'ianskoe dvizhenie v Rossii v 1917 g. mart–oktiabr* (Moscow, 1981), p. 88; Tan, 'Village social organisation', p. 69.

[96] Peter Pastor, 'Hungarian POWs in Russia during the revolution and civil war', in Samuel Williamson and Peter Pastor (eds.), *Essays on World War I: origins and prisoners of war* (Boulder, CO, 1983), pp. 149–62, and Reinhard Nachtigal, *Russland und seine osterreichisch ungarischen kriegsgefangenen (1914–1918)* (Grunbach, 2003).

[97] Rachamimov, *POWs*, pp. 122–5.

of war held in Germany. He declared that the demands of prisoners of war held in Russia to enjoy greater freedom were improper. He concluded that prisoners of war should have their position of captivity clarified.[98] In Nizhegorod province, prisoners of war were stationed in small groups in rural areas,[99] which made close supervision difficult. Local government officials submitted numerous reports of prisoners of war escaping or of enjoying too much freedom around their billets. The Nizhegorod provincial commissar sent a note round the militia captains and *uezd* commissars noting the 'epidemic' of prisoner of war escapes. There was no clear central system for supervising prisoners of war, and the commissar himself did not know how many were in the area, or what they were doing. It is pertinent that he contrasted this slack state of affairs with the reportedly terrible conditions in which Russian prisoners of war were held.[100] In Lukoianovskii *uezd*, an executive committee meeting at the end of June heard that prisoners of war didn't do anything but eat, while there was a terrible shortage of hands for harvesting.[101] Though it is not stated explicitly, this may have been a reference to officer prisoners of war, who were not expected to work, whereas rank-and-file soldiers were. In Spasskii *uezd*, Kazan, measures had to be taken in June to restore order as a result of the 'excesses' of prisoners of war stationed in the town.[102] Though it was not stated specifically, 'excesses' in this case probably referred to merrymaking and sleeping with soldiers' wives.[103]

We rarely hear the voices of the prisoners of war themselves in the narratives of revolution. Where we do, it is often in praise of Russia's revolution, or requesting access to the revolutionary free press. The socialist press tended to report any prisoner of war internationalist tendency or sympathy for Russia's revolution with gusto. A group of 180 Austrian officers held in the *uezd* capital of Tetiushi asked for access to the free Russian press, and the soviet paper printed their letter alongside an enthusiastic response from the editor.[104] At the May Day celebrations held in the village of Kliucha, Kazan, Austrian prisoners of war working in a nearby factory attended the meeting

---

[98] GANO, f. 733, op. 1, d. 1, l. 157; order from Moscow military region, regarding closer supervision over prisoners of war, 16 April 1917.

[99] *Izvestiia soveta rabochikh i soldatskikh deputatov* 16, 22 May 1917, p. 4.

[100] GANO, f. 815, op. 1, d. 8, ll. 1–3; two circulars from provincial commissar, dated early and late August 1917.

[101] GANO, f. 1887, op. 1, d. 17, l. 82; protocol of the meeting of Lukoianovskii *uezd* executive committee, 24–25 June 1917.

[102] NART, f. 1352, op. 1, d. 3, l. 178; protocol of Spasskii *uezd* committee of public safety, 13 June 1917.

[103] There were many cases of romantic attachments between Russian women and prisoners of war (Rachamimov, *POWs*, p. 109).

[104] *Kazanskaia rabochaia gazeta* 27, 13 May 1917, p. 3.

that was held. Their effusive support for the revolution was reported word for word: 'One of the prisoners of war held up a red flag with tears in his eyes, and said that if Germany and Austria did not take the Russian example and overthrow their monarchy, there would be nothing to return home for.'[105] Such examples of international proletarian solidarity overwhelming national allegiances provided useful support for Social Democrat Internationalists, who were predominant on the publishing newspaper's editorial board. Prisoners of war certainly added another layer of complexity to the presence of soldiers in Russia's rear.

SOLDIERS' WIVES

Soldiers' wives (*soldatki*) have been largely excluded from the master narrative of 1917 yet they were among the largest and most vocal of the interest groups to form in wartime.[106] Mark Baker concluded from his study of *soldatki* in Kharkiv that they represented the first active, mass, social movement of women in Russia, and that this demonstrated a transformation of gender roles as a result of mass mobilisation.[107] The evidence from Kazan and Nizhegorod does not point to a transformation of gender roles but does support the idea of *soldatki* as a mass social movement. Like soldiers, their wives encapsulated a diverse range of social, ethnic and national groups, and had a range of possible social identities. All those defining themselves as *soldatki* had other social categorisations that they could subscribe to, and some used a double barrel to describe themselves, such as worker-*soldatka* or peasant-*soldatka*. The prominence of the category *soldatka* in

[105] *Kazanskaia rabochaia gazeta* 15, 27 April 1917, pp. 2–3.
[106] My article on *soldatki* includes some material from Tambov not used here (Sarah Badcock, 'Women, protest, and revolution: soldiers' wives in Russia during 1917', *International Review of Social History* 49 (2004), 47–70). Emily E. Pyle's doctoral dissertation at the University of Chicago gives a detailed picture of soldiers' families' requests for aid and the implications for village social relations (E. E. Pyle, 'Village social relations and the reception of soldiers' family aid policies in Russia, 1912–1921', unpublished PhD thesis, University of Chicago (1997)). Barbara A. Engel, 'Not by bread alone: subsistence riots in Russia during World War I', *Journal of Modern History* 69 (1997), 696–721, deals extensively with the role of *soldatki* in food disorders in the pre-revolutionary wartime period. Mark Baker, 'Rampaging soldatki, cowering police, bazaar riots and moral economy: the social impact of the Great War in Kharkiv province', *Canadian-American Slavic Studies* 35 (2001), 137–56, offers a detailed and thorough analysis of the role of *soldatki* in wartime protest in Kharkiv province, Ukraine. Beatrice Farnsworth, 'The *soldatka*: folklore and court record', *Slavic Review* 49 (1990), 58–73, looks at the image and status of *soldatki* in pre-revolutionary Russia; A. G. Meyer, 'The impact of World War I on Russian women's lives', in Barbara Clements Evans, Barbara A. Engel, and Christine D. Worobec (eds.), *Russia's women: accommodation, resistance, transformation* (Berkeley, CA, 1991), pp. 208–24, pp. 216–18, deals briefly with *soldatki*. Wade, *The Russian revolution*, pp. 121–3, discusses *soldatki* activities in Petrograd.
[107] Baker, 'Rampaging soldatki', p. 143.

appeals and declarations indicates that a range of women chose it as a social definition.

Despite relatively low levels of formal organisation, *soldatki* made a significant mark on revolutionary politics at the local level. The moderate socialist leadership of local democratic organs was undermined by the disillusion of *soldatki* and prefigured the more politically significant alienation of many workers and soldiers. The disillusion and vocal protests of *soldatki* contributed significantly to the pervading sense of crisis and of breakdown of the lawful state. Though the formal translation of *soldatka* was a soldier's wife, the term was often used more broadly in 1917 to include other female dependents, and files of letters from *soldatki* often included correspondence from a range of family members. *Soldatki* had always been a significant minority group among married women,[108] but mass mobilisation caused *soldatki* numbers to swell dramatically.

Common grievances provided the central defining feature for *soldatki* as a group. These common grievances were locally defined, though they confirm Barbara Engel's observation that peasant women were most likely to participate in protest over household-related issues.[109] Kharkiv *soldatki* complained about separator peasants and local tariffs on food products that prevented them from selling their wares at market price, two grievances that were not voiced by *soldatki* in Nizhegorod or Kazan.[110] The most widely expressed demand from Nizhegorod and Kazan *soldatki* was for an increase in the allowance that was provided to the soldiers' families. This was often submitted by *soldatki* from a particular village or *volost* jointly. The dramatic increase of price on products of first necessity, alongside rampant inflation, left *soldatki* who relied on the state allowance for subsistence in an unenviable position of impoverishment, something commented upon by a range of sources. Semenovskii *uezd*'s executive committee, for example, commented on the 'scandalous distress' (*vopiushchaia nuzhda*) many *soldatki* were in,[111] while a writer in a Kazan newspaper commented that some *soldatki* were 'utterly destitute' (*gol perekatnaia*).[112] This state of crisis escalated in the course of 1917. Material need was perhaps the deciding factor in their drive to organise themselves collectively. Demands for supply of food products reflected the provisions situation in the locality, with calls for

---

[108] Farnsworth, 'The *soldatka*', p. 71.
[109] Barbara A. Engel, 'Women, men and the language of peasant resistance, 1870–1907', in Frank and Steinberg, *Cultures in flux*, pp. 34–53, p. 37.
[110] Baker, 'Rampaging soldatki', p. 137.
[111] GANO, f. 1887, op. 1, d. 2, l. 23; report of Semenovskii *uezd* executive committee to provincial meeting of *uezd* representatives, Nizhegorod province, 23 May 1917.
[112] *Izvestiia Kazanskago voenno-okruzhnago komiteta* 13, 4 June 1917, p. 1.

bread from deficit areas, and calls for sugar and white bread from surplus areas. Where there was a shortage, even if, like sugar, it did not threaten life, this shortage became a major issue of the day and took on equivalent or even greater force than demands for bread in a hungry province.[113]

There were many other categories of complaint. These included requests for free, or subsidised, fuel, refusal or inability to pay taxes, non-payment of state allowance, the status of common-law wives, shortage of housing, landlord attempts to evict *soldatki* and requests for husbands, fathers and sons to be given leave in order to help with fieldwork.[114] There were also more specific personal grievances. The Kazan provincial soviet of peasants' deputies, for example, asked the Voskresenskii *volost* committee to intercede on behalf of the *soldatka* Olga Makar'evna Egorova, of Gorkii village, Voskresenskii *volost*, whose father-in-law Semion Egorov had thrown her out of her house without compensation, forcing her and her young son to live with strangers.[115] Egorova's complaint demonstrates the willingness of *soldatki* to bring a host of grievances to the attention of the soviets.

The tsarist government had made some attempt to define the category *soldatka* more clearly, in order to establish who was to be eligible for state support. The resulting law of 25 June 1912 was ambiguous.[116] All wives and children of soldiers called into active service were theoretically eligible for state allowance, which was administered as a monetary sum. Common-law wives and their children were not, however, included in this remit, which was a significant omission.[117] The Provisional Government was put

---

[113] This issue is commented upon at length in Engel, 'Not by bread alone', esp. pp. 718–20. She comments that such demands for 'non-essential products' might be interpreted as signifying a rise in the standards of living and expectations of the lower-class population, or that it might, on the contrary, indicate that sugar and tea were being used as a replacement for more substantial subsistence foods. (See also S. Mintz, *Sweetness and power: the place of sugar in modern history* (New York, 1985), p. 149.) There were frantic cries across the spectrum of Kazan newspapers regarding the shortages of sugar, white flour and tea.

[114] For just a few examples of these complaints, see GANO, f. 2603, op. 1, d. 2; *fond* of Gorbatovskii *uezd* executive committee, *delo* of protocols of *volost* executive committees, esp. p. 169, p. 199, p. 200, p. 217.

[115] NART, f. 983, op. 1, d. 23, l. 235; letter from Kazan province soviet of peasants' deputies to Voskresenskii *volost* committee, August 1917. This reflects the degree of minutiae into which the soviet was drawn; their response to this plea, and innumerable others, many of a personal nature, are all carefully documented.

[116] See Pyle, 'Village social relations', chapter 2, pp. 105–75, for an assessment of the evolution of the 1912 law.

[117] GANO, f. 1101, op. 1, d. 23, l. 749; letter from the soviet of soldiers' deputies, Nizhegorod garrison, 23 March 1917, to the Nizhegorod *uezd* trusteeship for the assistance of soldiers' families, asking whether common-law soldiers' wives have the right to receive the state provisions grant. The trusteeship answered on reverse side, on 27 March 1917, and quoted the law of 15 June 1912 about the right of all lower military members' family, including common-law wives and offspring, to receive state allowance. This is a good example of the ambiguity of the 1912 law, which was here interpreted as including common-law wives in its remit.

under pressure to revise this statute, and in June 1917 it broadened the criteria for eligibility to include common-law wives, foster children and step-parents.[118] This broadening of the category, along with an increase in the number of applications for support, increased the already enormous financial burden *soldatki* support imposed on the state. The number of recipients of state allowance increased from 25 million in 1916 to 36 million by September 1917.[119] From the outbreak of the war until January 1917, aid to soldiers' families cost around 2 billion roubles, which was some 7 per cent of Russia's total military expenditure.[120] Between February and October 1917, 1.46 billion roubles were spent on allowances, which accounted for nearly 11 per cent of military expenditure.

This vast expenditure, and its effective allocation, was an enormous burden on Russia's overstrained economy and administration. The law of 1912 had established a network of committees to minister to *soldatki* needs, but even before the administrative and financial disarray that resulted from the February revolution, the state was unable to meet *soldatki* demands. The 'Nizhegorod provincial committee for the assistance of sick and wounded military and the families of drafted men' met on 13 February 1917 to discuss a potential increase in the allotment of money for the needs of families of drafted men. The chair of the meeting, P. A. Demidov,[121] pointed out that the debt incurred by the provincial *zemstvo* in providing assistance to needy families had risen to 650,000 roubles.[122] The meeting concluded that

The committees simply cannot fulfil their initially stated principle, to show assistance to all families requesting help, and the role of the committees now must be to show assistance to those groups of the population who are in the most unfavourable situations, for example those excluded from state allowance (common-law wives, families situated in active service) [. . .] Monetary assistance must have a place only in exceptional cases, since the population are needy, in the main, not for money, but for products, and in relation to this very question, both *uezd* and provincial committees are not in a position to assist. Any increase of money to the *uezd* organisations must be looked over thoroughly, as experience has shown that these *uezd* committees have not been very active locally, because their organisation suffers from grave insufficiencies.[123]

---

[118] Browder and Kerensky, *Russian Provisional Government*, vol. I, pp. 800–1, doc. 699, 'The extension of support for soldiers' families, 22 June 1917'.
[119] *Rossiia v mirovoi voine 1914–1918gg. v tsifrakh* (Moscow, 1925), table 41, p. 50.
[120] A. L. Sidorov, *Finansovoe polozhenie Rossii v gody pervoi mirovoi voiny* (Moscow, 1968), pp. 108–20.
[121] Demidov was head of the *zemstvo* and after the February revolution served as provincial commissar for around three months.
[122] GANO, f. 2603, op. 1, d. 2, l. 234; minutes of meeting of Nizhegorod provincial committee for the assistance of sick and wounded military and families of those called up, 13 February 1917.
[123] GANO, f. 2603, op. 1, d. 2, l. 234; minutes of meeting of Nizhegorod provincial committee for the assistance of sick and wounded military and families of those called up, 13 February 1917.

These committees continued to function in 1917 but were supplemented by the efforts of the soviets, Provisional Government organisations and ad hoc committees. This amalgam of organisations bearing some responsibility for administering aid to *soldatki* only contributed to the administrative confusion and inefficiency that was a theme of *soldatki* complaints. The main difficulty for the state in administering aid to the *soldatki* was not administrative confusion, however, but financial crisis.[124] Administrative bodies repeatedly stated that they would like to help *soldatki* more but had no funds available. Problems were compounded by the provisions situation, which deteriorated in the course of 1917.

Soldatki secured little direct representation in the myriad forms of government that were established in the wake of the February revolution. This is a reflection of the absence of women from all levels of administration, from the village *skhod* up to delegates for the Constituent Assembly. At lower levels of organisation, on *volost* and *uezd* executive committees, the delegates were almost exclusively male. The reasons for this have been discussed in chapter 4. There were even specific cases of *soldatki* being refused the right to participate in *volost* administration. A complaint was received from thirteen *soldatki* of Nizhnii Novgorod province that a deputy of their *volost* administration, in answer to their question of why a *soldatka* deputy had not been allowed to participate, answered, 'Obviously, it's unnecessary to allow riffraff (*svolochi*) into the workplace, and it is better to close the doors to keep such riffraff out.'[125]

Whilst the February revolution compounded the administrative and financial difficulties of administering aid to *soldatki*, it simultaneously heightened expectations of government, heralding significant changes in both the mechanics and in popular expectations of local administration. The rhetoric of revolution promised equality, freedom and justice. Like their soldier husbands and sons, *soldatki* clearly took this new rhetoric on board and expected the new democratic administration's lofty ideals to translate into real improvements in *soldatki* conditions. *Soldatki*, as a group sharing common grievances, formed an amorphous group that could place its requests and complaints to the administration at a level and a persistency that was not possible prior to the revolution.

Unlike their soldier husbands and sons, *soldatki* were left on the margins of power as women were excluded from the myriad power structures of 1917. They had significant impact on the course of local government,

---

[124] GANO, f. 27, op. 1, d. 3, l. 39; Duma records, 16 September 1917.
[125] GANO, f. 1101, op. 1, d. 23, l. 363; complaint to the soviet of soldiers' and workers' deputies, from thirteen *soldatki* of Goroulevskii *volost*, headed by Varvara Borynina, 20 April 1917.

but their participation was from the periphery, and not from the heart of local government. *Soldatki* formed autonomous organisations that did not work strictly within the sphere encompassed by the soviets, but over-lapped with it. There was a union of *soldatki* formed at national level by the Petrograd Soviet in June 1917,[126] but no reference was made to any central *soldatki* organisation in Kazan or Nizhnii Novgorod. The alliances of *soldatki* that formed in the provinces of Nizhegorod and Kazan shared common grievances within the context of local conditions, but developed in quite distinct directions, reflecting the importance of individual leadership in forming these organisations. The sources make almost no reference to the individuals who were prominent in the *soldatki* organisations, making any more detailed assessment of *soldatki* leaders impossible. It is, however, possible to present a broader picture of *soldatki* organisation and leadership, and to contrast the forms of *soldatki* organisation that developed in Kazan and Nizhnii Novgorod.

At an early stage of 1917 the Nizhegorod provincial soviet of workers' and soldiers' deputies was careful to embrace the *soldatki* in its remit. The women were invited to send a representative to the soviet's meetings. Though the demands of the *soldatki* in Nizhegorod province were numerous, and acknowledged across all levels of administration, they did not form their own autonomous association and did not put any external pressure on the soviet. The soviet's careful embracing of the *soldatki* at an early stage may well have given the *soldatki* a sufficient degree of public outlet and thus averted the build-up of sufficient discontent required for the *soldatki* to operate independently of the soviet. Their lack of vocal representation in public forums reflects a lack of concerted leadership for the Nizhegorod *soldatki*.

The *soldatki* of Kazan province, in contrast to those in Nizhegorod, had internal leaders, who from early stages organised and formed the women's movement. A formal association was created at the beginning of April, pre-dating the central *soldatki* organisation formed in Petrograd, with the aim to improve *soldatki* conditions of life.[127] A reflection of their self-awareness as a group was the formal photograph taken of the committee members together. The well-dressed, educated-looking women in the photograph give a rare indication of the social character of these organic *soldatki* leaders. Their dress and demeanour suggest that they were professional women, like teachers or clerks. The Kazan *soldatki* union was initiated by the women themselves, and not at the behest of the soviet as in Nizhnii Novgorod. The

[126] See Pyle, 'Village social relations', p. 293.   [127] *Kazanskaia rabochaia gazeta* 30, 17 May 1917, p. 3.

level of *soldatki* organisation in Kazan was accordingly at a much higher level. At their meeting in May, red flags were prepared, inscribed with 'bread' and 'increase the allowance for *soldatki*'.[128] The secretary of the union, Zinaida Matveevna Antonova, stood as a candidate for the Town Duma.[129]

Despite this higher level of executive organisation, a commentator remarked that 'the administration could not, however, restrain the poor, hungry, barely conscious women to whom it seemed that no measures had been taken for improvement of their situation'.[130] This comment must be read with caution; it may reflect the prejudices of the soviet reporter, and a desire to belittle *soldatki* organisation. It does, however, suggest that the leaders of the *soldatki* in Kazan were absolutely distinct from the *soldatki* themselves, confirming the impression from their photograph of educated professionals, far removed from the peasants and workers that made up the mass of *soldatki*. It also indicates that though the Kazan *soldatki* had internal leaders and administrators, this leadership was far more moderate and conventional than the majority of the Kazan *soldatki*, and was unable to restrain its 'followers'.

Soldatki in both Kazan and Nizhegorod operated on a number of levels in voicing their grievances, and attempting to extract concessions from the authorities. They submitted written statements, participated in administrative organisations and acted autonomously, outside these established organisations, in order to attract public support for their pleas, and to put direct pressure on the administration. A common feature of the presentation of these grievances was the women's enthusiasm to present their grievances collectively, rather than individually.[131] The majority of *soldatki* complaints and requests were addressed to the soviet of soldiers' deputies, and not to the provincial or *uezd* commissars. This is a telling reflection of the prestige of the soviets. The most common forms of address were written petitions, complaints or requests, submitted both independently and collectively. A large collection of *soldatki* letters of grievance has been preserved in the Nizhnii Novgorod State Archive.[132] Some of these were written by the women themselves, and others composed on their behalf by

[128] *Kazanskaia rabochaia gazeta* 31, 18 May 1917, p. 3.
[129] NART, f. 1246, op. 1, d. 102, l. 175; list of candidates to Town Duma elections.
[130] *Kazanskaia rabochaia gazeta* 31, 18 May 1917, p. 3.
[131] This may be a reflection of the tsarist policy to actively encourage the collective submission of petitions (Pyle, 'Village social relations', p. 186).
[132] GANO, f. 1101, op. 1, d. 23; a collection of 929 letters, mostly from soldiers' families, and a few from wounded soldiers. Many of these letters were from illiterate women and were written on their behalf by a scribe. Many more were barely legible.

a scribe or other literate person. In a number of cases, soldiers interceded personally on behalf of their wives, both singly and collectively. At a general meeting of the 183rd reserve infantry regiment, on 20 April, it was decreed after fierce discussion

[t]o commandeer a delegate and send a telegram to the war minister and to the soviet of soldiers' deputies in Petrograd, in order to quickly clarify the question about increase in *soldatki* pay, allowance for their families and pensions for invalids, declaring in all seriousness the reasons motivating this step.[133]

The collective action taken by *soldatki* shows that they found sufficient common ground, in the urgency of their pleas and in their lack of direct representation in government, to act together. There were instances where joint *soldatki* action was grouped by village or *volost*. In certain cases it was a response to a specific problem. The women of one *volost* used a pre-printed form to appeal about the non-payment of their allowances. Their husbands had been taken prisoner voluntarily, which classified them as deserters, thus leaving their families ineligible for state support. This excerpt from Daria Ivanovna Saiunovna's letter illustrates the powerless position of these women:

My husband, Ivan Vasilivech Saiunov of the 48th Siberian regiment, was taken prisoner and is still imprisoned. Since his capture I have not received allowance for his family, of myself and his two children aged five and four . . . the administration declared the last time I was given allowance that my husband gave himself over voluntarily as a prisoner and that is why I will receive no further allowance. I request to the soviet of soldiers' deputies to come to my family's aid, since I am not guilty of anything and must struggle with needy children in such difficult and hungry times, I don't actually know if my husband is guilty, and I cannot say anything about his motivations in handing himself over, but if he is guilty, then why are his innocent children going hungry in a state of poverty.[134]

The complaints submitted, even when individually written, rather than a mass complaint or a pre-printed form, were often very formulaic in their style. As in the pre-revolutionary period, petitioners invoked a combination of formal rules and moral principles in support of their claims.[135] The new expectations and rhetoric of revolution did have a significant impact on the form of these complaints. Petitioners frequently referred to their rights,

---

[133] GANO, f. 1101, op. 1, d. 5; protocols of the soviet of soldiers' deputies, 183rd infantry reserve regiment, p. 9.

[134] GANO, f. 1101, op. 1, d. 23, l. 173; pre-printed letter of complaint to the soviet of soldiers' deputies, with blank sections filled in by Daria Ivanovna Saiunovna.

[135] See Pyle, 'Peasant strategies', for a discussion of pre-revolutionary peasant strategies to obtain state aid, and the petitioners' tendency to ask in terms of charity, rather than 'rights'.

rather than just relying on moral principles and charity. It was usual for the *soldatka* to mention, in order, herself, the names and ages of her children, and the names and ages of dependent elderly parents (those mentioned were almost always the birth parents of the soldier, and not his wife). Nadezhda Grigorevna Fel'man's appeal to the soviet of soldiers' deputies, dated 19 May 1917, is typical in form:

> I humbly request that you consider carefully the situation of my family as stated below, and do not refuse my request. I am a weak, sick woman. My son Vladimir was taken into military service, and he is my sole source of nourishment and sustenance. I petitioned about the receipt of state allowance but was always refused. I have with me my daughter Maria aged nine, and as a result of poor health, and malnourishment through the rising cost of living, I am not able to work and feed myself. In this grave situation, I do not receive allowance.[136]

A relatively common phenomenon in these complaints was the direct relation presented by the *soldatki* of what they were giving to the state, and what they expected in return. The rhetoric of complaint blurred into the reality of their situation – they had given their sons and their husbands to the national interest, and their contribution to the state was the blood of their kin. The justification given to the Nizhegorodskii *uezd* commissar by *soldatki* for their non-payment of taxes was that since their husbands were away spilling their blood, the wives would not give any money to the state.[137] An appeal from the Kazan *soldatki* organisation directly declared to women that they had lost their sons and brothers and husbands to the war, and now were compelled to defend their own families, who faced want and hunger.[138] The language of the battlefield was directly employed in the domestic sphere.

While the Nizhegorod *soldatki* did not engage in any organised protests to uphold their complaints, the *soldatki* of Kazan employed the tactics as well as the language of the battlefield in forwarding their cause. Their demands were presented directly to the provincial administration, some-times in violent or threatening forms. The direct action of *soldatki* during 1917 was in some respects a continuation of the food riots seen through-out the war period in Russia, which were often led by women.[139] It also

---

[136] GANO, f. 1101, op. 1, d. 23, l. 574; letter from Nadezhda Grigorevna Fel'man to Nizhegorod soviet of soldiers' deputies, 19 May 1917.

[137] GANO, f. 1882, op. 1, d. 45, l. 288; report from Nizhegorodskii *uezd* commissar, 15 September 1917.

[138] Printed in *Rabochii* 14, 25 (12) May 1917. *Rabochii* was the organ of the Bolshevik organisation in Kazan town. Note that *soldatki* obligations regarding taxation were regarded as ambiguous anyway (Pyle, 'Village social relations', pp. 215–16).

[139] See Engel, 'Not by bread alone'; Baker, 'Rampaging soldatki', esp. pp. 150ff. The extreme violence of the Kharkiv *soldatki*, however, makes the Kazan activities look decidedly tame.

resonates with descriptions of peasant women's protest during the late 1920s and early 1930s.[140] In Kazan there was an atmosphere of open hostility, as *soldatki* consistently undermined and challenged decisions made by both town committees and the soviet. At a meeting held by the Kazan *soldatki* union in May, demands were voiced for provision of sugar and white flour, and for the increase of their allowance above the already agreed increase from three to seven roubles, up to a new sum of twenty roubles. The meeting's participants were counselled by one of the orators to go to the soviet to lay down their demands, since the soviet 'defended all toiling and impoverished people'. At this, the entire meeting marched to the gates of the palace where the soviet was in session. The besieged soviet sent a representative to pacify the women and entreated them to elect ten representatives to come into the soviet building and clarify their situation.

The soviet-sponsored newspaper afterwards reported that the women's anger was misdirected – they had received no response from the town administration to their pleas because they had provided no correspondence address, and their representative had not been present when the soviet discussed their case. The soviet clarified to the women's representatives that telegrams had been sent to the war minister about the plight of *soldatki*, and invited their representatives to the next soviet meeting, where *soldatki* grievances would be discussed. Whilst this was sufficient to diffuse the rising anger of the assembled women, it did not avert the women's march around the town, complete with banners and placards, demanding that their complaints be heard.[141] Such public demonstration of dissatisfaction with the soviet's actions in defending the working people was potentially damaging to the soviet's reputation.

The following week the Kazan soviet held a public session in the town theatre, in which *soldatki* issues were discussed. The decision to hold a public session is significant, as it reflected the degree of public concern and mistrust the *soldatki* issue raised, and the soviet's concern to address the grievances of its chosen constituents. The choice of a theatre as the meeting's location was a practical choice given the number of delegates and the size of the audience but was apt as the meeting developed into something of a public spectacle. A report of the meeting, written by an unnamed soviet

---

[140] Lynn Viola's work on women's protests during collectivisation shows that they shared many features of *soldatki* protests and the ways in which such protests were reported. See Lynne Viola, 'Babi-bunty and peasant women's protest during collectivisation', *Russian Review* 45 (1986), 23–42, esp. p. 33, regarding the reporting of women's protests, and pp. 38–9 on the well-organised nature of some women's protest, and its utilisation as a response to specific grievances.

[141] *Kazanskaia rabochaia gazeta* 31, 18 May 1917, p. 3.

member and published in *Kazanskaia rabochaia gazeta* gave an unsettling account of the stormy meeting. He declared, 'It is difficult and even useless to give a detailed report on the meeting.'[142] Soviet deputies, the supposed chosen representatives of the people (*narod*), were challenged and shouted down, most vocally by the *soldatki* and their supporters:

> Discussion of the *soldatki* question went on for more than four hours and by the end there was a storm even above the discussion. Amid worrying noise, shouts both from the public and from the soviet members, the meeting was closed at one in the morning. In the soviet there was no one who did not feel for the condition of the *soldatki*, and the speeches of the *soldatki* wrenched blood from the hearts of all that listened. But it was impossible for *soldatki* needs to be satisfied, because neither the state nor the soviet had the means. The soviet decided to do all that it could, but only what it could . . . attempts were made at heavy blows on the soviet; it was even said that the soviet had increased means for officers' wives but not for *soldatki*. There has never been discussion in the soviet about officers' wives. It was unconscious force against the soviet, rising anarchism and worrying provocation.[143]

Soldatki participation in the soviet resulted in the soviet losing its own decorum, rather than the *soldatki* gaining any. The plight of the Kazan *soldatki* was a real public issue; while their marches and noisy participation in meetings no doubt contributed to a prominent public profile, the effect was redoubled by the soviet's willingness to organise a range of public collections and charitable fund-raising events on behalf of the *soldatki*. For example, a concert-lottery was held on the 28 May, to be followed by a funfair (*narodnoe gulian'e*), with all funds raised going to the *soldatki*.[144] Such events were regular features in the town's public calendar but were a double-edged sword for the soviet. While they may well have been effective in collecting funds, and in publicly demonstrating that the soviet were active on behalf of *soldatki*, they also highlighted the women's continued demands and the inability of the soviet effectively to meet these demands.

RESPONSES TO *SOLDATKI* GRIEVANCES

The activism of Kazan *soldatki* proved to be highly effective in winning them a prominent public profile, and real concessions. The plight of *soldatki* was among the most persistent themes covered in the Kazan military district's

[142] *Kazanskaia rabochaia gazeta* 34, 21 May 1917, p. 4.
[143] *Kazanskaia rabochaia gazeta* 34, 21 May 1917, p. 4.
[144] *Kazanskaia rabochaia gazeta* 35, 24 May 1917, p. 1.

newspaper.[145] The *soldatki* union was granted use of the Zhuravlev building in the Kremlin as an office, and in August was provided with a house to operate as a hostel to house those *soldatki* with emergency housing needs.[146] Provincial and *uezd zemstva* were petitioned to set up cheap cafes for *soldatki*, and to take other measures to provide for needy *soldatki*. The town administration was commissioned to satisfy *soldatki* with firewood, and *soldatki* were given representation in the soviet, and on provisions and accommodation commissions.[147] Seven cheap cafes were established around Kazan town itself to satisfy *soldatki* needs. These cafes were forced to close in September, however, as a result of 'difficulties with the provisions situation, which made it more and more difficult to satisfy the lunchers, and in connection with the accusations of the *soldatki*, who were not satisfied with these lunches'.[148]

The prominence of *soldatki* in Kazan was particularly notable but was to some extent mirrored by the attention given to *soldatki* issues by resolutions of almost all local government organisations in Nizhnii Novgorod as well, from the village *skhod* and *volost* committees up to the provincial commissar. The plight of *soldatki* was widely acknowledged, and a range of measures proposed for their relief, including prioritising *soldatki* in receiving rented landowners' property,[149] providing assistance in fieldwork[150] and providing free or cheap firewood,[151] and preventing their eviction from rented accommodation.[152] The importance attributed by local government to the satisfaction of *soldatki* demands is apparent, and indicates the success of the *soldatki* in pressing their case.

---

[145] *Izvestiia Kazanskago voenno-okruzhnago komiteta. Ezhednevnaia politicheskaia gazeta.*
[146] *Kazanskaia rabochaia gazeta* 84, 29 July 1917, p. 3.
[147] *Kazanskaia rabochaia gazeta* 34, 21 May 1917, p. 4.
[148] *Kazanskaia rabochaia gazeta* 124, 13 September 1917, p. 3.
[149] NART, f. 983, op. 1, d. 23, l. 116; from the Kazan provincial soviet of peasants' deputies to Il'inskii *volost* committee, 4 July 1917.
[150] GANO, f. 1887, op. 1, d. 17, ll. 27–8; journal of the extraordinary meeting of Arzamasskii *uezd zemstvo*, 12 April 1917, p. 65 (from the resolutions of the first *Povolzhe* regional meeting of *uezd*, town and province executive committees, 30 May 1917); NART, f. 983, op. 1, d. 23, l. 82; from the Kazan soviet of peasants' deputies to the Administration of Land Affairs and State Property, June 1917, about the allotment of state horses for the needs of soldiers' families in fieldwork.
[151] GANO, f. 1887, op. 1, d. 2, l. 11; from the meeting of representatives of provincial and *uezd* executive committees and the provincial and *uezd* commissars, 23–25 May 1917; GANO, f. 1887, op. 1, d. 8, l. 32; from meeting of Nizhegorod provincial executive committee, 24 April 1917; NART, f. 983, op. 1, d. 17, l. 12; from the protocol of the meeting of Musliuminskii *volost* committee of public safety, 14 May 1917.
[152] GANO, f. 1887, op. 1, d. 8, l. 36; from meeting of Nizhegorod provincial executive committee, 1 May 1917; based on report of Naletov (who was also president of the soviet of workers' and soldiers' deputies) on the question of regularisation of accommodation for *soldatki*.

The ways in which the administration represented the *soldatki* and their plight gives some indication of their public image. Soviet and Provisional Government bodies alike employed the language of the battlefield, as the *soldatki* themselves did, in their attempts to raise public support for the *soldatki*. A common refrain was that it was society's responsibility to protect the families of those men who shed their blood for the motherland. A direct connection was made between the blood sacrifice made by the soldiers and the need for people to reciprocate in like, and thus to acknowledge their sacrifice. In a big advertisement appealing for help for the *soldatki*, run by the cultural-enlightenment committee of the soviet of soldiers and workers' deputies, it was repeatedly asked, 'What will we say to the soldiers suffering in the trenches about the hunger and suffering of their women and children?'[153] This language is important in understanding the prominent role played by symbolism. The complexities of the *soldatki* position were painted over by the broad brush strokes of national sacrifice and salvation. The perceivably avoidable suffering of their women and children mirrored the necessary suffering of the men in the trenches. The sufferings of *soldatki* contributed to the overall impression of a nation mobilised, a nation in deathly struggle.

Alongside these appeals to patriotic duty, the provincial administration and the press perpetuated 'poor victim' stereotypes of *soldatki*.[154] In the context of 1917, this can be regarded as an implicit attempt to depoliticise the *soldatki* agenda. Sympathy offered in the democratic press to these 'poor, illiterate women' implied or stated directly that the *soldatki* were a wholly unconscious group, who operated only on base instinct. *Soldatki* were routinely mentioned along with the poor, refugees and destitute.[155] By classifying the state of *soldatki* as deserving of charity, *soldatki* demands were depoliticised. The right of soldiers to receive polite treatments from their seniors and to be granted citizens' rights was accepted by all democratic organisations, in accordance with their status as politically active citizens. *Soldatki* considered their citizens' rights to include support from the state to maintain a tolerable standard of living, but their views were

---

[153] *Kazanskaia rabochaia gazeta* 35, 24 May, 1917, p. 1.
[154] For discussion of the 'poor *soldatka*' stereotype in pre-revolutionary period, see Pyle, 'Village social relations', pp. 198–217. There was also a need to counter the strongly rooted representation of *soldatki* as unrespectable members of the population, not least because of their associations with prostitution. For an example of the *soldatka* as a rough, abusive woman, see Steve A. Smith, 'The social meanings of swearing: workers and bad language in late Imperial and early Soviet Russia', *Past and Present* 160 (1986), 167–202, p. 177.
[155] See, for example, *Izvestiia Kazanskago gubernskago soveta krest'ianskikh deputatov* 4, 20 July 1917, p. 3: appeal from member of the executive committee of Kazan province soviet of peasants' deputies, Sukhanov, in which he asked that help be offered to 'the poor and *soldatki*'.

not acknowledged. Though it was practical difficulties that prevented the administration from fulfilling this demand, they did not portray *soldatki* as equal citizens, but as subjects for pity and for charity. The (exclusively male) local government leaders and journalists refused to recognise *soldatki* as a political force in their own right. This depoliticisation echoes the attitudes shown by Communist Party officials towards peasant women's protest during collectivisation.[156]

The *soldatki* movement did not self-consciously identify itself as 'political'; that is, it did not take up the programme of a political party, or try to present itself as a political organisation, in the way that other interest groups did.[157] None of the sources mention specific links between *soldatki* and political parties. The intransigent *soldatki* had potential affinity with the Bolshevik movement, but though they sometimes shared common ground in 1917, the Bolsheviks were little more than travelling companions with the *soldatki*.[158] There was an appeal published in a Kazan Bolshevik-controlled newspaper in May to join the *soldatki* union.[159] It is a fair assumption that *soldatki* support for the Bolsheviks probably related to the dynamic of heightened Bolshevik support among other social groups in the latter part of 1917.

The issue of the war was the one that most surely developed *soldatki* grievances and actions from local demands for satisfaction of material wants to national concerns. If the *soldatki* made specific association between their grievous material condition and the war, which widowed or beggared them, their complaints could take on a specifically political bent. There is, however, no evidence from the provinces considered that *soldatki* organisations addressed these national concerns in any coherent way. An unnamed soviet delegate,[160] reporting on a public meeting of the Kazan soviet of workers and soldiers' deputies on 18 May 1917, which discussed the *soldatki* question, implied that the *soldatki* were unknowing vehicles for counter-revolution and anarchy, and that their support for Bolshevik resolutions was a reflection

---

[156] Viola, 'Babi-bunty', p. 23.

[157] In Kazan, for example, the town employees complained that there was not a single town employee in any of the other lists standing for the Town Duma elections, so stood their own list of candidates (as reported in *Kazanskaia rabochaia gazeta* 132, 23 September 1917, p. 3) In the Duma elections of 8 October, they received 422 votes, which was enough to win them a seat.

[158] Farnsworth suggests that in the 1920s *soldatki* were most likely to be receptive to Bolshevik party activists, and most likely to attend meetings. (See Beatrice Farnsworth, 'Village women experience the revolution', in Gleason, Kenez and Stites, *Bolshevik culture*, pp. 238–60, p. 249.)

[159] *Rabochii* 14, 25 (12) May 1917.

[160] He was almost certainly a Menshevik, based on the political sympathies generally expressed by this paper.

of their 'dark unconsciousness'.[161] Notions of 'darkness', usually implying ignorance, illiteracy and lack of culture, were systematically applied to the rural population by its intelligentsia observers and were often particularly directed towards women.[162] Such language tells us more about the commentator's own fear and ignorance of unfamiliar or unwelcome societal norms and trends than about the allegedly 'dark' subjects.[163] A Bolshevik commentator in the paper *Rabochii* quite rightly challenged this unnamed author and asked what constituted anarchism. In the definition presented by the soviet delegate, anarchism was constituted by demands for bread and a conclusion to the war.

CONCLUSIONS

This chapter offers some insights into the impact of Russia's mass militarisation on ordinary people's lives. The experience of war permeated every section of Russian society in both urban and rural provincial life and was a major contributing factor to the pervading sense of crisis. Soldiers were not just 'peasants in greatcoats'. Their identities were complex and could involve ethnicity, religion, local identities and so on. Soldiers' wives also had complex identities, though their use of the '*soldatka*' label indicates that this category was a well-recognised and utilised identity. Both soldiers and their wives had their relationship with the state transformed by the February revolution. For soldiers, the revolution offered them the status of soldier-citizen, who could question authority and whose support for the state was conditional. For *soldatki*, the political revolution of February 1917 dramatically heightened popular expectations of what the state could deliver and offered a more open forum for expressing desires and concerns, but correspondingly worsened the economic and administrative problems Russia faced. This repositioning of the relationship between citizen and state lay at the heart of problems in governing Russia.

Soldiers and their wives contributed to Russia's sense of crisis in a number of ways. Soldier presence in the urban centres resulted in general disorder that disturbed the local population and heightened a sense of lawlessness. The July soldiers' rising in Nizhnii Novgorod is an extreme case of the impact soldiers could have on public order in the towns. When soldiers

---

[161] *Kazanskaia rabochaia gazeta* 34, 21 May 1917, p. 4.
[162] The word '*baba*', a colloquial expression meaning 'woman' and often referring specifically to rural women, had just such connotations of ignorance, irrationality and hysteria. (See Viola, 'Babi-bunty', p. 23.)
[163] See Frierson, *Peasant icons*, esp. pp. 32–127.

chose to disobey orders explicitly, they constituted a wilful and dangerous force that could only be controlled with more troops. In the countryside, soldiers in various guises, as deserters, prisoners of war and on leave, all heightened social dislocation and a sense of lawlessness. Though some particular soldiers' groups played a major role in disturbances, the problem was more general than just isolated 'hooligan elements' among the military. All soldiers, armed with their new rhetoric of rights and freedoms, contributed to a heightened sense of crisis in towns and countryside. Regional administrations were effectively unable to control soldiers in the towns and in the countryside, and this contributed to a sense of lawlessness.

In many instances soldiers and workers acted in harmony and formed the 'proletarian bloc' idolised by subsequent Soviet iconography and memoirists. They did not, however, stand unerringly united in 1917, and in Nizhegorod in particular we find evidence of hostility and conflict between workers and soldiers, centred around the sense of injustice that some soldiers harboured towards workers. Soldiers complained that workers were avoiding the military draft. Workers' complaints about the length of hours, conditions of labour and pay rang false with soldiers, who were expected to risk and if necessary sacrifice their lives in defence of the state. This injustice, in a climate when equality and fairness was stressed, resulted in some divisions and hostility among the natural alliance of workers and soldiers. The political elite tried to gloss over these conflicts, but they existed nevertheless.

The relationship of soldiers with their leaders was transient and conditional. Though in principle soldiers, with their well-developed committees and soviet, had an extensive network of representation and well-defined leadership, in practice they often bypassed their elected leadership and acted autonomously. *Soldatki* lacked the soldiers' network of representation, but by their forceful organisation and actions also effectively bypassed soviet leadership. The nature of the directly democratic soviets, and the problem of where their power and authority really lay, is brought into relief. The soviets' popular image as the body representing all toiling and impoverished people placed a massive burden of expectation on them. Their requirement to be responsive to national concerns, however, along with the pressure laid upon them by Russia's financial crisis, left them in an ambiguous position, whereby they were practically unable to satisfy the demands laid on them by their constituents. *Soldatki* rejected the leadership of both Provisional Government bodies and the soviets, leaving them as political 'loose cannon'. This contributed to the sense of political crisis that pervaded the latter months of 1917.

Finally, *soldatki* offer an unusual example of female participation in revolutionary politics. Recognising their importance as political actors cannot alter the picture of revolution as defined and directed predominantly by male workers and soldiers, but it does help us to hear those often lost voices of the female, the civilian and the rural dweller. While *soldatki*, along with all women, were on the periphery of formal power structures in 1917, they organised themselves and placed significant pressure on these formal power structures.

CHAPTER 7

'Water is yours, light is yours, the land is yours, the wood is yours'

The power and authority of the Provisional Government crumbled palpably on the land question, as state policies were sidelined and local initiatives came to dominate discourse and action on land use. Preceding chapters have explored the role of political parties and leaders, and the ways in which the political elite tried to communicate with the population. Peasant responses to the land question allow us to explore grass-roots perspectives of the revolution, perceptions of duty and responsibilities towards government and state, and broader conceptions of justice. This chapter explores the practical political interactions both among local power structures, and between peasants and government, and reveals the irregularity of power and authority structures at all levels, as central government was unable to impose their orders, or even to intervene significantly. Connections between central and regional power frayed as regional administrations made autonomous decisions to resolve land relations. The inability of central authorities to control these independent initiatives accentuated the devolution of power and authority in Nizhegorod and Kazan, away from the centre and the provincial administration, and towards lower-level organisations.

This analysis of land policies formulated at regional level reveals that the divisions that emerged were not only between central government and ordinary people, but also between central government and local government. Local leaders played a key role in forming and directing land relations. Both central government and local leaders struggled to recognise peasants' political autonomy and agency, preferring to mask their alarm at peasant action with explanations of ignorance and 'misunderstanding' in the first months of revolution. Peasants sought to work creatively in constructing new

---

NART, f. 1246, op. 1, d. 52, l. 369; declaration of Moshtaushskii village *skhod*, by Kronstadt sailor-agitator, Khalapsin, at village meeting in Cheboksarskii *uezd*, Kazan, 14 June 1917.

structures and legitimising their actions and were not only forces of destruction.[1] Peasants behaved rationally and operated intelligently in political spheres, but consciously rejected imprecations from the centre.

There has been relatively little historical study focusing solely on land relations in 1917. A number of Soviet historians dedicated themselves to work on the Russian countryside in revolution, but their work is difficult to relate to this study both because of its ideological basis and because of its unwillingness to engage with regional specificity.[2] The emphasis of Soviet works tended to be on class, and more specifically inter-peasant class struggle, as the key delineator of peasant behaviour in 1917. Like Kabanov's post-Soviet writing, class divisions among the peasantry are not evident here.[3] Soviet historiography tended to ignore geographical differences in eastern Europe.[4] Pershin, for example, mentioned specific regions in his examples of peasant action in 1917, but he did not place them in any sort of context or explain their practical distinctions. Western historiography, meanwhile, has moved increasingly towards a study of the peasantry on a regional basis. John Keep's work considered regional variations in rural revolution. Orlando Figes' first monograph made an important contribution to understandings of rural revolution in 1917, but focused on the post-October period. Mike Hickey's seminal works on Smolensk in 1917 include an article surveying rural revolution in Smolensk. The most important recent works are Mark Baker's work on Kharkiv's peasantry, and Aaron Retish's thesis on Viatka's peasantry. Baker identifies land as the most important issue for Kharkiv peasants, while Retish does not focus on land relations, which were less troubled in Viatka than in some of Russia's other European provinces.[5] Graeme Gill's 1979 monograph is the only Western work to date which focuses solely on peasant action in 1917. Whilst this book made an

---

[1] This view accords with that of Michael Hickey, who saw land redistribution as a sphere of peasant autonomy, rather than an obsession with landlords and destruction (Hickey, 'Urban *zemliachestva*', p. 19).

[2] Two key Soviet works include Maliavskii, *Krest'ianskoe dvizhenie*; P. N. Pershin, *Agrarnoe revoliutsiia v Rossii: kniga 1: ot reformy k revoliutsii* (Moscow, 1966).

[3] V. V. Kabanov, *Krest'ianskaia obshchina i kooperatsiia Rossii XX veka* (Moscow, 1997).

[4] L. V. Milov, 'Prirodno-klimaticheskii faktor i mentalitet Russkogo krest'ianstva', in V. P. Danilov (ed.), *Mentalitet i agrarnoe razvitie Rossii (XIX–XX vv.): materialy mezhdunarodnoi konferentsii Moskva. 14–15 Iiunia 1994 g.* (Moscow, 1994), pp. 40–56, p. 40.

[5] S. P. Melgunov, *The Bolshevik seizure of power* (Oxford, 1972), pp. 198–204, discusses how figures relating to peasant unrest are agreed. J. L. H. Keep, *The Russian revolution: a study in mass mobilisation* (London, 1976), pp. 186–99. Figes, *Peasant Russia, civil war*; Graeme Gill, *Peasants and government in the Russian revolution* (London, 1979); L. A. Owen, *The Russian peasant movement, 1906–1917* (London, 1937); Retish, 'Peasant identities in Russia's turmoil'; Hickey, 'Urban *zemliachestva*'; Mark Baker, 'Beyond the national: peasants, power and revolution in Ukraine', *Journal of Ukrainian Studies* 24 (1999), 39–67; Baker, 'Peasants, power and revolution'.

important contribution to the field, Gill himself tacitly acknowledged his work's avoidance of regional factors. In order to understand land relations and peasant behaviour in 1917, we need to be aware of regional diversity of both landholding and land interests.

The patterns of peasant action both in Nizhegorod and Kazan provinces share characteristics shown in other regional and national studies of peasant direct action, which included seizure of land and wood, attacks on peasant separators and enthusiasm to 'validate' peasant actions and infractions. These general trends, when explored more closely, reflected local conditions and varied from *uezd* to *uezd* within each province. We cannot make general comparisons of land relations in Nizhegorod and Kazan, because of the diversity of types of agriculture and landholding, which varied from one *uezd* to another. Figures 7.1 and 7.2, showing patterns of land use and livestock holding in the different *uezds* of Nizhegorod and Kazan, reveal that although Kazan was a bigger agricultural producer overall than Nizhegorod, and had more livestock, the distinctions between *uezds* were more significant than the distinctions between provinces. The preconditions of land relations lay in the geography of each particular region, and the history of landholding there. One area where comparisons can be drawn more clearly is in the agrarian policies carried out at provincial level in Nizhegorod and Kazan, which were to have a significant impact in shaping the nature of land relations, and the levels of land-related conflict in the provinces.

In figures 7.1 and 7.2, the first twelve *uezds* listed are in Kazan province, the second eleven in Nizhegorod province. Chistopolskii *uezd* in Kazan province has a significantly larger sown area than any of the other *uezds*, but also had a comparably larger population. The data in figure 7.2 show that although Kazan was a bigger agricultural producer overall, crop types and levels of production varied significantly from *uezd* to *uezd*, and some *uezds* in Nizhegorod province, for example, were larger crop producers than some *uezds* in Kazan province. Rye, usually grown for home consumption rather than export, was the major crop for all *uezds* in both Nizhegorod and Kazan provinces. Figure 7.2 offers us a glimpse of specific local variations in agriculture. While most of the *uezds* grew negligible quantities of hemp, for example, Arzamasskii and Lukoianovskii *uezds*, both in Nizhegorod province, grew significant quantities, no doubt reflecting local conditions and the needs of local cottage industry. These figures confirm that our understandings of local land relations must be informed by local agricultural conditions, that varied significantly from place to place.

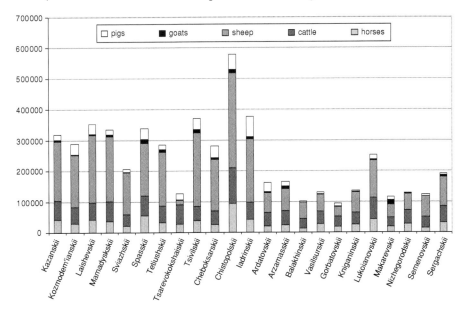

Figure 7.1. Livestock (per head) held in Nizhegorod and Kazan provinces, by *uezd*, for 1916
Source: *Predvaritel'nye vserossiiskoi sel'skokhoziaistvennoi perepisi 1916 goda (Po podschetam, proizvedennym mestnymi perepisnymi uchrezhdeniiami)* (Petrograd, 1916), pp. 94–123.

PRIVATELY OWNED LAND

The land question dominated peasant revolutionary discourse and priorities in Kazan and Nizhegorod, as it had in the pre-revolutionary period. Nizhegorod and Kazan were among Russia's most active regions in terms of the volume of recorded peasant risings.[6] Figures on numbers of peasant disturbances are, however, notoriously unreliable, as they depend on how peasant disturbances are defined, and the judgements of the list compilers.[7] The dominance of the land question in Nizhegorod and Kazan reflected the geography and economy of these provinces, both of which had large tracts of arable land. Aaron Retish's work on Viatka shows that interest in the land question was dependent on the presence of land hunger and of non-peasant ownership, neither of which applied to Viatka.[8] While it is important, as Retish notes, to acknowledge that peasant interest in land

[6] Maliavskii, *Krest'ianskoe dvizhenie*, pp. 374–80.
[7] For a discussion of the problems of quantifying peasant unrest, see Baker, 'Peasants, power and revolution', chapter 2, and Figes, *Peasant Russia, civil war*, p. 47.
[8] Retish, 'Peasant identities in Russia's turmoil', p. 180ff.

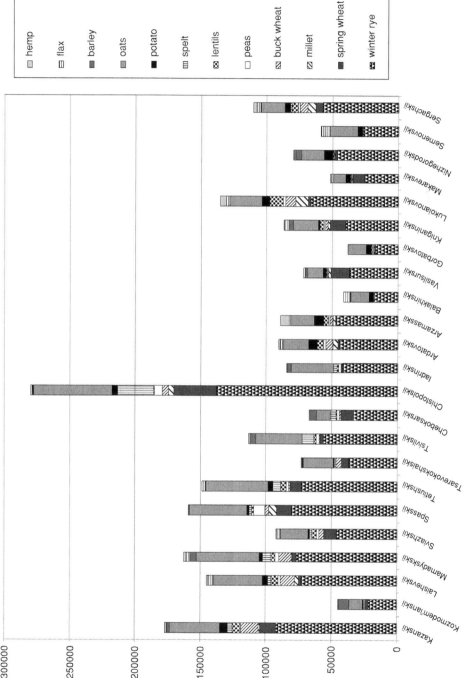

Figure 7.2. Sown areas (in *desiatins*) in Nizhegorod and Kazan provinces, by *uezd*, showing crop types, for 1916

Source: Predvaritel' nye vserossiiskoi sel' skokhoziaistvennoi perepisi 1916, pp. 94–123.

was entirely rational, we must also recognise that where land was an issue, its significance went much deeper than political affiliations, ownership or improved conditions of living; it was closely associated with peasant notions of *volia* (will or freedom). An undated appeal from Tsarevokokshaiskii *uezd* soviet of peasants' deputies, Kazan province, declared that 'the most important question [for the Constituent Assembly] is the life of the peasantry and their riches. Their riches are the land. A peasant without land is like a person without hands.'[9] This highly emotional language reflected the significance of landholding as beyond economic concerns, and encapsulating essential peasant desires. A village teacher, D. Kuznetsov, described peasant discourse in Lukoianovskii *uezd*, Nizhegorod province:

Peasants are silent about the schools, about the state structure and about *zemstva*, but they talk and talk about who is to get the most land. The general mood is very certain. The source of land is unquestionably to come from landowners, without payment . . . the second question, on how the land is to be used, provokes more disagreement. The elders say that we will live communally . . . others say that land must be collectivised . . . a third dream is the creation of *khutors* . . .[10]

Both the Provisional Government and the soviets demanded that peasants wait for decision of the land question by the Constituent Assembly. This policy of waiting was not accepted by much of the peasant population. Land was not only an economic concern, it was a matter of fulfilling peasants' 'just will'. An educational 'question and answer' section in the Left SR-dominated Kazan soviet of peasants' deputies' newspaper asked rhetorically; 'But is Russia's salvation harmed by the just will of the peasantry being fulfilled? *(A razve vredit spaseniiu Rossii to, chto spravedlivaia volia krest'ianstva budet ispolnena?)*'[11]

In both Nizhegorod and Kazan provinces, by 1916 less than 5 per cent of arable land was in non-peasant hands, and figure 7.3 shows that private land-owning was statistically insignificant in both provinces.[12] Private land-ownership was concentrated in two *uezds* of each province, Spasskii (14 per cent privately owned) and Laishevskii (13 per cent privately owned) in Kazan, and Kniagininskii (seven percent privately owned) and Lukoianskii (8 per cent privately owned) in Nizhegorod.[13] It was in these *uezds* that seizure of non-peasant land was most frequently seen. The seizure of privately held land by peasants is an enduring image of 1917, but the

[9] NART, f. 983, op. 1, d. 18, ll. 53–4; appeal of Tsarevokokshaiskii *uezd* peasants' deputies, undated.
[10] *Nizhegorodskaia zemskaia gazeta* 31–32, 10 August 1917, pp. 15–16.
[11] *Izvestiia Kazanskago gubernskago soveta krest'ianskikh deputatov* 15, 20 August 1917, pp. 2–3.
[12] *Predvaritel'nye vserossiiskoi sel'skokhoziaistvennoi perepisi 1916*, pp. 94–123.
[13] Figures from *Predvaritel'nye vserossiiskoi sel'skokhoziaistvennoi perepisi 1916*, pp. 94–123.

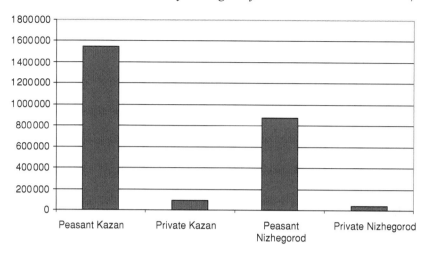

Figure 7.3. Land sown (in *desiatins*) by peasant and private owners, 1916
Source: *Predvaritel'nye vserossiiskoi sel'skokhoziaistvennoi perepisi 1916*, pp. 94–123.

stereotype of violent seizure and even destruction of landlords' property was infrequently seen. In many cases, transition of land into peasant hands was made without open conflict. Peasants were able to utilise a range of 'pseudo-legal' and intimidating tactics to gain use of land, before the use of violence, which was usually a last resort measure.

The actions of peasants from Aryshkadza village, Kazan province, is a typical example of peasant seizure of land by threat of violence rather than by its actual application. Acting under the auspices of the *skhod*, Aryshkadza peasants declared on 26 August that the land of the local owner Korsakov would be sown by them for winter grain, and that Korsakov's employees had one day to leave the property. The peasants worked the fields the following day.[14] Applied violence became more likely when there was a history of bad relations between peasants and a landowner, or if the landowner resisted the taking of inventories or the transfer of his land. In Chistopolskii *uezd*, the owner of the Mamykovskii estate, Shults, refused to co-operate with the land committee, and the *uezd* commissar warned that without soldiers it would not be possible to preserve the estate.[15] Natalia Neratova, a landowner in Laishevskii *uezd*, reported to the provincial commissar at the end of May that she had left her property because of threats from soldiers and a group

---

[14] *Kazanskaia rabochaia gazeta* 119, 6 September 1917, p. 3.
[15] NART, f. 1246, op. 1, d. 50, ll. 44–5; report to the *uezd* provisions administration, Chistopolskii *uezd*, late May 1917.

of women and boys, who came to her house at midnight and carried out a search of the whole property. They reportedly grew angry when nothing was found, and boys threw stones at the windows.[16]

Landowners were virtually powerless to resist incursions on their property, though they protested vociferously to regional and central government. Their vigour in protesting to the authorities may well explain the dominance of seizure of privately owned land in accounts of the revolutionary situation, even in provinces like Nizhegorod and Kazan, where levels of private land-ownership were so low. The Provisional Government supported private landholders' claims in principle, but in practice could not prevent peasant incursions. Local government tended to be more hostile to landowners' claims, and would not allow them to hold arms for self-defence. In Chistopolskii *uezd*, the military committee issued a decree in the spring announcing that all landowners were to be disarmed, and left only with small arms for hunting.[17] Where landowners were intransigent in their relations with local land committees, their own position was often made worse. In Kazan *uezd*, several landowners refused to allow inventories to be taken of their property, which resulted in some of their property going missing, without any means for them to account for it.[18] Landowners in Spasskii *uezd*, Kazan province, put up concerted resistance to peasant attempts to seize their land and property on 27 April but were unable to prevent the theft of their cattle and the appropriation of their meadowland.[19]

Peasants shared some common attitudes towards land, but conflict was not only between peasant and landlord, but also among peasants themselves. Other studies have pointed to hierarchies and divisions within peasant communities, though these conflicts were not conducted along class lines.[20] The new freedoms of 1917 offered a forum for open conflicts between

---

[16] NART, f. 1246, op. 1, d. 54, ll. 331–2; letter from landowner Natalia Neratova, to the provincial commissar, 27 May 1917.

[17] NART, f. 1246, op. 1, d. 50, ll. 136–7; two letters from Chistopolskii *uezd* commissar to provincial commissar, 13/18 August 1917.

[18] NART, f. 174, op. 1, d. 9, l. 23; journal of the meeting of the Kazan provincial land committee, 22 and 23 July 1917.

[19] NART, f. 1246, op. 1, d. 41, l. 58; appeal to minister for land regarding seizure of Butlerovka estate, 27 April 1917.

[20] See, for example, Orlando Figes, 'Peasant farmers and the minority groups of rural society: peasant egalitarianism and village social relations during the Russian revolution', in E. Kingston-Mann, T. Mixter and Jeffrey Burds (eds.), *Peasant economy, culture and politics of European Russia 1860–1921* (Princeton, NJ, 1991), pp. 379–401; Maureen Perrie, 'The Russian peasant movement of 1905–1907: its social composition and revolutionary significance', *Past and Present* 57 (1972), 123–55; Maureen Perrie, 'The Russian peasant movement of 1905 – its composition and significance', in Ben Eklof and Stephen P. Frank (eds.), *The world of the Russian peasant* (1996), pp. 193–208. Mark Baker's work on Ukrainian peasants found that inter-peasant conflict was the norm (Baker, 'Beyond the national').

peasant communities, both across villages and within village communities. Though communality characterised much peasant activity in 1917, conflict among peasants was also an important feature. Inter-village rivalries, interspersed by outbreaks of violence, often featured in pre-revolutionary village life.[21] There were violent conflicts between peasants in some communities during 1917. In some cases, conflicts arose between wealthy and less-well-off peasants, as in June in Almeteva, where wealthy Tatars from Kulbaev village seized land from the Ostrovskii estate that was rented by landless peasants.[22] In other cases, the origins of violent conflict were unclear. One village in Chistopolskii *uezd* appealed directly to then Minister of Justice Kerensky to send military force to protect them from the robbing and violence against them by peasants of three neighbouring villages.[23]

Those peasants who had left the commune to farm independently (separators) were often the targets of inter-peasant violence. Attacks on separators formed the bulk of inter-peasant conflict and confirmed communal peasants' desires to maintain traditional landholding patterns, and to resist the changes of the last fifteen years.[24] Separators were targets for communal peasant action throughout 1917, whether they were pressured back into the commune, had 'surplus' lands requisitioned, or were driven from their land. Orlando Figes' work suggested that in the middle-Volga region peasant direct action was more bitter where directed against separators from the commune than against gentry landowners.[25] The incidence of reports on action against separators in both Kazan and Nizhegorod provinces confirms this. In Kazan province, numerous reports noted that in many *uezds*

---

[21] Stephen Frank comments that 'violence in general was more typical of rural than urban areas' (Frank, 'Popular justice', p. 243). Group fist-fighting contests, for example, that sometimes degenerated into scenes of extreme violence, were regarded as a form of recreation by both urban and rural working classes. (See Daniel R. Brower, 'Labor violence in Russia in the late nineteenth century', *Slavic Review* 41 (1982), 417–31, p. 425.)

[22] NART, f. 1246, op. 1, d. 53, l. 194; telegram reporting disturbance in village, 26 June 1917.

[23] NART, f. 1246, op. 1, d. 50, l. 154; urgent telegram to Kerensky from peasants of Kutushskoi *volost*, Chistopolskii *uezd*, Kazan province, undated. For other examples, see NART, f. 1246, op. 1, d. 51, l. 176; report from assistant provincial commissar to Mamadyshskii *uezd* commissar, undated; NART, f. 1246, 1, d. 50, l. 24; report from captain of Chistopol militia to Chistopolskii *uezd* commissar, 24 June 1917.

[24] For pre-revolutionary peasant resistance to changes in land tenure, see Judy Pallot, *Land reform in Russia 1906–1917: peasant responses to Stolypin's project of rural transformation* (New York, 1999), esp. chapters 3 and 6. Figes, *Peasant Russia, civil war*, pp. 56–61, considered the movement of communal peasants against separators in the Volga region.

[25] Figes, 'Peasant farmers', p. 384. Also, see Orlando Figes, 'The Russian peasant community in the agrarian revolution, 1917–18', in Roger Bartlett (ed.), *Land commune and peasant community in Russia* (New York, 1990), pp. 237–53, p. 240. Note, however, that action against separators was regionally specific; Michael Hickey has found that in Smolensk, for example, the number of *khutori* and *otruba* actually increased in 1917.

and *volosts* the commune seized separators' land.[26] Commune attacks on separators were not simply anarchic assaults on the better off. They reflected deeper notions about justice, land holding and society. The village committee of Novo-Shchelkinskii, Staro-Arabinskii *volost*, Tsivilskii *uezd*, issued a 'verdict' on 13 August. Its language is unusual for rural pronouncements, and strongly suggestive of a party political influence, with repeated use of Social Democratic terminology. That said, its sentiment on the position of separators is clear:

> We, the undersigned citizens of Novo-Shchelkinskii village committee, Staro-Arabinskii *volost*, Tsivilskii *uezd*, at a general people's meeting discussed the problem that several citizens with larger families and young people from the age of 18, some of whom bear the burden of military and government service, do not currently have a scrap of land, while such land is occupied by the bourgeoisie, that is, by rich people who strengthened their own holdings after the death and resettlement in Siberia of several individuals, with the support of the now overthrown government . . . the bourgeoisie illegally enticed neighbouring people to rent their land to them. Giving them loans of money and grain, and treating them to beer and wine, [a practice] which continues now. This is why it is unanimously declared – to take from the bourgeoisie both strengthened rented land and church land, and to grant this land to the landless and the young. They have the right to sow this with winter grain as of 1917. The current verdict is signed . . . (list of illiterates' names)[27]

The role of the village committee in this declaration, stating common interest and unifying community response to separators, was a feature of many communal incursions on separator land. The *skhod* of Zakharave village, Khvostikovskii *volost*, Semenovskii *uezd*, Nizhegorod province, declared on 17 April that there would be no more separate landholding in the commune but allowed separators to return their land to communal use only after the harvest of the spring sowing they had already planted, and that they would be guaranteed the use of their pastures for one year. This allowed for a period of transition for separators but was emphatic in concluding that after the transition period, 'all *otrubnik* land will again be made communal'.[28]

---

[26] NART, f. 1246, op. 1, d. 64, l. 143; circular from Kazan province executive committee, undated. See also NART, f. 1246, op. 1, d. 48, l. 135; telegram to Kozmodem'ianskii *uezd* commissar from provincial commissar, 27 May 1917; NART, f. 1246, op. 1, d. 49, ll. 120–1; letter from Staro-Arabosinskoi *volost* committee, Tsivilskii *uezd*, to provincial commissar, 17 August 1917; NART, f. 1246, op. 1, d. 51, ll. 264–6; letters from separators to provincial commissar, 16–19 June 1917.

[27] NART, f. 1246, op. 1, d. 49, l. 121; joint appeal from thirteen separators of Ziurinskii *volost*, Mamadyshskii *uezd*, to provincial commissar, 19 June 1917.

[28] GANO, f. 815, op. 1, d. 30, l. 8; decree from peasants of Zakharave village, Khvostikovskii *volost*, Semenevskii *uezd*, 17 April 1917.

The extent of action against separators depended in part on the numbers of separators in the area. In Siukeev village, Tetiushskii *uezd*, it was reported that there were more than 700 separators in a village of 2,171 people. The separators had reportedly taken the best land, and the *skhod* ordered the separators' arrest.[29] Some separators had their lives as well as their livelihoods threatened. Separators in Chistopolskii *uezd* were physically threatened by their communal neighbours, and a Tatar was killed in Chistopolskii *uezd* during disputes over use of separators' land.[30] A group of separators in Chistopolskii *uezd* formed a small landowners' society in July and appealed to the provincial commissar about the threats of violence they endured. Local land committees had turned down their appeals, though the provincial commissar ruled in their favour.[31] Separators' appeals and petitions illuminate their troubled position in post-revolutionary village life. The commune targeted Badamshin, a Trudovik and former member of the first two State Dumas who had been imprisoned twice for his resistance to the old regime. In a telegram to Kerensky at the end of April, Badamshin explained that neighbouring communal peasants had seized the seventy-seven *desiatins* of land that had been worked by him and his family for more than forty years. His brother had been threatened with murder and the family faced ruin.[32] The kudos of an old revolutionary hero was inadequate protection against communal incursions on his property.

Provisional Government, soviets and local government were unanimous in their support for separators who worked their own land but had limited means available to intervene on their behalf. Separators from Makar'evskii *uezd* came in person to the provincial meeting of *uezd* commissars, to complain about threats and violence against them by peasants from the commune. Despite a supportive hearing at this meeting, reports of violence against separators continued into October.[33] Separators in Mamadyshskii

[29] NART, f. 1246, op. 1, d. 74, ll. 221–2; from the instructor-account of the office of petty credit of Kazan provincial *zemstvo* to the Kazan province provisions committee and the committee of public safety regarding his travels around Tetiushskii *uezd*, 29 May 1917.

[30] NART, f. 1246, op. 1, d. 50, l. 25; report of Chistopolskii *uezd* land committee to the *uezd* commissar, 26 June 1917.

[31] NART, f. 1246, op. 1, d. 50, ll. 121–2; from members of Nikolskii land society, Chistopolskii *uezd*, to provincial commissar, 21 July 1917.

[32] NART, f. 1246, op. 1, d. 41, ll. 103–4; telegram to Kerensky, 30 April 1917. For a similar example, see NART, f. 983, op. 1, d. 23, ll. 102–7, 127; appeals of separators against land seizures in Tsivilskii, Kozmodem'ianskii, Cheboksarskii *uezds*, June–July 1917.

[33] GANO, f. 1882, op. 1, d. 13, ll. 155–9; protocol of the meeting of *uezd* commissars in Nizhegorod province, 10–11 April 1917; GANO, f. 1882, op. 1, d. 28, l. 445: report of the provincial commissar to the Ministry of Internal Affairs, 23 October 1917.

uezd were targeted by communal peasants and attacked as 'dead souls',[34] and had all their land seized.[35] Kazan's committee of public safety sent a delegate, Stepanov, to intervene, but though he claimed to have resolved the problems, bitter complaints from separators to the provincial commissar continued through the summer.[36] Mamadyshskii *uezd*'s militia captain reported to the *uezd* commissar in August that a member of Kazan's soviet of peasant deputies, Nikoforov, had visited the *uezd* and had incited the crowd against Stepanov, a member of the committee of public safety, and against other local leaders.[37]

WOODLAND

Woodcutting was the most widespread and insidious of all forms of agrarian disorder in Nizhegorod province and was also a prominent feature of Kazan's agrarian disorder. Several thousand telegrams reporting agrarian unrest in Nizhegorod province referred predominantly to woodcutting.[38] Woodcutting featured in the reports of most *uezd* commissars from March through to October.[39] Seizure of private and state-owned woodlands was commonplace, because, as we see in figure 7.4, while only a tiny proportion

[34] NART, f. 1246, op. 1, d. 51, l. 207; report to Kazan committee of public safety from delegate sent to Mamadyshskii *uezd*, 23 May 1917.

[35] NART, f. 1246, op. 1, d. 43, l. 73; letter to provincial commissar from group of separators in Mamadyshskii *uezd*, 15 July 1917.

[36] NART, f. 1246, op. 1, d. 43, l. 243; report of soviet of peasants' deputies delegate Stepanov, on the situation in Mamadyshskii *uezd*, 10 July 1917; NART, f. 1246, op. 1, d. 43, l. 101; Matvei Svechnikov, a soldier and *khutorian* who bought land after the Russo-Japanese war in Shemobrashskii *volost*, Mamadyshskii *uezd*, had his land seized by neighbouring communal peasants and was left without any means for his family. He appealed to the provincial commissar on 26 July. NART, f. 1246, op. 1, d. 43, l. 69; on 15 July, *otrubniki* in Shemorbash village, Mamadyshskii *uezd*, requested that a command of soldiers be sent to protect them and their property. They warned that if the seizures were not halted, there would be widespread riots across the *uezd*.

[37] NART, f. 1246, op. 1, d. 43, l. 301; report to Mamadyshskii *uezd* commissar from captain of militia, 27 August 1917.

[38] GANO, f. 1882, op. 1, d. 44, ll. 57–384; telegrams from the *uezds* to the provincial commissar, reporting peasant unrest, almost all of which was manifested as woodcutting, in March and April 1917. GANO, f. 1882, op. 1, d. 14, ll. 1–339; most of these pages are telegrams about peasant action for the period 1 June–25 July 1917. GANO, f. 1882, op. 1, d. 23; telegrams and letters about agrarian risings (seizure of land, woodcutting, cattle requisition), for the period 27 April–12 September 1917. GANO, f. 1882, op. 1, d. 28; 480 pages included telegrams about reports on agrarian disorder. GANO, f. 1882, op. 1, d. 42; 512 pages of writings about the risings of the peasantry against the Provisional Government. Most of these were reports of woodcutting. GANO, f. 1882, op. 1, d. 45; 847 pages, writings about peasant seizure of land, 6 April–25 October 1917.

[39] GANO, f. 1882, op. 1, d. 28, l. 6; telegram from provincial commissar Demidov to Ministry for Internal Affairs, 13 March 1917; GANO, f. 1882, op. 1, d. 28, l. 312; report from Lukoianovskii *uezd* commissar, 23 September 1917; GANO, f. 1882, op. 1, d. 28, l. 314; report from Balakhninskii *uezd* commissar, October 1917; GANO, f. 1882, op. 1, d. 28, l. 435; report of Makar'evskii *uezd* commissar, October 1917.

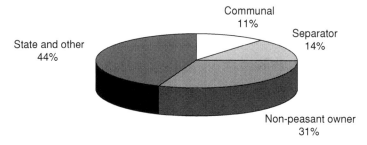

Figure 7.4. Ownership of woodland in Nizhegorod province
Source: *Nizhegorodskaia zemskaia gazeta*, 31–32, 10 August 1917, pp. 8–9.

of farm land was in communal hands, 75 per cent of woodland was held by non-peasants and the state.[40] Woodcutting did not occur at specific times of year, as seen in the seizure of arable and meadowland, but could take place whenever the cutter had time and inclination. Woodland made up 44 per cent of all land in Nizhegorod province, but more than 70 per cent of it was privately or state-owned. Non-peasant woodland became the prime target for peasant seizure. Some *uezds* had very little woodland, while others were heavily forested; more than 75 per cent of Makar'evskii *uezd* was woodland, for example, while Vasil'skii *uezd* was only 3 per cent woodland. The type and extent of peasant action depended very heavily on local conditions.

Some works have suggested that the peasants themselves often regulated widespread woodcutting.[41] The picture in Kazan and Nizhegorod was rather more complex. There were instances where the village administration acted against unauthorised woodcutting. In Varvarinskii commune, Sviazhskii *uezd*, Kazan, the *skhod* decreed that woodcutting and land seizure had to end and arrested a number of individuals as a result of their woodcutting activities.[42] In other areas, however, woodcutting was condoned or ignored by land committees, and was carried out both by individuals and by the whole commune.[43]

The motives for woodcutting were complex. Fuel shortages offered a prosaic explanation for woodcutting. In Laishevskii *uezd*, Kazan, the *uezd* commissar appealed to the provincial commissar on 27 April to permit

---

[40] Figures from *Nizhegorodskaia zemskaia gazeta* 31–32, 10 August 1917, pp. 8–9.

[41] Gill, *Peasants and government*, p. 43; Maliavskii, *Krest'ianskoe dvizhenie*, pp. 167–8.

[42] NART, f. 1246, op. 1, d. 45, l. 212; decree of *skhod* in Varvarinskii obshchestvo, Sviazhskii *uezd*, 5 June 1917.

[43] Graham Tan's study of right bank Ukraine found that peasant woodcutting took the character of 'uncontrolled despoiling' (Tan, 'Village social organisation', p. 78).

some woodcutting, in order to satisfy the population's urgent needs. He warned that there would be major disturbances as a result of winter fuel shortages if measures were not taken to ameliorate the situation.[44] In some areas peasants cut wood in order to stockpile or sell. In Nizhegorod, much of the population urgently needed money in order to purchase grain at 1917's ever-inflating prices, which made the felling of wood for sale particularly attractive. Whole villages participated in woodcutting in Semenovskii *uezd*, and cut wood for sale as well as for personal use. Peasants resolutely ignored the appeals and imprecations of the local land committee, and the militia was unable to cope.[45] Landowners in Balakhninskii *uezd* were accused of intensifying uncontrolled woodcutting by chopping their own wood to prevent wood from falling into the hands of the peasantry.[46]

Corruption of militia and wood guards also played a part in facilitating the movement. In Alatskoi *volost*, Kazan *uezd*, the chief of militia Akimov was alleged to be the most active figure in the illicit cutting and sale of wood.[47] Forest guards were bribed or overwhelmed by the volume of resistance. The foresters of Cheremshanskii forest, in Spasskii *uezd*, noted that even their increased pay of ten roubles per month was not enough to persuade employees to stay at their posts when they saw land redistribution going on around them.[48] From early in 1917, M. E. Sumgin, Nizhegorod provincial commissar, reported on the situation of the province for the period August–September and offered a feasible overall explanation for woodcutting:

The agrarian movement manifests itself in arbitrary woodcutting on privately owned and state land in the province; the cutting of wood is carried out by the population partly with aims of preparation of firewood for winter, and in the majority of cases cut to take advantage of the high prices of wood.[49]

As with the seizure of private land, regional administrators recognised that regulation rather than unenforceable prohibition was the best way to deal with the crisis. They were unable to prevent the wanton cutting of

[44] NART, f. 1246, op. 1, d. 54, l. 180; report from Laishevskii *uezd* commissar to provincial commissar, 27 April 1917.
[45] GANO, f. 815, op. 1, d. 30, ll. 82–3; protocol of the restoration of order in Semenov town, 20 September 1917.
[46] GANO, f. 1882, op. 1, d. 13, ll. 155–9; protocol of the meeting of *uezd* commissars in Nizhegorod province, 10–11 April 1917.
[47] NART, f. 174, op. 1, d. 44, l. 96; meeting of Kazan *uezd* land committee, 25 September 1917.
[48] NART, f. 1246, op. 1, d. 41, l. 354; report from Foresters of Cheremshanskii forestry, to Kazan administration of land affairs and state property, 1 June 1917.
[49] GANO, f. 1882, op. 1, d. 43, l. 361; report from provincial commissar to the Ministry of Internal Affairs on situation in the province. Undated.

wood from private and state woodlands. The Nizhegorod soviet of peasants' deputies proposed control by regulation, with the establishment of
fixed prices on woodland, and the power of requisition for *uezd* executive
committees if private owners resisted such fixed prices.[50] The provincial
commissar supported these measures, but it was not until 23 October that
he was emboldened to act against the Provisional Government's orders and
transfer land and wood to the hands of the land committees.[51] The Kazan
provincial land committee decided at its meeting on 20 June to form a special wood use commission to try and control the burgeoning wood crisis.[52]
Sviazhskii *uezd*'s land committee tried to pre-empt and control 'predatory'
woodcutting in private and state-woods by declaring all such woodland
to be the property of the *uezd*, and guarded by *uezd* administration.[53]
The Kazan soviet of peasants' deputies passed a provisional law about the
defence of woodland and its timber in response to the wholesale felling
of private and state-owned land. Committees were to be formed at *uezd*
and province level.[54] As in other aspects of rural governance, few practical
measures were available to protect woodland.

GOVERNING THE COUNTRYSIDE

Peasants sought to protect themselves, and to define their position in
relation to central authorities. Peasants tried to legitimise their actions
in pseudo-legal forms,[55] and some incursions into private property were
organised 'in the belief that such acts complied with the needs of the revolution'.[56] Other regional studies on peasant behaviour in 1917 have noted
the enthusiasm with which peasants pursued legal means to acquire land,
or to use legal vindications and trappings with their seizures.[57] Peasants
acted rationally in their attempts to resolve land relations. They utilised the
language of revolutionary rights and citizens' norms to justify and vindicate

[50] GANO, f. 1882, op. 1, d. 13, l. 103; excerpt from the decree of the Nizhegorod soviet of peasants'
deputies, 29 May 1917.
[51] GANO, f. 1882, op. 1, d. 28, l. 445; report of provincial commissar Sumgin to Ministry of Internal
Affairs, 23 October 1917.
[52] NART, f. 1353, op. 1, d. 1, ll. 56–60; protocol of the meeting of the committee of public safety, 20
June 1917. See also NART, f. 983, op. 1, d. 23, l. 83; request from the soviet of peasants' deputies to
Kazan provincial commissar, 13 June 1917.
[53] NART, f. 1246, op. 1, d. 71, ll. 63–5; meeting of the Sviazhskii *uezd* land committee, 18–19 June 1917.
[54] NART, f. 174, op. 1, d. 1, l. 171; provisional law issued by the soviet of peasants' deputies about
the defence of woodland and its timber, undated but contemporaneous with the Kazan soviet of
peasants' deputies land law, 13 May 1917.
[55] See Figes, *Peasant Russia, civil war*, p. 51; Tan, 'Village social organisation', p. 85.
[56] Hickey, 'Urban *zemliachestva*', p. 151.
[57] Retish, 'Peasant identities in Russia's turmoil', p. 185; Baker, 'Peasants, power and revolution',
chapter 2.

their own behaviour. A report from Vasil'skii *uezd* in April commented on the careful list making and organisation that accompanied peasant demands and actions; 'The population made up a list of private landowners' provision reserves, calculating according to them what they, the peasants, were to receive in their decree.'[58]

In Kazan, peasants often acquired written validation of land transfer from 'harassed landlords'.[59] In one village in Kozmodem'ianskii *uezd*, Kazan, the village inhabitants sent an elegantly worded appeal to the Kazan soviet of workers and soldiers' deputies asking that former state land alongside the village should be appropriated by them.[60] This showed that the community sometimes sought approval and affirmation from some form of authority before they took any action. A more extreme example of such action was the decisions taken by Shemobarskii *volost* committee of public safety in Mamadyshskii *uezd* in Kazan at their meeting in April. Taking on a mantle of great authority, they declared that all land was to be transferred to the hands of local land committees prior to the convocation of the Constituent Assembly.[61] A similar decree was issued by Spasskii *uezd* provisions committee on 29–30 May, with an additional clause that the population was to be supplied with wood.[62] This declaration predated a similar decree later issued by the Kazan soviet of peasants' deputies on a province-wide basis.

In the enactment of these 'pseudo-legal' decisions, peasants often used coercion by means of threatened violence. The peasants of Ivanovko village in Kazanskii *uezd*, for example, made a formal declaration in May that the landowner Bashkirov had agreed, in the presence of the president of the *volost* executive committee, to transfer all his land to peasants with the exception of five *desiatins* for his own use, and that he would supply the peasants with grain. He was to be paid with part of the 1918 harvest.[63] Bashkirov, however, in a letter to the Union of Agriculturalists, asserted that the peasants had forced him to agree to this transfer, and that he feared a beating or murder if he had refused. Though the president of the *volost* executive committee had destroyed the protocol on 19 May,

[58] GANO, f. 1882, op. 1, d. 13, ll. 155–9; protocol of the meeting of *uezd* commissars in Nizhegorod province, 10–11 April 1917.
[59] NART, f. 983, op. 1, d. 23, l. 208; protocol of soldier-peasant meeting, 6 May 1917.
[60] NART, f. 983, op. 1, d. 23, l. 157; protocol from peasants to soviet of peasants, workers and soldiers' deputies, 21 July 1917.
[61] NART, f. 983, op. 1, d. 16, l. 19; decree of Shemobarskii *volost* committee of public safety, Mamadyshskii *uezd*, 14 April 1917.
[62] NART, f. 1246, op. 1, d. 41, l. 354; report from Foresters of Cheremshanskii forestry to Kazan administration of land affairs and state property, 1 June 1917.
[63] NART, f. 1246, op. 1, d. 75, l. 224; resolution of peasants of Ivanovko village, Kazanskii *uezd*, 19 May 1917.

peasants demanded that the agreement be remade.[64] Panovskii *volost* committee arrested a landowner from Laishevskii *uezd*, Petr Alekseev, in May for refusing to sign the document affirming 'voluntary' transfer of his land to peasants. His land was taken regardless and redistributed, and the villagers appropriated the prisoners of war on his property.[65] The intervention of the *uezd* commissar caused Alekseev to be freed and initiated an investigation into the incident.[66]

In some cases there was open conflict in interpretations of events according to landowners and peasants. A report from the owner of nearby woodland told the provincial commissar that the peasants of Vydreevka and Dydrei villages, acting in consort, mowed the meadows owned by a peasant from a neighbouring village, relying only on 'the people's right' (*narodnik prav*) as their justification.[67] An investigation into this accusation suggested that the matter was not a deliberate infringement, but a 'misunderstanding', and that the villagers involved had collected money to pay for the meadows. The villagers' payment was clearly a post-factum validation of their actions.[68]

There were instances of peasants withdrawing their claims openly, again using pseudo-legal documentation, where they recognised that they had transgressed proper norms. The landowner Molostvov had his cattle seized in the name of the local land committee, but when the peasants 'became conscious of their incorrect actions' the cattle were returned.[69] In an instance of illicit woodcutting in Sviazhskii *uezd*, Kazan province, in June, the peasants involved issued a detailed and apologetic explanation:

We citizens of Seitova village, Tashevskii *volost*, gathered on 7 June 1917 at the *skhod* in the presence of the captain of the militia, the assistant of Sviazhskii *uezd* commissar, the president of the *volost* committee and the president of Seitovskii village committee declare – we the undersigned citizens of Seitova village acknowledge that we are guilty in the unauthorised theft of wood which formerly belonged to citizen Pauluchchi, and which is now NATIONAL (NARODNYI) property. And in order to

[64] NART, f. 1246, op. 1, d. 75, l. 225; letter from landowner Mukhamediia Galeevicha Bashirova to Kazan Union of Agriculturalists, 26 July 1917.

[65] NART, f. 1246, op. 1, d. 54, l. 375; letter from Kazan Union of Agriculturalists to provincial commissar, 6 June 1917.

[66] NART, f. 1246, op. 1, d. 54, l. 380; report from Laishevskii *uezd* commissar to provincial commissar, 8 June 1917.

[67] GANO, f. 815, op. 1, d. 30, l. 106; from Baranikhovskii forestry administration, Semenov town, to Nizhegorod provincial commissar, 3 July 1917.

[68] GANO, f. 815, op. 1, d. 30, l. 108; provincial commissar response to Baranikhovskii forestry administration.

[69] NART, f. 1246, op. 1, d. 183, ll. 44–5; from journal of the meeting of the Kazan provincial land committee, 23–24 September 1917.

wash this stain from ourselves, [which was made] THROUGH IGNORANCE, and which we cannot with honour leave on ourselves – we ask the provincial commissar to take from us this fine gathered voluntarily from those guilty of wood theft, and use the money for the needs of a school. We have gathered the fine at 50 kopeks for every one of us guilty of stealing wood. Altogether have been gathered 280 roubles. (SIGNED)[70]

The peasants of Seitovo recognised that the new freedoms of 1917 were balanced against requirements to uphold the law and maintain the state. This example of peasants withdrawing from their initial cause is unusual. The pseudo-legal justifications used by peasants to support their claims showed that they engaged with the language of revolution and used this language to support their own interpretations of the new order.

As 1917 progressed, a clear division emerged between the policies made and supported by the Provisional Government, and the policies enacted by regional government. Central government's attitudes towards peasants evolved in the course of 1917, but they were confused and consistently failed to address peasant interests or to show any real understanding of peasant motivations and actions. The Provisional Government's position on the land question was echoed by other central and regional organisations. It reasserted that the Constituent Assembly was the only body that would be authorised and empowered to make full and fair land redistribution. Until its convocation, peasants were to wait peacefully. Regional government policy was more dynamic and responded more closely to peasants' needs, both because its personnel were more closely linked with the peasants they governed, and because proximity to real problems forced administrators to take practical measures to best control the situation.

Victor Chernov's appointment as minister for agriculture in the first coalition government was very popular among the peasantry and raised expectations that land reform would be forthcoming.[71] The challenges to Chernov's position in government from the Kadets in July and August evoked a fierce response from regional peasant assemblies, who clearly regarded Chernov as 'their' minister.[72] The results of Chernov's appointment, from a peasant perspective, were disappointing. He carried the banner of social revolution alone in the new coalition government, and was isolated

[70] NART, f. 1246, op. 1, d. 45, l. 209; decree of Seitovo village, Tashevskii *volost*, Sviazhskii *uezd*, 7 June 1917.

[71] See *Izvestiia Kazanskago gubernskago soveta krest'ianskikh deputatov* 18, 1 October 1917, pp. 2–3; Chernov's instructions are discussed at length by Kolegaev as of enormous significance.

[72] For example, NART, f. 983, op. 1, d. 36, ll. 302–3; telegrams from Kazan soviet of peasants' deputies' executive committee, to Kerensky; NART, f. 1246, op. 1, d. 71, ll. 71–5; protocols of Sviazhskii *uezd* land administration, 14 August 1917, singles out Chernov as the 'true defender' of the working peasantry.

in cabinet. The central land committee was united in its dislike for Chernov's perceived 'Zimmerwaldist' outlook. Right of centre SRs, who offered very little concrete support for Chernov's initiatives, also dominated the executive committee of the All-Russian peasants' soviet. Chernov had no experience of government, and he admitted that though he was an able theoretician, he was an awful politician.[73] Chernov's exit from the Provisional Government after the August crisis enabled him to salvage his personal reputation as a champion for peasants' rights.

Chernov believed that only concessions to peasant demands for land could protect the land fund from serious erosion. He proposed three specific measures in his tenure as minister for agriculture; to suspend the Stolypin reforms, to suspend all land transactions and to place all land in the hands of the local land committees. The Provisional Government approved the suspension of the Stolypin reforms immediately, but key figures opposed the suspension of land transactions, on the grounds that they formed the basis of the monetary economy. Chernov bypassed his cabinet colleagues and sent a circular around the provinces asking notaries to withhold acknowledgement of land deals on 17 May. He was forced by cabinet to rescind this on 23 June, and it was not until 12 July that a Kerensky-sponsored bill was passed by the Provisional Government, which placed severe restrictions on land transactions.[74] Even then, the liberal press resisted this fiercely.[75] Chernov's third and most important proposal, to place all land in the hands of the land committees, was not even considered by the first coalition. His attempt to bypass the Provisional Government and to broaden the powers of the land committees regardless of Provisional Government policy contributed to confusion in the countryside over 'correct' land policy.[76]

The attitudes of the political elite towards the rural population evolved steadily but dramatically in the course of 1917, from faith in the transformative powers of education on the perceivedly ignorant but good-natured peasantry, towards frustration and use of repressive measures against the apparently irredeemable peasant population. In the first months of revolution, declarations from the Provisional Government, and from the whole gamut of local administrative structures, sought to 'excuse' peasant disorder with

---

[73] Victor M. Chernov, *The great Russian revolution* (New Haven, CT, 1936), pp. 397–8.
[74] Browder and Kerensky, *Russian Provisional Government*, vol. II, doc. 485, pp. 556–7; law of the Provisional Government, 12 July 1917.
[75] *Russkaia vedomosti* 172, 29 July 1917, p. 1; editorial, commented that 'We regard this measure [the ban on land transactions] as one of most unsuccessful actions of the Provisional Government.'
[76] Browder and Kerensky, *Russian Provisional Government*, vol. II, doc. 487, pp. 558–62; Chernov's instructions to the land committees, issued on 16 July 1917, which authorised a significant strengthening of the land committees' powers. Doc. 488, pp. 562–3, published on 17 July, presents the response of Tsereteli, the minister of the interior, which overruled Chernov's instructions.

explanations of peasant ignorance and misunderstanding. The political elite
viewed the Russian revolution almost as a 'sacred' event, and this is reflected
in their optimistic vision of how it was to be implemented.[77] The political
elite implied that if peasants only knew what their duties were and were
allowed to participate in government, they would support the new order.
Any unpleasantness could be resolved with explanation and education. In
Semenovskii *uezd*, this faith in education and reconciliation was particularly
apparent. The *uezd* commissar reported that at the outset of revolution,
between 3 and 26 March, there were several cases of 'misunderstandings'
between peasants and separators, which were resolved by committee members who travelled around the regions and drew up agreements between
communal peasants and separators.[78] Tetiushskii *uezd* commissar wrote to
the provincial commissar on 19 May to request that significant numbers
of agitators be sent to the village Ananasovo-Ieshtebnevo, where there had
been significant disturbances between separators and communal peasants.[79]

In the first months of revolution, the political elite faithfully repeated
the mantra that representative local government was fundamental to the
establishment of rural order, and that peasant disorders could be resolved
through transforming the system of local government on democratic bases.
The statement issued by the Kazan soviet of workers and soldiers' deputies
in April, for example, declared that 'it was necessary to liquidate peasant
lawlessness by means of changing the system of local self-government and
zemstva on a democratic basis'.[80] This belief was supplemented by the idea
that peasant actions against state decrees were founded on misunderstanding and ignorance, and could therefore be resolved through education. In
March and April in Nizhegorod province, the political elite frequently noted
peasant incomprehension at the meanings and limitations of their new-
found revolutionary freedom: 'Vasil'skii *uezd* commissar T. M. Burushkin
reported that in the *uezd* in general it was peaceful, but that the population,
owing to their ignorance, are badly oriented in questions of their rights and
laws and resort to such excesses, which have not been reduced in limits set
out by the new renovated state structure'[81] (10–11 June 1917).

---

[77] On elite perceptions of Russia's 'sacred' and 'great' revolution, see Kolonitskii, 'The Russian idea',
p. 56.
[78] GANO, f. 1887, op. 1, d. 2, l. 22; report of Semenovskii *uezd* executive committee to the meeting of
Nizhegorod provincial commissars, 23–25 May 1917.
[79] NART, f. 1246, op. 1, d. 74, l. 146; letter from Tetiushskii *uezd* commissar to provincial commissar,
19 May 1917.
[80] *Kazanskaia rabochaia gazeta* 5, 14 April 1917, p. 3.
[81] GANO, f. 1882, op. 1, d. 13, ll. 155–9; protocol of the meeting of *uezd* commissars in Nizhegorod
province, 10–11 April 1917.

This belief was to be fundamentally undermined in the course of 1917, as peasants flexed their new-found political muscle and increasingly directed their affairs in wilful transgression of central policy. In some cases, peasants were indeed unaware of central policies. In Kozmodem'ianskii *uezd*, Kazan, for example, disputes between peasants from the villages Largoty and the neighbouring Bolshaia Chuvaki meant that the peasants refused to work the land that divided the two villages.[82] Fighting that broke out between these two villages in May was so serious that the *uezd* commissar requested that a command of soldiers be sent to support the militia, who were unable to stem the fighting.[83] Tatarinskoi *volost* provisions committee later explained that the grounds for 'misunderstandings' had been that the Largoty villagers did not attend the meeting held explaining the provincial commissar's 16 May decree, so that they were not informed of central policy.[84]

More often, however, peasant disorder was based on well-informed interpretations of the new order. Spasskii *uezd*, Kazan province, provides among the most distinctive examples of self-directed policies. In April, peasants demanded the land of the owner Molovtsev, and were granted it by the committee of public safety, which predated the peasant soviet in Spasskii.[85] A meeting of delegates from the *uezd*'s villages on 24 June declared itself to be the Spasskii soviet of peasants' deputies. This meeting explicitly prioritised local interests over national interests. A newspaper report commented that:

This meeting carried great significance for the population, which would be fine if it supported a general-state point of view. But above all the discussion at the meeting showed that it considered itself to be defending Spasskii interests, which meant that it passed decrees not only against the Provisional Government, but also against the all-Russian and the Kazan soviet of peasants' deputies . . . [It called for] the non-recognition of fixed prices, the rapid transfer of landowner land to all the people, and the clearance sale of all landowner inventory, working horses and cattle for the needs of the population.[86]

In Lukoianovskii *uezd*, Nizhegorod province, by June numerous seizures of wood, land and buildings had been reported. Rather than resort to

---

[82] NART, f. 1246, op. 1, d. 48, l. 190; report of Dmitrii Fedorovich Ilugin, member of executive committee of soviet of workers, soldiers and peasants' deputies, to provincial commissar, 25 May 1917.

[83] NART, f. 1246, op. 1, d. 48, l. 90; telegram from Kozmodem'ianskii *uezd* commissar to provincial commissar, 9 May 1917.

[84] NART, f. 1246, op. 1, d. 48, l. 189; letter from Tatarkasinskoi *volost* provisions committee to provincial commissar, 25 May 1917.

[85] NART, f. 174, op. 1, d. 9, ll. 63–4; journal no. 9 of the meeting of Kazan provincial land committee, 23–24 September 1917.

[86] *Kazanskaia rabochaia gazeta* 69, 5 July 1917, p. 4.

calls for soldiers, as many *uezd* administrators did, Sumgin, Lukoianovskii *uezd* commissar, proposed that those villages participating in illegal actions should be boycotted, that their seized goods would be requisitioned by force, and that guilty individuals would be tried in court. It placed special emphasis on the pursuit of those individuals considered to be instigating these actions.[87] That said, the *uezd* committee asserted that the *uezd* was doing better than many of its neighbours with regard to preparation for land reforms, thanks to the leadership of Sumgin and despite the 'wilful and violent seizure of private landowners' land'.[88]

Across both Kazan and Nizhegorod provinces, official responses were characterised in the first months after revolution by calls for the resolution of disorder through conciliation and education, and from late May 1917 by calls for soldiers to reassert authority in the countryside, often in association with provisions disorder. As the earlier section on peasant actions has shown, both national and regional governments had limited means to resolve peasant unrest. The resort to soldiers can be regarded as a measure of desperation, and the failure of 'educational' measures to resolve the crisis. The immediate response of the Kazan provincial committee of public safety in April to the 'rising of peasants on an agrarian basis' was to send its members out to the regions to calm the population. They suggested that education was the key to resolving disputes. Administrators struggled to understand and respond to rural events, basing their responses on limited and sometimes inaccurate information. One committee member, Talashenko, commented that the information the committee received on risings was unreliable, as it came from individuals and was uncorroborated.[89]

The decrees sent by central and regional government were often swamped by the orders and decrees issued by various village, *volost* and *uezd* committees. On 10 July, the Kazan provincial commissar, Chernyshev, tried to control this phenomenon by stating that all decrees and decisions at village and *volost* level had to be signed and confirmed by the *uezd* commissar.[90] Such a measure was futile in the face of multitudinous sources of authority. One comedic instance of misinformation was the report that peasants in

[87] GANO, f. 1887, op. 1, d. 17, l. 81; protocol of the meeting of Lukoianovskii *uezd* executive committee, 24–25 June 1917.

[88] GANO, f. 1887, op. 1, d. 18, ll. 29–30; protocol of general meeting of Lukoianovskii *uezd* executive committee, 27–28 May 1917.

[89] NART, f. 1353, op. 1, d. 1, ll. 3–4, 7–8; protocol of meeting of the provincial committee of public safety, 10 April 1917.

[90] NART, f. 1246, op. 1, d. 64, l. 310; officially printed postal-telegram to all *volost* and village commissars from provincial commissar, 10 July 1917.

Kadyk-Kuperskoi *volost*, Mamadyshskii *uezd*, had murdered Balovnev, a member of the provincial provisions committee, on 4 July.[91] A hundred soldiers were sent to the area that day to arrest the ringleaders,[92] and it was only on 7 July that a letter was published in the newspaper *Kamsko-Volzhskaia rech* reporting that Balovnev had not been murdered and was alive and well in Mamadysh town.[93]

In Nizhnii Novgorod M. E. Sumgin, a PSR stalwart and provincial commissar from early in 1917, recognised that drastic action had to be taken if a semblance of legitimacy and control in the countryside was to be maintained. An undated, pre-October 1917 report from the provincial commissar Sumgin to the minister for internal affairs demanded that land committees take over control of privately owned land.[94] Sumgin's proposal echoed Chernov's July proposal to the Provisional Government.[95] Like Chernov, Sumgin was thwarted. Unlike Chernov and his fellow theorists in the Central Committee, however, Sumgin was directly responsible for maintaining order in the province. On 23 October 1917, the provincial commissar took the measures he had proposed on his own initiative, in a desperate attempt to control seizure of land and wood:

The anarchy that exists in most of the province is manifested absolutely everywhere in the seizure of grain; cutting of wood continues along with arson of property. I am taking these measures, on the one hand actually transferring all land and woods to the keeping of the land committees to show the population the undoubted victories of the revolution, and on the other hand, using ranks of soldiers to cut short counter-revolutionary calls to burn and rob.[96]

Kazan set itself apart from the national situation by having a particularly radical and proactive soviet of peasants' deputies, whose decree of 13 May pre-empted the Provisional Government's prognostications and transferred all land, privately held and otherwise, into the hands of the local *volost* committees prior to the decision on land by the Constituent Assembly.[97] The

[91] NART, f. 1246, op. 1, d. 51, l. 279; telephonogram from Mamadysh to province provisions committee, 4 July 1917.
[92] NART, f. 1246, op. 1, d. 51, l. 281; telegram confirming dispatch of soldiers, 4 July 1917.
[93] NART, f. 1246, op. 1, d. 51, l. 292; letter to editor of *Kamsko-Volzhskaia rech*, 7 July 1917.
[94] GANO, f. 1882, op. 1, d. 28, l. 299; report from the Sormovo *uezd* commissar, 10 October 1917.
[95] Browder and Kerensky, *Russian Provisional Government*, vol. II, doc. 487, pp. 558–62; Chernov's instructions to the land committees, issued on 16 July 1917, which authorised a significant strengthening of the land committees' powers. Doc. 488, pp. 562–3, published on 17 July, presents the response of Tsereteli, the minister of the interior, which overruled Chernov's instructions.
[96] GANO, f. 1882, op. 1, d. 28, l. 445; report of provincial commissar Sumgin to Ministry of Internal Affairs, 23 October 1917.

Kazan provincial land committee supported this decree. In many respects this decree validated and confirmed statements already made by local land committees who sought to regulate land seizure through regional control.[98] The move enraged local landowners and drove a rift between the soviet and the infuriated Provisional Government authorities, but it also had the effect of ameliorating the violence and irregularity of land seizure. All local reports from Kazan province point to diminished rural unrest as a result of orderly transfer of land to peasant hands. This contradicts statistics for peasant unrest in 1917, which indicate that Kazan saw among the highest levels of agrarian unrest in the country, topped only by Saratov and Astrakhan on the lower Volga.[99] This contradiction highlights the difficulties of quantifying rural unrest. Local reports may have been misleading, as local administrators had an interest in portraying a sense of order. This study indicates, however, that the figures reflect the number of complaints from disgruntled landowners, rather than levels of 'disorder' in terms of land use and public unrest.

Andrei Kolegaev was the driving force behind the Kazan soviet's land law. The son of political exiles, Kolegaev had been repeatedly imprisoned for his political activities in the pre-revolutionary period and was eventually exiled to Paris, where he worked for four years in a range of different trades. A member of the PSR since 1906, Kolegaev became a leading light of the Left SR faction from its inception in October 1917 and played a major role in the drafting of the Soviet 'fundamental law of land socialisation', issued on 19 February 1918.[100] In an article in the province peasants' soviet newspaper, Kolegaev clarified and defended his position on so-called land seizures in Kazan. He commented that while 'many write and shout about land seizure in Kazan province, there are different sorts of land seizure; the Constituent Assembly will transfer all land to peasants, and then the state will seize the land. In Kazan all know that almost all landowner land has been transferred to the land committees.'[101] Kolegaev reasoned that the soviet-authorised seizure in Kazan was no less legitimate than decisions made by the Constituent Assembly.

---

97   NART, f. 1246, op. 1, d. 51, ll. 275–7; Kazan soviet of peasants' deputies' decree on land, 13 May 1917.
98   NART, f. 1246, op. 1, d. 41, l. 52; telegram from Trekh ozera village, 15 April, declaring that all land was to be transferred to land committees prior to the decision of the Constituent Assembly.
99   Maliavskii, *Krest'ianskoe dvizhenie*, pp. 374–80. Maliavskii produced his figures on peasant disorder from a wide range of sources.
100 Kolegaev resigned from his duties in the Soviet government as protest against the treaty of Brest Litovsk, but by November 1918 joined the Bolshevik Party, and after the civil war worked in agriculture. He was executed in 1937. (Information from autobiography in *Izvestiia kazanskago soveta krest'ianskikh deputatov* 6, 23 July, p. 4, and Shelokhaev, *Politicheskii partii Rossii*, pp. 258–9.)
101 *Izvestiia Kazanskago gubernskago soveta krest'ianskikh deputatov* 8, 28 July 1917, p. 2.

Kazan peasant soviet's land law was used as a basis for land seizure across the province.[102] The extent to which these seizures constituted 'anarchy' is very much a matter of perspective. For the victims of the seizures, the loss of their private property constituted anarchy. The regional administration, on the other hand, argued that the law enabled controlled and systematic utilisation of land stocks, and regulated land seizures, reducing the risk of violence. An undated report from the provincial commissar to the minister for land declared that the soviet decree had spread across the province very rapidly, and there had been a swell of land seizures, woodcutting and violence against landlords as a result.[103] Tetiushskii *uezd* commissar reported to the provincial commissar at the end of July that the land seizures in the *uezd* had been justified by the peasants concerned with reference to the peasant soviet land law, and that in Prolei Kashinskoi *volost*, the land committees had acted specifically on the basis of the soviet decree. He noted that 'if such land seizures were not lawful, then the publication of such a declaration should not have been allowed'.[104]

A meeting of the Kazan provincial land committee on 15 June noted that there was no anarchy in the province, and that this vindicated their decision to go along with the peasant soviet's land decree.[105] The membership of the Kazan provincial land committee was supplemented by fifteen representatives from the Kazan soviet of peasants' deputies at the demand of the soviet, which offered the soviet of peasants' deputies an additional base of power in the province.[106] The main land committee wrote to protest about events in Kazan on 16 October, but the Kazan land committee stood by its actions, again pointing to the much improved land relations in the region.[107]

The Kazan soviet of peasants' deputies sent a telegram to the Ministry of Internal Affairs, the Ministry of Land and the All-Russian soviet of

[102] For example, in Marasinskii *volost*, Spasskii *uezd* (*Izvestiia Kazanskago gubernskago soveta krest'ianskikh deputatov* 20, 7 October 1917, pp. 2–3).
[103] NART, f. 983, op. 1, d. 23, l. 209; telegram from Kazan soviet of peasants' deputies to the minister of land, undated.
[104] NART, f. 1246, op. 1, d. 70, l. 31; letter from Tetiushskii *uezd* commissar to provincial commissar, 24 July 1917.
[105] NART, f. 1246, op. 1, d. 183, ll. 34–46; journal of the meeting of the Kazan provincial land committee, 23–24 September 1917. See also NART, f. 174, op. 1, d. 9, l. 9; meeting of Kazan provincial land committee, 22 June 1917. For an example of exceptionally orderly and equitable decisions about land use, see NART, f. 1351, op. 1, d. 10, l. 38; report of Chistopolskii *uezd* committee of public safety, 15 June 1917.
[106] NART, f. 983, op. 1, d. 22, l. 35; from Kolegaev, president of Kazan soviet of peasants' deputies, to Petrograd soviet of peasants' deputies, Chernov, and the main land committee, undated.
[107] NART, f. 1246, op. 1, d. 183, ll. 47–50; journal of the meeting of Kazan provincial land committee, 16 October 1917.

peasants' deputies in an attempt to justify their actions to central authority. The telegram reiterated that the land law had produced calm in land
relations, and had averted rural anarchy.[108] In some areas, like the Chuvash-
dominated Cheboksarskii *uezd*, the land committee heard reports from the
volost committees at the beginning of August that indicated that there had
been almost no disorders, and that privately owned land had been taken and
redistributed via the *volost* land committees. Separators and small landowners who wished to work their own land were allowed to do so. In some *volosts*
there had been 'misunderstandings' between commune peasants and separators, but these had been resolved.[109] These positive reports do not of
course reflect the experiences of landowners, who were no doubt forced to
relinquish their property.

Reports from the *uezds* to the provincial land committee on 22 and
23 July offered a broader picture of the law's impact. In Kazan *uezd*, all
privately owned land that could not be worked by the owner's own labour
had been redistributed by the land committees and inventories taken. This
example was followed across the *uezds*, with some variety as to whether
any rent was paid to the legal landowner. Overall, the picture was one of
controlled and economical land use, and total transgression of the norms of
private land-ownership.[110] The *uezd* land committees gave the impression
that every available area of land was being sown.[111] Such reports of peaceful
and productive land use supported the law-makers' claim that their radical
action was justified. In Chistopolskii *uezd*, a meeting of the committee of
public safety on 26 July stated that all land issues in the region had been
resolved, because both the *uezd* committee and the commissariat supported
the PSR platform.[112] This is confused, since the PSR position in itself was
unclear and divided, but we can infer from this that it referred to the Kazan
peasants' soviet land decree authored by Kolegaev. In Tsivilskii *uezd*, the
uezd committee of public safety looked over the soviet's land decree on

[108] NART, f. 983, op. 1, d. 21, ll. 121–2; telegram from Kolegaev, president of Kazan soviet of peasants'
deputies, to the All-Russian soviet of peasants' deputies, Chernov, and the Ministry of Internal
Affairs, undated.

[109] NART, f. 174, op. 1, d. 55, ll. 50–2; journal of the meeting of general meeting of members of
Cheboksar *uezd* land committee, 1 August 1917.

[110] NART, f. 174, op. 1, d. 9, ll. 23–8; journal of the meeting of the Kazan province land committee,
22–23 July 1917.

[111] NART, f. 174, op. 1, d. 9, ll. 45–63; meeting of the Kazan province land committee, 23–24 August
1917.

[112] NART, f. 983, op. 1, d. 16, ll. 101–6; protocol of the meetings of the executive *uezd* committee
of public safety, the soviet of peasants' deputies, *volost* commissars, soviet of workers and soldiers'
deputies and representatives of the town committee of public safety, 26 July 1917.

3 June and decided in the most part to accept it, though they also sent a telegram to the Provisional Government reiterating the reasons for their decision to accept the decree.[113]

Once the land law had been disseminated, those opposing it could only take retrospective measures to control its implementation.[114] A group of landowners from Tetiushi village, Tetiushskii *uezd*, appealed to the Kazan soviet of peasants' deputies on 29 June that they should receive payment for meadows given to the use of the army. The soviet of peasants' deputies responded that in accordance with the Kazan peasants' soviet land decree of 13 May, no compensation would be given.[115] Sviazhskii *uezd* had exceptionally radical, political and pro-active administrators, which may have been a reflection of the *uezd*'s history of exceptional radicalism.[116] Sviazhskii *uezd* committee of public safety issued a whole range of measures just after the land committee's announcements, on 22 June, attempting to establish a firm rule of law in the *uezd*. It announced the length of jail terms and size of fines for a range of public-order offences, from general hooligan behaviour, abusive language, public drunkenness and theft from woodlands. Those abusing or threatening public officials were particularly targeted, with jail for two to ten days, and a fine of between two and twenty roubles.[117] That such measures were issued at *uezd* level is an important indicator of the ways in which power was being appropriated locally, and how in some places the restoration of order was being defined and determined by small groups of local leaders.

Sviazhskii *uezd* land committee's meeting on 18–19 June showed how the administration acted retrospectively in order to legitimise and control peasant interpretation of the soviet land law. It stated that 'several peasant communes wilfully seized all baronial land, not considering the land needs of neighbouring villages', and that in order to ensure the more just distribution of land, *volost* land committees were to be formed quickly, to distribute land to peasants justly, and to ensure that all land was sown. Land already seized was not to be subject to distribution, but all remaining

[113] NART, f. 1246 op. 1, d. 53, ll. 157–8; meeting of Chistopolskii *uezd* committee of public safety, 3 June 1917.

[114] NART, f. 1246, op. 1, d. 41, l. 182; appeal from land renter in Spasskii *uezd* to Kazan provincial provisions committee, 2 June 1917.

[115] NART, f. 983, op. 1, d. 13, l. 69; protocol of executive committee of Kazan soviet of peasants' deputies, 29 June 1917.

[116] For a description of the dramatic unrest that occurred in Sviazhsk after the emancipation edict was announced in 1861, see Venturi, *Roots of revolution*, pp. 214–17.

[117] NART, f. 1246, op. 1, d. 71, ll. 330–2; protocol of meeting of Sviazhskii *uezd* committee of public safety, 10 September 1917.

privately owned land was to be taken over by land committees in order to prevent disagreements between peasants. These were measures of damage limitation. There was no means available to prevent land seizure, so the best course of action was clearly to intervene to ensure that redistribution progressed as fairly as possible and maximised sown land.

Sviazhskii *uezd* land committee did not stop at these retrospective measures, however. In a radical move, it proposed that all pedigree cattle were to be transferred to the *uezd* land administration, and were to be kept on three farm properties, which were to have a paid staff. All produce from these cows was to go 'for the satisfaction of other general *uezd* cultural needs'. All privately owned horses were to be distributed to peasants to assist in working the land, and any livestock in private hands not working their own land were also to be transferred to the *uezd* farms.[118] These decrees emphasised the importance of individual labour, mirroring in some respects PSR policy. The extent to which this committee appropriated state authority is particularly noticeable and points to ambitious and highly motivated local leaders. The provincial commissar responded to their grandiose appropriations of power promptly. In a statement to the provincial land committee on 14 July, he reiterated that the soviet land law was not legitimate, that land and property seizure was in no way sanctioned, that cattle were to stay with their original owners, that wood was state property not *uezd* property, and overall condemned the Sviazhskii *uezd* land committee's unacceptable and unorthodox use of their power.[119]

It is a reflection of the Sviazhskii *uezd* committee's self-confidence and righteousness that they offered firm and unswerving resistance to the provincial commissar's condemnation of their actions. In a protocol on 14 August, the Sviazhskii *uezd* land committee accused the provincial commissar of protecting big landowners and defended the righteousness of its actions at length. This declaration revealed an unusual and unconciliatory tone that allied the committee firmly with a Left SR and even Bolshevik position. They accused the Provisional Government of being an enemy of the working peasantry.[120] The radicalism of Sviazhskii *uezd*'s committee was exceptional, but it does reflect the broader problems of local administration challenging the authority of their regional superiors.

---

[118] NART, f. 1246, op. 1, d. 71, ll. 63–5; protocol of meeting of Sviazhskii *uezd* land committee, 18–19 June 1917.

[119] NART, f. 1246, op. 1, d. 71, l. 66; letter from provincial commissar to provincial land committee, 14 July 1917.

[120] NART, f. 1246, op. 1, d. 71, ll. 71–5; declaration of meeting of Sviazhskii *uezd* land administration, 14 August 1917.

CONCLUSIONS

This snapshot of peasant relations with regional and national authority reveals that peasants exercised a high degree of autonomy in deciding their affairs. Far from being passive or blindly violent, peasant actions rationally responded to local conditions. Peasants attempted to secure material gains for their communities, and they utilised the language of revolution, in particular the rhetoric of rights and freedoms, to do this. Their actions against fellow peasants were not defined by any straightforward class distinctions among the peasantry, but on what they perceived to be the best interests of the community, or on personal antagonisms.

The upper reaches of the political elite showed themselves unwilling or unable to recognise peasant political agency. Their initial response to rural disorder was to call for more education to 'enlighten' the 'dark' rural people who obviously had not understood the Provisional Government's policies. Peasants interpreted the revolution as they chose and tried to benefit from the change of regime, but this does not necessarily mean that they did not understand Provisional Government policy. The self-conscious, careful and measured ways in which peasants took control over land in many places in fact indicates that they fully understood their situation, and the implications of their actions. Not all rural people were fully aware of all the ramifications of new revolutionary terminology that was formed and utilised by the political elite. Peasants' actions in 1917, however, showed that they were able to utilise the language and rhetoric of revolution in order to defend and justify their actions.

While the Provisional Government, supported by the Petrograd Soviet, instructed peasants to wait calmly for resolution of the land question, regional administrators recognised that regulation rather than unenforceable prohibition was the best way to deal with peasant actions, and they were forced by practical exigencies to negotiate a course between demands from peasants and demands from central government. Divisions emerged not just between the political elite and ordinary people, but also between the political elite and local leaders. This need for regional government to respond to local conditions meant that local leaders played a significant role in defining and directing land action. In the case of Kazan, authoritative leadership from the soviet of peasants' deputies revolutionised land relations. According to local landowners, this measure accelerated 'anarchy' in the province. The impression given by administrators and reporters, however, suggests that the Kazan peasant soviet's policies regularised land use and avoided mass disorder.

The nature and form of land unrest was defined by local conditions, and these varied significantly from *uezd* to *uezd* around the two provinces. Direct comparisons of land relations between the two provinces are unhelpful, as such comparisons would obscure the local diversity of land relations. We can, however, make some meaningful comparison between the ways in which regional leaders responded to the challenges of rural land use in 1917. While both Nizhegorod and Kazan found regional leaders initiating policies that did not accord with those laid out by the Provisional Government in their attempts to control and contain rising levels of civic disorder in the countryside, the boldness shown by Kazan's regional leaders in tackling land use questions resulted in significantly lower levels of public violence and disorder in land use. The radical policies of Kazan's regional government were initiated by the Kazan soviet of peasants' deputies and accepted by other branches of government in Kazan. By responding to popular concerns and largely disregarding the rights of private land-ownership, Kazan's administration was able to regulate land and reduce incidents of civil disorder.

CHAPTER 8

Feeding Russia

The question of provisions provided a dark heart for the economic and political crises that beset 1917. Russia was not fundamentally short of food-stuffs, but problems of administration and transport conspired to produce food shortages and threats of famine in some areas. Provisions problems steadily worsened through 1917. Russia followed nineteenth-century trends in famines, in that human and institutional factors were more significant than natural scarcity in causing distress and starvation.[1] The government faced concerted resistance from peasant producers in implementing the grain monopoly, and hostility from consumers who were threatened by famine. The split between consumers and producers was between surplus and deficit regions among the peasantry, as well as between town and country. The food crisis also accentuated vertical and horizontal tensions in regional administration and was the issue that provoked most hostility and violence against administrators.

Peter Gatrell's work provides a valuable synthesis of Russia's provisions situation during the First World War, while Lars Lih's study of the provisions crisis during 1917 lucidly explained why and in what form the crisis manifested itself.[2] This chapter explores the mechanics of crisis at grass-roots level, and in doing so exposes some of its peculiarities more clearly. As we have seen in earlier chapters, the panacea to the problems facing Russia in February 1917 was seen to be in enabling Russia's population to rule themselves. It was convenient to blame corrupt and venal tsarist bureau-cracy for Russia's woes. Democratisation, or as Lih calls it the 'enlistment of the population', was the means utilised by the Provisional Government to administer the grain monopoly. This faith in the population relied on the presumption that the population would choose to strengthen central power

---

[1] Martin Ravallion, *Markets and famines* (Oxford, 1987), p. 6.
[2] Gatrell, *Russia's first world war*, chapter 7; Lars. T. Lih, *Bread and authority in Russia, 1914–1921* (Berkeley, 1990).

over defending local interests, the decision Lih aptly described as 'Hobbes' choice'. This study of provisions questions confirms that centrifugal forces overwhelmed reconstituting forces, as the population rationally chose to protect their own interests in so far as was possible and refused the many sacrifices asked of them by the fledgling state. This finding supports Mark Baker's findings on the peasantry of Kharkiv province, whose behaviour he found to be defined by personal economic interests and local concerns.[3] Far from being 'dark' and 'unconscious', peasant behaviour in Kazan and Nizhegorod demonstrated rational responses to the choices that were made available to them.[4] As Peter Holquist pointed out, in the pre-revolutionary period the political elite had blamed the autocratic state for the supposed 'benightedness' of the Russian population. In 1917 the elite based their policies around a faith in ordinary people's ability to recognise the necessity of provisions policy. As 1917 drew on, this faith was undermined, and the political elite increasingly looked to the state to impose order over ordinary people.[5] In this chapter we will see how and why this loss of faith played itself out in the towns and villages of Nizhegorod and Kazan provinces.

This chapter will overuse the word 'crisis'. It is worth considering that crisis denoted different things to different parts of the population. The popular press, for example, devoted a lot of column space to discussion of sugar shortages, as shortages afflicted rural and urban regions. In Kazan province, many of the reported 'dangerous' and 'severe' shortages were in white flour, which was considered particularly necessary for the elderly and children, even though supplies of rye were sufficient to avert hunger. In the context of impending hunger in some regions, these 'critical' shortages seem, in retrospect, trivial. They do, however, reveal something of the norms and expectations of ordinary people, and we must respect these expectations if we are to understand popular mood. If the sugar shortage in Kazan provoked popular anxiety and concerns, then this sugar shortage constituted a crisis.[6]

---

[3] Baker, 'Peasants, power and revolution', chapter 2.

[4] Lih, *Bread and authority*, p. 68.

[5] See Peter Holquist, 'Violent Russia, deadly Marxism? Russia in the epoch of violence, 1905–1921', *Kritika* 4 (2003), 627–52, p. 642.

[6] In Kazan town, there were fears about white bread shortage, and in May ten wagons were received from Samara, 'to be distributed among the sick and children' (*Kazanskaia rabochaia gazeta* 36, 25 May 1917, p. 3). The general meeting of Kazan's soviet of workers' and soldiers' deputies at the end of May proposed the requisitioning of all confectionery and a ban on the sale of expensive confectionery goods (*Kazanskaia rabochaia gazeta* 39, 28 May 1917, p. 3).

ROOTS OF THE PROBLEM

The provisions crisis was one of supply and distribution rather than pro-duction. National figures on Russia's grain output are misleading. They indicate that though food production reduced steadily from 1914 to 1917, it was still only 30 per cent below the pre-war average by 1917.[7] As Russia was one of the world's biggest grain exporters at the turn of the century, a drop of 30 per cent in production should not have left Russia in shortfall for domestic consumption. These figures are misleading, however, not least because local conditions in terms of geography, population and forms of agriculture defined the problems that were faced from region to region. There are three fundamental explanations for the food crisis, all of which were intimately connected to Russia's involvement in the First World War. First, the needs of providing for the army increased demand for food prod-ucts and other goods compared to the pre-war period. Secondly, transport of provisions around Russia, from her surplus provinces, and to her deficit provinces and the front, proved to be a serious logistical problem. Most of Russia's consuming provinces were situated in north-west European Russia, and most of the producing provinces were in south-east Russia. It is less generally understood that even in the parts of surplus provinces that needed to import grain, supply and transport of provisions were a serious problem. Finally, perhaps most significant in driving Russia's provisions crisis was the disruption of trade, because of government intervention in grain prices and movement, and because of a shortage of consumer goods available for producers to buy.

Nizhegorod and Kazan provinces illustrate these problems. Nizhegorod was an importer of grain, and Kazan an exporter, though both were on a small scale. Based on averages between 1909 and 1913, Nizhegorod needed to import 5.82 *puds* of grain per person to satisfy consumer needs, while Kazan exported 5.79 *puds* per person. Nizhegorod was one of the smallest importers of grain of the consuming provinces, thirteenth out of sixteen, and Kazan was in the lower ranks of Russia's exporting provinces, twenty-first out of thirty-three. Nizhegorod was in a strong geographical position to acquire grain, as most of its neighbouring provinces, with the exception of

7 S. S. Demosthenov, 'Food prices and the market in foodstuffs', in Peter Struve (ed.), *Food supply in Russia during the World War* (New Haven, CT, 1930), pp. 268–411, p. 311. N. Kondratev, *Rynok khlebov i ego regulirovanie vo vremia voiny i revoliutsii* (Moscow, 1991), pp. 124–5; figures cited here differ from Demosthenov's, suggesting that though 1914 and 1917 were rather weak years, 1915 and 1916 were well above the average from the period 1909–13.

Astrakhan and Viatka, were big exporters of grain.[8] Some *uezds* in Nizhe-gorod were exporters of grain, which offered another important source of grain for the province as a whole. Despite these advantages, Nizhe-gorod province faced serious shortages and extreme difficulties in acquir-ing food products. Kazan province, meanwhile, was expected to export significant quantities of grain for the army, as well as feeding itself. In fact its towns, especially the capital Kazan, faced serious shortages throughout 1917. Provisions shortages had been a problem in Kazan town before the revolution. Police reports in January 1917 stated that the provisions cri-sis in Kazan town was 'critical', and that there were widespread fears of famine.[9]

The tsarist regime had restricted its involvement in wartime food sup-ply to supplying the army and fixed grain prices only on army supplies.[10] The Provisional Government took over the tsarist government's provision-ing structures but vastly expanded their scope, and superseded the needs of supplying the army with the needs of supplying the country at large. There had been consensus for a grain monopoly, with fixed prices on all grain, not just that supplied to the army, before the February revolution.[11] A comparison of the government's fixed grain prices with market values, however, immediately reveals the problems such a system faced. The Provi-sional Government established its first fixed price on 25 March 1917, which at 235 kopeks per *pud* was 48 kopeks lower than market price in Kazan. The increase of fixed prices on 27 August to 470 kopeks did not keep pace with market prices, which by the end of August were 847 kopeks above the fixed price.[12] Prices were higher in the mid-Volga region, which included Kazan and Nizhegorod, and increased more rapidly in the course of 1917 than almost anywhere outside the industrial region and Belorussia.[13] These figures show the chronological dynamic of the food crisis, which became progressively worse in the course of 1917.

The Volga region's spiralling prices came in part from the intermingling of surplus and deficit regions. Kazan, with its unrealisable surpluses, and Nizhegorod, with its unfulfilled wants, were located alongside one another. The movement of walkers and 'sack men' between provinces and *uezds*

[8] Kondratev, *Rynok khlebov*, pp. 95–6. N. D. Kondratev was of peasant stock, an SR who was made president of the All-Russian soviet of peasants' deputies in June 1917.

[9] NART, f. 1246, op. 1, d. 140, l. 106; report of reasons for strike at Alafuzovskii factory, 30 January 1917; NART, f. 1246, op. 1, d. 140, l. 107; report on the state of Kazan, 20 January 1917.

[10] K. I. Zaitsev and N. V. Dolinsky, 'Organisation and policy' in Struve, *Food supply in Russia*, pp. 5–17.

[11] Lih, *Bread and authority*, p. 84.   [12] Kondratev, *Rynok khlebov*, p. 400.

[13] Demosthenov, 'Food prices', pp. 269, 271, 275, 278.

was identified as a feature of 1917 by Lars Lih and characterised relations between the two provinces.[14] Alongside formal requests from one provincial commissar to another to provide grain, and personal letters from starving Nizhegorod citizens printed in the local press appealing to the Kazan peasants to release their grain, Kazan was inundated with individuals seeking to buy grain.[15] A telegram from Kazan's provincial provisions administration to the provincial commissar on 5 July encapsulated the hopelessness of trying to control grain movement: 'Situation desperate. Militia powerless to struggle with the speculators and needy from Nizhegorod province. This morning a crowd of several hundred people gathered at the building of the provisions administration demanding distribution of grain from town reserves. Disorder threatened. We ask for help. Please send soldiers rapidly.'[16]

Administrators in Iadrinskii *uezd*, Kazan province, were unable to prevent speculation on grain, as Nizhegorod citizens were 'ready to pay any prices so that they can receive grain. The fixed prices seem too low.'[17] Despite one hundred soldiers sent, and permanent watches being set on all roads leaving the *uezd*, the administration was unable to prevent 'leakage' of grain into Nizhegorod province.[18] Chistopol town, the capital of Chistopolskii *uezd* in Kazan, was 'flooded by more than a thousand walkers from hungry provinces every day'. All these walkers had permissions from their *volost* administration to seek grain, as they were hungry, but instead of approaching the Chistopol authorities, they bought from illicit traders at high prices, preventing any grain from reaching army supplies or the hungry parts of Kazan province.[19] Kazan's provincial commissar complained to Nizhegorod provincial commissar in September about Nizhegorod citizens coming to Kazan to try to buy grain, which threatened to cause civil

---

[14] Lih, *Bread and authority*, pp. 77–81. Mark Baker's work on Ukraine also recognised that the pressure of 'walkers' from surrounding provinces was a significant factor in food supplies (Baker, 'Beyond the national').

[15] An example of such letters can be found in *Kazanskaia rabochaia gazeta* 137, 30 September 1917, p. 3; letter to the editor from Vladimir citizens, with a request that their appeal for grain be translated into Chuvash and Tatar. An example of more formal requests is printed in *Kazanskaia rabochaia gazeta* 77, 15 July 1917, p. 3, where Kazan's Town Duma discussed a request from Nizhegorod for 25,000 *puds* of rye.

[16] NART, f. 1246, op. 1, d. 44, l. 16; telegram from the provincial provisions administration to the provincial commissar, 5 July.

[17] *Kazanskaia rabochaia gazeta* 75, 13 July 1917, p. 3.

[18] NART. f. 1246, op. 1, d. 44, l. 111; letter from Iadrinskii *uezd* commissar to provincial commissar, 12 August 1917; NART, f. 1246, op. 1, d. 44, l. 16; telegram from Kazan provisions administration to provincial commissar, 14 July 1917.

[19] *Kazanskaia rabochaia gazeta* 146, 11 October 1917, p. 4.

disturbance.[20] The provincial provisions committee in September blamed speculators explicitly for Kazan's failure to fulfil its grain quotas.[21]

Nizhegorod blamed the problem on Kazan's refusal to supply provisions. Nizhegorod provincial commissar appealed directly to the minister of internal affairs in an attempt to make Kazan sell its grain:

I report first, that provisions hunger has come to the province, especially Balakhninskii, Semenovskii, Makar'evskii and Gorbatovskii *uezds*, where already hunger is seen. It is necessary to transport grain from other provinces before the closure of navigation [*i.e. before waterways freeze and become impassable. SB*]. I request that the minister of provisions gives permission for the regional *volost uezd* provisioning committees to buy grain from Kazan province, because purchase of grain is prohibited. I ask the Kazan provincial commissar to urgently confirm that permission is given to the provincial provisions committee for free purchase of grain for export to Nizhegorod province.[22]

This report had no discernible effect on Nizhegorod's position. Vladimir Ganchel, Nizhnii Novgorod's town mayor, gave a gloomy general report on the provisions situation in September:

Nothing has come of attempts to purchase grain in Kazan, Simbirsk and Viatka provinces. The last two have almost no grain, but Kazan is withholding grain, which is antisocial and goes against the Provisional Government . . . Ganchel proposes sending a delegate to Kazan for talks with the Kazan provisioning organisations, and to explain the serious situation in Nizhegorod province.[23]

The grain purchasing commission, established to buy grain from neighbouring provinces, failed to deliver:

Despite all measures taken by the Nizhegorod Purchasing Commission, they have not been successful in providing bread for Nizhegorod province, because of the resistance of Kazan, Viatka, Simbirsk, Ufimsk and Samara provinces to protocols of the regional *volost* and *uezd* committees. The situation of the town in the populated factory area of the breadless *uezds* is catastrophic. The town is not supplied with bread even for a day. Tobolsk and Kuban evade the fulfilment of October and September orders; Ufimsk and Kazan also refused to fulfil October orders.[24]

Even within Nizhegorod province, *volost* and *uezd* provisions committees did not work to ease hunger in the province generally but protected

[20] GANO, f. 1882, op. 1, d. 22, l. 87; report from Kazan about the provisions crisis, with a note written by Nizhegorod provincial commissar on the reverse, 26 September 1917.
[21] *Kazanskaia rabochaia gazeta* 143, 7 October 1917, p. 3.
[22] GANO, f. 1882, op. 1, d. 28, l. 305; letter from Nizhegorod provincial commissar to the Ministry of Internal Affairs, undated but probably September 1917.
[23] GANO, f. 27, op. 1, d. 3, l. 19; from Town Duma records, 12 September 1917.
[24] GANO, f. 27, op. 1, d. 4, l. 5; from Town Duma records, telegram sent to D. V. Sirotkin of the Nizhegorod purchasing commission and read out in the Duma chamber on 5 October 1917.

the interests of their own local citizens. Makar'evskii *uezd* commissar complained bitterly in a report to the provincial commissar in September about the selfishness of the *uezds* surrounding Makar'evskii *uezd*, which was dangerously hungry:

Regarding the extremely severe situation of the provisions question in the village Lyskov; there is absolutely no grain at the regional markets; the *volost* provisions boards of neighbouring Vasil'skii and Kniagininskii *uezds*, where the peasant population is incomparably better supplied with bread than the population of Makar'evskii *uezd*, delay and requisition every *pud* of provisions products transported to Lyskov village in the most senseless way, in spite of all common sense, on the basis of a total misunderstanding of their functions. This makes the population terribly angry . . .The most immediate measures must be taken for the cessation of the totally unjustified and terribly damaging anarchist activities of these boards.[25]

Speculation on grain prices was not the only explanation for the scarcity of grain on the market. Part of the conundrum of rising grain prices and reluctance of peasant producers to surrender their produce came from scarcity and high prices of manufactured goods.[26] The belief that fixed prices on all goods of first necessity could alleviate the food supply crisis was widely held, and calls for fixed prices were made from national down to village levels. Even the food commissioners' convention held in August 1916 expressed the wish for fixed prices on all articles of prime necessity.[27] The All-Russian soviet of peasants' deputies in May 1917 declared: 'The peasantry surrenders all the produce of its labour and economy at established prices. Without further delay, fixed prices must be introduced on manufactured goods to correspond with the prices on grain . . .This must be done to correct the injustice, also to prevent the ruin of the working peasantry.'[28]

Supply of manufactured goods to the peasantry was identified in Kazan as a key explanation for peasant hostility and resistance to the grain monopoly. A meeting of all Kazan *uezd* and *volost* commissars in June demanded that while the grain monopoly was to be carried out firmly, fixed prices had to be set on all products of first necessity.[29] In Kazan *uezd*, the commissar took the initiative in attempts to improve grain monopoly implementation, and in July tried to buy butter, salt and matches through the provincial provisions

[25] GANO, f. 1882, op. 1, d. 45, l. 170; Makar'evskii *uezd* commissar report, 23 September 1917.
[26] Demosthenov, 'Food prices', p. 427.
[27] Zaitsev and Dolinsky, 'Organisation and policy', p. 157.
[28] Browder and Kerensky, *Russian Provisional Government*, vol. II, doc. 545, p. 631; report from *Den* 61, 17 May 1917.
[29] NART, f. 1246, op. 1, d. 52, l. 5; published resolutions of the meeting of *uezd* and *volost* commissars and secretaries, 15–17 June 1917.

committee, and to organise points of sale for these items around the *uezd*. It is unlikely that these measures were ever implemented, as he required large cash advances from the provincial provisions committee for his purchases.[30]

The belief that prices had to be fixed on all products was widely held, but not universal. When Nizhegorod Town Duma discussed the need to fix prices on products other than grain in August, conflict arose between the socialists who favoured state control of the economy, and the liberal Kadets who sought to avoid restrictions on free-market economy.[31] In Spasskii *uezd*, Kazan, the committee of public safety invited seventeen local traders to discuss with them the possibility of lowering prices. After discussion with the traders, they came up with a novel conclusion: the need to open barriers and allow absolutely free trade in goods. High flour prices were also blamed on the limitations to free trade.[32] Defence of the free market was, however, rarely found in the socialist press.

The Provisional Government proposed an attempt to fix prices on the goods required in the countryside, and to make them available in order to facilitate the exchange of goods between town and country.[33] This monumental enterprise required nothing less than control over the whole economy and never got beyond committee stage.[34] The proposed state control of agriculture and industry was beyond the authority of the Provisional Government, which had no state mechanism of control available. This was symptomatic of the ad hoc measures that the Provisional Government took without having the means or the motivation to make the measures effective. There was an essential dichotomy between the use of anti-market, administrative levers to stabilise the economy, and the use of norms and procedures carried out by representative local government to implement them.[35]

HUNGER IN TOWN AND COUNTRY

The Provisional Government sought to harness popular strength in the great task of provisioning, by making local administration fully accountable

[30] *Kazanskaia rabochaia gazeta* 78, 16 July 1917, p. 3.
[31] GANO, f. 27, op. 1, d. 2, ll. 172–8; from Town Duma records, 2 August 1917.
[32] NART, f. 1352, op. 1, d. 2, ll. 46–7, 68; protocol of meeting of Spasskii *uezd* committee of public safety, 11–12 March 1917.
[33] Browder and Kerensky, *Russian Provisional Government*, vol. II, doc. 535, p. 621; announcement of the Provisional Government regarding the grain monopoly, 28 March 1917.
[34] V. Mau, 'Bread, democracy and the Bolshevik coup', *Revolutionary Russia* 7 (1994), 34–7, p. 37.
[35] Mau, 'Bread, democracy', p. 36.

at every level, and by involving ordinary people in administration. Provisions committees were to be set up at every level from *volost* to province. These bodies were set the formidable tasks of collecting information about reserves and population needs, overseeing the collection of grain from producers and transporting this grain to its destinations, both in the army and needy provinces. The Provisional Government gravely underestimated the task that such committees faced, and the self-preserving attitudes adopted by ordinary people. Without a functioning committee network, the provisions administration could not function effectively. In practice, though provisions committees were formed everywhere at provincial level, at lower levels they only operated in consuming areas, where the role of the committees was to make censuses, and distribute provisions. In surplus areas, where the role of the committees was to make censuses and arrange for the sale or requisition of grain, the committees were either not formed, or faced stern resistance. In the course of 1917, provisions committees in consuming areas were the most beleaguered part of the whole administrative structure, and the group most liable to harassment, de-selection and violence. They were placed in an impossible position as in implementing central government policy they often faced the wrath of the very people who had elected them.

At provincial level in both Nizhegorod and Kazan, provisions committees encapsulated the full gamut of democratic representatives, with the soviets and Provisional Government bodies working closely together. Nizhnii Novgorod provisions committee was formed in March and included representatives from a range of town organisations, including the Duma, *zemstva*, soviet of workers' deputies, Peasants' Union, refugee committee and town co-operatives.[36] A united provisions meeting held in Kazan on 23 May numbered almost six hundred people, including representatives from the provincial provisions committee, the Town Duma, *zemstva*, soviets and the committee of public safety.[37] Despite their broad and democratic constituency, provisions organisations in both Nizhegorod and Kazan faced persistent suspicion and accusations of incompetence. In Nizhegorod province, even the moderate socialists who headed provincial administration called for new provisions administration by August.[38] On 12 September the Nizhegorod Town Duma decided, following the precedent set by the Petrograd Town Duma, to take over the provisions committees.[39] The complex structures of provisions organisation in Nizhegorod province were perceived to be

[36] GANO, f. 27, op. 1, d. 1, l. 282; from Town Duma records, 24 April 1917.
[37] *Kazanskaia rabochaia gazeta* 34, 24 May 1917, p. 3.
[38] GANO, f. 27, op. 1, d. 2, ll. 172–8; from Town Duma records, 2 August 1917.
[39] GANO, f. 27, op. 1, d. 3, l. 19; from Town Duma records, 12 September 1917.

failing. The army grain-requisitioning organisation, a carry-over from the tsarist regime, was taken over by a soviet-delegated commission in October in a desperate attempt to supply the province with provisions.[40]

In Kazan, the soviet of workers', soldiers' and peasants' deputies formed a control commission for investigation into Kazan's provisions affairs in July.[41] By 22 September, Kazan town, which should have been well supplied, had only one or two days of grain reserves in stock. The head of the town provisions administration had to defend the right of the town to buy grain to other grain-hungry provinces including Nizhegorod, Moscow and Smolensk.[42] The critical provisions situation in Kazan town prompted a general meeting of soviets, military and factory committees and socialist parties. This meeting demanded that an All-Russian meeting of soviets of workers', soldiers' and peasants' deputies be formed to take power without any coalition with 'bourgeois' forces and presented detailed measures for the total reorganisation of provincial provisions affairs. This included requisition of products of first necessity, and the use of armed force in the countryside to implement grain seizure.[43]

The connection between provisions crisis and 'bourgeois' participation in government structures that was drawn confirms a general suspicion that the crisis was the result of incompetence and perhaps villainy. The president of the provincial provisions committee resigned on 30 September, declaring that the situation was hopeless and that hunger was unavoidable.[44] The provisions committee petitioned the Provisional Government for permission to buy 50,000 *puds* of grain from Ufa. Despite the soviet's firebrand rhetoric about the evils of collaboration with bourgeois forces, they co-operated with the existing provincial provisions administration. The old administration, supplemented with a large contingent of soviet representatives, met on 30 September to tackle the crisis.[45] By 3 October, the provincial provisions committee had completely new membership and resolved to use military units to extract grain from the villages.[46] This new provincial provisions committee had the support of the Bolsheviks and Left SRs in the soviet, which by October held a small majority.[47]

[40] *Izvestiia soveta rabochikh i soldatskikh deputatov* 54, 15 October 1917, p. 2; from the meeting of the executive committee of the soviet of workers' and soldiers' deputies, 13 October 1917.
[41] *Kazanskaia rabochaia gazeta* 74, 12 July 1917, p. 3.
[42] *Kazanskaia rabochaia gazeta* 133, 24 September 1917, p. 3; reported in the Town Duma meeting.
[43] *Kazanskaia rabochaia gazeta* 135, 28 September 1917, p. 3.
[44] *Kazanskaia rabochaia gazeta* 139, 3 October 1917, p. 3.
[45] *Kazanskaia rabochaia gazeta* 140, 4 October 1917, p. 3.
[46] *Kazanskaia rabochaia gazeta* 146, 11 October 1917, p. 3.
[47] *Kazanskaia rabochaia gazeta* 159, 19 October 1917, p. 3.

Popular hostility towards provisions committees was commonplace in both Nizhegorod and Kazan, though the grounds for this hostility varied from place to place. In areas without severe need of provisions, the very establishment of provisions committees was resisted. In areas that were grain-hungry, provisions committees were established but faced hostility from the population for their perceived failings in ameliorating food shortages in the area. Provisions committees were set up in most *volosts* around Nizhegorod province, many of which were grain-hungry. These committees were not widespread or successful in Kazan, in principle an exporting region. Despite their 'democratic' status, provisions administrations faced concerted challenges. Suspicion of incompetence and corruption shadowed *uezd* and *volost* provisions committees closely, especially in the areas most seriously threatened with hunger.

The problem was not widespread incompetence on the part of these committees, but rather a complex interaction between the population's high expectations of their new administration to deliver, and the newly elected representatives' accountability. As the peasants of Sotnurskaia *volost*, Tsarevokokshaiskii *uezd*, told their village provisions commissar, 'We elected you, you must listen to us.'[48] Minutes from Lukoianovskii *uezd* provisions committee meeting in May exposed the extreme mistrust and hostility the *uezd* provisions committee provoked.[49] They were accused of inactivity and corruption, and threatened with violence. They denied the charges against them, blaming the provisioning problems in the area on the national situation and the policies of the provincial provisions committee. The committee struggled to obtain grain, even though they had funds available, and waited for deliveries from neighbouring regions. In Cheboksarskii *uezd*, one of Kazan's most politically tumultuous provinces, the provisions committee was accused by the committee of public safety of gross incompetence and inactivity, and it was proposed that the public safety committee take over some of its functions.[50]

Though Nizhegorod, as a grain importer, was in a weak position given the national provisions crisis, the problem was not clear-cut. Some *uezds* in the province had a surplus but, as in Kazan province, resisted the grain monopoly and either hung onto their produce or sold it at higher prices to

---

[48] NART, f. 1246, op. 1, d. 73, l. 146; note to Tsarevokokshaiskii *uezd* provisions committee from Sotnurskaia *volost* provisions administration, 1 September 1917.

[49] GANO, f. 1887, op. 1, d. 18, ll. 27–33; general meeting of Lukoianovskii *uezd* executive committee, 27 May 1917.

[50] NART, f. 1353, op. 1, d. 1, ll. 56–60; journal of Cheboksarskii *uezd* committee of public safety, 4 September 1917.

speculators. Reports from the *uezds* repeatedly linked fears about provisions to a rise in extremist actions, and the population's divorce from the work of public organisations. At the provincial meeting of *uezd* commissars in April, references to high grain prices, insufficiency of supplies and the urgency of the provisions situation were common factors in *uezd* commissar reports.[51] Shortages beset some areas early in the year. In March, Khoklomskii *volost*, Semenovskii *uezd*, had no wheat available at any price, and little rye, and 'even the churches did not have enough flour for the host'.[52] The worst-affected areas were in the north and north-west of the province, the *uezds* Balakhninskii, Semenovskii, Makar'evskii and Gorbatovskii. These *uezds* were mostly forested and had very little arable land, so they urgently needed to import large quantities of grain.[53]

Reports came in from all over the province of attacks on provisions administration. Direct action against the provisions administration occurred in similar forms in different *uezds* around the province. This report from Ardatov town in April is a good example of the forms of such action.

A market was held in Ardatov town on 3 April, and a meeting of people from peasant villages was held. Under the influence of speeches of citizen A. E. Kurov, clearly directed to the undermining of authority and trust in individuals standing at the head of regional *uezd zemstva* and administration . . . [a] crowd drawn of approximately 1000 people, some of whom were drunk, showed up at the building of the regional *zemstvo* court and began to knock at the door, wishing to carry out stocktaking and searches. The situation was particularly threatening to safety because documents and sums of money were preserved in that building, as well as members of the *uezd zemstvo*. The captain of the regional garrison, *uezd* military captain Colonel Nekhliudov, was compelled to send a command of soldiers from the 62nd infantry reserve regiment under the command of warrant officer Ivanov and forced the crowd, without the use of weapons, to disperse. The court was sealed up.

On 8 April these very events were played out again, but the crowd went still further, forcing the *uezd* commissar to go to the meeting of the *uezd* executive committee. He was asked to free citizen Kurov, who was still imprisoned then. The commissar pleaded that he could not do this, but was ignored. The crowd declared that the commissar was arrested and demanded that he be directed to the prison . . . the commissar sat in the prison office for 15 minutes . . . The captain

---

[51] GANO, f. 1882, op. 1, d. 13, ll. 155–9; protocol of the meeting of *uezd* commissars in Nizhegorod province, 10–11 April 1917.

[52] GANO, f. 815, op. 1, d. 20, l. 7; protocol of the meeting of Khoklomskii *volost* executive committee, 19 March 1917.

[53] Details of land use in the *uezds* found in *Nizhegorodskaia zemskaia gazeta* 31–32, 10 August 1917, pp. 8–9. The shortages in these four *uezds* can be clearly explained when looking at figure 7.2 showing grain production in the *uezds*.

of the garrison was again compelled to take decisive measures and with the help of a command of soldiers situated in Ardatov town on leave, freed the arrested commissar and restored order, again without weapons.[54]

The characteristics of protest here were repeated in reports from other *uezds*. The protests usually involved a gathering of peasants, often on market day, outside the provisions administration buildings. There were demands for immediate distribution of foodstuffs, or searches, or the resignation of the administration, alongside threats of violence against administrators, and often attacks as well.[55] Deficit *uezds* of Kazan province saw very similar patterns of unrest. In Cheboksarskii *uezd*, Kazan, a deficit region, the president of the *uezd* provisions committee was threatened by a crowd of 200 people, many of whom were women. They forced him to grant permission for the immediate distribution of white flour among the population, threatening to throw him out of the window if he refused. The crowd subsequently demanded that he carry out searches of the station for provisions reserves and threatened to throw him into the Volga.[56] Such forms of protest are comparable to urban workers' conflicts with factory owners in the late nineteenth century and suggest that to some extent ordinary people were following a 'script' of how to conduct open contestation with the state.[57]

In Gorbatovskii *uezd*, provisioning provoked open public disorder by July 1917,[58] which persisted through August and September. The geographical location of the *uezd* meant that after the river navigation season closed at the onset of autumn, there were no effective means of getting grain into the *uezd*.[59] Orchestrated demonstrations against the provisions administration in Gorbatov town went on for four days in August and culminated in the crowd demanding the resignation of the provisions administration.[60] Individuals came from different *volosts* in the *uezd* to participate in the protest,

[54] GANO, f. 1882, op. 1, d. 42, l. 124; from the journal of the meeting of Ardatovskii executive committee, 10 April 1917.

[55] For more examples, see GANO, f. 1882, op. 1, d. 13, ll. 155–9; protocol of the meeting of *uezd* commissars in Nizhegorod province, 10–11 April 1917; GANO, f. 851, op. 1, d. 2, l. 245; journal of general meeting of Makar'evskii *uezd* hilly section executive committee, 6 August 1917.

[56] NART, f. 1246, op. 1, d. 52, l. 349; from president of Cheboksarskii *uezd* provisions administration Kozlenkov to provincial commissar, 9 June 1917.

[57] For comparable forms of protest among textile workers in the late nineteenth century, see Brower, 'Labor violence', p. 421.

[58] *Izvestiia soveta rabochikh i soldatskikh deputatov* 30, 16 July 1917, p. 4.

[59] *Izvestiia soveta rabochikh i soldatskikh deputatov* 42, 27 July 1917, p. 4, 'resolution of the seven soviets of Gorbatovskii *uezd* '.

[60] *Narod* 61, 3 September 1917, p. 4.

and the crowd met at ten o'clock in the morning for four consecutive mornings.

The demands of the crowd were 'Give us grain. You will make us starve.' The crowd would not accept explanations from members of the administration. A voice was heard from the crowd, cursing foully, and threatening members of the administration with murder. At that moment several members of the administration ran away. The crowd seized the president of the administration, intending to lynch him, but the commissar and armed soldiers persuaded the crowd to leave him untouched. He was then arrested by the militia, together with another administration member, Sokolov, who, on the way to the guardhouse, had his beard pulled by the crowd, and the key of the provisions warehouse taken.[61]

These demonstrations of dissatisfaction with provisions administration intensified and increased in number as the summer wore on, and food shortages became increasingly urgent. The provincial section of the Nizhe-gorod soviet of workers' and soldiers' deputies reported a desperate shortage of provisions in almost all *uezds* by the end of August.[62] There were reports of harvest failures around the Volga region due to weather conditions. More than 60 per cent of Balakhninskii *uezd* was forested, and only 25 per cent of its land was set to arable. This helps explain why it was among the worst hit, with widespread expectation of starvation by the winter. Even mushrooms, a traditional supplementary winter food, had not grown in 1917.[63] The Town Duma and the provincial commissar sought to blunt the province's impending hunger by acquiring 500,000 *puds* of potatoes 'to procure cheap potato flour for the poor'.[64] This measure was fraught with difficulties, as the preparation of the potatoes was very slow, and the price of potatoes rose steadily. A wave of pogroms swept the province's towns and villages at the end of September, linked to fears of food shortages and pogroms in neighbouring Tambov. Shops and warehouses were raided.[65] The soviet supported the town administration in its attempts to control the situation and organised armed commands to defend the town's grain reserves.[66]

In his masterful study of refugees in Russia during the First World War, Peter Gatrell commented that the situation of refugees steadily deteriorated during the economic collapse that characterised 1917 and the civil war

---

[61] *Narod* 61, 3 September 1917, p. 4.

[62] *Izvestiia soveta rabochikh i soldatskikh deputatov* 44, 10 September 1917, pp. 1–3.

[63] *Nizhegorodskaia zemskaia gazeta* 36, 7 September 1917, p. 14.

[64] GANO, f. 27, op. 1, d. 3, l. 18; from Town Duma records, 12 September 1917.

[65] *Izvestiia soveta rabochikh i soldatskikh deputatov* 52, 8 October 1917, p. 1.

[66] *Izvestiia soveta rabochikh i soldatskikh deputatov* 53, 12 October 1917, p. 4; from the meeting of the executive committee of the soviet of workers' and soldiers' deputies, 7 October 1917. For examples from Balakhninskii *uezd*, see GANO, f. 1882, op. 1, d. 28, l. 314; report to provincial commissar, 10 October 1917; GANO, f. 1882, op. 1, d. 45, l. 205; copy of writings from the journal of the meeting of Balakhninskii town Duma on the question of preparation of provisions, 28 September 1917.

period.[67] This was certainly the case for the large numbers of refugees situated in Nizhegorod and Kazan provinces and related particularly to the provisions situation. Refugees were settled disproportionately in urban areas, and in Nizhnii Novgorod made up 15 per cent of the town's population.[68] References to refugees from official and newspaper sources in the March–May period were generally sympathetic, and increases to their allowances were granted or requested by a number of *uezd* committees.[69] Many of the refugees were young children, women and elderly people.[70] By July, the situation of Kazan's 60,000 refugees was critical. Only half of them received an allowance, and they were driven out of several *uezds*. Only Laishevskii and Chistopolskii *uezds* continued to take refugees.

The non-Russian population was particularly hostile to refugees. A representative of the largely Tatar Tsarevokokshaiskii *uezd* petitioned for removal of refugees from the *uezd*, as the *uezd* was, he claimed, already replete with 'newcomers'. The committee of public safety there petitioned the government to recommend that citizens in war zones remain where they are, and not flee.[71] Slobodo-Streletskii *volost* in Iadrinskii *uezd* requested in August that the refugees in the *volost*, a total of 375 people, be transferred to other *volosts*, as they had insufficient provisions.[72] The situation for refugees in Nizhegorod was even more acute, as the province's food shortages heightened unease about newcomers. There were some 63,000 refugees in Nizhegorod province, and it was proposed in September that they be moved to neighbouring provinces of Viatka, Ufimsk and Simbirsk by barge.[73] Increasingly, demands were heard from individual *uezds* that refugees be removed.[74] The sense of crisis evoked by food shortages caused

---

[67] Peter Gatrell, *A whole empire walking: refugees in Russia during World War I* (Bloomington, IN, 1999), p. 179.

[68] Gatrell, *A whole empire walking*, p. 3.

[69] See NART, f. 1352, op. 1, d. 2, l. 83; meeting of Spasskii *uezd* committee of public safety, 20 March 1917, reporting the refugees' allowances had been increased; NART, f. 1246, op. 1, d. 73, l. 55; protocol of Tsarevokokshaiskii *uezd*, 10 May 1917, asking that refugees' allowances be increased as they were in a pitiful state. This request for an increase in allowances was no doubt prompted in part by the reductions in refugee allowance of up to 50 per cent that were made at the beginning of 1917 (Gatrell, *A whole empire walking*, p. 173).

[70] For evidence of this, see NART, f. 406, op. 3, d. 3; lists of refugees receiving allowance in Kazan province.

[71] *Kazanskaia rabochaia gazeta* 85, 25 July 1917, p. 3; report of the provincial committee of public safety, 23 July 1917.

[72] NART, f. 1246, op. 1, d. 44, ll. 117–18; minutes from the general meeting of Iadrinskii *uezd* committee of public safety, 7 August 1917.

[73] *Nizhegorodskaia zemskaia gazeta* 36, 7 September 1917, p. 10.

[74] For examples in Makar'evskii *uezd*, parts of which were experiencing shortages, the executive committee demanded in October that refugees be removed from Lyskov village (GANO, f. 851, op. 1, d. 2, l. 355; meeting of the general meeting of Makar'evskii *uezd* executive committee, hilly region, 10 October 1917).

local communities to withdraw support from newcomers to their areas, and demand their removal.

Industrial workers relied on purchased grain supplies, and as a politically significant group within the urban population were of particular importance. Workers, like the rest of the population, focused on the problem of acquiring provisions, and their organisations played a prominent role in urban grain acquisition. Of ten reports from Nizhegorod's *uezd* worker soviets, six named the provisions question as the most important facing the local soviet.[75] In Arzamasskii *uezd*, for example, the workers' soviet, representing 3,000 workers, had successfully defended workers' interests in all public organisations. By September, however, crowds of hungry people were regularly laying siege to the soviet. The workers' soviet, having taken a position of authority, was then blamed, like other public organisations, for the provisions crisis. Kulebakskii soviet of workers' deputies, on the other hand, heightened its prestige and authority by successfully acquiring flour from neighbouring areas and distributing it among the worker population.

The administration of the Sormovo factories in Nizhnii Novgorod faced a daunting problem in finding supplies for its 25,000 workers. On 13 March the Sormovo factories only had reserves for three days, and the factory's provisions situation was reportedly critical.[76] Worker-led organisations in Sormovo proved to be very effective in tackling this problem. Indeed, the success of the Sormovo workers' organisations in acquiring provisions was such that it provoked hostility from other town residents and soldiers. Sormovo's approach to the provisions question demonstrated the extent to which workers' organisations acted autonomously and without regard to other branches of town administration. The Sormovo factory complex had its own provisions committee, which worked independently of other *uezd* organisations in the province. Workers were supplied provisions through the factory provisions committee, but also through the *volost zemstvo* provisions administration. Malyshev, a member of the factory provisions committee, declared on 16 October that the committee's intensive work had succeeded in purchasing 235,000 *puds* of grain, much of which had already been received, with the remainder being sent on a steamer.[77] Town organisations suspected Sormovo of appropriating an unfair share of provisions. The barge containing 27,000 *puds* of grain obtained by the

[75] *Izvestiia soveta rabochikh i soldatskikh deputatov* 56, 22 October 1917, pp. 2–3.
[76] GANO, f. 1882, op. 1, d. 25, l. 115; telegram sent by director of Sormovo factories Khrenikov, to provincial commissar, 13 March 1917.
[77] *Izvestiia rabochikh i soldatskikh deputatov* 57, 26 October 1917, p. 4, Sormovo life.

Sormovo factories was seized by the town administration, causing an out-cry from Sormovo administration and soviet.[78] On 17 October, the factory director reported to the Ministry of Defence that: 'Malicious rumours have been disseminated about non-existent reserves in Sormovo. I, in my duty as a citizen, report promptly to the military . . . the legends about provisions reserves of Sormovo factories do not have any foundation: Not one *pud* of flour and not one *pud* of grain is currently in the storehouses.'[79]

Despite these protestations, it is apparent that Sormovo's success in acquiring grain far outstripped the town's provisions organisations. Even by mid-December, the factories still had reserves of 150,000 *puds* of flour, rye and oats.[80] It was later acknowledged that because Sormovo was sup-plied both by the factory committee and the *zemstvo*, Sormovo workers were better supplied than the non-worker population. Sormovo workers were therefore blamed when insufficient foodstuffs were distributed to Sormovo's non-worker population. Attempts were made in December to amalgamate the provisions administrations to allay this problem.[81] The provisions question brought tensions to a head all over the province but in the case of Sormovo highlighted a sense that workers were unfairly privileged.

RESISTANCE TO THE GRAIN MONOPOLY

Of all Russia's surplus provinces, Kazan was one of the worst providers of grain for the front in 1917. For February and March 1917, Kazan pro-vided 12 per cent of its grain quota to the army. Only the Don region per-formed worse.[82] The general explanation for a shortage of grain for the grain monopoly has already been discussed – the collapse of internal markets, the problems of transport and the challenges of internal speculation. Only by investigating incidences of resistance to the grain monopoly at closer quarters, however, can these problems really be understood. Kazan province offered virulent and often violent resistance to the grain monopoly, fuelled in places by particular intransigence from the non-Russian population.

---

[78] *Izvestiia rabochikh i soldatskikh deputatov* 55, 19 October 1917, p. 2.
[79] GANO, f. 1442, op. 1, d. 9, l. 226; telegram to the commissar for defence from the director of Sormovo factories, 17 October 1917.
[80] GANO, f. 442, op. 1, d. 7, ll. 173–5; report from the director of Sormovo factories to the Sormovo office of the soviet of workers' deputies, 15 December 1917.
[81] *Krasnoe znamia* 16, 8 December 1917, p. 3; report on the provisions situation in Sormovo.
[82] Kondratev, *Rynok khlebov*, pp. 419–21. Ukraine also did poorly. Mark Baker's study of Kharkiv peasants indicates that, as in Kazan, peasants refused to co-operate with food-supply organs (Baker, 'Peasants, power and revolution', chapter 2).

A meeting of Kazan province's provisions committee on 5 July offered detailed reports on the provisions situation in eight of Kazan's twelve *uezds*. All these eight reported fierce resistance to the grain monopoly, and in many areas provisions committees had not been organised at all. Some *volosts* in Kozmodem'ianskii *uezd* destroyed the whole provisions administration.[83] Cheboksarskii, Kozmodem'ianskii and Tsarevokokshaiskii *uezds* in the north-west of the province were the most unruly of all, and 'there was in practice no grain monopoly'.[84] These three *uezds* had a significantly lower sown area than the rest of the province (see figure 7.2, p. 185).

Contemporaries' explanations for this heated resistance tended to emphasise that peasants 'misunderstood' or were 'ignorant' of the grain monopoly, or were led astray by 'dark' forces operating in the villages, or wealthy peasants.[85] The non-Russians were singled out in particular as being 'dark' and especially hostile to the imposition of the grain monopoly. Complaints were also made of excessive demands for grain being made on villagers, who were not left enough to feed themselves and their livestock.[86] The political elite claimed that the solution to these problems was education and understanding. As 1917 progressed, attempts at educating villagers on provisions matters were repeatedly rebuffed, and peasants made increasingly 'conscious' statements of resistance to the grain monopoly. From summer onwards, we correspondingly see explanations for provisions disorder being given as the evils of market forces and of dark counter-revolutionary force in the villages, and the solution was seen increasingly to be the use of armed force. The peasants' titular leaders became increasingly disillusioned with the people they had looked towards to help the country out of provisions crisis. In Tsarevokokshaiskii *uezd*, reports initially talked of 'misunderstandings'. These so-called 'misunderstandings' escalated into 'open risings against the provisions and land committees, and against the militia captain' by mid-September. The only solution open to the provincial commissar was to send in more soldiers.[87]

[83] *Kazanskaia rabochaia gazeta* 75, 13 July 1917, p. 3.
[84] *Kazanskaia rabochaia gazeta* 77, 15 July 1917, p. 3. Extreme hostility to the grain monopoly was also manifested in Kharkiv (Baker, 'Beyond the national', p. 51).
[85] *Kazanskaia rabochaia gazeta* 75, 13 July 1917, p. 3; see also *Kazanskaia rabochaia gazeta* 128, 19 September 1917, p. 4, for accusations that peasants were led astray by 'kulaks'.
[86] See, for example, *Kazanskaia rabochaia gazeta* 67, 2 June 1917, p. 4, letter from Spasskii *uezd*; *Kazanskaia rabochaia gazeta* 87, 27 July 1917, p. 4, letter from Chistopolskii *uezd*; NART, f. 1246, op. 1, d. 43, l. 77; report of outside agitator brought to Mamadyshskii *uezd* to resolve conflict in Kabyk-Kuperskoi *volost*, 16 July 1917.
[87] NART, f. 1246, op. 1, d. 73, l. 146; note to Tsarevokokshaiskii *uezd* PC from Sotnurskaia *volost* provisions administration, 1 September 1917; NART, f. 1246, op. 1, d. 73, l. 137; letter from Tsarevokokshaiskii *uezd* commissar to provincial commissar, 16 September.

Attempts to win villagers' co-operation with education programmes routinely failed. Kazan *uezd* provisions administration reported to the provincial provisions committee on 12 July that the population categorically refused to implement the grain monopoly, and that only strong military force would enable the grain monopoly to be enacted. In a number of *volosts*, provisions educators had been beaten and terrorised. Most communities refused to organise provisions committees, and where they did exist, as in Baltasynskii *volost*, they were re-elected and themselves opposed the grain monopoly.[88] When a provisions instructor came to Baltasynskii in August, he was told to address 'requests' for fixed prices to the commune council, and the Tatar villagers said, 'we will submit to the law, but we won't submit to norms of consumption and fixed prices'.[89] This situation did not improve in the *uezd*. Kazan's *uezd* commissar wrote to the provincial commissar at the start of September that he had met extreme hostility when trying to defend the grain monopoly in Kliuchei village, Kudmorskii *volost*, and had been forced to run away.[90]

Another example of villagers' negative responses to education attempts can be found in Iadrinskii *uezd*, where large quantities of grain were being illegally exported to neighbouring *uezds*. In most *volosts* of Iadrinskii *uezd*, there had been categorical refusals to carry out the grain monopoly or to organise *volost* provisions committees. In a number of villages, the mood was described as 'extremely dangerous'.[91] Representatives of the Kazan soviet of workers' and soldiers' deputies visited Alikovskii *volost*, Iadrinskii *uezd*, in an attempt to educate the population on the grain monopoly. A meeting was held in the Chuvash village Al'kov on 25 July. Around 2,000 people attended, and when delegates began to speak of the need to organise committees, a crowd of around 200 people, reportedly dominated by deserters armed with sticks and bottles, came forward and beat up three of the delegates. When the local intelligentsia, including teachers and a priest, protested at the violence, they were also attacked. Only one of the soviet delegates managed to run away. The disorder went on from ten in the morning till three in the afternoon. By the time armed assistance turned up at four in the afternoon, the crowd had mostly dispersed. Thirty-seven

[88] NART, f. 1246, op. 1, d. 75, l. 53; letter from Kazanskii *uezd* provisions administration to Kazan province provisions committee, 12 July 1917, p. 60; telegram from *uezd* commissar to provincial commissar, 19 July 1917; *Kazanskaia rabochaia gazeta* 86, 26 July 1917, p. 4.

[89] *Kazanskaia rabochaia gazeta* 100, 12 August 1917, p. 4.

[90] NART, f. 1246, op. 1, d. 75, l. 295; report from Kazan *uezd* commissar to provincial commissar, September 1917.

[91] NART, f. 1246, op. 1, d. 44, ll. 52–7; journal of the meeting of Iadrinskii *uezd* committee and soviet, 10 July 1917.

people were subsequently arrested and taken to Iadrinskii prison by an armed convoy of soldiers.[92]

The Provisional Government's decision to claim all grain above subsistence norms as state property relied on local food-supply organs to take successful inventories and establish sound links with producers. The first step of this process was the gathering of complete information on the population and provisions stocks. This first step proved to be unrealisable. A survey from Moscow soviet of workers and soldiers' deputies revealed that only two of thirty-eight provinces had completed a census.[93] In Kazan, census taking, sometimes undertaken alongside the updating of electoral registers, met with fierce resistance. A *volost* provisions committee in Tsarevokokshaiskii *uezd* noted that the population refused to abide by its decrees and was unwilling to give any information about the number of residents and quantity of grain. The report noted the refusal of villagers there to consider national interests: 'Russia is forgotten: the word *rodina* [motherland] is understood only as their village.'[94]

Kolegaev, the Left SR president of the Kazan peasants' soviet, journeyed around the notoriously restless Kozmodem'ianskii *uezd* in early summer. He noted that peasants in many *volosts* of the *uezd* had no grain and feared the census, as they believed it would take away what little they had. This, Kolegaev argued, revealed their lack of understanding; a full census would actually benefit them. The Cheremis were particularly 'dark' and fearful. They associated the census listings with ration cards from the towns and believed they would have to queue for grain: 'Peasants from a range of villages ran to the woods and lived there. Few residents remain . . . Terrible rumours circulate and they are believed. The peasantry is afraid of everything. When the censors came, they found empty houses and stores.'[95]

In Mamadyshskii *uezd*, the explanation for refusals of census taking in a number of *volosts* was that the population, many of whom were *soldatki*, lived solely on black bread and were being asked to give more than they had.[96] The *uezd* committee responded by increasing the allowance of retained grain.[97] Some peasant resistance shown to census-takers

[92] *Kazanskaia rabochaia gazeta* 87, 27 July 1917, p. 3; a more detailed report of events produced in *Kazanskaia rabochaia gazeta* 109, 24 August 1917, p. 4.
[93] Zaitsev and Dolinsky, 'Organisation and policy', p. 105.
[94] NART, f. 1246, op. 1, d. 73, l. 145; note from *volost* provisions committee to Tsarevokokshaiskii *uezd* provisions administration, September 1917.
[95] *Izvestiia Kazanskago gubernskago soveta krest'ianskikh deputatov* 14, 18 July 1917, pp. 2–3.
[96] NART, f. 1246, op. 1, d,. 43, l. 77; report of outside agitator brought to Mamadyshskii *uezd* to resolve conflict in Kabyk-Kuperskoi *volost*, 16 July 1917.
[97] NART, f. 1246, op. 1, d. 43, l. 30; letter from Mamadyshskii *uezd* commissar to provincial commissar, 18 July 1917.

demonstrated their consciousness and awareness. In Sandyrskii *volost*, the provisions administration had its paperwork, with details of the census, particularly targeted by crowds of rioters who broke into buildings and destroyed all books, papers and documentation on 18 September.[98] Destruction of paperwork was a common feature of peasant attacks on provisions administration in surplus areas. The captain of the soldiers sent to carry out the census in Tsarevokokshaiskii *uezd* reported that in one *volost*, Abranskii, not a single resident would give any information, even their names. They threw stones at soldiers, burnt all the paperwork of the *volost* provisions administration and threatened to murder those who defended the grain monopoly.[99] In the Chuvash village of Bolshoi Sundir, Kozmodem'ianskii *uezd*, Zapolskii, the president of the provisions administration, was murdered on 14 August. Peasants had gathered outside the administration building and demanded the destruction of land and provisions census listings. When Zapolskii refused, the crowd dragged him out onto the street and beat him to death with sticks and stakes.[100] In Toraevskii *volost*, Iadrinskii *uezd*, Kazan, soldiers were sent in September to protect the beleaguered provisions administration and carry out censuses. Despite soldier presence, however, on 28 September crowds dispersed the provisions committee and destroyed all its paperwork. A further eighty soldiers were sent to quell the disorder.[101]

The villagers demonstrated their ability to organise very effectively if they felt it necessary. In Karmyshkii *volost*, land and provisions committees had been organised, but while the land committees operated effectively and energetically, the provisions committee was completely inactive, as the population would not allow a census of grain to be taken. The organiser concluded that 'where there is no grain, the population organises committees; where there is grain, the population resists'.[102] Where provisions committees were formed in surplus areas, if they were to survive they too opposed the grain monopoly. In Bol'she-Iuginskii *volost*, Kozmodem'ianskii *uezd*, members of the *volost* provisions committee themselves incited crowds against the

---

[98] NART, f. 1246, op. 1, d. 73, l. 148; letter from Sandyrskii *volost* provisions administration to province provisions administration, 18 September 1917.

[99] NART, f. 1246, op. 1, d. 73, l. 176; from Captain of command in Tsarevokokshaisk town to Tsarevokokshaiskii *uezd* provisions administration, 28 September 1917.

[100] *Kazanskaia rabochaia gazeta* 128, 19 September 1917, p. 4.

[101] NART, f. 1246, op. 1, d. 44, l. 167; telefonogram from captain of militia to Iadrinskii *uezd* commissar, 19 September 1917, p. 167; telegram from provincial commissar to *uezd* commissar, 20 September 1917, p. 171; telegram from provincial commissar to *uezd* commissar, 21 September 1917, p. 188; telefonogram from provincial commissar to *uezd* commissar, 28 September 1917, p. 211; telegram to provincial commissar from captain of militia, 7 October 1917.

[102] *Kazanskaia rabochaia gazeta* 86, 26 July 1917, p. 4.

grain monopoly.[103] Resistance shown to the grain monopoly was in no way uniformly 'elemental' or arising from ignorance, as reporters implied. The *volost* provisions administration in Koshklovskii *volost*, Tsarevokokshaiskii *uezd*, resigned en masse in August, as they faced total non-co-operation from the local population. A gathering of peasants from the *volost* met on 11 August and declared:

1. The *volost* provisions committee and administration has no jurisdiction over us, and we do not consider them to be official individuals.
2. We do not wish to carry out the grain monopoly in the *volost*.
3. We will not permit the listing of the population's grain and cattle.
4. We cannot permit the requisition of 25 head of cattle, since they are all we have left for our households.
5. All demands from the *volost* will be fulfilled only when the war is quickly ended.[104]

These demands calmly and categorically laid out the villagers' attitude towards the provisions question, and towards the authority of the local administration. Faced with such conscious and open hostility, the provincial commissar sent troops to seize cattle forcibly.[105] The authorities resorted to soldiers with increasing frequency as the summer wore on.

Intimidation and violence towards those who tried to enact the grain monopoly ranged from the mundane to the serious, even in the same *volost*. The population of Mamadyshskii *uezd* resisted even census taking with fearsome force. The situation was worsened by the presence of large numbers of deserters in the area.[106] Provisions administrators repeatedly requested armed military support to protect them and enforce their will.[107] A visit from an external agitator in July to Kabyke-Kuperskoe *volost*, Mamadyshskii *uezd*, suggested that the local official there, Balovnev, had needlessly provoked the population, and had had his cheek slapped by a *soldatka* as a result.[108] Things escalated, however, in July, when more soviet agitators

[103] NART, f. 1246, op. 1, d. 48, l. 204; note from Bol'she-Iuginskii *volost* PC to Kozmodem'ianskii *uezd* provisions administration, 20 June 1917.
[104] NART, f. 1246, op. 1, d. 73, ll. 88–90; letter from Koshklovskaia *volost* provisions administration to Tsarevokokshaiskii *uezd* provisions administration, 15 August 1917.
[105] NART, f. 1246, op. 1, d. 73, ll. 89–90; telegrams between provincial commissar and provincial provisions administration, 2 September 1917.
[106] NART, f. 1246, op. 1, d. 43, l. 65; telegram to captain of military from provincial commissar, 19 July 1917; NART, f. 1354, op. 2, d. 5, ll. 69–70; journal of the meeting of Mamadyshskii *uezd* committees of provisions and public safety, 1 August 1917.
[107] NART, f. 1246, op. 1, d. 43, l. 134; letter from Kazan provincial provisions administration to Kazan provincial commissar, 25 July 1917.
[108] NART, f. 1246, op. 1, d. 43, l. 77; report of outside agitator in Mamadyshskii *uezd*, 16 July 1917.

were sent in to the area, and two newspapers reported that Balovnev had been murdered.[109] More delegates were sent into the area in August. They were driven away three times by resistant villagers and were rescued from their public by an armed command. The *uezd* provisions committee was unable to offer any help.[110] A united meeting of the Mamadyshskii provisions administration and the *uezd* committee of public safety found that the basis for this severe hostility to the grain monopoly was founded on the insufficient norms allowed by the monopoly for the feeding of livestock and for the population's sustenance.[111]

Whether the source of resistance was excessive demands from government, ignorance or rampant self-interest, the violence meted out to those trying to support the grain monopoly in Kazan's *uezds* intensified. As the summer progressed, the region effectively broke away from central government control, and local people acted autonomously in accordance with their own interests. In Arkhangel'skii *volost*, Cheboksarskii *uezd*, neither the Provisional Government nor the soviets were recognised. Provisions delegates were beaten and it was threatened that anyone sent to teach in the village would be murdered.[112] Spasskii *uezd* had been tumultuous from March onwards, and soldiers sent there arrested a number of local citizens.[113] At the beginning of June, army delegates were sent to the *uezd* for grain-monopoly agitation, and in one village were cursed, 'given grief', kicked, threatened with drowning and dragged to jail.[114] In July, the military chief of the region was beaten very severely, almost to death, by a crowd, and then dragged to prison.[115] In Tsarevokokshaiskii *uezd*, the *volost* administration in Petrikovskii was totally overrun by peasants and soldiers on leave, who besieged the administrative buildings, broke in and dragged the committee

---

[109] *Kamsko-volzkskaia rech*, 7 July 1917, and *Kazanskaia rabochaia gazeta* 72, 8 July 1917, p. 3; both reported that Balovnev had been murdered. In fact, Balovnev was alive and well and living in Mamadysh (NART, f. 1246, op. 1, d. 48, l. 292; letter to the editors).

[110] NART, f. 1246, op. 1, d. 43, l. 104; report of the military controller Pavlov regarding the situation in Mamadyshskii *uezd*, undated; NART, f. 1246, op. 1, d. 43, l. 160; letter to the president of the provincial provisions administration from delegates of Kazan soviet of workers' and soldiers' deputies commandeered to Mamadyshskii *uezd*, 11 August 1917.

[111] NART, f. 1246, op. 1, d. 43, l. 253; report of the united meeting of the Mamadyshskii *uezd* provisions administration and the committee of public safety, 14 July 1917.

[112] *Kazanskaia rabochaia gazeta* 77, 15 July 1917, p. 3.

[113] NART, f. 1246, op. 1, d. 41; papers about the introduction of the new regime into Spasskii *uezd*, pp. 10, 327.

[114] NART, f. 1246, op. 1, d. 41, l. 224; letter to provincial commissar from delegate of the seventh army, 9 June 1917.

[115] NART, f. 1246, op. 1, d. 41, ll. 323, 326, 327, 331; series of telegrams describing the incident and appealing for more military backing.

members into the street, where they were beaten till they lost consciousness.[116] This violence needs to be understood in the context of traditional village use of violence. Stephen Frank's work has shown that violence in village society was generally deployed strategically and pragmatically. Extreme violence was usually employed only when the village community felt itself to be under threat. The grain monopoly was clearly regarded as a mortal threat to the village community, which had to be combated with the most extreme measures.[117]

The non-Russian population was often singled out as being particularly resistant to the grain monopoly. In a report from Chistopolskii *uezd*, for example, Tatars in Eriklinskii *volost* refused to give any information for the provisions census.[118] This was explained partly by problems in communication. Kazan's numerous ethnic groups, including Tatars, Chuvash and Cheremis, had different languages and alphabets, and many did not understand Russian. Another explanation for the particular intransigence of the Tatar community was its history of hostility to state and external influences. From 1827 onwards, clumsy efforts were made by the state to convert apostatised Tatars, and defectors were forcibly resettled or exiled. This experience left the Tatar community particularly hostile to state intervention.[119] The Kazan committee of Chuvash military decided to send its representatives to Chuvash villages to disseminate information and proposed that the provincial provisions committee be reorganised along national lines.[120] A member of a *volost* provisions committee in Tsarevokokshaiskii *uezd* appealed specifically for agitators with Cheremis language skills.[121] Just as with the Russian population, however, as the summer wore on, explanations of 'misunderstandings' became less and less credible, and force was increasingly called for to suppress risings.

In July, Kazan's united provisions meeting was forced to conclude that seizure of grain backed by armed force was the only way to extract grain from the region's peasants.[122] Even where armed force was resorted to, the Kazan peasantry did not back down. In Kozmodem'ianskii *uezd*, peasants in many *volosts* refused outright to comply with the grain monopoly. Kolegaev, after

---

[116] NART, f. 1246, op. 1, d. 73, l. 162; letter from Petrikovskii *volost* provisions administration to Tsarevokokshaiskii *uezd* provisions administration, 25 September 1917.

[117] See the discussion of popular justice in Frank, 'Popular justice'.

[118] NART, f. 983, op. 1, d. 16, ll. 101–6; minutes of the Chistopolskii *uezd* committee of public safety and other *uezd* representatives, 26 June 1917.

[119] Geraci, *Window on the east*, p. 28.

[120] *Kazanskaia rabochaia gazeta* 120, 7 September 1917, p. 4.

[121] NART, f. 1246, op. 1, d. 73, l. 145; note from *volost* provisions committee to Tsarevokokshaiskii *uezd* provisions administration, September 1917.

[122] *Kazanskaia rabochaia gazeta* 73, 11 July 1917, p. 3.

visiting Bol'she-Iunginskii *volost* in Kozmodem'ianskii *uezd* in July, argued that the beating and violence meted out to those trying to administer the census and grain monopoly had its origins in ignorance, or 'darkness', and that the presence of soldiers had in itself worsened the situation as there was great animosity towards soldiers. Kolegaev's impression was that dialogue, without the presence of soldiers, would resolve matters.[123] The situation in Kozmodem'ianskii *uezd* by September indicates that Kolegaev's faith in education was misplaced. Violence and resistance in the *uezd* continued unabated. Soldiers surrounded Akramov village. The Akramov peasants, some 4,000 in number, guarded the village in disciplined lines, and on the approach of any soldier towards the village, bells sounded to raise the alarm. The *uezd* commissar, N. A. Rodionov, who camped out with the soldiers, declared that though he was prepared to allow the soldiers to threaten the peasants, he would not actually authorise them to shoot.[124]

By September, a coalition of Left SRs and Bolsheviks had taken control of Kazan's provincial provisions administration. Their attitude towards the use of armed force and arrests in the countryside was ambiguous. While in principle they supported the use of force as their predecessors had, they laboured under the delusion that resistance to the grain monopoly was carried out by a minority, and that most peasants were simply unenlightened. Kolegaev, commenting on the unrest in Spasskii *uezd* in July, argued that arrests and the sending of soldiers only heightened resentment in the villages against the provisions committees. He stated that the soviet of peasants' deputies did not oppose arrests in general but protested against the 'arbitrary' arrests that he alleged had been taking place. He reiterated that 'even if they are dark, they are still our comrades. We cannot go to them with armed force.'[125] As the summer progressed, and the grain monopoly continued to crumble, Kolegaev and his comrades came to support punitive measures in the countryside, which they justified as actions against the 'wealthy minority' that they asserted to be behind the problems. The Nizhegorod soviet of workers' and soldiers' deputies also called for the use of soldiers against peasants withholding grain as the summer progressed.[126] This reflected a national shift towards desperate measures for grain procurement.[127]

[123] *Izvestiia Kazanskago gubernskago soveta krest'ianskikh deputatov* 14, 18 August 1917, pp. 2–3.
[124] *Kazanskaia rabochaia gazeta* 128, 19 September 1917, p. 4.
[125] *Izvestiia Kazanskago gubernskago soveta krest'ianskikh deputatov* 8, 28 July 1917.
[126] *Izvestiia soveta rabochikh i soldatskikh deputatov* 53, 12 October 1917, p. 4, meeting of the executive committee of soviet of workers' and soldiers' deputies, 9 October 1917.
[127] George L. Yaney, *The urge to mobilise: agrarian reform in Russia 1861–1930* (London, 1982), p. 442.

CONCLUSIONS

Regional government lost control of the countryside in 1917, and this loss of control was precipitated by the provisions crisis. Government policies on grain procurement exposed the gulf between the political elite's vision of how the countryside operated, and the realities. The Provisional Government's faith in the democratisation of local government to resolve the problems of supply and distribution proved to be mistaken. Local interests overwhelmed national interests in ordinary people's priorities. The Provisional Government had little in the way of either coercive or encouraging methods to encourage people to abide by the grain monopoly, short of appeals and imprecations.

This chapter substantiates the argument in chapter 6 that the cultural-enlightenment campaigns of 1917 ultimately failed not because of the method of delivery or of misunderstood language, but because they preached a message that was not accepted by ordinary rural people. Both Provisional Government and soviet sources believed initially that peasant hostility to the grain monopoly and provisions administration was founded in ignorance and misunderstandings, which could be resolved through explanation and education. This faith in education waned as the summer of 1917 progressed, and troops were increasingly used in attempts to enforce the grain monopoly and public order. The Provisional Government's grain monopoly policy was a logical one, that sought to make best use of national grain production and distribute the grain to where need was greatest. For the grain monopoly to be a success, it needed effective administration, and the willingness of the grain-producing population to make economic sacrifices in the name of Russia's greater good. The grain monopoly failed to operate effectively precisely on these two points. The political elite's optimistic faith in the power of local self-government to mobilise and efficiently administer the population was misplaced, as its success was predicated on the local population being obedient to central authority, and willing to make personal sacrifices. Attempts to 'educate' the local population about the efficacy of the grain monopoly failed because the local population refused to make the personal sacrifices required, not because they failed to understand the message.

Studying the nature of the food crisis in Nizhegorod and Kazan highlights that straightforward comparisons of the two provinces are misleading. By investigating local conditions more closely, as with land relations, we see that the situation varied from *uezd* to *uezd*. It makes more sense to make comparisons between grain deficit and grain surplus areas, some of which were in Nizhegorod, and some in Kazan. Provisions committees were not formed in surplus areas, or were formed and then resisted the grain monopoly they had been created to implement. Provisions committees were formed in deficit areas and became a focus of popular hostility about food shortages. Popular hostility took common forms in different deficit areas. It invariably involved threats or acts of violence against provisions administrators. In deficit areas, popular hostility and violence was directed against educators and agitators as well as administrators of the grain monopoly. Rural violence can be explained by setting it in its cultural context, as a means to protect the community's interests, but this explanation did not help the Provisional Government or local administrators in their futile attempts to implement national policy. At provincial level in both Nizhegorod and Kazan, provisions committees had a wide and 'democratised' membership but were repeatedly reformed and accused of incompetence and corruption. Soviet participation in these committees was, however, unable to improve on their effectiveness. Soviet leaders were forced to condone the use of troops in the countryside in their attempts to support the grain monopoly. The use of troops by regional administration was essentially an admission that attempts at educating the population to accept the grain monopoly had been a failure.

Conclusions

These chapters are intended to highlight the confusion and imprecision of power relations and social interactions in 1917 rather than to offer conclusive answers and clear models. Russia's revolutionary year generated multiple sources of power, with non-institutional, decentralised power challenging state and central power. Local considerations defined regional power relations. Authorities, be they central, regional or party political, struggled and ultimately failed to define revolutionary discourse, communicate their messages and control political power. Recognising the blurred lines and ambiguity of locations of power helps us move towards a more nuanced understanding of 1917 and demonstrates that the political elite's alternatives were circumscribed by the desires and demands of ordinary people. Historians face serious problems in trying to 'hear the voices' of ordinary people, and of ordinary rural people in particular, as this work tries to do. Despite all efforts, ordinary people's voices remain elusive, and muffled by the voices of the political elite and politically dominant social groups. The best we can do is to be conscious of the diversity and confusion of ordinary people's responses to revolution, and to try and pick up on the myriad of different perspectives held by ordinary people in 1917.

This study highlights areas that help us to understand the failure of democratic party politics in 1917. The boundaries of behaviour defined as political have been enlarged here beyond the political elite and the urban and organised sections of the population, in order to understand the ways in which ordinary people behaved as political actors. The assumption that political behaviour had to relate to party politics, or to engage with some centrally defined master narrative, is deep rooted in historical understandings of the revolutionary period. This assumption, along with the problems of elite-dominated sources, has effectively excluded many ordinary people from our conceptions of the political process. This book presents a much-expanded cast of political actors for 1917.

Party politics had shallow roots in Russian popular consciousness, and these roots were not sufficient to provide the foundations for a new political system. As we see from their participation in the electoral process, ordinary people understood and adopted the party political system, which at national level required that they select their representative from party lists. Party politics did not, however, structure most ordinary people's day-to-day lives and political decisions. Historians cling to voting figures as 'evidence' of popular support and mood, mainly because they are our only quantifiable measuring stick of ordinary people's political affiliations. Unfortunately, what voting figures measure are really only fleeting glimpses of popular political identities, which for much of the population did not relate closely to party politics. Ordinary people understood and utilised the party political system, but voting for a candidate did not imply full agreement with the programmatic details of that candidate's party platform. Their vote at most represented a loose association between the voter's sense of public identity or priorities and their sense of which candidate or group best represented their aspirations at that moment. The political elite envisaged that democratic party politics would involve voters selecting parties based on their programme, and providing the winning party mandate to carry out that programme, and it did to some degree. This conception of democratic party politics required the voting public to embrace some degree of party loyalty and identification with party programmes if it was to operate in a stable way. Party loyalty and identification were not prominent features of 1917's political environment.

By embracing the notion of ordinary people as political actors, we are able to reconsider the channels of communication between ordinary people and the political elite. If Russia's attempts at democratic party politics were to flourish, communication of their political messages and their projected social and national goals had to be effective. This book has highlighted the failure of communication and understanding between the political elite and ordinary people and can help us to outline how and in what ways these lines of communication failed. Communication between the political elite and ordinary people was on the whole stymied not by any failings or ignorance on the part of ordinary people, but because some aspects of the political elite's messages were not accepted by ordinary people, and because the political elite were unwilling or unable to identify or respond to the needs and demands of ordinary people. Ordinary people displayed a pragmatic refusal to obey orders or requests that they did not consider to be in their best interests. Where appeals went unanswered or orders thwarted, this reflected a conscious decision on the part of ordinary folks to protect what they regarded as their best interests.

The political elite expected the rural intelligentsia to be their main conduit for communication with ordinary people. Their role is discussed repeatedly in this book, and it was an ambivalent one. The Provisional Government's attempt to found popular, democratic local government needed the rural intelligentsia to man the administrative network. In some instances, the rural intelligentsia were reluctant to take their allotted roles as the revolutionary village vanguard. There is plenty of evidence, too, that the rural population excluded the rural intelligentsia from participation in local government. Some members of the rural intelligentsia did play a prominent role in cultural-enlightenment programmes and in local leadership. When local leaders remained responsive to their constituents' needs and demands, however, they inevitably diverged from the aims of the political elite.

Localism and economic interests dominated ordinary people's responses to 1917 in Nizhegorod and Kazan. Ordinary people in both urban and rural areas were pragmatic in their responses to revolution, and acted according to their own perceived best interests. Peasants, like workers, were able to organise and to act in concerted fashion where it was recognised that such organisation was in their own best interests. This refusal of ordinary people to act in the interests of the state, as defined by local government and the Provisional Government, was, however, a key feature of the ultimate failure of democratic party politics. This is most apparent when we look at responses to the food crisis, and the land question, and does not apply only to peasants, but to workers and soldiers as well.

The drive for democratisation in local government that characterised 1917 reflected the wave of popular and elite optimism in the wake of the February revolution, and the utopianism of Russia's new administrators. For the political elite, February optimism was manifested in their faith in the 'goodness' of the Russian people, and this faith and optimism informed the first six months of the Provisional Government's administration. Democratisation of local government was a reflection of demands from below, and a demonstration of the political elite's faith that ordinary people would act in national interests. Underlying this faith was the naïve understanding that many of Russia's problems were predicated on the failings of the tsarist regime and administration. Remove this administration, hand over control to democracy, and Russia could function freely once more. Such faith was misplaced and reflects the political elite's lack of experience in the exercise of political power.

Like almost every other study of Russia's revolution, this book has reiterated that Russia's participation in the First World War affected every aspect of social and political life and compounded the Provisional Government's problems in administering Russia. The other warring nations, including the relatively stable democracies of Britain and France, actually increased the power and penetration of the state in daily life in the strained conditions produced by wartime, and even they struggled with popular dissent. To decentralise and democratise local government in a period of economic and social crisis as the Provisional Government did was counter-intuitive, and it resulted in the almost complete loss of central government's ability to govern the provinces. On the provisions question, on land relations, on the forms of local government, the Provisional Government was powerless to enforce its will. It was ultimately unwilling or unable to use force to make ordinary people stay in line with the state. The crumbling economy, collapsed social hierarchies and democratised local government all generated powerful centrifugal forces, pushing Russia's regions apart and heightening individuals' interest in their own needs.

The Provisional Government, and the local government administration, was concerned with what can be described as responsible politics. Their policies in 1917 were centred around determination to continue Russia's defence of her borders by participation in the war, to maintain public calm and order, and to establish a democratic political system to replace the collapsed tsarist regime. Chasms emerged, however, between local and central government on how to achieve these goals. While the moderate socialists that dominated local government tended to share the Provisional Government's aims and principles, their means and actions had to respond to local conditions. This often meant sidelining national policy, and carrying out independent initiatives. Local government's pragmatic and necessary responses to the challenges they faced deepened the gulf between central power and local power, and revealed the virtual impotence of central authority.

This work's study of two provinces has helped us recognise the importance of locality in defining the shape of the revolutionary year. As the numbers of regional studies of the revolutionary period increase, so our understanding of the interrelations between local conditions and national concerns will become clearer. The experience of revolution in the capital towns of Nizhnii Novgorod and Kazan are comparable, though both had very specific problems and conditions. Party politics were well developed and combative in both towns. Both had relatively well-developed networks of educated society that were to form a significant factor in the province's administration. They both had problems with food shortages and with the practical problems of housing large garrisons. Such comparability between these two major towns is to be expected. A more interesting dynamic emerges in the complex differences, conflicts and comparisons between town and countryside in both places. Studies of the revolutionary period have tended to focus either on urban or on rural areas. By looking at urban and rural together, we see that in some respects, the capital towns might as well have been in another country, so great were the dissonances between townspeople's and rural dwellers' experiences. While in the big towns, the February revolution was news of immediacy that had immediate and massive reverberations, in the countryside, the news of February events was more slowly dispersed and produced a more muted initial reaction. Nizhnii Novgorod and Kazan both had highly developed party political organisations, which campaigned intensively, and succeeded to some extent in engaging the town population. Outside larger towns, party political activity was sparser and more sporadic, and was less effective in penetrating popular consciousness.

Some aspects of the revolutionary year, however, were common to town and country. Rural areas were reached by the cultural-enlightenment campaigns of 1917, though the intensity of campaigns was less focused than in the towns. Soldiers and their wives made their presence felt in town and countryside alike and played a part in generating a sense of crisis in both places. The issue that connected towns and country most closely was provisions. The shortages in the big towns were matched by shortages in some rural areas, and urban and rural people alike shared fears of food shortages and hunger. Provisions questions also sharpened conflicts between urban and rural areas, as the urban administrations sought without much success to extract grain from an increasingly insular rural population. These conflicts and dissonances between urban and rural experiences of revolution were warnings of the centrifugal forces generated by the breakdown of central power and authority, which only intensified in the civil war that followed the Bolsheviks' seizure of power.

This study does not intend to romanticise the responses of ordinary people to revolution, but it emphasises the complexity and variety of ordinary people's lives. If we take those soldiers discussed in chapter 6, for example, some were moderate and cautious and supported the Provisional Government. Some became thoroughly politically radicalised. But many more bumped along the bottom, swept along with the new climate of social and political freedom. Some soldiers deserted, stole, drank, harassed women, got onto trains without paying. Though many of the peasants of chapter 5 may have utilised revolutionary language and legal affirmations in their quest to control land and wood and the local economy, they also on occasion used intimidation and violence to support their claims. The Sormovo workers' administration showed in its response to the food-supply crisis that ultimately they sought to protect their own constituents and disregarded the needs of other townspeople. Ordinary people responded consciously to 1917. They acted in what they perceived to be their own best interests, and these actions did not correspond with the political elite's idealised visions of democratic and responsible political behaviour.

Party politics did not define ordinary people's behaviour, but it was one of a range of different factors that shaped their understandings of 1917. Life was volatile, uncertain and potentially dangerous. Apparently simple tasks like buying bread or getting on a train could be fraught with difficulties and danger. For ordinary people, the political transformation wrought by 1917 did bring the social and political freedoms heralded by the Provisional Government, but it also brought disorder and confusion. The tragic breakdown of living conditions was not a necessary consequence of democratisation in and of itself, but in the conditions of 1917 democratisation resulted in an acceleration of chaos. In the welter of revolutionary rhetoric, ordinary people sought to defend their own interests and get on with their lives as best they could.

Bibliography

ARCHIVAL SOURCES CONSULTED

STATE ARCHIVE OF NIZHEGOROD REGION, NIZHNII NOVGOROD (GANO)

f. 27: Nizhnii Novgorod Town Duma
f. 442: Sormovo factory records
f. 713: Fokinskii, Vasil'skii *uezd*
f. 715: Makar'ev, Makar'evskii *uezd*
f. 733: Elizarovskii, Gorbatovskii *uezd*
f. 815: Semenovskii *uezd* commissar for the Provisional Government
f. 830: Nizhegorodskii *uezd* commissar for the Provisional Government
f. 851: Lysovskii, Makar'evskii *uezd*
f. 1100: Nizhegorod soviet of workers' deputies
f. 1101: Nizhegorod soviet of soldiers' deputies
f. 1102: Nizhegorod soviet of workers' and soldiers' deputies
f. 1882: Nizhegorod provincial commissar for the Provisional Government
f. 1887: Nizhegorod province executive committee for the Provisional Government
f. P-4653: Nizhegorod provincial commissar for labour

NATIONAL ARCHIVE OF THE REPUBLIC OF TATARSTAN, KAZAN (NART)

f. 174: Kazan provincial land administration
f. 406: Kazan provincial committee for showing assistance to refugees
f. 983: Kazan soviet of peasants' deputies
f. 1153: Factory inspectorate of Kazan province, 1896–1919
f. 1246: Chancery of Kazan provincial commissar for the Provisional Government
f. 1351: Chistopolskii *uezd* committee of public safety
f. 1352: Spasskii *uezd* committee of public safety
f. 1353: Kazan provincial committee of public safety
f. 1354: Mamadyshskii *uezd* committee of public safety

STATE ARCHIVE OF THE RUSSIAN FEDERATION, MOSCOW (GARF)

f. 9591c: Collection of files of petty-bourgeois parties

RUSSIAN STATE ARCHIVE OF SOCIAL AND POLITICAL HISTORY, MOSCOW (RGASPI)

f. 274: Central Committee of the Socialist Revolutionary Party, 1891–1923

RUSSIAN STATE HISTORICAL ARCHIVE, ST PETERSBURG (RGIA)

f. 1278: State Duma

RUSSIAN STATE MILITARY-HISTORICAL ARCHIVE, MOSCOW (RGVIA)

f. 366: War Ministry cabinet's political administration

NEWSPAPERS CONSULTED

Biulletin Nizhegorodskago Vremmenago Revoliutsionnago Komiteta (Bulletin of the Nizhegorod Provisional Revolutionary Committee, Nizhnii Novgorod)

Chasovoi na revoliutsionnom postu (Publication of the Kazan military region executive committee, Kazan)

Delo derevne (Publication of Tambov provincial PSR committee, the provincial soviet of peasants' deputies and members of the provincial *zemstva* administration, Tambov)

Delo naroda (Publication of PSR Central Committee, Petrograd)

Golos truda (Publication of the Kazan PSR organisation, Kazan)

Izvestiia Kazanskago gubernskago soiuza sel'skikh khoziaev (Publication of Kazan provincial Union of Agriculturalists, Kazan)

Izvestiia Kazanskago gubernskago soveta krest'ianskikh deputatov (Publication of Kazan provincial soviet of peasants' deputies, Kazan)

Izvestiia Kazanskago voenno-okruzhnago komiteta (Publication of Kazan military region committee, Kazan)

Izvestiia soveta rabochikh deputatov, continued as *Izvestiia sovetov rabochikh i soldatskikh deputatov* (Publication of Nizhegorod soviet of workers' and soldiers' deputies, Nizhnii Novgorod)

Izvestiia Tambovskago soveta rabochikh, krest'iasnksikh i soldatskikh deputatov (Publication of Tambov soviet of workers', soldiers' and peasants' deputies, Tambov)

Kazanskaia rabochaia gazeta, continued as *Kazanskaia rabochaia gazeta i Izvestiia soveta rabochikh i soldatskikh deputatov* (Publication of Russian Social Democrat Workers' Party, Kazan)

Kazanskoe slovo (Published without party affiliation, Kazan)

Krasnoe znamia (Publication of the Nizhegorod soviet of workers' and soldiers' deputies, Nizhnii Novgorod)

Narod (Publication of the Nizhegorod provincial PSR committee)

Narodnaia svoboda (Publication of the Nizhegorod provincial Constitutional Democrat Party committee, Nizhnii Novgorod)

Nizhegorodskaia zemskaia gazeta (Publication of the Nizhegorod provincial zemstvo, Nizhnii Novgorod)
Partiinaia izvestiia (Journal published by the PSR Central Committee, Petrograd)
Rabochii (Publication of the Kazan committee of Russian Social Democrat Workers' Party, Kazan)
Simbirskaia narodnaia gazeta (No formal party affiliation, Simbirsk)
Sotsialist-Revoliutsioner (Publication of the Kazan PSR committee, Kazan)
Sotsialist-Revoliutsioner (Publication of the Penza provincial PSR committee, Penza)
Tambovskii zemskii vestnik (Publication of Tambov *zemstva*, Tambov)
Volia naroda (Publication of Rightist group within PSR, Petrograd)
Za zemliu i voliu (Publication of the Kazan provincial PSR committee, the Kazan town PSR committee, the soviet of peasants' deputies, and the PSR Military Organisation, Kazan)
Zemlia i volia (Publication of the Simbirsk provincial soviet of peasants' deputies and the Simbirsk PSR committee)

SECONDARY SOURCES CITED

Antonov-Saratovski, V. P., *Pod stiagom proletarskoi bor' by: otryvki iz vospominnanii o rabote v Saratove za vremia s 1915g. do 1918g.* (Moscow and Leningrad, 1925)
Anweiler, Oskar, *The soviets: the Russian workers', peasants' and soldiers' councils 1905–1921* (New York, 1958)
Badcock, Sarah, '"We're for the muzhiks' party!" Peasant support for the Socialist Revolutionary Party during 1917', *Europe Asia Studies* 53 (2001), 133–50
   'From saviour to pariah: a study of the role of Karl Ianovich Grasis in Cheboksary during 1917', *Revolutionary Russia* 15 (2002), 69–96
   'Women, protest, and revolution: soldiers' wives in Russia during 1917', *International Review of Social History* 49 (2004), 47–70
Baker, Mark, 'Beyond the national: peasants, power and revolution in Ukraine', *Journal of Ukrainian Studies* 24 (1999), 39–67
   'Peasants, power and revolution in the village: a social history of Kharkiv province, 1914–1921', unpublished PhD thesis, Harvard University (Cambridge, MA, 2001)
   'Rampaging soldatki, cowering police, bazaar riots and moral economy: the social impact of the Great War in Kharkiv province', *Canadian-American Slavic Studies* 35 (2001), 137–56
Bezberezh'ev, S. V., 'Mariia Aleksandrovna Spiridonova', in Golikov, A. G. and Korelin, A. P., *Rossiia na rubezhe XIX–XX vekov: Materialy nauchnikh chtenii* (Moscow, 1999), pp. 335–55
Boniece, Sally, 'Mariia Spiridonova, 1884–1918: feminine martyrdom and revolutionary mythmaking', unpublished PhD thesis, Indiana University (Bloomington, 1996)
   'The Spiridonova case, 1906: terror, myth and martyrdom', *Kritika* 4 (2003), 571–606

Brooks, Jeffrey, *When Russia learned to read: literacy and popular literature, 1861–1917* (Princeton, NJ, 1985)

Brovkin, Vladimir N., *The Mensheviks after October: socialist opposition and the rise of the Bolshevik dictatorship* (Ithaca, NY, 1987)

Behind the front lines of the civil war (Princeton, NJ, 1994)

Browder, Robert P. and Kerensky, Alexander F., *The Russian Provisional Government of 1917; documents*, 3 vols. (Stanford, CA, 1961)

Brower, Daniel R., 'Labor violence in Russia in the late nineteenth century', *Slavic Review* 41 (1982), 417–31

'The Penny Press and its readers', in Frank, Stephen P. and Steinberg, Mark D. (eds.), *Cultures in flux: lower-class values, practices and resistance in late Imperial Russia* (Princeton, NJ, 1994), pp. 147–67

Burds, Jeffrey, *Peasant dreams and market politics: labour migration and the Russian village, 1861–1905* (Pittsburgh, 1998)

Carr, E. H., *The Bolshevik revolution 1917–1923* (Harmondsworth, 1983)

Channon, John, 'The peasantry in the revolutions of 1917', in Frankel, J., Frankel, E. G. and Knei-Paz, B. (eds.), *Revolution in Russia: reassessments of 1917* (Cambridge, 1992), pp. 105–30

Chanyshev, Ia., '1917 god v Kazani', *Druzhba Narodov* 5 (1957), 121–38

Chernov, Victor M. [under pseudonym 'O.'], 'Bibliografia', *Nakanune* 3, 28 (1901), 343–4

The great Russian revolution (New Haven, CT, 1936)

Chugaev, D. A. Gaponenko, L. S., Smuchebnikov, M. D., Tomashevich, I. U., Chernov, A. V. and Iakovlev, L. E., *Revoliutsionnoe dvizhenie v Rossii v iiule 1917g.: Iiulskii krizis* (Moscow, 1959)

Chulos, Chris J., *Converging worlds: religion and community in peasant Russia 1861–1917* (DeKalb, IL, 2003)

Clark, Charles, 'Uprooting Otherness: Bolshevik attempts to refashion rural Russia via the reading rooms', *Canadian Slavonic Papers* 38 (1996), 305–30

Clements, Evans Barbara, *Bolshevik women* (Cambridge, 1997)

Demosthenov, S. S., 'Food prices and the market in foodstuffs', in Struve, Peter (ed.), *Food supply in Russia during the World War* (New Haven, CT, 1930), pp. 268–411

Eklof, Ben, *Russian peasant schools: officialdom, village culture, and popular pedagogy, 1861–1914* (Berkeley, CA, 1983)

Engel, Barbara A., 'Women, men and the language of peasant resistance, 1870–1907', in Frank, Stephen P. and Steinberg, Mark D. (eds.), *Cultures in flux: lower-class values, practices and resistance in late Imperial Russia* (Princeton, NJ, 1994), pp. 34–53

'Not by bread alone: subsistence riots in Russia during World War I', *Journal of Modern History* 69 (1997), 696–721

Ezhov, N., *Voennaia Kazan v 1917 g.* (Kazan, 1957)

Farnsworth, Beatrice, 'Village women experience the revolution', in Gleason, A., Kenez, Peter and Stites, Richard (eds.), *Bolshevik culture: experiment and order in the Russian revolution* (Bloomington, IN, 1985), pp. 238–60

'The *soldatka*: folklore and court record', *Slavic Review* 49 (1990), 58–73

Field, Daniel, *Rebels in the name of the tsar* (Boston, 1989)

Figes, Orlando, *Peasant Russia, civil war: the Volga countryside in revolution* (Oxford, 1989)

'The Russian peasant community in the agrarian revolution, 1917–18', in Bartlett, Roger (ed.), *Land commune and peasant community in Russia* (New York, 1990), pp. 237–53

'Peasant farmers and the minority groups of rural society: peasant egalitarianism and village social relations during the Russian revolution', in Kingston-Mann, E., Mixter, T. and Burds, Jeffrey (eds.), *Peasant economy, culture and politics of European Russia 1860–1921* (Princeton, NJ, 1991), pp. 379–401

A people's tragedy: the Russian revolution 1891–1924 (London, 1996)

'The Russian revolution and its language in the villages', *Russian Review* 56 (1997), 323–45

Figes, Orlando, and Kolonitskii, Boris I., *Interpreting the Russian revolution: the language and symbols of 1917* (New Haven, CT, 1999)

Fitzpatrick, Sheila, *Stalin's peasants: resistance and survival in the Russian village after collectivisation* (Oxford, 1994)

Frank, Stephen P., 'Popular justice, community and culture among the Russian peasantry, 1870–1900', *Russian Review* 46 (1987), 239–65

'Confronting the domestic Other: rural popular culture and its enemies in fin de siècle Russia', in Frank, Stephen P. and Steinberg, Mark D. (eds.), *Cultures in flux: Lower-class values, practices and resistance in late Imperial Russia* (Princeton, NJ, 1994), pp. 74–107

Frank, Stephen P. and Steinberg, Mark D., *Cultures in flux: Lower-class values, practices and resistance in late Imperial Russia* (Princeton, NJ, 1994)

Frierson, Cathy A., 'Crime and punishment in the Russian village: rural concepts of criminality at the end of the nineteenth century', *Slavic Review* 46 (1987), 55–69

Peasant icons: representations of rural people in late nineteenth century Russia (Oxford, 1993)

Galili, Z., *The Menshevik leaders in the Russian revolution: social realities and political strategies* (Princeton, NJ, and Guildford, 1989)

Gatrell, Peter, *A whole empire walking: refugees in Russia during World War I* (Bloomington, IN, 1999)

Russia's first world war: a social and economic history (London, 2005)

Geifman, Anna, *Thou shalt kill: revolutionary terrorism in Russia, 1894–1917* (Princeton, NJ, 1993)

Geraci, Robert, *Window on the east: national and Imperial identities in late tsarist Russia* (Cornell, 2001)

Gill, Graeme, *Peasants and government in the Russian revolution* (London, 1979)

Gleason, A., 'The terms of Russian social history', in Kassow, Samuel D., West, James L. and Clowes, Edith W. (eds.), *Educated society and the quest for public identity in late Imperial Russia* (Princeton, NJ, 1991), pp. 15–27

Glickman, R. L., *Russian factory women* (Berkeley, CA, 1984)

Golikov, A. G. and Korelin, A. P., *Rossiia na rubezhe XIX–XX vekov: materialy nauchnikh chtenii* (Moscow, 1999)

Golovine, N. N., *The Russian army in the World War* (New Haven, CT, 1931)

Golub, P. A., Korabliev, I. E., Kuznetsov, M. E. and Fignater, I. I., *Velikaia Oktiabr'skaia Sotsialisticheskaia Revoliutsiia: entsiklopediia* (Moscow, 1987)

Good, J. E. and Jones, D. R., *Babushka: the life of the Russian revolutionary E. K. Breshko-Breshkovskaia* (Newtonville, MA, 1991)

Haimson, Leopold J., *The making of three Russian revolutionaries* (Cambridge, 1987)
'The problem of social identities in early twentieth century Russia', *Slavic Review* 47 [1] (1988), 1–20

Hasegawa, Tsuyoshi, 'The problem of power in the February revolution of 1917 in Russia', *Canadian Slavonic Papers* 14 (1972), 611–33
The February revolution: Petrograd 1917 (Seattle, 1981)
'Crime, police and mob justice in Petrograd during the Russian revolutions of 1917', in Wade, Rex A. (ed.), *Revolutionary Russia: new approaches* (New York, 2004), pp. 46–72

Herrlinger, Page, 'Orthodoxy and the experience of factory life in St Petersburg, 1881–1905', in Melancon, Michael and Pate, Alice K. (eds.), *New labor history: worker identity and experience in Russia, 1840–1918* (Bloomington, IN, 2002), pp. 77–94

Hickey, Michael C., 'Discourses of public identity and liberalism in the February revolution: Smolensk, Spring 1917', *Russian Review* (1996), 615–37
'Local government and state authority in the provinces: Smolensk, February–June 1917', *Slavic Review* 55 (1996), 863–81
'Urban *zemliachestva* and rural revolution: Petrograd and the Smolensk countryside in 1917', *Soviet and Post Soviet Review* 23 (1996), 142–60
'Moderate socialists and the politics of crime in revolutionary Smolensk', *Canadian-American Slavic Studies* 35 (2001), 189–218
'The rise and fall of Smolensk's moderate socialists: the politics of class and the rhetoric of crisis in 1917', in Raleigh, Donald J. (eds.), *Provincial landscapes: local dimensions of Soviet power, 1917–1953* (Pittsburg, 2001), pp. 14–35

Hildermeier, M., *Die Sozialrevolutonare partei Russlands: Agrarosozialismus und Moderisierung in Zarenreich (1900–1914)* (Cologne, 1978)

Holquist, Peter, *Making war, forging revolution: Russia's continuum of crisis, 1914–1921* (Cambridge, MA, 2002)
'Violent Russia, deadly Marxism? Russia in the epoch of violence, 1905–1921', *Kritika* 4 (2003), 627–52

Iskhakov, Salavat, *Rossiiskie musul'mane i revoliutsiia* (Moskva, 2004)

Kabanov, V. V., *Krest'ianskaia obshchina i kooperatsiia Rossii XX veka* (Moscow, 1997)
'Oktiabr'skaia revoliutsiia i krest'ianskaia obshchina', *Istoricheskii zapiski* 3 (1984), 100–50.

Kassow, Samuel D., West, James L. and Clowes, Edith W., 'The problem of the middle in late Imperial Russian society', in Kassow, Samuel D., West, James

L. and Clowes, Edith W. (eds.), *Educated society and the quest for public identity in late Imperial Russia* (Princeton, NJ, 1991), pp. 3–14

Katz, M. B., 'Occupational classification in history', *Journal of Interdisciplinary History* (1972), 63–88

Keep, J. L. H., *The Russian revolution: a study in mass mobilisation* (London, 1976)

Kelly, Catriona, *Refining Russia: advice literature, polite culture, and gender from Catherine to Yeltsin* (Oxford, 2001)

Kirillov, V. K., *Karl Ianovich Grasis* (Cheboksary, 1969)

Klier, John, 'The pogrom paradigm in Russian history', in Klier, John and Lambroza, S. (eds.), *Pogroms* (Cambridge, 1992), pp. 13–38

Knight, A., 'Female terrorists in the Russian Socialist Revolutionary Party', *Russian Review* 38 (1979), 139–59

Koenker, Diane P., 'The evolution of party consciousness in 1917: the case of the Moscow workers', *Soviet Studies* 30 (1978), 38–62

  Moscow workers and the 1917 revolution (Princeton, NJ, 1981)

  'Men against women on the shop floor in early Soviet Russia: Gender and class in the socialist workplace', *American Historical Review* 100 (1995), 1438–64

Kokhn, M. P., *Russkie indeksi tsen* (Moscow, 1926)

Kolonitskii, Boris I., 'Antibourgeois propaganda and anti-"Burzhui" conciousness in 1917', *Russian Review* 53 (1994), 183–96

  'The Russian idea and the ideology of the February revolution', in Hara, Teruyaki and Matsuzato, Kimitaka (eds.), *Empire and society: approaches to Russian history* (Sapporo, 1997), pp. 41–71

  '"Democracy" as identification: towards the study of political consciousness during the February revolution', in Palat, Madhavan K. (ed.), *Social identities in revolutionary Russia* (London, 2001), pp. 161–73

Kondratev, N., *Rynok khlebov i ego regulirovanie vo vremia voiny i revoliutsii* (Moscow, 1991)

Konstantinov, M. M. and Tochilin, F. M., *Politicheskaia katorga i ssylka: biograficheskii spravochnik chlenov obshchestva politkatorzhan i ssyl'no-poselentsev* (Moscow, 1934)

Krasovitskaia, T. Iu., *Rossiiskoe obrazovanie mezhdu reformatorstvom i revoliutsionerizmom, fevral 1917–1920 god* (Moscow, 2002)

Kuromiya, Hiroaki, *Freedom and terror in the Donbas: a Ukrainian-Russian borderland, 1870s–1990s* (Cambridge, 1998)

Lane, D., *The roots of Russian communism: a social and historical study of Russian Social-Democracy, 1898–1907* (Assen, 1969)

Lenin, V. I., *What is to be done?* (Peking, 1973)

  Polnoe sobranie sochinenii, 55 vols. (Moscow, 1977)

Leonov, M. I., *PSR v 1907–1914 gg.* (Moscow, 1997)

Lih Lars, T., *Bread and authority in Russia, 1914–1921* (Berkeley, CA, 1990)

Lohr, Eric, 'Patriotic violence and the state: the Moscow riots of May 1915', *Kritika* 4 (2003), 607–26

Magnov, K., 'Dni Oktiabria', *Kommunisticheskii put* 12 (1922), 98–117

Maliavskii, A. D., *Krest'ianskoe dvizhenie v Rossii v 1917 g. mart–oktiabr* (Moscow, 1981)

Mau, V., 'Bread, democracy and the Bolshevik coup', *Revolutionary Russia* 7 (1994), 34–7

Medynskii, E. N., *Kak i pochemu narod unichtozhil staruiu vlast i za chto on boretsia* (Moscow, 1917)

    Kak vesti besedi po politicheskam voprosam: metodicheskie ukazaniia, konspekti i spiski literaturi dlia lektorov, uchitelei i pr. (Moscow, 1917)

    Ot temy k svetu! Nashe neumyn'e i nasha bednota. Nasha temnota. Kak borot'sia s nashei temnotoi (Nizhnii Novgorod, 1917)

    Revoliutsiia i vneshkol'noe obrazovanie. S prilozheniem konspektov besed s krest'ianami na temy, sviazannym s revoliutsiei (Moscow, 1917)

    Kak organizovat i vesti selskie prosvetitel'nye obshchestva i kruzhki (Nizhnii Novgorod, 1918)

Melancon, Michael, 'The Socialist Revolutionaries from 1902 to 1907: peasant and workers' party', *Russian History-Histoire Russe* 12 (1985), 2–47

    'Who wrote what and when? Proclamations of the February revolution in Petrograd, 23 Feb.–1 March 1917', *Soviet Studies* 40 (1988), 479–500

    The Socialist Revolutionaries and the Russian anti-war movement, 1914–17 (Columbus, OH, 1990)

    '"Marching together!" Left bloc activities in the Russian revolutionary movement, 1900 – February 1917', *Slavic Review* 49 (1990), 239–52

    'The syntax of Soviet power: the resolutions of local soviets and other institutions, March–October 1917', *Russian Review* 52 (1993), 486–505

    'Soldiers, peasant-soldiers, and peasant-workers and their organisations in Petrograd: ground-level revolution during the early months of 1917', *Soviet and Post Soviet Review* 23 (1996), 161–90

    'The Left Socialist Revolutionaries and the Bolshevik uprising', in Brovkin, Vladimir N. (ed.), *The Bolsheviks in Russian society* (New Haven, CT, 1997), pp. 59–82

    Rethinking Russia's February revolution: anonymous spontaneity or socialist agency? (Pittsburg, 2000)

    'The Neopopulist experience: default interpretations and new approaches', *Kritika* 5 (2004), 195–206

Melgunov S. P., *The Bolshevik seizure of power* (Oxford, 1972)

Meyer, A. G., 'The impact of World War I on Russian women's lives', in Clements Evans, Barbara, Engel, Barbara A. and Worobec, Christine D. (eds.), *Russia's women: accommodation, resistance, transformation* (Berkeley, CA, 1991), pp. 208–24

Mikhailov, Nikolai V., 'The collective psychology of Russian workers and workplace: self-organisation in the early twentieth century', in Melancon, Michael and Pate, Alice K. (eds.), *New labor history: worker identity and experience in Russia, 1840–1918* (Bloomington, IN, 2002), pp. 77–94

Mill, J. S., *Utilitarianism, liberty, representative government* (London, 1960)

Milov, L. V., 'Prirodnoe-klimaticheskii faktor i mentalitet Russkogo krest'ianstva', in Danilov, V. P. (ed.), *Mentalitet i agrarnoe razvitie Rossii (XIX–XX vv.): materialy mezhdunarodnoi konferentsii Moskva. 14–15 Iiunia 1994 g.* (Moscow, 1994), pp. 40–56

Mintz, S., *Sweetness and power: the place of sugar in modern history* (New York, 1985).

Morozov, K. N., *Partiia sotsialistov-revoliutsionerov v 1907–1914gg.* (Moscow, 1998)

Morrisey, Susan K., *Heralds of revolution: Russian students and the mythologies of radicalism* (Oxford, 1998)

Mukhamedov, S. E. and Timofeev, V. P., *Za vlast sovetov: sbornik vospominanii uchastnikov revoliutsionnikh sobytii v Tatarii* (Kazan, 1960)

Muliukov, Iskandr Maratovich, 'Rukovodstvo sovetov kul'turno-prosvetitel'nymi uchrezhdeniami v pervye gody Sovetskoi vlasti, 1917–1920gg. po materialam Kazanskoi gubernii', unpublished PhD thesis, Institut iazyka, literatury i istorii imeni G. Ibragimova Kazanskogo filiala ANSSSR (Kazan, 1990)

Murphy, Kevin, *Revolution and counter-revolution: class struggle in a Moscow metal factory* (New York, 2005)

Nachtigal, Reinhard, *Russland und seine osterreichisch ungarischen kriegsgefangenen (1914–1918)* (Grunbach, 2003)

Neuberger, J., *Hooliganism: crime, culture and power in St Petersburg, 1900–1914* (London, 1993)

Nikolaev, A. B., *Gosudarstvennaia Duma i fevral'skoi revoliutsii: ocherki istorii* (Riazan, 2002)

Noack, Christian, 'The Tataro-Bashkir Feud in 1917' (Conference paper given at Conference of the Study Group on the Russian Revolution, University of Durham, 2001)

'Ob osvobozhdenii M.A. Spiridonovoi', *Izvestiia TsK KPSS* (1991), 178–80

Oganovskii, N. P. (ed.), *Sel'skoe khoziaistva. Rossii v XX veke: sbornik statistikaekonomicheskikh svodenie za 1901–1922g.* (Moscow, 1923)

Orlovsky, Daniel T., 'The Provisional Government and its cultural work', in Gleason, A., Kenez, Peter and Stites, Richard (eds.), *Bolshevik Culture: experiment and order in the Russian revolution* (Bloomington, IN, 1985), pp. 39–56

Owen, L. A., *The Russian peasant movement, 1906–1917* (London, 1937)

Pallot, Judy, *Land reform in Russia 1906–1917: peasant responses to Stolypin's project of rural transformation* (New York, 1999)

'Imagining the rational landscape in late Imperial Russia', *Journal of Historical Geography* 26 (2000), 273–91

Pape, C., 'On the margins of utopia? Zemstvo liberals and the peasant commune', *Russian History-Histoire Russe* 11 (1984), 220–35

Pastor, Peter, 'Hungarian POWs in Russia during the revolution and civil war', in Williamson, Samuel and Pastor, Peter (eds.), *Essays on World War I: origins and prisoners of war* (Boulder, CO, 1983), pp. 149–62

Perrie, Maureen, 'The Russian peasant movement of 1905–1907: its social composition and revolutionary significance', *Past and Present* 57 (1972), 123–55

'The social composition and the structure of the Socialist Revolutionary Party before 1917', *Soviet Studies* 24 (1972), 223–50

'The Russian peasant movement of 1905: its composition and significance', in Eklof, Ben and Frank, Stephen P. (eds.), *The world of the Russian peasant* (1996), pp. 193–208

Pershin, P. N., *Agrarnoe revoliutsiia v Rossii, kniga I: ot reformy k revoliutsii* (Moscow, 1966)

Pethybridge, R. W., 'The significance of communications in 1917', *Soviet Studies* 19 (1967), 109–14

Phillips, Hugh, '"A bad business": the February revolution in Tver', *Soviet and Post Soviet Review* 23 (1996), 120–41

Poliakov, U. A., *Naselenie Rossii v XX veke: istoricheskie ocherki, vol. I* (Moscow, 2000)

Povarov, N., *Revoliutsionnyi period v g. Nizhnem* (Nizhnii Novgorod, 1918)

Predvaritel'nye vserossiiskoi sel'skokhoziaistvennoi perepisi 1916 goda (Po podschetam, proizvedennym mestnymi perepisnymi uchrezhdeniiami) (Petrograd, 1916)

Protasov, L. G., *Vserossiskoe uchreditel'noe sobranie: istoriia rozhdeniia i gibeli* (Moscow, 1997)

Pyle, E. E., 'Peasant strategies for obtaining state aid: a study of petitions during World War I', *Russian History-Histoire Russe* 24 (1997), 41–64

'Village social relations and the reception of soldiers' family aid policies in Russia, 1912–1921', unpublished PhD thesis, University of Chicago (1997)

Rabinowitch, A., 'Spiridonova', in Acton, Edward, Cherniaev, V. U. and Rosenberg, William G. (eds.), *Critical companion to the Russian revolution* (Bloomington, IN, 1997), pp. 182–7

Rachamimov, Alon, *POWs and the Great War* (Oxford, 2002)

Radkey, Oliver H., *The agrarian foes of Bolshevism: promise and default of the Russian Socialist Revolutionaries, February to October 1917* (New York, 1958)

The sickle under the hammer: the Russian Socialist Revolutionaries in the early months of Soviet rule (New York, 1963)

Rakhmatullin, A., 'Mulla-Nur Vakhitov', *Kommunisticheskii put* 11 (1922), 34–40

Raleigh, Donald J., *Revolution on the Volga: 1917 in Saratov* (New York, 1986)

'The revolution of 1917 and the establishment of Soviet power in Saratov', in Wade, Rex A. and Seregny, Scott J. (eds.), *Politics and society in provincial Russia: Saratov, 1590–1917* (Columbus, OH, 1989), pp. 277–306

Ravallion, Martin, *Markets and famines* (Oxford, 1987)

Read, Christopher, *From tsar to soviets: the Russian people and their revolution* (London, 1996)

Retish, A., 'Peasant identities in Russia's turmoil: status, gender and ethnicity in Viatka province, 1914–1921', unpublished PhD thesis, Ohio State University (Columbus, OH, 2003)

Rice, C., *Russian workers and the SR Party through the revolution of 1905–7* (Basingstoke, 1988)

Rigby, T. H., *Communist Party membership in the USSR, 1917–1967* (Princeton, NJ, 1968)

Rittersporn, Gabor, 'The omnipresent conspiracy: on Soviet imagery of politics and social relations in the 1930s', in Getty, J. Arch and Manning, Roberta (eds.), *Stalinist terror: new perspectives* (Cambridge, 1993), pp. 99–115

Rohe, Karl, *Elections, parties and political traditions: social foundations of German parties and party systems, 1861–1917* (Oxford, 1990)

Rosenberg, William G., 'The Russian Municipal Duma elections of 1917', *Soviet Studies* (1969), 131–63

Rossiia v mirovoi voine 1914–1918gg. v tsifrakh (Moscow, 1925)

Sanborn, Joshua A., *Drafting the Russian nation: military conscription, total war, and mass politics, 1905–1925* (DeKalb, IL, 2003)

'Unsettling the empire: violent migrations and social disaster in Russia during World War I', *Journal of Modern History* 77 (2006), 290–324

Scott, James, *Weapons of the weak: everyday forms of peasant resistance* (New Haven, CT, 1985)

Seregny, Scott J., 'Revolutionary strategies in the Russian countryside: rural teachers and the SR Party on the eve of 1905', *Russian Review* 44 (1985), 221–38

Russian teachers and peasant revolution: the politics of education in 1905 (Bloomington, IN, 1989)

'Power and discourse in Russian elementary education: the school inspectorate, 1869–1917', *Jahrbucher für Geschichte Osteuropas* 47 (1999), 161–86

'Peasants, nation, and local government in wartime Russia', *Slavic Review* 59 (2000), 336–42

'Zemstvos, peasants, and citizenship: the Russian adult education movement and World War I', *Slavic Review* 59 (2000), 290–315

Service, Robert, *Lenin: a biography* (Basingstoke, 2000)

Shanin, Teodor, *The awkward class: political sociology of peasantry in a developing society: Russia 1910–25* (Oxford, 1972)

Shelokhaev, V. V., *Politicheskii partii Rossii, konets 19– pervaia tret' 20 veka. Entsiklopediia* (Moscow, 1996)

Shelokhaev, V. V., Volobuev, V. V., Gorshkov, M. K. et al., *Programmi politicheskikh partii Rossii konets XIX–XX vv* (Moscow, 1995)

Shnurovskii, K., 'Vospominaniia o tovarishche Ol'kentskom', *Kommunisticheskii put* 11 (1922), 20–30

Shul'gin, P. E., *Za vlast sovetov: vspominaet uchastniki bor' bi za vlast v Nizhegorodskoi gubernii* (Gorky, 1967)

Sidorov, A. L., *Finansovoe polozhenie Rossii v gody pervoi mirovoi voiny* (Moscow, 1968)

Smith, Steve A., *Red Petrograd: revolution in the factories 1917–18* (Cambridge, 1983)

'The social meanings of swearing: workers and bad language in late Imperial and early Soviet Russia', *Past and Present* 160 (1986), 167–202

The Russian revolution: a very short introduction (Oxford, 2002)

Smuchebnikov, M. D., Chugaev, D. A., Kovalenko, D. A., Reuzhberg, G. E. and Vladimitsev, E. N., *Revoliutsionnoe dvizhenie v Rossii v mai–iiune 1917g. Iiunskaia demonstratsiia* (Moscow, 1959)

Spiridovich, A. E., *Partiia sotsialistov revoliutsionerov i ee predshestvenniki, 1886–1916* (Petrograd, 1916)

Steinberg, Mark D., *Voices of revolution. 1917* (New Haven, CT, 2001)

Sukhanov, N. N., 'Iz proshlogo: etiudi fevralskoi revoliutsii', *Kommunisticheskii put* 2 (1923), 61–5

Suny, R. G., 'Towards a social history of the October revolution', *American Historical Review* 88 (1983), 31–52

Surh, Gerald D., 'The Russian pogroms of October 1905' (Conference paper given at Labour History of Russia and the Soviet Union: Work in Progress, Amsterdam, 2005)

Swift, Anthony E., 'Workers' theater and "proletarian culture" in prerevolutionary Russia, 1905–1917', in Zelnik, Reginald E. (ed.), *Workers and intelligentsia in late Imperial Russia: realities, representations, reflections* (Berkeley, CA, 1999), pp. 260–91

Tan, Graham, 'Village social organisation and peasant action: right-bank Ukraine during the revolution, 1917–1923', unpublished PhD thesis, School of Slavonic and East European Studies, University of London (1999)

Thurston, Gary, 'The impact of Russian popular theatre, 1886–1915', *Journal of Modern History* 55 (1983), 237–67

Trotsky, Leon, *What next?: vital questions for the German proletariat* (New York, 1932)

Venturi, F., *Roots of revolution: a history of the populist and socialist movements in nineteenth-century Russia* (London, 1960)

Verner, Andrew, 'Discursive strategies in the 1905 revolution: peasant petitions from Vladimir province', *Russian Review* 54 (1995), 65–90

Viola, Lynne, 'Babi-bunty and peasant women's protest during collectivisation', *Russian Review* 45 (1986), 23–42

Peasant rebels under Stalin: collectivisation and the culture of peasant resistance (New York, 1996)

Vladimirov, V., *Maria Spiridonova* (Moscow, 1906)

Volkov, I., 'Vania Volkov (Vospominaniia tovarishcha)', *Kommunisticheskii put* 11 (1922), 31–3.

Von, Geldern, *Entertaining tsarist Russia* (Bloomington, IN, 2000)

Wade, Rex A., *The Russian revolution, 1917* (Cambridge, 2000)

Wartenweiler, David, *Civil society and academic debate in Russia, 1905–1914* (Oxford, 1999)

Weinberg, R., 'Workers, pogroms, and the 1905 revolution in Odessa', *Russian Review* 46 (1987), 53–75

The revolution of 1905 in Odessa: blood on the steps (Bloomington, IN, 1993)

Wildman, Alan, *The old army and the soldiers' revolt (March–April 1917)*, vol. I of *The end of the Russian Imperial army* (Princeton, NJ, 1980)

The road to Soviet power and peace, vol. II of *The end of the Russian Imperial army* (Princeton, NJ, 1987)

Wixman, Ronald, *The peoples of the USSR: an ethnographic handbook* (London, 1984)

Worobec, Christine D., *Peasant Russia: family and community in the post emancipation period* (Princeton, NJ, 1991)

Wynn, Charters, *Workers, strikes and pogroms: the Donbas-Dnepr bend in late Imperial Russia, 1870–1905* (Princeton, NJ, 1992)

Yaney, George L., *The urge to mobilise: agrarian reform in Russia 1861–1930* (London, 1982)

Zaitsev, K. I. and Dolinsky, N. V., 'Organisation and policy', in Struve, Peter (ed.), *Food supply in Russia during the World War* (New Haven, CT, 1930), pp. 5–17

Zhakov, A., 'Nasha partiia v period ot fevralia do oktiabria v Kazani', *Kommunisticheskii put* 26 (1923), 86–92

Index

Alcohol, 129, 155
  and soldiers, 151, 152, 160–1
Anti-semitism, 52

Breshko-Breshkovskaia, Ekaterina, 46, 106, 139

Cheremis (Marii), 234
  and the February revolution, 37
Chernov, Victor Mikhailovich, 68, 72, 75, 106,
  114, 198–9, 203
Chernyshev, V.N, 19
Chuvash, 6, 8, 128, 206, 234
  and the February revolution, 37
  as local leaders, 96, 97, 103
Clergy, 135, 141, 142
  and the February revolution, 36, 41–2, 45
  as local leaders, 89, 93, 95
  and the Provisional Government, 41
Constituent Assembly, 13, 88, 196, 198
  candidates to, 91, 92, 113–16
    joint lists from PSR and peasants' soviets,
    112
  selection of candidates, 111–12
  women candidates, 106
Constitutional Democrats (Kadets), 11, 40, 98
  in the Kazan Town Duma, 26
Cultural enlightenement campaigns
  funding for, 136–7
  urban/rural distinctions, 124–5, 133, 142

Denike, Iu.P., 20, 24
Deserters, 158–9, 160, 161–2
Dual power, 13, 19, 21

Economic crisis, 10, 136, 165, 168
Education, 125, 128, 133, 200–1, 202
  and the grain monopoly, 229
  and non-Russians, 128
  reading rooms, 129
  role of party politics in, 135–6, 142, 143
  soldiers, 128

Elections, 58, 79
  apathy towards, 77, 84, 117–18
  to Constituent Assembly, 58, 116, 127, 135
  to Kazan Town Duma, 23, 26–7
  to Nizhnii Novgorod Town Duma, 23, 25
  non-Russians and, 118–19, 122
  preparations for, 101–2
  resistance to, 118
    from non-Russian communities, 118–21
  role of intelligentsia in, 116–17
  socialist bloc, 25, 26
  women as voters, 118

February revolution, 9, 14, 16, 30
  and Cheremis (Marii), 37
  and Chuvash, 37
  and the clergy, 36, 41–2, 45
  intelligentsia and, 36
  interpretations of, 38, 42, 43
  national minorities and, 37–8
  news of, 31
    in the countryside, 35–8
    in Kazan town, 32–3
    in Nizhnii Novgorod town, 33–5
  and Nizhnii Novgorod Town Duma, 34
  and the Provisional Government, 39
  rumours and, 42
  and Sormovo workers, 34
  and Tatars, 37
  villains of, 49–51
  zemstvo committees, 40
Figner, Vera, 115
Food supply, 158
  fear of famine, 216–7, 220
    in Nizhegorod province, 222, 224, 225–6
  grain monopoly, 215
  hoarders, 50–1, 52
  origins of 1917 crisis, 213
  Provisional Government and, 214, 218–9, 236
  refugees, 224–6
  shortages, 165–6

Food supply (*cont.*)
  Sormovo workers, 226–7
  violence, 222–3, 229–30
  workers, 226
Fuel shortage, 166, 175, 193, 194

Ganchel, Vladimir Genrikhovich, 98–100, 216
'Going to the people' movement, 131
Grain monopoly
  census for, 230
  and education, 229
  and non-Russians, 227, 228, 234
  resistance to, 160, 161, 227
Grasis, Karl Ianovich, 54, 153

Intelligentsia, 240
  as educators, 131, 134–5
  in February revolution, 36
  popular hostility to, 94, 229
  as local leaders, 89, 93–102
  role in preparing elections, 116–17
  Socialist Revolutionary Party, 62

Jews, 27

Kashmenskaia, Maria, 109–11
Kazan soviet of peasants' deputies, 97, 186, 195,
    205, 207, 210
  land law, 196, 201
  payment of, 105
Kazan soviet of workers' deputies, 38
Kazan soviet of workers and soldiers' deputies,
    73, 177, 196, 200, 229, 233
Kazan committee of public safety, 17, 19, 24
Kazan town August fire, 21, 22
Kazan Town Duma, 22, 23, 24, 136
  candidates for, 89, 170
  and Constitutional Democrats (Kadets), 26
  elections to, 23
  Left SRs and, 27
  Social Democrat Party (Bolsheviks), 27
  socialist bloc, 27
  women in, 106
Kazan town garrison, 145–6
Kazan University, 6, 32, 33, 115, 126
Kerensky, Alexander Feodorovich, 21, 44, 97, 99,
    189
Kolegaev, Alexander Lukich, 27, 70, 73, 204,
    230, 234, 235

Land relations
  historiography of, 182–3
  private ownership, 184–7
  Provisional Government and, 181, 188, 198,
    199

regional government response
  in Kazan, 203–4, 205–7
  in Nizhegorod, 203
  violence and, 186–8, 196–7
  woodland and, 192–5
  regulation of, 195
Land rental, 42, 190, 206
Latvian committee of refugees, 19
Left SRs, 27, 70, 73, 204, 220, 235
  in Kazan Town Duma, 27
  in Sormovo, 82
Lenin, Vladimir Ilich, 68, 156
Libin, V.I., 23
Local leaders, 17, 18, 181
  Chuvash, 96, 103
  Clergy, 89, 93, 95
  education of, 90–1
  intelligentsia as, 93
  occupation of, 91–3
  payment for, 104–5
  shortage of, 101–4
  soldiers, 95–8, 153
  Tatar, 103

May Day, 142
Music and song, 33, 48, 137, 138, 139–40, 141–2,
    151
Muslims, 7, 8–27, 38, 118, 119, 120–1, 126,
    143
  as soldiers, 148–9

Narodnyi dom, 129, 130
Nizhegorod provincial executive committee, 17,
    18, 25
Nizhegorod soviet of peasants' deputies, 19, 59,
    195
Nizhegorod soviet of soldiers' deputies, 98
Nizhegorod soviet of workers and soldiers'
    deputies, 133, 224, 235
Nizhegorod soviet of workers' deputies, 134
Nizhnii Novgorod garrison, 146
Nizhnii Novgorod Town Duma, 23, 25–7, 31, 98,
    110, 219
  candidates for, 89, 110
  elections, 23
  February revolution, 34
  women in, 106
Non-Russians, 6–9, 24, 37, 38, 103, 120, 126, 143,
    161–2, 225
  education of, 128
  and elections, 118–19, 122
  and grain monopoly, 227, 228, 234
  and soldiers, 147–8

Officers, 21, 22, 33, 50, 128, 152–3, 163, 174

Peasantry
  administrative structures of, 15, 17, 106, 135
  communication with, 130–1, 133, 134, 239–40
  elite preconceptions of, 131, 132–3, 199–200,
    228
  illciit woodcutting, 193–4
  importance of land relations for, 184–6
  inter peasant conflict, 188–9
  as political actors, 181–2, 187, 195–6, 201, 231
Peasants' union, 20
Petrograd Soviet, 11, 64, 169
Political exiles, 33, 47–9, 78, 115
  donations for, 48–9
Prisoners of war, 162–4
Provisional Committee of the State Duma, 39
Provisional Government, 10
  and the clergy, 41
  and cultural enlightenment campaigns, 124
  and February revolution, 39
  and food supply, 214, 218–19, 236
  and land relations, 181, 188, 198, 199
    use of force, 202–3
  popularity of, 11
Provisions committees
  hostility towards, 221, 222–3
  membership of, 219–20

Reading rooms, 129
Refugees, 10, 103, 176
  and food supply, 224–6

Separators, 165, 206
  violence towards, 189–92
Social Democrat Party (Bolsheviks), 54, 57, 68,
    126, 155, 156, 157, 220, 235
  in Kazan Town Duma, 27
  and October seizure of power, 25, 99–100
  and *soldatki*, 177
  in Sormovo, 80, 81
  women in, 108
Social Democrat Party (Mensheviks), 11, 20, 32,
    69, 126, 143, 155
Social Democrats, 35, 143
Socialist bloc, 26, 77
  divisions in, 77–8
  Kazan Town Duma, 27
Socialist Revolutionary Party, 11, 35, 43, 46, 56,
    79, 98, 111, 126, 136, 139, 143, 155, 208
  affinity with peasant milieu, 112
  attitudes towards World War One, 70–1, 74
  before 1917, 63–5
  candidates to Constituent Assembly, 114
  divisions in, 26, 27–61, 62–3, 67–76, 82, 115–16
    Kazan PSR organisation, 73–6
  finances of, 65

  intelligentsia, 62
  organisation of, 66–7
  participation in Kazan Town Duma, 27
  participation in Nizhnii Novgorod Town
    Duma, 23
  participation in Provisional Government, 11
  and political exile, 64
  popular image of, 60
  publications of, 32
  Sormovo PSR group, 34, 80–2, 143
  support in countryside, 61–2
  support in Nizhnii Novgorod, 25
  teachers, 62
  women in, 108
  and workers, 60–1
Soldatki, 164
  grievances of, 165–6, 230
  organisation and leadership, 168–70
  and party politics, 177
  petitions, 170–2
  Provisonal Government policy towards,
    166–8
  and Social Democrat Party (Bolsheviks), 177
  violence of, 172–3
Soldiers, 15, 21, 145–4, 171
  and alcohol, 151, 152, 160–1
  and black market trading, 151
  conflict with workers, 154
  and crime, 149–50, 155
  deserters, 158–9, 160, 161–2
  education, 128, 140
  evacuees, 126, 149, 153, 156–7
  invalids, 149
  July rising, Nizhnii Novgorod, 18, 153–7
  Kazan town garrison, 145–6
  local leaders, 95–8, 153
  Muslims, 148–9
  Nizhnii Novgorod garrison, 146
  non-Russian, 147–8
  organisation of, 15
  peasant identities of, 147
  as political agitators, 158
  problems of leadership, 150, 152–3, 155, 157
  transport, 150
  violence, 54, 145, 146, 151–2, 159–60
Sormovo PSR group, 34, 143
Sormovo soviet of workers' deputies, 82
Sormovo workers, 32, 34, 49, 99, 142, 157
  February revolution, 34
  food supply, 226–7
  party politics, 79–83
  and Socialist Revolutionary Party, 80–2
soviets, 15, 16, 17, 18, 32
  cultural enlightenment work of, 126, 127, 133,
    136, 137, 138

soviets (*cont.*)
  Kazan soviet of peasants' deputies, 104
    land law, 205–7
  Kazan soviet of workers' and soldiers'
    deputies, 19, 97, 173–4
  membership of, 88–9
  Nizhegorod soviet of peasants' deputies, 19,
    195
  Nizhegorod Soviet of soldiers' deputies,
    98
  Nizhegorod soviet of workers' and soldiers'
    deputies, 100, 169
  Nizhegorod soviet of workers' deputies, 25, 79
  payment of members, 105
  peasant soviets' affiliation with PSR, 112
  Sormovo soviet of workers' deputies, 82
  women in, 105–6
Spiridonova, Maria, 46, 47, 70
State Duma, 11, 13, 25, 38, 39, 40, 42, 58, 107, 118,
    130, 153, 159, 191
Students, 33, 99, 120, 126, 131, 153
  Kazan University, 32

Tatars, 6, 8, 128, 143, 234
  and the February revolution, 37
  as local leaders, 103
  resistance to elections, 119
Teachers, 92, 93, 106, 126, 135
  and the Socialist Revolutionary Party, 62
  women, 105, 107
Transport, 5–6, 10, 31, 146, 150, 211, 213

Violence, 51, 119, 157

and food supply, 222–3, 229–30, 231, 232–34,
    235
inter peasant conflict, 189, 201
land relations, 186–8, 196–7
pogroms, 49, 224
separators, 189–92
soldatki, 172–3
soldiers, 54, 145, 146, 151–2

Women, 126, 150–1
  in public life, 105–11
    exclusion from, 107–8, 135, 168
    on peasant committees, 107
  role in elections, 118
  teachers, 105
Woodland, 192–5, 197, 207
Workers, 15
  and food supply, 226
  as leaders, 22
  organisation of, 15
  party politics among, 79–80
    apathy, 83
  role in February revolution, 34, 35
  and Socialist Revolutionary Party, 60–1
  women, 108

zemliachestva, 16
zemstva, 14, 16, 17, 18, 19, 25, 93, 98, 119, 136
  selection of candidates, 112
  work in cultural enlightenment, 126, 136
    in February revolution, 40
    unpopularity of, 53, 54
Zenzinov, Vladimir Mikhailovich, 64, 69

NEW STUDIES IN EUROPEAN HISTORY

Books in the series

Royalty and Diplomacy in Europe, 1890–1914
RODERICK R. McLEAN

Catholic Revival in the Age of the Baroque
Religious Identity in Southwest Germany, 1550–1750
MARC R. FORSTER

Helmuth von Moltke and the Origins of the First World War
ANNIKA MOMBAUER

Peter the Great
The Struggle for Power, 1671–1725
PAUL BUSHKOVITCH

Fatherlands
State-Building and Nationhood in Nineteenth-Century Germany
ABIGAIL GREEN

The French Second Empire
An Anatomy of Political Power
ROGER PRICE

Origins of the French Welfare State
The Struggle for Social Reform in France, 1914–1947
PAUL V. DUTTON

Ordinary Prussians
Brandenburg Junkers and Villagers, 1500–1840
WILLIAM W. HAGEN

Liberty and Locality in Revolutionary France
Rural Life and Politics, 1760–1820
PETER JONES

Vienna and Versailles
The Courts of Europe's Dynastic Rivals, 1550–1780
JEROEN DUINDAM

From Reich to State
The Rhineland in the Revolutionary Age, 1780–1830
MICHAEL ROWE

Re-Writing the French Revolutionary Tradition
Liberal Opposition and the Fall of the Bourbon Monarchy
ROBERT ALEXANDER

Provincial Power and Absolute Monarchy
The Estates General of Burgundy, 1661–1790
JULIAN SWANN

People and Politics in France, 1848–1870
ROGER PRICE

Nobles and Nation in Central Europe
Free Imperial Knights in the Age of Revolution, 1750–1850
WILLIAM D. GODSEY, JR

Technology and the Culture of Modernity in Britain and Germany, 1890–1945
BERNHARD RIEGER

The Russian Roots of Nazism
White Émigrés and the Making of National Socialism, 1917–1945
MICHAEL KELLOGG

The World Hitler Never Made
Alternate History and the Memory of Nazism
GAVRIEL D. ROSENFELD

Madness, Religion and the State in Early Modern Europe
A Bavarian Beacon
DAVID LEDERER

Fascism's European Empire
Italian Occupation During the Second World War
DAVID E RODOGNO, translated by ADRIAN BELTON

Family and Community in Early Modern Spain
The Citizens of Granada, 1570–1739
JAMES CASEY

Popular Culture and the Public Sphere in the Rhineland, 1800–1850
JAMES M. BROPHY

Politics and the People in Revolutionary Russia
A Provincial History
SARAH BADCOCK

20835339R00157

Printed in Great Britain
by Amazon